Emanuel Swedenborg

Heaven and Its Wonders and Hell from Things Heard and Seen

BAMBOO BOOKS

Emanuel Swedenborg

Heaven and Its Wonders and Hell from Things
Heard and Seen

Original published in 1875
Republished by Bamboo Books, 2020
Cover Design: Bamboo Books

ISBN: 978-5-519-70134-1

Dear Reader,

This is an exact replica of a book published in 1899. The book reprint was manually improved by a team of professionals, as opposed to automatic processed used by some companies. However, the book may still have imperfections such as missing pages, poor pictures, errant marks, etc. that were a part of the original text. We appreciate your understanding if the imperfection which can not be improved, and hope you will enjoy reading this book.

Our contacts:
✉ request@bamboo-publishing.com
𝐟 fb.com/bamboobooks

HEAVEN

AND ITS WONDERS

AND

HELL.

FROM

THINGS HEARD AND SEEN.

BY

EMANUEL SWEDENBORG.

ORIGINALLY PUBLISHED IN LATIN AT LONDON, A. D. 1758.

PHILADELPHIA
J. B. LIPPINCOTT & CO.
1875.

CONTENTS.

HEAVEN.

THE WORLD OF SPIRITS, AND THE STATE OF MAN AFTER DEATH.

HELL.

HEAVEN AND HELL.

HEAVEN AND HELL.

N the Lord's discourse with His disciples concerning the Consummation of the Age,* which is the last time of the church,[1] at the close of His predictions concerning its successive states as to love and faith,[2] He says: "*Immediately after the tribulation of those days, the sun shall be darkened, and the moon shall not give her light, and the stars shall fall from heaven, and the powers of the heavens shall be shaken. And then shall appear the sign of the Son of man in heaven: and then shall all the tribes of the earth wail; and they shall see the Son of man coming in the clouds of heaven with power and great glory. And he shall send his angels with the loud-sounding trumpet, and they shall gather*

---

* [*The consummation of the Age* is the correct rendering of the original Greek, which, in our common English Bibles, is translated *the end of the world.* The Greek word Αιων has no such meaning as our word *world;* but it means an age, a period of time, or a dispensation.—Tr.]

From the ARCANA CŒLESTIA.

[1] That the consummation of the age is the last time of the church, n. 4535, 10622.

[2] The things which the Lord predicted in Matt. chap. xxiv. xxv. concerning the consummation of the age, and concerning His advent, thus concerning the successive vastation of the church and concerning the last judgment, are explained in the articles which precede several of the chapters of Genesis, namely, chap. xxvi. to xl. See n. 3353 to 3355, 3486 to 3489, 3650 to 3655, 3751 to 3757, 3897 to 3901, 4056 to 4060, 4229 to 4231, 4332 to 4335, 4422 to 4424, 4635 to 4638, 4661 to 4664, 4807 to 4810, 4954 to 4959, 5063 to 5071.

2

A*

9

*together his elect from the four winds, from one end of the
heavens even to the other.*"—Matt. xxiv. 29, 30, 31.   They who
understand these words according to the literal sense, suppose
that, at the final consummation, which is called the last judgment,
all these things will happen as they are described in that sense;
thus they imagine, not only that the sun and moon will be darkened, and that the stars will fall from heaven, and that the sign
of the Lord will appear in heaven, and that they shall see Him
in the clouds attended by the angels with trumpets, but they
also imagine, agreeably to what is predicted elsewhere, that the
whole visible world will perish, and that afterwards a new heaven
and a new earth will be created.   This is the opinion of most
persons within the church at this day.   But they who entertain
such notions, are unacquainted with the arcana which lie concealed in every part of the Word; for in every part of the Word
there is an internal sense, which treats not of natural and worldly
things, such as are treated of in the literal sense, but of things
spiritual and celestial; and not only is this the case in regard
to the meaning of several expressions, but even in regard to every
single expression;[1] for the Word is written by pure correspondences,[2] in order that there may be an internal sense in every part
of it.   What the nature of that sense is, may appear from all the
things said and shown concerning it in the ARCANA CŒLESTIA;
which may also be seen collected together in the little work on the
WHITE HORSE spoken of in the Apocalypse.   What the Lord
said in the passage just quoted concerning His coming in the
clouds of heaven, is to be understood according to the same sense.
By the sun there mentioned, which shall be darkened, is signified
the Lord as to love;[3] by the moon, the Lord as to faith;[4] by the

---

[1] That in all and each of the things of the Word there is an internal or
spiritual sense, n. 1143, 1984, 2135, 2333, 2395, 2495, 4442, 9048, 9063, 9086.

[2] That the Word is written by pure correspondences, and that hence all,
and each of, the things therein signify spiritual things, n. 1404, 1408, 1409,
1540, 1619, 1659, 1709, 1783, 2900, 9086.

[3] That the sun, in the Word, signifies the Lord as to love, and thence
love to the Lord, n. 1529, 1837, 2441, 2495, 4060, 4696, (4996), 7083, 10809.

[4] That the moon, in the Word, signifies the Lord as to faith, and thence
faith in the Lord, n. 1529, 1530, 2495, 4060, 4696, 7083.

stars, the knowledges of good and truth, or of love and faith;[1] by the sign of the Son of man in heaven, the manifestation of divine truth ; by the tribes of the earth which shall wail, all things of truth and good, or of faith and love ;[2] by the coming of the Lord in the clouds of heaven with power and glory, His presence in the Word, and revelation ;[3] by clouds is signified the literal sense of the Word,[4] and by glory its internal sense ;[5] by the angels with the loud-sounding trumpet is signified heaven, whence comes divine truth.[6] From this it is plain that, by these words of the Lord is meant that, at the end of the church, when there is no longer love, and thence no longer faith, the Lord will open the Word as to its internal sense, and reveal the arcana of heaven.

The arcana which are revealed in the following pages, are those concerning heaven and hell, together with the life of man after death. The man of the church at this day knows scarcely anything about heaven and hell, nor yet about his own life after death, although these things are all treated of in the Word ; yea, many even among those who were born within the church deny these things, saying in their hearts, Who has ever come thence and told us ? Lest, therefore, such a negative principle, which rules especially among those who possess much worldly wisdom, should also infect and corrupt the simple in heart and faith, it has been granted me to associate with angels and to converse with them as one man with another, and also to see the things which are in the heavens as well as those which are in the hells,

---

[1] That stars, in the Word, signify the knowledges of good and of truth, n. 2495, 2849, 4697.

[2] That tribes signify all truths and goods in the complex, thus all things of faith and of love, n. 3859, 3926, 4060, 6335.

[3] That the coming of the Lord is His presence in the Word and revelation, n. 3900, 4060.

[4] That clouds, in the Word, signify the Word in the letter, or the sense of its letter, n. 4060, 4391, 5922, 6343, 6752, 8106, 8781, 9430, 10551, 10574.

[5] That glory, in the Word, signifies divine truth as it is in heaven, and as it is in the internal sense of the Word, n. 4809, (5292), 5922, 8267, 8427, 9429. 10574.

[6] That a trumpet signifies divine truth in heaven, and revealed from heaven, n. 8815, 8823, 8915; the same is signified by voice, n. 6971, 9926.

and this for the space of thirteen years, and so to describe these things from what I have myself seen and heard,—in the hope that ignorance may thus be enlightened and incredulity dissipated. The reason that such immediate revelation is made at this time, is, that this is what is meant by the coming of the Lord.

THE LORD IS THE GOD OF HEAVEN.

2. It ought, first of all, to be known who is the God of heaven; since everything else depends on this. In the universal heaven no other than the Lord alone is acknowledged as the God of heaven. They say there, as He himself taught, *that He is one with the Father; that the Father is in Him and He in the Father; and that whosoever seeth Him seeth the Father;* and that everything holy proceeds from Him.—John x. 30–38; xiv. 10, 11; xvi. 13, 14, 15. I have often conversed with the angels on this subject, and they constantly said, that they cannot in heaven distinguish the Divine into three, because they know and perceive that the Divine is one, and that it is one in the Lord. They said also, that those belonging to the church who come from the world, and have entertained an idea of three Divines, cannot be admitted into heaven, because their thought wanders from one to another; and it is not allowable there to think three and say one,[1] because every one in heaven speaks from his thought. Speech there is what is revolved in the mind, or it is thought speaking. Wherefore they who in the world have distinguished the Divine into three, and have conceived a distinct idea of each, and have not made and concentrated it into one in the Lord, cannot be received; for in heaven there is a communication of the thoughts of all; wherefore if any one should come

---

[1] That Christians in the other life were explored as to the idea they had concerning one God, and that it was discovered that they had an idea of three Gods, n. 2329, 5256, 10736, 10738, 10821. That a Divine Trinity in the Lord is acknowledged in heaven, n. 14, 15, 1729, 2005, 5256, 9303.

thither thinking of three and confessing one, he would be immediately discovered and rejected. It is, however, to be observed
that all those who have not separated truth from good, or faith
from love, when they are instructed, receive in the other life the
heavenly idea concerning the Lord, namely, that He is the God
of the universe; but it is otherwise with those who have separated faith from life, that is, who have not lived according to the
precepts of a true faith.

3. Those within the church who have denied the Lord, and
have acknowledged only the Father, and have confirmed themselves in such a faith, are out of heaven; and as no influx from
heaven where the Lord alone is adored, can be received by them,
they are deprived by degrees of the faculty of thinking what is
true on any subject whatever; and at length they become either
as mutes, or speak foolishly, and wander around, their arms
hanging down and dangling about as if they were deprived of
all strength in the joints. Those also who have denied the
Divine of the Lord, and have acknowledged only His Human,
like the Socinians, are likewise out of heaven. They are carried forward a little toward the right,* and let down into the
deep; and thus they are completely separated from the rest
who come from the Christian world. They, too, who profess to
believe in an invisible Divine, which they call the animating
principle [*Ens*] of the universe, from which all things existed,
and who reject faith in the Lord, have found by experience that
they believe in no God; because an invisible Divine is, to them,
like nature in its first principles, which is no object of faith and
love, because it is no object of thought.[1] These have their lot

---

* [The situation of spirits in the other world, as also their ascent into
heaven or descent into hell, is constantly described by the author with
reference to the body of the spectator. The meaning in this passage is,
that the spirits here mentioned appear to sink down in front, a little
toward the right, into the particular place appointed for them. This will
be more fully comprehended when the reader understands what is said
hereafter concerning the *Quarters* in Heaven, n. 141-154.—Tr.]

[1] That a Divine which is not perceptible by any idea, cannot be an object
of faith, n. 4733, 5110, (5633), 6982, 6996, 7004, 7211, (9267), 9359, 9972,
10067.

among those who are called naturalists. It is otherwise with those who are born without the church, and are called Gentiles, of whom more will be said hereafter.

4. All infants, of whom a third part of heaven consists, are initiated into the acknowledgment and faith that the Lord is their Father; and afterwards that He is the Lord of all, thus the God of heaven and earth. That infants grow up in the heavens, and are perfected by knowledges, even to angelic intelligence and wisdom, will be seen in what follows.

5. Those who are of the church cannot doubt that the Lord is the God of heaven; for He Himself taught, *that all things of the Father are His*, Matt. xi. 27; John xvi. 15; xvii. 2; and that *He hath all power in heaven and in earth*, Matt. xxviii. 16. He says in heaven and in earth, because He who rules heaven rules the earth also, for one depends on the other.[1] To rule heaven and earth, signifies to receive from Him all the good which is of love, and all the truth which is of faith, thus all intelligence and wisdom, and therefore all happiness; in short, eternal life. The Lord also taught this when He said: " *He that believeth on the Son, hath eternal life; but he that believeth not the Son, shall not see life.*" John iii. 36. Again: "*I am the Resurrection and the Life; he that believeth in Me, though he die, shall live; and every one that liveth and believeth in Me, shall not die to eternity.*" John xi. 25, 26. And again: "*I am the Way, the Truth, and the Life.*" John xiv. 6.

6. There were certain spirits, who, while they lived in the world, professed to believe in the Father, and had no other idea concerning the Lord, than as of another man, and consequently did not believe him to be the God of heaven. They were, therefore, permitted to wander about, and to inquire wherever they pleased, whether there be any other heaven than the Lord's. They inquired for several days, but found none. They were of

---

[1] That the universal heaven is the Lord's, n. 2751, 7086. That He has all power in the heavens and on earth, n. 1607, 10089, 10827. That since the Lord rules heaven, He also rules all things which thence depend, and thus all things in the world, n. 2026, 2027, 4523, 4524. That the Lord alone has the power of removing the hells, of withholding from evils, and of keeping in good, and thus of saving, n. 10019.

that class who supposed the happiness of heaven to consist in glory and dominion; and because they could not obtain what they desired, and were told that heaven does not consist in such things, they were indignant, and wished to have a heaven in which they could domineer over others, and excel them in glory in like manner as in the world.

THE DIVINE OF THE LORD MAKES HEAVEN.

7. THE angels taken collectively are called heaven, because they constitute heaven. Nevertheless it is the Divine proceeding from the Lord, which flows-in with the angels, and is received by them, which makes heaven in general and in particular. The Divine proceeding from the Lord is the good of love and the truth of faith. As far, therefore, as they receive good and truth from the Lord, so far they are angels, and so far they are heaven.

8. Every one in the heavens knows and believes, yea, perceives, that he wills and does nothing of good from himself, and that he thinks and believes nothing of truth from himself, but from the Divine, thus from the Lord; and that the good and truth which are from himself, are not good and truth, because there is not in them life from the Divine. The angels of the inmost heaven also clearly perceive, and are sensible of, the influx; and so far as they receive it, they seem to themselves to be in heaven, because they are so far in love and faith, and so far in the light of intelligence and wisdom, and thence in heavenly joy. Since these things all proceed from the Divine of the Lord, and the angels possess heaven in them, it is evident that the Divine of the Lord makes heaven, and not the angels by virtue of anything properly their own.[1] Hence it is that heaven

---

[1] That the angels of heaven acknowledge all good to be from the Lord, and none from themselves; and that the Lord dwells with them in what is His own, and not in their *proprium*, n. 9338, 10125, 10151, 10157. That

in the Word is called the habitation of the Lord, and His throne; and that the dwellers there are said to be in the Lord.[1] But how the Divine proceeds from the Lord and fills heaven, will be shown in what follows.

9. The angels, by virtue of their wisdom, go still further. They say that not only are all good and truth from the Lord, but also the all of life. They confirm this by the consideration that nothing can exist from itself, but from what is prior to itself; consequently, that all things exist from a First, which they call the very *Esse* of the life of all things; and that in like manner they subsist, because subsistence is perpetual existence; and that what is not continually kept in connection with the First by intermediates, is forthwith dissolved, and utterly dissipated. They say, moreover, that there is only one Fountain of life, and that the life of man is a stream thence issuing, which would instantly cease to flow if it were not continually supplied from that Fountain. They say further, that from that one Fountain of life which is the Lord, nothing proceeds but divine good and divine truth, and that these affect every one according to his reception of them; that those who receive them in faith and life have heaven in them; but those who reject or suffocate them, turn them into hell; for they turn good into evil, and the true into the false, thus life into death. That the all of life is from the Lord, they also confirm by this consideration: that all things in the universe have reference to good and truth,—the life of man's will, which is the life of his love, to good, and the life of his understanding, which is the life of his faith, to truth; wherefore, since every thing good and true comes from above, it follows that thence also comes the all of life. Because the angels believe this, therefore they refuse all thanks on account of the

---

therefore, by angels in the Word, is meant something of the Lord, n. 1925, 2821, 3039, 4085, 8192, 10528; and that therefore they are called gods, from reception of the Divine from the Lord, n. 4295, 4402, 7268, 7873. 8301, 8192. That all good which is good, all truth which is truth, and consequently all peace, love, charity, and faith, are also from the Lord, n. 1614, 2016, 2751, 2882, 2883, 2891, 2892, 2904; and all wisdom and intelligence, n. 109, 112, 121, 124.

[1] That they who are in heaven are said to be in the Lord, n. 3637, 3638

good they do, and are displeased and withdraw themselves if any one attributes good to them. They wonder how any one can believe that he is wise from himself, and that he does good from himself. Good done for the sake of one's self, they do not call good, because it is done from self; but good done for the sake of good, this they call good from the Divine; and they say that this good is what makes heaven, because this good is the Lord.[1]

10. Spirits who, while they lived in the world, confirmed themselves in the belief that the good which they do and the truth which they believe are from themselves, or appropriated to them as their own, (in which belief are all those who place merit in their good actions, and attribute righteousness to themselves), are not received into heaven. The angels shun them; they regard them as stupid and as thieves; as stupid, because they continually look to themselves, and not to the Divine; and as thieves, because they rob the Lord of what is His. These spirits are opposed to the faith of heaven, which is, that the Divine of the Lord received by the angels makes heaven.

11. That they who are in heaven and in the church, are in the Lord and the Lord in them, He also teaches where He says, *"Abide in me, and I in you; as the branch cannot bear fruit of itself, except it abide in the vine, no more can ye except ye abide in Me. I am the vine, ye are the branches; he that abideth in Me, and I in him, the same bringeth forth much fruit; for without Me ye can do nothing."* John xv. 4, 5.

12. From these considerations it may now be evident, that the Lord dwells in His own with the angels of heaven, and thus that the Lord is the All in all of heaven. The reason is, because good from the Lord is the Lord with the angels, for what is from Him is Himself; consequently, good from the Lord is heaven to the angels, and not anything proper to themselves.

---

[1] That good from the Lord has the Lord within it, but not good from the proprium, n. 1802, 3951, 8480.

2

THE DIVINE OF THE LORD IN HEAVEN IS LOVE TO HIM AND CHARITY TOWARD THE NEIGHBOR.

13. THE Divine proceeding from the Lord is called in heaven divine truth, for a reason which will appear in what follows. This divine truth flows into heaven from the Lord out of His divine love. Divine love and divine truth thence proceeding are, comparatively, like the fire of the sun and the light thence proceeding in the world; love being as the fire of the sun, and truth thence proceeding, as light from the sun. Fire also signifies love from correspondence; and light, the truth thence proceeding.[1] Hence it may appear what is the quality of divine truth proceeding from the divine love of the Lord; namely, that in its essence it is divine good conjoined to divine truth; and because it is conjoined, it vivifies all things of heaven, as the heat of the sun conjoined to light in the world fructifies all things of the earth in spring- and summer-time. It is otherwise when heat is not conjoined to light, thus when the light is cold; then all things are torpid and lifeless. This divine good, which is compared to heat, is the good of love with the angels; and the divine truth, which is compared to light, is that by means of which they receive the good of love.

14. The Divine in heaven which makes heaven, is love, because love is spiritual conjunction. Love conjoins the angels with the Lord and with each other; and it conjoins them in such a manner, that they are all as one in the Lord's sight. Moreover, love is the very *esse* of every one's life; wherefore both angels and men derive their life from it. That the inmost vital principle of man is from love, must be obvious to every one who considers the subject; for he grows warm from its presence, cold

---

[1] That fire, in the Word, signifies love either heavenly or infernal, n. 934, 4906, 5215. That sacred and celestial fire signifies divine love, and every affection which is of that love, n. 934, 6314, 6832. That the light thence derived signifies truth proceeding from the good of love, and that light in heaven is divine truth, n. (3395), 3485, 3636, 3643, 3993, 4302, 4413, 4415, 9548, 9684.

from its absence, and from its privation he dies.[1] But it is to be observed that the quality of every one's life is as the quality of his love.

15. There are two distinct loves in heaven, love to the Lord and love toward the neighbor. In the inmost or third heaven is love to the Lord; in the second or middle heaven, love toward the neighbor. Each proceeds from the Lord, and each makes heaven. How these two loves are distinguished, and how they are conjoined, appears very clearly in heaven, but only obscurely in the world. In heaven, to love the Lord does not mean to love Him as to His person, but to love the good which is from Him; and to love good, is to will and do good from love: and to love the neighbor does not mean to love a fellow-being as to his person, but to love the truth which is from the Word; and to love truth is to will and do it. Hence it is evident, that these two loves are distinguished like good and truth, and that they are conjoined just as good is conjoined with truth.[2] But these things are not easily comprehended by one who is ignorant of what love is, what good is, and what the neighbor is.[3]

16. I have conversed with the angels on this subject a number of times, and they have expressed astonishment that the men of the church do not know, that to love the Lord and the neighbor is to love good and truth, and to do them from the heart; when yet they might know, that every one manifests his love for another by willing and doing what the other desires; and that he is loved in return, and conjunction with him is effected in this way, and not by loving him and constantly disregarding his will,

---

[1] That love is the fire of life, and that life itself is actually derived from love, n. 4906, 5071, 6032, 6314.

[2] That to love the Lord and the neighbor is to live according to the Lord's precepts, n. 10143, 10153, 10130, 10578, 10648.

[3] That to love the neighbor is not to love the person, but to love that which appertains to him, and which constitutes him, thus truth and good, n. 5025, 10336. That they who love the person, and not what appertains to another, and constitutes him, love alike what is evil and what is good, n. 3820. That charity consists in willing truths and in being affected by truths for the sake of truths, n. 3876, 3877. That charity toward the neighbor is to do what is good, just, and right in every work, and in every employment, n. 8120, 8121, 8122.

which, in reality, is not to love him; and that they might also know, that the good proceeding from the Lord is His likeness, because He is in it; and that those become likenesses of Him, and are conjoined to Him, who make good and truth [constituents] of their life by willing and doing them. To will also is to love to do. This the Lord also teaches in the Word, where He says, " *He that hath My commandments and doeth them, he it is that loveth Me;—and I will love him, and make My abode with him.*" John xiv. 21–23. And again: " *If ye keep My comm.andments, ye shall abide in my love.*" John xv. 10.

17. That the Divine proceeding from the Lord, which affects the angels and makes heaven, is love, all experience in heaven testifies; for all who are there are forms of love and charity. They appear of ineffable beauty, and love beams forth from their faces, from their discourse, and from every single act of their lives.[1] Moreover, from every angel and spirit proceed spiritual spheres of life which encompass them, whereby they are known as to the quality of the affections of their love, even when they are a great way off; for these spheres flow forth from the life of each one's affection, and thence of his thought, or from the life of his love and thence of his faith. The spheres proceeding from the angels are so full of love, that they affect the inmosts of the life of those present. They have several times been perceived by me, and have affected me in this wise.[2] That love is that from which the angels derive their life, is also manifest from this circumstance, that every one in the other life turns himself according to his love; they who are in love to the Lord and in love toward the neighbor, turn themselves constantly to the Lord; but they who are in the love of self, turn themselves constantly backward from the Lord. This occurs in every turning of their bodies; for in the other life spaces are according to the states of the interiors of those there; in like manner the quar-

---

[1] That the angels are forms of love and charity, n. 3804, 4735, 4797, 4985, 5199, 5530, 9879, 10177.

[2] Tnat a spiritual sphere, which is a sphere of life, flows forth and diffuses itself from every man, spirit, and angel, and encompasses him, n. 4464, 5179, 7454, 8630. That it flows from the life of his affection and thence of his thought, n. 2489, 4464, 6206.

ters, which are not determined there as in the world, but according to the aspect [or direction] of people's faces. It is not, however, the angels who turn themselves to the Lord, but the Lord who turns to Himself those who love to do the things which are from Him.[1] But more will be said on this subject hereafter, when the quarters in the other life come to be treated of.

18. The Divine of the Lord in heaven is love, because love is the receptacle of all things of heaven, which are peace, intelligence, wisdom, and happiness: for love receives all things whatsoever, which are in agreement with itself; it longs for them, seeks after them, imbibes them as it were spontaneously; for it continually desires to be enriched and perfected by them.[2] This is also known to man; for his love inspects as it were the stores of his memory, and draws forth thence all things which are in agreement with it; and these it collects together and arranges in and under itself,—in itself, that they may be its own, and under itself that they may be subservient to it; but whatever is not in agreement with itself, it rejects and exterminates. That every faculty for receiving truths congenial to itself, and the desire of conjoining them to itself, are inherent in love, is manifest also from those who were elevated into heaven; these, although simple in the world, when they came among the angels, entered at once into angelic wisdom, and into the felicities of heaven: the reason was, because they loved good and truth for their own sake, and implanted them in their lives, and thereby acquired the faculty of receiving heaven with every ineffable thing there. But they who are in the love of self and the world, are incapable of receiving heavenly things. They hold them in aversion, reject them, and at the first touch and influx of them, they associate themselves with those in hell who are in loves

---

[1] That spirits and angels turn themselves constantly to their loves, and they who are in the heavens constantly to the Lord, n. 10130, 10189, 10420, 10702. That the quarters in the other life are according to the aspect of the face, and are thence determined, otherwise than in the world, n. 10130, 10189, 10420, 10702.

[2] That innumerable things are in love, and that love takes to itself all things which are in agreement with itself, n. 2500, 2572, 3078, 3189, 6323, 7490, 7750.

similar to their own.   There were certain spirits who doubted if
such things were inherent in heavenly love, and wished to know
whether it were so ; wherefore they were led into a state of heavenly love,—their opposing principles being meanwhile removed,
—and were carried forward some distance where there was an
angelic heaven ; and from thence they conversed with me, saying
that they perceived a more interior happiness than could be expressed in words, lamenting greatly that they must return to their
former state.   Others also were elevated into heaven, and in
proportion as their elevation became more interior or exalted, they
entered into such intelligence and wisdom as to be able to understand things which before were incomprehensible to them.
Hence it is evident, that love proceeding from the Lord is the
receptacle of heaven and of all things there.

19. That love to the Lord and love toward the neighbor comprehend in themselves all divine truths, may be manifest from
what the Lord Himself spoke concerning these two loves, saying : " *Thou shalt love the Lord thy God with all thy heart
and with all thy soul.   This is the first and greatest commandment.   The second, which is like unto it, is, Thou shalt
love thy neighbor as thyself.   On these two commandments
hang. the law and the prophets.*" Matt. xxii. 37—40.   The law
and the prophets are the whole Word, thus all divine truth.

HEAVEN IS DISTINGUISHED INTO TWO KINGDOMS.

20. Since there are infinite varieties in heaven, and no society
is exactly like another, nor indeed any angel like another,[1] there-

---

[1] That variety is infinite, and that one thing is never the same as another,
n. 7236, 9002.   That in the heavens also there is infinite variety, n. 684,
690, 3744, 5598, 7236.   That the varieties in the heavens are varieties of
good, n. 3744, 4005, 7236, 7833, 7836, 9002.   That thus all the societies in
the heavens, and every angel in a society, are distinct from each other, n.
690, 3241, 3519, 3804, 3986, 4067, 4149, 4263, 7236, 7833, 7836; but that still
all make a one by love from the Lord, n. 457, 3986.

fore heaven is distinguished generally, specifically, and particularly; generally, into two kingdoms; specifically, into three heavens; and particularly, into innumerable societies. We shall speak of each in what now follows. The general divisions are styled kingdoms, because heaven is called the kingdom of God.

21. Some angels receive the Divine proceeding from the Lord, more, and others less, interiorly. They who receive it more interiorly, are called celestial angels; but they who receive it less interiorly, are called spiritual angels. Hence heaven is distinguished into two kingdoms, one of which is called the CELESTIAL KINGDOM, the other the SPIRITUAL KINGDOM.[1]

22. The angels who constitute the celestial kingdom, because they receive the Divine of the Lord more interiorly, are called interior, and also superior angels; and thence also the heavens which they constitute are called interior and superior heavens.[2] They are called superior and inferior, because interior and exterior things are so named.[3]

23. The love in which they are who belong to the celestial kingdom, is called celestial love; and the love in which they are who belong to the spiritual kingdom, is called spiritual love. Celestial love is love to the Lord, and spiritual love is charity toward the neighbor. And since all good is of love—for what one loves is good to him—therefore also the good of one kingdom is called celestial, and the good of the other spiritual. Hence it is evident in what respect those two kingdoms are distinguished; namely, that they are distinguished like the good of love to the Lord, and the good of charity toward the neigh-

---

[1] That the whole heaven is distinguished into two kingdoms, the celestial kingdom and the spiritual kingdom, n. 3887, 4138. That the angels of the celestial kingdom receive the Divine of the Lord in the will-part, thus more interiorly than the spiritual angels, who receive it in the intellectual part, n. 5113, 6367, 8521, 9936, 9995, 10124.

[2] That the heavens which constitute the celestial kingdom are called superior, and those which constitute the spiritual kingdom are called inferior, n. 10068.

[3] That interior things are called superior, and that superior things signify interior, n. 2148, 3084, 4599, 5146, 8325.

bor :[1] and since the former good is interior good, and the former love interior love, therefore the celestial angels are interior angels, and are called superior.

24. The celestial kingdom is also called the priestly kingdom of the Lord, and in the Word His habitation; and the spiritual kingdom is called His regal kingdom, and in the Word His throne. The Lord also in the world was called Jesus from the Divine-celestial, and CHRIST from the Divine-spiritual.

25. The angels in the Lord's celestial kingdom far excel in wisdom and glory those in His spiritual kingdom, because they receive the Divine of the Lord more interiorly; for they are in love to Him, and thence nearer and more closely conjoined to Him.[2] These angels are such, because they have received and do receive divine truths immediately into life, and not, as the spiritual, first into the memory and thought; wherefore they have them inscribed on their hearts, and comprehend them, and as it were see them in themselves; nor do they ever reason about them whether it be so or not.[3] They are like those described in Jeremiah : "*I will put My law in their mind, and write it on their heart: they shall not teach any more every one his friend, and every one his brother, saying, Know ye Jehovah: they shall all know Me from the least of them even unto the greatest.*" xxxi. 33, 34. And they are called in Isaiah, "*The taught of Jehovah.*" liv. 13. That they who are taught of Jehovah are they who are taught of the Lord, the Lord Himself teaches in John, chap. vi. 45, 46.

26. It was said that these angels possess wisdom and glory above the rest, because they have received, and do receive, divine

---

[1] That the good of the celestial kingdom is the good of love to the Lord, and the good of the spiritual kingdom is the good of charity toward the neighbor, n. 3691, 6435, 9468, 9680, 9683, 9780.

[2] That the celestial angels are immensely wiser than the spiritual angels, n. 2718, 9995. What is the distinction between the celestial angels and the spiritual angels, n. 2088, 2669, 2708, 2715, 3235, 3240, 4788, 7068, 8521, 9277, 10295.

[3] That the celestial angels do not reason concerning the truths of faith, because they perceive them in themselves, but that the spiritual angels reason concerning them whether it be so, or not so, n. 202, 337, 597, 607, 784, 1121, 1384, (1398), 1919, 3246, 4448, 7680, 7877, 8780, 9277, 10786.

truths immediately into life; for as soon as they hear them, they also will and do them; they do not lay them up in the memory, and then think whether they be true or not. They who are of such a character know instantly, by influx from the Lord, whether the truth which they hear be truth; for the Lord flows-in immediately into man's will, and mediately through the will into his thought; or, what is the same, the Lord flows-in immediately into good, and mediately through good into truth;[1] for that is called good which is of the will and thence of the act, but that is called truth which is of the memory and thence of the thought. All truth likewise is turned into good, and implanted in the love, as soon as it enters the will; but so long as truth is in the memory and thence in the thought, it does not become good, nor does it live, nor is it appropriated to man; since man is man from the will and thence from the understanding, and not from the understanding separate from will.[2]

27. Because there is such a distinction between the angels of the celestial and those of the spiritual kingdom, therefore they do not dwell together, nor do they hold intercourse with each other. There is communication between them only by intermediate angelic societies, which are called celestial-spiritual;

---

[1] That the Lord's influx is into good, and by good into truth, and not *vice versa;* thus into the will, and by it into the understanding, and not *vice versa,* n. 5482, 5649, 6027, 8685, 8701, 10153.

[2] That the will of man is the very *esse* of his life, and is the receptacle of the good of love; and that the understanding is the *existere* of life thence derived, and is the receptacle of the truth and good of faith, n. 3619, 5002, 9282. Thus that the life of the will is the principal life of man, and that the life of the understanding proceeds from it, n. 585, 590, 3619, 7342, 8885, 9282, 10076, 10109, 10110. That those things become principles of life, and are appropriated to man, which are received by the will, n. 3161, 9386, 9393. That man is man by virtue of his will and thence of his understanding, n. 8911, 9069, 9071, 10076, 10109, 10110. That every one, also, is loved and valued by others who possesses a sound will and understanding, and that he is rejected and held in light estimation who understands well, but does not will accordingly, n. (8911), (10075). That man also after death remains such as his will is, and his understanding thence derived; and that the things of the understanding, which are not at the same time things of the will, vanish, because they are not in the man, n. 9069, 9071, 9282, 9386, 10153.

4 B

through these the celestial kingdom flows into the spiritual.[1] Hence it is, that, although heaven is divided into two kingdoms, still it makes one; for the Lord always provides such intermediate angels, through whom there may be communication and conjunction.

28. Much is said in the following pages about the angels of both kingdoms; therefore it is needless to enter into particulars here.

THERE ARE THREE HEAVENS.

29. THERE are three heavens, and these are most distinct from each other; the inmost or third, the middle or second, and the ultimate or first. They follow in order and are mutually related like the highest part of man, which is called the head, his middle, which is the body, and the lowest, which is the feet; and like the highest, middle, and lowest stories of a house. The Divine which proceeds and descends from the Lord is also in similar order; therefore, from the necessity of order, heaven is threefold.

30. The interiors of man, which belong to his rational mind [*mens*] and his natural mind [*animus*],* are also in similar order; he has an inmost, a middle, and an ultimate; for when man was created, all things of divine order were collated into him, so that he was made divine order in form, and thence a

---

[1] That there is communication and conjunction between the two kingdoms by means of angelic societies, which are called celestial-spiritual, n 4047, 6435, 8787, 8802. Concerning the influx of the Lord through the celestial kingdom into the spiritual, n. 3669, 6366.

* [The author frequently employs two Latin words together (*mens* and *animus*) to denote the mind,—meaning by the former the rational mind, which is relatively internal, and by the latter the natural mind, which is relatively external. A similar distinction, common also with the philosophers, is indicated in the Apostolic writings by the two Greek words *pneuma* and *psyche*—TR.]

heaven in miniature.[1] For this reason also, man, as to his interiors, communicates with the heavens; and he also comes among the angels after death,—among those of the inmost, middle, or lowest heaven, according to his reception of divine good and truth from the Lord, during his life in the world.

31. The Divine which flows-in from the Lord, and is received in the third or inmost heaven, is called celestial; and therefore the angels in that heaven are called celestial angels. The Divine which flows-in from the Lord, and is received in the second or middle heaven, is called spiritual; and therefore the angels in that heaven are called spiritual angels. The Divine also which flows-in from the Lord, and is received in the ultimate or first heaven, is called natural; but because the natural of that heaven is not like the natural of the world—for it has a spiritual and celestial within it—therefore that heaven is called spiritual- and celestial-natural, and the angels there, spiritual- and celestial-natural angels.[2] Those are called spiritual-natural who receive influx from the second or middle heaven, which is the spiritual heaven; and those are called celestial-natural who receive influx from the third or inmost heaven, which is the celestial heaven. The spiritual-natural and the celestial-natural angels are distinct from each

---

[1] That all things of Divine Order were collated into man, and that man from creation is Divine Order in form, n. 4219, 4222, 4223, 4523, 4524, 5114, (5368), 6013, 6057, 6605, 6626, 9706, 10156, 10472. That with man his internal man was formed to the image of heaven, and his external to the image of the world, and that on this account man was called by the ancients a microcosm, n. 4523, 5368, 6013, 6057, 9279, 9706, 10156, 10472. That thus man from creation, as to his interiors, is a heaven in its least form, according to the image of the greatest, and that this also is the case with the man who is created anew, or regenerated by the Lord, n. 911, 1900, 1928, 3624 to 3631, 3634, 3884, 4041, 4279, 4523, 4524, 4625, 6013, 6057, 9279, 9632.

[2] That there are three heavens, the inmost, the middle, and the ultimate; or the third, the second, and the first, n. 684, 9594, 10270. That the goods in each heaven follow also in a threefold order, n. 4938, 4939, 9992, 10005, 10017. That the good of the inmost or third heaven is called celestial, the good of the middle or second heaven spiritual, and the good of the ultimate or first heaven spiritual-natural, n. 4279, 4286, 4938, 4939, 9992, 10005, 10017, 10068.

other; but still they constitute one heaven, because they are in the same degree.

32. There is in each heaven an internal and an external. They who are in the internal, are called internal angels; but they who are in the external, are called external angels. The external and internal in the heavens, or in each heaven, are like the voluntary and its intellectual with man; the internal being as the voluntary, and the external as its intellectual. Every voluntary has its intellectual; one does not exist without the other. The voluntary is comparatively as flame, and its intellectual as the light thence derived.

33. It is to be carefully noted, that the interiors of the angels are what determine their situation in one or the other of these heavens; for the more their interiors are open to the Lord, the more interior is the heaven in which they dwell. There are three degrees of the interiors with every one, whether angel, spirit, or man. They with whom the third degree is open, are in the inmost heaven; they with whom the second degree is open, are in the middle heaven; and they with whom only the first degree is open, are in the lowest heaven. The interiors are opened by the reception of divine good and divine truth. They who are affected with divine truths, and admit them immediately into the life, thus into the will, and thence into act, are in the inmost or third heaven, and are situated in that heaven according to their reception of good from the affection of truth; but they who do not admit them immediately into the will, but into the memory and thence into the understanding, and from that will and do them, are in the middle or second heaven; while they who live a moral life, and believe in a Divine Being, and care but little about being instructed, are in the lowest or first heaven.[1] Hence it may be manifest that the states of the interiors make heaven, and that heaven is within every one, and not without him; as the Lord also teaches, where he says, "*The kingdom*

---

[1] That there are as many degrees of life in man, as there are heavens, and that they are opened after death according to his life, n.3747, 9594. That heaven is in man, n. 3884. Consequently that he who receives heaven in himself during his abode in the world, comes into heaven after death, n. 10717.

*of God cometh not with observation: neither shall they say,
Lo here! or, Lo there! for, behold, the kingdom of God is
within you.*" Luke xvii. 20, 21.

34. All perfection also increases toward the interiors and decreases toward the exteriors, because interior things are nearer
the Divine, and in themselves purer; but exterior things are
more remote from the Divine, and in themselves grosser.[1] Angelic perfection consists in intelligence, wisdom, love and every
good, and thence in happiness; but not in happiness without the
former; for without them happiness is external, and not internal.
Since the interiors of the angels of the inmost heaven are open
to the third degree, therefore their perfection immensely surpasses the perfection of the angels in the middle heaven, whose
interiors are open to the second degree. In like manner the
perfection of the angels of the middle heaven surpasses the perfection of the angels of the ultimate heaven.

35. In consequence of this difference, an angel of one heaven
cannot enter-in among the angels of another heaven; in other
words, one cannot ascend from an inferior heaven, nor descend
from a superior one. Whoever ascends from an inferior heaven,
is seized with painful anxiety; nor can he see those who are
there, still less converse with them; and whoever descends from
a superior heaven, is deprived of his wisdom, stammers in his
speech, and is filled with despair. Some angels of the ultimate
heaven, who had not yet been instructed that heaven consists in
the interiors of the angels, believed that they should come into
superior heavenly happiness, if they could only come into a
heaven of superior angels. They were therefore permitted to
enter; but when they were there, they saw no one however they
searched, although a great multitude were present; for the interiors of the strangers were not opened in the same degree as the

---

[1] That interior things are more perfect, because nearer to the Divine, n.
3405, 5146, 5147. That in the internal there are thousands and thousands
of things, which in the external appear as one general thing, n. 5707.
That in proportion as man is elevated from external things toward interior, he comes into light, and thus into intelligence; and that this elevation is like passing out of a mist into a clear atmosphere, n. 4598, 6183,
6313.

interiors of the angels who lived there; hence neither was their sight. Shortly after, they were seized with such intense anguish that they scarcely knew whether they were alive or not. Wherefore they quickly returned to the heaven whence they came, glad to come among their own, and promising that they would no more covet higher things than were in agreement with their life. I have also seen some let down from a superior heaven, and so entirely deprived of their wisdom, as not to know what their own heaven was. It is otherwise when the Lord, as frequently happens, elevates angels from an inferior to a superior heaven, that they may see its glory; in such cases they are first prepared and encompassed with intermediate angels, through whom communication is effected. It is evident from these things, that the three heavens are most distinct from each other.

36. Those, however, who belong to the same heaven, can hold intercourse with every one there; but the delights of their intercourse are according to their affinities for good. But of these in the following chapters.

37. But, although the heavens are so distinct that the angels of one heaven cannot associate with those of another, still the Lord conjoins all the heavens by immediate and mediate influx; by immediate influx from Himself into all the heavens, and by mediate influx from one heaven into another;[1] and thus He accomplishes His purpose, that the three heavens may be one, that all may be in connection from First to last, and that nothing be unconnected; whatever is not connected by intermediates with THE FIRST, cannot subsist, but is dissipated and becomes nothing.[2]

----

[1] That influx from the Lord is immediate from Himself, and also mediate through one heaven into another, and that the Lord's influx into the interiors of man is in similar order, n. 6063, 6307, 6472, 9682, 9683. Concerning the immediate influx of the Divine from the Lord, n. 6058, 6474 to 6478, 8717, 8728. Concerning mediate influx through the spiritual world into the natural world, n. 4067, 6982, 6985, 6996.

[2] That all things exist from things prior to themselves, thus from the First, and that in like manner they subsist,—because subsistence is perpetual existence,—and that therefore there is nothing unconnected, n. 3626 to 3628, 3648, 4523, 4524, 6040, 6056.

38. He who is unacquainted with the nature of divine order as to degrees, cannot comprehend in what manner the heavens are distinct, nor even 'what is meant by the internal and external man. Most people have no other idea concerning things interior and exterior, or concerning things superior and inferior, than as of something continuous, or cohering by continuity from purer to grosser: whereas things interior and exterior are not continuous with respect to each other, but discrete. Degrees are of two kinds; namely, degrees continuous and degrees not continuous. Degrees continuous are as the degrees of the waning light from flame even to its extinction; or as the degrees of the waning sight, from things which are in light to those which are in shade; or as the degrees of the purity of the atmosphere, from its lowest to its highest parts. Distances determine these degrees. Whereas degrees not continuous, but discrete, are distinguished like prior and posterior, like cause and effect, and like what produces and what is produced. The careful inquirer will discover, that in all created things whatsoever, and in every part of them, there are such degrees of production and composition; namely, that from one thing proceeds another, and from that a third, and so on. Whoever fails to comprehend these degrees, cannot possibly understand the distinctions of the heavens, and the distinctions of the interior and exterior faculties of man; nor the distinction between the spiritual world and the natural world; nor the distinction between the spirit of man and his body; and consequently he cannot understand what and whence correspondences and representations are, nor what influx is. Sensual men do not comprehend these distinctions, for they make increments and decrements, even according to these degrees, continuous; hence they are unable to conceive of what is spiritual, otherwise than as a purer natural. Wherefore they also stand without, and far removed from intelligence.[1]

---

[1] That things interior and exterior are not continuous, but distinct and discrete according to degrees, and that each degree has a distinct termination, n. 3691, 5145, 5114, 8603, 10099. That one thing is formed from another and that the things which are so formed are not purer and grosser by continuity, n. 6326, 6465. That he who cannot perceive the distinction of things interior and exterior, according to such degrees, cannot compre-

39. Lastly, I am permitted to relate a certain arcanum concerning the angels of the three heavens, which has never before entered the mind of any one, because no one has hitherto understood the subject of degrees. The arcanum is this: that with every angel, and also with every man, there is an inmost or supreme degree, or an inmost or supreme something, into which the Divine of the Lord first or proximately flows, and from which it arranges the other interior things which succeed according to the degrees of order with the angel or man. This inmost or supreme [region] may be called the Lord's entrance to angels and men, and His veriest dwelling-place with them. By virtue of this supreme or inmost, man is man, and is distinguished from brute animals; for these do not possess it. Hence it is that man, different from animals, can, as to all the interiors of his rational and natural minds (*mentis et animi ejus*) be elevated by the Lord to Himself, can believe in Him, be affected with love toward Him, and thus see Him; and that he can receive intelligence and wisdom, and converse in a rational manner. It is for this reason also that he lives forever. But what is disposed and provided by the Lord in this inmost [region] does not come manifestly to the perception of any angel, because it is above his thought, and transcends his wisdom.

40. These are general truths concerning the three heavens; but in what follows I shall speak of each heaven specifically. ·

THE HEAVENS CONSIST OF INNUMERABLE SOCIETIES.

41. THE angels of each heaven do not all dwell together in one place, but are distinguished into larger and smaller societies, according to the differences of the good of love and faith in which they are. They who are in similar good form one soci-

hend the internal and external man, nor the interior and exterior heavens, n. 5146, 6465, 10099, 10181 ety. Goods in the heavens are of infinite variety; and every angel is such, in character, as is his own good.[1]

42. The angelic societies in the heavens are also distant from each other according to the general and specific differences of their goods; for distances in the spiritual world are from no other origin than from a difference in the state of the interiors, consequently, in the heavens, from a difference in the states of love. Those are far apart who differ much, and those are near who differ little. Similarity brings them together.[2]

43. All in each society are arranged among themselves according to the same law. The more perfect ones, that is, those who excel in good, consequently in love, wisdom, and intelligence, are in the middle. Those who excel less, are round about them, at a distance varying with the degrees of their perfection. This arrangement may be compared to light decreasing from the centre toward the circumference. Those in the middle are also in the greatest light, and those near the circumference, in less and less.

44. Those of like character are brought together as it were spontaneously; for with their like, they are as with their own [relations], and at home; but with others, as with strangers and abroad. When they are with their like, they are also in their freedom, and thence in every delight of life.

45. Hence it is evident that good consociates all in the heavens, and that all are distinguished according to its quality:

---

[1] That variety is infinite, and that in no instance is one thing the same as another, n. 7236, 9002. That there is also an infinite variety in the heavens, n. 684, 690, 3744, 5598, 7236. That the varieties in the heavens, —which are infinite,—are varieties of good, n. 3744, 4005, 7236, 7833, 7836, 9002. That these varieties exist by means of the multiplicity of truths from which every one has good, n. 3470, 3804, 4149, 6917, 7236. That hence all the societies in the heavens, and every angel in a society, are distinct from each other, n. 690, 3241, 3519, 3804, 3986, 4067, 4149, 4263, 7236, 7833, 7836; but that still all act in unity by love from the Lord, n. 457, 3986.

[2] That all the societies of heaven have a fixed position according to the differences of the state of life, thus according to the differences of love and of faith, n. 1274, 3638, 3639. Wonderful things in the other life, or in the spiritual world, concerning distance, situation, place, space, and time, n. 1273 to 1277.

B*

nevertheless it is the Lord, the Source of all good, who thus joins the angels in consociation,. and not the angels themselves. He leads them, conjoins them, arranges them, and keeps them in freedom, so far as they are in good ; thus He preserves every one in the life of his love. faith, intelligence, and wisdom, and thence in happiness.[1]

46. All who are in similar good also know each other—although they had never met before—just as men in the world know their kindred, relations and friends ; the reason is, because in the other life there are no kindreds, relationships, and friend ships, but such as are spiritual, that is, of love and faith.[2] I have several times been permitted to see this, when I have been in the spirit, withdrawn as it were from the body, and thus in company with angels. On such occasions, I have seen some who seemed as if I had known them from infancy ; but others seemed wholly unknown to me. They who seemed as if known from infancy, were those who were in a state similar to the state of my spirit ; but they who were unknown, were in a dissimilar state.

47. All who belong to the same angelic society resemble each other in general, but not in particular. How likenesses in general can coexist with variations in particular, may in some measure be comprehended from examples of a like nature in the world. It is well known that every race of people have some common resemblance in the face and eyes, whereby they are known and distinguished from other races ; and the distinction between families is still more marked ; but it is more perfect in the heavens, because there all the interior affections appear and

---

[1] That all freedom is of love and affection, because what a man loves, that he does freely, n. 2870, 3158, 8990, 9585, 9591. That since freedom is of the love, thence also it is the life of every one, and its delight, n. 2873. That nothing appears to be a man's own, but what is from freedom, n. 2880. To be led of the Lord is essential liberty, because this is to be led by the love of good and truth, n. 892, 905, 2872, 2886, 2890, 2891, 2892. 9096, 9586 to 9591.

[2] That all proximities, relationships, affinities, and as it were consanguinities, in heaven, are from good, and according to its agreements and differences, n. 605, 917, 1394, 2739, 3612, 3815, 4121.

shine forth from the face,—for the face in heaven is the external and representative form of those affections. No one in heaven is permitted to have a face that is not in correspondence with his affections. It has also been shown me how the general resemblance is particularly varied in the individuals of one society. There appeared to me a face like that of an angel, which was varied according to the affections of good and truth, as they exist with those who are in one society. These variations continued a long time; and I observed that the same face in general remained as the plane [or groundwork], and that the rest were only derivations and propagations from that. By this face were also shown me in like manner the affections of the whole society, according to which the faces of those belonging to it are varied; for, as was said above, the faces of angels are the forms of their interiors, thus of affections which are of love and faith.

48. Hence also it is, that an angel who excels in wisdom, instantly discerns the character of another from his face. No one in heaven can conceal his interiors by his countenance, and it is absolutely impossible for him to dissemble and deceive through craft and hypocrisy. It sometimes happens that hypocrites insinuate themselves into societies, having learned to conceal their interiors, and to compose their exteriors so as to appear in the form of the good in which the members of that society are, and thus to feign themselves angels of light; but they cannot remain there long; for they begin to experience interior pain, to be tortured, to grow livid in the face, and to become as it were half-dead; these sufferings arise from the contrariety of the life which flows-in and operates [upon them]; wherefore they quickly cast themselves down into the hell inhabited by their like; nor do they any more desire to ascend. These are they who are meant by the man who was found among the invited guests, not having on a wedding-garment, and was cast into outer darkness. (Matt. xxii. 11, and following verses).

49. All the societies of heaven communicate with each other; not by open intercourse, for few go out of their own society into another, since to go out of their own society is like going out of themselves, or out of their own life, and passing into another which is not so agreeable. But they all communicate

oy an extension of the sphere which proceeds from the life of every one. The sphere of one's life is the sphere of his affections, which are of love and faith. This sphere extends itself far and wide into the surrounding societies, and in proportion as the affections are more interior and perfect.[1] The angels are intelligent and wise according to the measure of that extension. They who are in the inmost heaven, and in the centre of it, have extension into the whole heaven. Hence there is in heaven a communication of all with each, and of each with all.[2] But this extension will be more fully treated of hereafter, when we come to speak of the heavenly form according to which the angelic societies are arranged, and also where we treat of the wisdom and intelligence of the angels; for all extension of the affections and thoughts proceeds according to that form.

50. It was said above that there are larger and smaller societies in the heavens; the larger consist of myriads of angels, the smaller of some thousands, and the least of some hundreds. There are some also who live apart, as it were in separate house and families; these, although they live so dispersed, are still ar ranged in like manner as those who live in societies; that is, the wiser of them are in the midst, and the more simple in the boun daries. These are more immediately under the divine auspices of the Lord, and are the best of the angels.

---

[1] That a spiritual sphere, which is a sphere of life, flows forth from every man, spirit, and angel, and encompasses them, n. 4464, 5179, 7454, 8630. That it flows forth from the life of their affection and thought, n. 2489, 4464, 6206. That those spheres extend themselves far into angelic societies according to the quality and quantity of good, n. 6598 to 6613, 8063, 8794, 8797.

[2] That in the heavens there is given a communication of all goods, inasmuch as heavenly love communicates all its own to another, n. 549, 550, 1390, 1391, 1399, 10130, 10723.

EVERY SOCIETY IS A HEAVEN IN A LESS FORM, AND EVERY ANGEL IN THE LEAST.

51. EVERY society is a heaven in a less form, and every angel in the least, because the good of love and faith is what makes heaven; and this good is in every society of heaven, and in every angel of the society. It matters not that this good is everywhere different and various; it is still the good of heaven; the only difference is, that heaven is of one quality in one part, and of another in another. It is therefore said, when one is elevated into any society of heaven, that he is gone to heaven; and of those who are there, that they are in heaven, and every one in his own heaven. This is known to all in the other life; therefore they who stand without or beneath heaven, and view the angelic societies from afar, say that heaven is there and also there. It is, comparatively, as with governors, officers, and servants, in a royal palace or court; although they live by themselves in separate apartments or chambers, one above and another below, still they are all in one palace or court, each one ready to serve the king in his respective function. Hence is evident what is meant by the words of the Lord, "*In my Father's house are many mansions;*" John xiv. 2; and what by the *habitations of heaven*, and by the *heavens of heavens* in the prophets.

52. That every society is a heaven in a less form is also evident from this, that the heavenly form of each one is similar to that of the whole heaven. In the whole heaven, they who excel the rest are in the centre; and around them, even to the boundaries, in a decreasing order, are they who excel less, as may be seen in a preceding section, n. 43. The same is evident from this also, that the Lord leads all in the whole heaven as if they were one angel; in like manner those in each society. Hence an entire angelic society sometimes appears as a single individual in the form of an angel, which also the Lord has permitted me to see. When also the Lord appears in the midst of the angels, He does not appear encompassed by a multitude, but as one in an angelic form. Hence it is that the Lord in the Word is called

an angel; as is also an entire society. Michael, Gabriel, and Raphael, are only angelic societies, which are so named from their functions.[1]

53. As an entire society is a heaven in a less form, so likewise is every angel a heaven in the least; for heaven is not without an angel, but within him; for his interiors, which belong to his mind, are arranged into the form of heaven, and thus for the reception of all things of heaven which are without him. He also receives them according to the quality of the good which is in him from the Lord. Hence an angel is also a heaven.

54. It can in no case be said that heaven is without one, but that it is within him; for every angel receives the heaven which is without him according to the heaven which is within him. This plainly shows how much he is deceived, who believes that to go to heaven is merely to be elevated among the angels, without regard to the quality of one's interior life; thus that heaven may be given to every one from immediate mercy;[2] when yet, unless heaven be within a person, nothing of the heaven which is without him flows-in and is received. Many spirits entertain this opinion; and because of their belief, they have been taken up into heaven; but when they came there, because their interior life was contrary to that of the angels, they grew blind as to their intellectual faculties till they became like idiots, and were tortured as to their will faculties so that they behaved like madmen; in a word, they who go to heaven after living wicked lives, gasp there for breath, and writhe about like fishes taken from the

[1] That the Lord in the Word is called an angel, n. 6280, 6831, 8192, 9303. That an entire angelic society is called an angel; and that Michael and Raphael are angelic societies so named, from their functions, n. 8192. That the societies of heaven, and the angels, have not any name, but that they are distinguished by the quality of their good, and by an idea concerning it, n. 1705, 1754.

[2] That heaven is not granted from unconditional mercy, but according to the life, and that the all of that life, by which man is led of the Lord to heaven, is from mercy, and that this is the meaning of mercy, n. 5057, 10659. That if heaven were granted from immediate mercy, it would be granted to all, n. 2401. Concerning some evil spirits cast down from heaven, who believed that heaven was granted to every one from immediate mercy, n. 4226.

water into the air, and like animals in the ether of an air-pump, after the air has been exhausted. Hence it is evident that heaven is not without one, but within him.[1]

55. Since all receive the heaven which is without them according to the quality of the heaven which is within them, therefore they receive the Lord in like manner, since the Divine of the Lord makes heaven. Hence it is, that when the Lord presents Himself in any society, He appears there according to the quality of the good in which the society is principled, thus not the same in one society as in another : not that the dissimilitude is in the Lord, but in those who see Him from their own good, thus according to that good. The angels are also affected at the sight of the Lord according to the quality of their love ; they who love Him deeply, are deeply affected ; they who love Him less, are less affected ; and the evil who are out of heaven, are tormented at His presence. When the Lord appears in any society, He appears there as an angel ; but He is distinguished from others by the Divine which shines through Him.

56. Heaven also exists wherever the Lord is acknowledged, believed in, and loved. Variety in the worship of Him, arising from the variety of good in different societies, is not injurious, but advantageous ; for the perfection of heaven results from such variety. It is difficult to explain intelligibly how the perfection of heaven is the result of such variety, unless we employ some terms familiar to the learned world, and by means of these show how a perfect one is formed of various parts. Every whole is composed of various parts ; for a whole which is not composed of various parts is nothing, therefore it has no form, and no quality. But when a whole is composed of various parts, and these are arranged in a perfect form, wherein each part joins itself to another as a sympathizing friend in the series, then it is complete. Now heaven is a whole composed of various parts arranged in the most perfect form ; for the heavenly form is the most perfect of all forms. That all perfection results from this harmonious arrangement of parts that are different, is evident from all the beauty, pleasantness, and delight, which affect both the senses

---

[1] That heaven is in man, n. 3884.

and the mind (*animus*); for these exist and flow from no other source than from the concert and harmony of many concordant and sympathizing parts, either coexistent or successive, and not from one thing alone; hence it is said that variety is charming, and it is known that its charms depend upon its quality. From these considerations it may be seen as in a mirror how perfection results from variety, even in heaven; for from the things existing in the natural world, those in the spiritual world may be seen as in a mirror.[1]

57. The same may be said concerning the church as concerning heaven; for the church is the Lord's heaven upon earth. There are also many churches, and yet each one is called a church, and likewise is a church, so far as the good of love and faith rules therein. There also the Lord makes a whole from different parts, thus from several churches makes one church.[2] The same, too, may be said of each member of the church in particular, as of the church in general; namely, that the church is within him and not without him, and that every man, in whom the Lord is present in the good of love and faith, is a church.[3] The same may also be said of a man in whom the church is, as of an angel in whom heaven is, that he is a church in the least form, as an angel is a heaven in the least form; and further, that a man in whom the church is, is a heaven equally with an angel; for man was created that he might go to heaven and become an angel; wherefore he who receives good from the Lord, is a man-angel.[4]

---

[1] That every whole [*unum*] results from the harmony and agreement of various parts, and that otherwise it has no quality, n. 457. That hence the universal heaven is a one, n. 457. Because all therein regard one end, which is the Lord, n. 9828.

[2] That if good were the characteristic and essential of the church, and not truth without good, the church would be a one, n. 1285, 1316, 2982, 3267, 3445, 3451, 3452. That all churches also make one church before the Lord, by virtue of good, n. 7396, 9276.

[3] That the church is in man, and not out of him, and that the church at large consists of men in whom the church is, n. 3884.

[4] That a man who is a church, is a heaven in the least form, after the image of the greatest, because his interiors, which are of the mind, are arranged after the form of heaven, and consequently for the reception of

I am permitted to tell what man has in common with an angel, and what he has more than the angels. *Man has in common with an angel*, that his interiors are alike formed in the image of heaven, and also that he becomes an image of heaven in proportion as he is in the good of love and faith. But *man has more than the angels*, in that his exteriors are formed in the image of the world, and in proportion as he is in good, the world with him is subordinate to heaven and serves it;[1] and then the Lord is present with him in both as in His heaven; for He is in His own divine order everywhere, for God is order.[2]

58. Lastly, it is to be observed, that whoever has heaven in himself, not only has heaven in his greatest or general principles, but also in his least or most particular ones; and that the least things in him are an image of the greatest. This results from the fact, that every one is his own love, and is of the same quality as his ruling love; whatever rules flows into and arranges all the particulars, and everywhere induces a likeness of itself.[3] The ruling love in the heavens is love to the Lord, because the Lord

all things of heaven, n. 911, 1900, 1928, 3624 to 3631, 3634, 3884, 4041, 4279, 4523, 4524, 4625, 6013, 6057, 9279, 9632.

[1] That man has an internal and an external, and that his internal from creation is formed after the image of heaven, and his external after the image of the world, and that on this account man was called by the ancients a microcosm, n. 4523, 4524, 5368, 6013, 6057, 9279, 9706, 10156, 10472. That therefore man was so created that the world in him might serve heaven, which also it does in the good, but that with the evil the case is inverted, and heaven serves the world, n. 9283, 9278.

[2] That the Lord is order, because the divine good and truth, which proceed from the Lord, make order, n. 1728, 1919, (2201), 2258, (5110), 5703, 8988, 10336, 10619. That divine truths are laws of order, n. 2247, 7995. That so far as man lives according to order, thus so far as he is in good according to divine truths, so far he is a man, and the church and heaven are in him, n. 4839, 6605, (8067).

[3] That the ruling or governing love with every one is in all and each of the things of his life, thus in all and each of the things of his thought and will, n. 6159, 7648, 8067, 8853. That man is such as the ruling principle of his life is, n. (918), 1040, 1568, 1571, 3570, 6571, 6934, 6938, 8854, 8856, 8857, 10076, 10109, 10110, 10284. That love and faith, when they rule, are in the minutest particulars of the life of man, though he does not know it, n. 8854, 8864, 8865.

6

is there loved above all things.   Hence the Lord is there the All in
all ; He flows into all and each of the angels, arranges them, and
induces in them a likeness of Himself, and causes Heaven to be
wherever He is.   Hence an angel is a heaven in the least form, a
society in a greater, and all the societies taken together in the
greatest.   That the Divine of the Lord makes heaven, and that
it is the all in all there, may be seen above, n. 7 to 12.

THE WHOLE HEAVEN IN ONE COMPLEX RESEMBLES ONE MAN.

59.   THAT heaven in its whole complex resembles one man, is
an arcanum not yet known in the world ; but in the heavens it is
very well known.   To know this, together with the specific and
particular things relating to it, is the chief article of the intelligence of the angels.   On this knowledge also depend many
more things which, without it as their general principle, could
not enter distinctly and clearly into the ideas of their minds.
Because they know that all the heavens, together with their societies, resemble one man, therefore also they call heaven THE
GREATEST and THE DIVINE MAN ;[1] Divine from this, that the
Divine of the Lord makes heaven ; see above, n. 7 to 12.

60. That celestial and spiritual things are arranged and conjoined into that form and image, cannot be conceived by those
who have no just idea respecting things spiritual and celestial ;
they imagine that the terrestrial and material things which compose the ultimate of man, are what make man, and that he would
not be man without them.   But be it known to such, that man is
not man by virtue of those things, but by virtue of this, that he
can understand what is true, and will what is good ; these are the

[1] That heaven in the whole complex appears in form as a man, and that
heaven itself is hence called the GRAND MAN [or Greatest Man], n. 2996,
2998, 3624 to 3649, 3741 to 3745, 4625.

spiritual and celestial things which make man. It is also generally known, that every man is such as is the character of his understanding and will; and it might also be known, that his earthly body is formed to serve these faculties in the world, and to perform uses in accordance with their dictates, in the ultimate sphere of nature. Therefore also the body has no activity of itself, but acts altogether obsequious to the nod of the understanding and the will, insomuch that whatever a man thinks, he utters with the tongue and lips, and whatever he wills, he performs with the body and its members; so that understanding and will are the active agent, and the body does nothing itself. Hence it is evident, that the things of the understanding and the will are what make the man; and that these are in the human form, because they act upon the most minute parts of the body, as what is internal acts upon what is external; by virtue of these faculties, therefore, man is called an internal and spiritual man. Heaven is such a man, in the greatest and most perfect form.

61. Such is the idea of the angels concerning man. Wherefore they never attend to the things which man does with the body, but to the will from which the body does them. This they call the man himself, and the understanding so far as it acts in unison with the will.[1]

62. The angels, indeed, do not see heaven in the whole complex in the form of a man, for the whole heaven does not fall under the view of any angel; but they sometimes see remote societies, consisting of many thousands of angels, as one in such a form: and from a society, as from a part, they form a conclusion concerning the whole, which is heaven. For in the most perfect form, the whole is as the parts, and the parts as the whole; the only difference being like that between similar things of greater and less magnitude.[*] Hence they say, that the whole heaven is

---

[1] That the will of man is the very esse of his life, and that the understanding is the existere of life thence derived, n. 3619, 5002, 9282. That the life of the will is the principal life of man, and that the life of the understanding proceeds thence, n. 585, 590, 3619, 7342, 8885, 9282, 10076, 10109, 10110. That man is man from his will, and thence from his understanding, n. 8911, 9069, 9071, 10076, 10109, 10110.

[*] [This may be illustrated by the configuration of salts of the same

such in the sight of the Lord, [as a single society is when seen
by them], because the Divine, from the inmost and supreme, be-
holds all things.

63 Such being the form of heaven, it is therefore ruled by the
Lord as one man, and thence as one whole; for it is well known,
that although man consists of an innumerable variety of things,
both in the whole and in part,—*in the whole*, of members, organs,
and viscera; *in part*, of series of fibres, nerves, and blood vessels,—thus of members within members and parts within parts,
yet still the man, when he acts, acts as a unit.   Such also is heaven under the auspices and guidance of the Lord.

64. The reason why so many different things in man act as
one, is because there is nothing whatever in him which does not
contribute something to the common weal, and perform some
use.   The whole performs use to its parts, and the parts perform
use to the whole; for the whole is made up of the parts, and the
parts constitute the whole; wherefore they provide for each
other, have respect to each other, and are conjoined in such a
form, that all and each have reference to the whole and its good.
Hence it is that they act as one.   The consociations in the heavens are similar.   They are joined together there according to
their uses in a like form; wherefore they who do not perform use
to the community, are cast out of heaven as things foreign to its
nature.   To perform use, is to desire the welfare of others for the
sake of the common good; and not to perform use, is to desire
the welfare of others, not for the sake of the common good, but
for the sake of self.   These latter love themselves supremely, but
the former love the Lord above all things.   Hence it is that they
who are in heaven act in unison, not from themselves but from
the Lord; for they regard Him as the one only Source of all
things, and His kingdom as the community whose good is to be
sought.   This is meant by the Lord's words, " *Seek ye first the
kingdom of God, and His righteousness, and all things shall
be added unto you.*"   Matt. vi. 33.   To seek His righteousness

_____

species; thus, for example, whether they consist of parts of a triangular,
hexagonal, cylindrical, or any other form, it is well known that the minutest particles o those parts are of the same figure.—Tr.]

is [to seek] His good.[1] They who, in the world, love the good of their country more than their own, and the good of their neighbor as their own, are they who, in the other life, love and seek the kingdom of the Lord,—for there the kingdom of the Lord is in the place of their country; and they who love to do good to others, not for their own sake, but for the sake of the good, love their neighbor,—for in the other life good is the neighbor.[2] All of this character are in the GRAND MAN, that is in heaven.

65. Since the whole heaven resembles one man, and likewise is a divine-spiritual man in the greatest form, even as to figure, therefore heaven is distinguished, like man, into members and parts; and these are also named like the members and parts of man. The angels likewise know in what member one society is, and in what another; and they say, that one society is in the member or some province of the head, another in the member or some province of the breast, another in the member or some province of the loins; and so on. In general, the highest or third heaven forms the head down to the neck: the middle or second heaven forms the breast down to the loins and knees; the ultimate or first heaven forms the legs and feet down to the soles, and also the arms down to the fingers,—for the arms and hands are ultimates of man, although at the sides. Hence it is further evident why there are three heavens.

66. The spirits who are beneath heaven are greatly surprised when they hear and see that heaven is beneath, as well as above; for they think and believe, like men in the world, that heaven is nowhere but over head; for they do not know that the situation of the heavens is like that of the members, organs, and viscera

---

[1] That justice in the Word is predicated of good, judgment of truth, and that hence to do justice and judgment is to do what is good and true, n. 2235, 9857.

[2] That in the supreme sense the Lord is the neighBor, and hence that to love the Lord is to love that which is from Him, because in all which is from Him, He is; thus it is to love what is good and true, n. 2425, 3419, 6706, 6711, 6819, 6823, 8123. Hence that all good which is from the Lord is the neighbor, and that to will and to do that good is to love the neighbor, n. 5026, 10336.

in man, some of which are above and some beneath; and that
it is like the situation of the parts in each member, organ, and
viscus, some of which are within and some without.   Hence
they have confused ideas concerning heaven.

67. These things concerning heaven as the GRAND MAN are
adduced, because, without this previous knowledge, what follows
concerning heaven cannot be comprehended; nor can any distinct idea be had of the form of heaven, of the conjunction of
the Lord with heaven, of the conjunction of heaven with man,
nor of the influx of the spiritual world into the natural, and none
whatever concerning correspondence.   Yet these subjects will be
treated in order in what now follows; wherefore this is pre-
mised for the purpose of throwing light upon them.

EVERY SOCIETY IN THE HEAVENS RESEMBLES ONE MAN.

68. THAT every society of heaven resembles one man, and is
likewise in the form of a man, I have several times been permitted to see.   There was a society into which many insinuated
themselves, who knew how to assume the appearance of angels
of light.   They were hypocrites.   When these were being separated from the angels, I saw that the whole society at first appeared as one indistinct mass; then by degrees in the human
form, yet obscurely; and at length distinctly as a man.   They
who were in that man, and composed him, were such as were in
the good of that society; but the rest, who were not in that man,
and did not compose him, were hypocrites.   These were rejected,
but the former were retained; and thus separation was effected.
Hypocrites are they who talk well, and likewise do well, but
regard themselves in everything.   They talk like angels about
the Lord, about heaven, about love, and about heavenly life.
They also do well, that they may appear as they talk, but they
think otherwise; they believe nothing, nor do they will good to
any but themselves: when they do good, it is for the sake of

themselves; and if for the sake of others, it is only that they may be seen; so it is still for the sake of themselves.

69. That an entire angelic society, when the Lord exhibits Himself present, appears as one in a human form, has also been granted me to see. There appeared on high, toward the east, as it were a reddish white cloud, encompassed with little stars. which was descending; and in its descent it gradually became more lucid, until at length it appeared in a form perfectly human. The little stars encompassing the cloud were angels, who appeared as stars by virtue of light from the Lord.

70. It is to be observed, that although all in one heavenly society, when viewed collectively, appear as one in the likeness of a man, still each society is a different man from every other. They differ like the faces of different individuals of the same family, and for a similar reason; of which above, n. 47; that is, they differ according to the varieties of good in which they are, and which determines the form. The societies which are in the inmost or supreme heaven, and in the centre there, appear in the most perfect and beautiful human form.

71. It is worthy of remark, that the greater the number in a society of heaven, and the more they act as one, the more perfectly human is the form of that society; for variety, arranged in a heavenly form produces perfection, as was shown above, n. 56; and where there are many, there is variety. Every society of heaven also increases in number daily, and as it increases it becomes more perfect; and not only does the society become more perfect in this way, but the whole heaven also, because heaven is composed of societies. Since increasing numbers make heaven more perfect, it is evident how much deceived they are, who believe that heaven will be shut when full. When yet the contrary is true, that it will never be shut, and that the greater its fullness, the greater its perfection; wherefore the angels desire nothing more earnestly than the arrival of new angelic guests.

72. Every society when viewed as a whole, appears in the human form, because the universal heaven is in that form, as was shown in the preceding chapter; and in the most perfect form, which is the form of heaven, the parts bear the likeness of the whole, and the least reflects the greatest. The smaller constituents and parts

of heaven are the societies of which it is composed; and that
these are also heavens in a less form, may be seen above, n. 51,
to 58. This likeness is perpetual, because in the heavens the
goods of all are from one love, thus from one origin. The one
love, from which the goods of all in heaven have their origin, is
love to the Lord from the Lord. Hence it is, that the whole
heaven is a likeness of Him in general; every society, less generally; and every angel, in particular. See also what was said
above on this subject, n. 58.

THEREFORE EVERY ANGEL IS IN A PERFECT HUMAN FORM.

73. In the two preceding chapters it was shown that heaven
in the whole complex resembles one man, and in like manner
every society in heaven; and from the sequence of causes there
adduced, it follows that every angel also is in the human form.
As heaven is a man in the greatest form, and a society of heaven
in a less, so is an angel in the least; for in the most perfect form,
which is the form of heaven, there is a likeness of the whole in
every part, and of every part in the whole. The reason is, because heaven is a communion, for it communicates all its own to
each one, and each one receives all that he has from that communion. An angel is a receptacle [of all heavenly things], and
thence a heaven in the least form, as was also shown above in its
proper chapter. Man, too, so far as he receives heaven, is also a
receptacle, a heaven, and an angel; see above, n. 57. This is described in the Apocalypse in these words: "*He measured the
wall of the holy Jerusalem, a hundred and forty-four cubits,
the measure of a man, that is, of an angel.*" xxi. 17. In this
passage, Jerusalem is the Lord's church, and, in a more eminent
sense, heaven;[1] the wall is truth which protects from the assault

---

[1] That Jerusalem is the church, n. 402, 3654, 9166.

of falses and evils;[1] a hundred and forty-four are all truths and goods in the complex;[2] the measure is its quality;[3] man is the subject in whom reside all these things in general and particular, and therefore heaven is in him; and because an angel also is a man from these same things, therefore it is said, the measure of a man, which is that of an angel. This is the spiritual sense of these words. Without that sense, who could understand what is meant by the wall of the holy Jerusalem being the measure of a man, which is that of an angel?[4]

74. But to proceed now to experience. I have seen a thousand times that angels are human forms, or men; for I have conversed with them as man with man, sometimes with one alone, sometimes with many in company; nor did I discover in their form any thing different from the form of man; and I have repeatedly wondered that they were such. And lest it should be said that it was a fallacy, or a visionary fancy, I have been permitted to see them in a state of full wakefulness, when I was in the exercise of every bodily sense, and in a state of clear perception. I have also frequently told them that men in the Christian world are in such blind ignorance concerning angels and spirits, as to believe them to be minds without form, and mere thoughts, concerning which they have no other idea than as of something ethereal, in which there is somewhat vital; and because they thus ascribe to them nothing human except a thinking principle, they

---

[1] That a wall denotes truth protecting from the assault of falses and evils, n. 6419.

[2] That twelve denotes all truths and goods in the complex, n. 577, 2089, 2129, 2130, 3272, 3858, 3913; and in like manner seventy-two, and a hundred and forty-four; since a hundred and forty-four arises from twelve multiplied into itself, n. 7973. That all numbers, in the Word, signify things, n. 482, 487, 647, 648, 755, 813, 1963, 1988, 2075, 2252, 3252, 4264, 4495, 5265. That numbers multiplied signify the same as the simple numbers from which they arise by multiplication, n. 5291, 5335, 5708, 7973.

[3] That measure, in the Word, signifies the quality of a thing as to truth and good, n. 3104, 9603.

[4] Concerning the spiritual or internal sense of the Word, see the tract ON THE WHITE HORSE IN THE APOCALYPSE, and the Appendix to the article on the Word, in that ON THE NEW JERUSALEM AND ITS HEAVENLY DOCTRINE.

imagine that they cannot see, because they have no eyes ; nor hear, because they have no ears ; nor speak, because they have neither mouth nor tongue.   The angels said in reply, that they knew such a belief exists with many in the world, and that it is the prevail· ing belief among the learned, and also, to their astonishment, among the clergy.   They also assigned as a reason for this, that the learned, who were the leaders, and who first broached such ideas concerning angels and spirits, thought of them from the sen· sual conceptions of the external man ; and they who think from these, and not from interior light, and the general idea implanted in every one, must of necessity adopt such fictions ; because the sensuals of the external man can comprehend only what is within nature, but not what is above it, thus nothing whatever of the spiritual world.[1]   From these leaders as guides, the false notion concerning the angels was communicated to others, who did not think for themselves, but from them ; and they who first think from others, and make the things so thought matters of their faith, and afterwards view them as such from their own un-derstanding, can with difficulty recede from them ; wherefore they generally acquiesce in confirming them.   They further said that the simple in faith and heart have no such idea concerning the angels, but think of them as heavenly men, because they have not extinguished by erudition what was implanted in them from heaven, nor can they conceive of anything without a form. Hence it is that angels are always represented in temples, both in sculpture and painting, as men.   Concerning what is thus implanted from heaven, they added, that it is the Divine commu-nicated by influx to those who are in the good of faith and life.

75. From all my experience, which is now of many years, I can declare and affirm that the form of the angels is in every re-spect human ; that they have faces, eyes, ears, breasts, arms,

---

[1] That man, unless he be elevated above the sensual principles of the external man, makes little progress in wisdom, n. 5089.   That a wise men thinks above those sensual principles, n. 5089, 5094.   That when man is elevated above those sensual principles, he comes into a clearer light, and at length into heavenly light, n. 6183, 6313, 6315, 9407, 9730, 9922.   That elevation and abstraction from those sensual principles was known to the ancients, n. 6313.

hands, feet; that they see, hear, and converse with each othei ; in a word, that they lack nothing which belongs to man, except the material body. I have seen them in a light, which exceeds by many degrees the noon-day light of the world; and in that light I observed all parts of their faces more distinctly and clearly than ever I did the face of men on earth. I have also been per-mitted to see an angel of the inmost heaven. His countenance was brighter and more resplendent than the faces of the angels of the inferior heavens. I examined him closely, and his form was perfectly human.

76. It is, however, to be observed, that angels cannot be seen by man with his bodily eyes, but with the eyes of the spirit which is within him ;[1] because the spirit is in the spiritual world, and all things of the body are in the natural world. Like sees like, because from like. Besides, every one knows that the organ of bodily vision, which is the eye, is so gross that it cannot see even the smaller things of nature except by the aid of optical glasses ; much less, then, can it discern those which are above the sphere of nature, as are all things in the spiritual world: never-theless, these are seen by man when he is withdrawn from the bodily sight, and the sight of his spirit is opened. This is ef-fected in a moment, when it pleases the Lord that man should see spiritual things. And then he is not aware, but that he sees them with the eyes of the body. Thus angels were seen by Abraham, Lot, Manoah, and the prophets. Thus the Lord also was seen by His disciples after His resurrection; and in like manner, too, have angels been seen by me. The prophets were called seers, and men whose eyes were open,—1 Sam. ix. 9 ; Numb. xxiv. 3,—because they saw with the eyes of the spirit ; and the opening of this spiritual sight was called opening the eyes. This was the case with the servant of Elisha, of whom we read, "Elisha prayed and said, JEHOVAH, *open, I pray thee, his eyes, that he may see: and* JEHOVAH *opened the eyes of the young man, and he saw; and behold, the mountain was*

---

[1] That man, as to his interiors, is a spirit, n. 1594. And that the spirit is the man himself, and that the body lives from it, n. 447, 4622, 6054.

full of horses and chariots of fire round about Elisha." 2
Kings vi. 17.

77. Good spirits, with whom I have also conversed on this
subject, were deeply grieved that there should be such ignorance
within the church concerning the nature of heaven, and concerning spirits and angels ; and being displeased, they charged me by
all means to make it known, that they are not formless minds,
nor ethereal breaths, but that they are men in form, and that they
see, hear, and feel, the same as men in the world.[1]

IT IS FROM THE DIVINE HUMAN OF THE LORD, THAT THE WHOLE HEAVEN AND EVERY PART OF IT RESEMBLES A MAN.

78. THAT heaven in the whole and in every part resembles a
man, because it exists from the Divine Human of the Lord, follows
as a conclusion from all that has been said and shown in the preceding chapters ; for it was shown, I. *That the Lord is the God
of heaven.* II. *That the Divine of the Lord makes heaven.*
III. *That heaven consists of innumerable societies; and that
every society is a heaven in a less form, and every angel in the
least.* IV. *That the whole heaven in one complex resembles
one man.* V. *That every society in the heavens also resembles
one man.* VI. *That hence every angel is in a perfect human
form.* These propositions all lead to the conclusion, that the
Divine which makes heaven is human in form. That this is the
Divine Human of the Lord, may be still more clearly seen, be-

---

[1] That every angel, because he is a recipient of divine order from the
Lord, is in a human form, perfect and beautiful according to the measure
of his receptivity, n. 322, 1880, 1881, 3633, 3804, 4622, 4735, 4797, 4985,
5199, 5530, 6054,-9879, 10177, 10594. That the divine truth is the principle by which order is effected, and that the divine good is the essential
of order, n. 2451, 3166, 4390, 4409, 5232, 7256, 10122, 10555.

cause in a compendious form, from the extracts which are given
as a corollary to this chapter from the ARCANA CŒLESTIA. That
the Lord's Humanity is Divine, and not merely human, as the
church at this day believes, may also be seen from those extracts,
as well as from those at the end of the chapter on the Lord, in
the work ON THE NEW JERUSALEM AND ITS HEAVENLY DOC-
TRINE.

79. The truth of this has been made evident to me from much
experience, of which something shall now be told. No angel
in all the heavens, ever conceives of the Divine under any other
than the human form ; and what is wonderful, those in the superior heavens are unable to think otherwise of the Divine. This
necessity of their thought flows from the Divine itself, and also
from the form of heaven, according to which their thoughts extend themselves around ; for every thought which the angels
have, has extension into heaven, and their intelligence and wisdom is in proportion to that extension. Hence it is that all there
acknowledge the Lord, because in Him alone is the Divine Human. These things have not only been told me by the angels,
but it has also been given me to perceive them, when I have been
elevated into the interior sphere of heaven. Hence it is evident,
that the wiser the angels are, the more clearly do they perceive
this truth ; and hence it is that the Lord appears to them ; for the
Lord appears in a Divine-angelic form, which is the human, to
those who acknowledge and believe in a visible Divine, but not
to those who acknowledge and believe in an invisible Divine ; for
the former can see their Divine, but the latter cannot.

80. Because the angels have no conception of an invisible
Divine, which they call a Divine without form, but of a visible
Divine in a human form, therefore it is common with them to
say, that the Lord alone is Man, and that they are men from
Him ; and that every one is a man so far as he receives the Lord.
By receiving the Lord, they understand receiving good and truth
which are from Him, since the Lord is in His own good and
His own truth. This also they call intelligence and wisdom.
They say that every one knows that intelligence and wisdom
make the man, and not the face without them. This is manifest
also from the angels of the interior heavens ; because they are in

good and truth from the Lord, and thence in wisdom and intelligence, they are therefore in the most beautiful and most perfect human form ; whilst the angels of the inferior heavens are in a form less perfect and less beautiful. It is the opposite in hell ; those there, when viewed in the light of heaven, scarcely appear as men, but as monsters ; for they are not in good and truth, but in evil and the false, and thence in the opposites of intelligence and wisdom ; wherefore also their life is not called life, but spiritual death.

8˙ Because the whole heaven and every part of it resembles a man from the Divine Human of the Lord, therefore the angels say that they are in the Lord, and some that they are in His body, by which they mean that they are in the good of His love ; as the Lord Himself also teaches, where He says: "*Abide in Me, and I in you. As the branch cannot bear fruit of itself except it abide in the vine, no more can ye, except ye abide in Me ;—for without Me ye can do nothing.— Continue ye in My love : if ye keep my commandments, ye shall abide in My love.*" John xv. 4 to 10.

82. Such being the conception of the Divine in the heavens, it is therefore implanted in every man who receives any influx from heaven, to think of God under a human shape. So thought the ancients, and so the moderns likewise think, both those without and those within church. The simple see Him in thought as an old man encompassed with brightness. But all those have extinguished this implanted perception, who have removed the heavenly influx by their self-derived intelligence, or by a life of evil. They who have extinguished it by self-derived intelligence, are not willing to acknowledge any but an invisible God ; but they who have extinguished it by a life of evil, are not willing to acknowledge any God. Nor is either class aware that any such implanted perception exists, because it no longer exists with them ; when yet this is the Divine celestial itself, which primarily flows from heaven into man, because man was born for heaven, and no one enters heaven without an idea of the Divine.

83. Hence it follows, that one who has no true idea of heaven, that is, of the Divine from whom heaven exists, cannot be elevated to the first threshold of heaven. As soon as he approaches

it, he is sensible of a resistance and a strong repulsion. The reason is, because his interiors, which ought to receive heaven, are closed, since they are not in the form of heaven ; yea, the nearer he approaches heaven, the more tightly are they closed. Such is the lot of those within the church who deny the Lord, and who, like the Socinians, deny His Divinity. But what is the lot of those who are born out of the church, to whom the Lord is not known because they have not the Word, will be seen in what follows.

84. That the ancients had an idea of the Human [linked with their idea] of the Divine, is manifest from the appearances of the Divine to Abraham, Lot, Joshua, Gideon, Manoah, his wife, and others, who, although they saw God as a man, still adored Him as the God of the universe, calling him the God of heaven and earth, and Jehovah. That it was the Lord who was seen by Abraham, He Himself teaches in John, chap. viii. 56 ; that it was He, also, who was seen by the rest, is evident from the Lord's words, "*That no one has seen the Father, and His shape, and heard His voice,*" John, chap. i. 18 ; v. 37.

85. But that God is a Man, can with difficulty be comprehended by those who judge everything from the sensual conceptions of the external man ; for the sensual man cannot think of the Divine, except from the world and the objects therein ; thus he cannot think otherwise of a Divine and Spiritual Man, than as of a corporeal and natural one : hence he concludes that, if God were a Man, He would be as large as the universe ; and if He ruled heaven and earth, He would do it by means of many subordinate officers, after the manner of kings in the world. If he were told, that in heaven there is no extension of space as in the world, he would not at all comprehend it ; for he who thinks solely from nature and its light, thinks of no other sort of extension than that which is visible before him. But people commit a great mistake when they think in this manner concerning heaven. Extension there is not like extension in the world. Extensior. in the world is determinate, and therefore measurable ; but in heaven extension is not determinate, and therefore not measurable. But more will be said hereafter about extension in heaven, when we come to treat of space and time in the spiritual world. Be-

sides, every one knows how far the sight of the eye extends, even
to the sun and stars which are so far distant. He who thinks
more deeply knows also that the internal sight, which is that of
the thought, reaches still further, and hence that a still more interior sight must have a still wider range. What then must be
the Divine sight, which is the inmost and highest of all? Since
the thoughts are capable of such extension, therefore—as has
been shown in preceding chapters—all things of heaven are communicated with every one there, consequently all things of the
Divine which makes heaven and fills it.

86. The inhabitants of heaven are astonished that men should
imagine themselves intelligent, who think of an invisible Being,
that is, of a Being incomprehensible under any form, when they
think of God; and that they should call those not intelligent and
even simple, who think otherwise; when yet the contrary is the
truth. They suggest, that if those who imagine themselves intelligent because they think God has no form, would examine themselves, would they not find that they regard nature as God, some of
them nature as manifest to the sight, others nature in her invisible
recesses? And are they so blind as not to know what God is,
what an angel is, what a spirit is, what their own soul is which is
to live after death, what the life of heaven in man is, and many
other things of intelligence? When yet those whom they call
simpletons know all these things in some measure. Their idea is,
that God is the Divine in a human form; that an angel is a heavenly man; that their own soul, which is to live after death,
is like an angel; and that the life of heaven in man is to live according to the divine precepts. These, therefore, the angels call
intelligent, and fitted for heaven; but the others, on the contrary,
not intelligent.[1]

---

[1] Extracts from the ARCANA CŒLESTIA, concerning the Lord and concerning His Divine Human.

That the Divine was in the Lord from His very conception, n. 4641,
4963, 5041, 5157, 6716, 10125. That Divine seed was in the Lord alone, n.
1438. That His soul was Jehovah, n. 1999, 2004, 2005, 2018, 2025. That
thus the inmost of the Lord was the Divine Itself, and that the clothing
was from the mother, n. 5041. That the Divine Itself was the Esse of the

THERE IS A CORRESPONDENCE OF ALL THINGS OF HEAVEN, WITH ALL THINGS OF MAN.

87. IT is unknown at this day what correspondence is. This ignorance arises from various causes, the chief of which is, that

---

Lord's life, from which the Human afterwards went forth, and was made the Existere from that Esse, n. 3194, 3210, 10269, 10372.

That within the church, where the Word is, by which the Lord is known, the Divine of the Lord ought not to be denied, nor the Holy [Spirit] proceeding from Him, n. 2359. That they within the church who do not acknowledge the Lord, have no conjunction with the Divine, but that it is otherwise with those who are out of the church, n. 10205. That it is an essential of the church to acknowledge the Divine of the Lord, and His union with the Father, n. 10083, 10112, 10370, 10728, 10730, 10816, 10817, 10818, 10820.

That the glorification of the Lord is the subject treated of in many passages of the Word, n. 10828; and that this subject is everywhere treated of in the internal sense of the Word, n. 2249, 2523, 3245. That the Lord glorified His Human, but not the Divine, because the Divine was glorified in Itself, n. 10057. That the Lord came into the world that He might glorify His Human, n. 3637, 4286, 9315. That the Lord glorified His Human by the divine love which was in Him from conception, n. 4727. That the love of the Lord toward the universal human race, was the life of the Lord in the world, n. 2253. That the Lord's love transcends all human understanding, n. 2077. That the Lord saved the human race by glorifying His Human, n. 4180, 10019, 10152, 10655, 10659, 10828. That otherwise the whole human race would have perished in eternal death, n. 1676. Concerning the state of the Lord's glorification and humiliation, n. 1785, 1999, 2159, 6866. That glorification, when predicated of the Lord, denotes, the uniting of His Human with His Divine, and that to glorify is to make Divine, n. 1603, 10053, 10828. That the Lord, when he glorified His Human, put off all the human derived from the mother, until at length He was not her son, n. 2159, 2574, 2649, 3036, 10830.

That the Son of God from eternity was the divine truth in heaven, n. (2628), (2798), 2803, 3195, 3704. That the Lord also made His Human divine truth from the divine good which was in Him, when He was in the world, n. 2803, 3194, 3195, 3210, 6716, 6864, 7014, 7499, 8127, 8724, 9199 That the Lord at that time arranged all things appertaining to Himself into a celestial form, which is according to divine truth, n. 1928, 3633. That on this account the Lord was called the Word, which is divine truth, n. 2533, 2818, 2859, 2894, 3393, 3712. That the Lord alone had perception

8   C*

man has removed himself from heaven by the love of self and
the world ; for he who loves himself and the world above all else,

---

and thought from Himself, and above all angelic perception and thought,
n. 1904, 1914, 1919.

That the Lord united the divine truth, which was Himself, with the divine good, which was in Himself, n. 10047, 10052, 10076. That the union
was reciprocal, n. 2004, 10067. That the Lord, when He departed from
the world, made His Human also divine good, n. 3194, 3210, 6864, 7499,
8724, 9199, 10076. That this is meant by His coming forth from the
Father and returning to the Father, n. 3736, 3210. That thus He was
made one with the Father, n. 2751, 3704, 4766. That since that union,
divine truth proceeds from the Lord, n. 3704, 3712, 3969, 4577, 5704, 7499,
8127, 8241, 9199, 9398. In what manner divine truth proceeds, illustrated,
n. 7270, 9407. That the Lord, by His own proper power, united the Human with the Divine, n. 1616, 1749, 1752, 1813, 1921, 2025, 2026, 2523, 3141,
5005, 5045, 6716. That hence it may be manifest, that the Human of the
Lord was not as the human of another man, because He was conceived
from the Divine Itself, n. 10125, 10826. That His union with the Father,
from whom He had His soul, was not like a union between two persons,
but like that of soul and body, n. 3737, 10824.

That the most ancient people could not adore the Divine Esse, but the
Divine Existere, which is the Divine Human, and that the Lord, therefore,
came into the world, that He might be made the Divine Existere from the
Divine Esse, n. 4687, 5321. That the ancients acknowledged the Divine,
because He appeared to them in a human form, and that this was the Divine Human, n. 5110, 5663, 6846, 10737. That the Infinite Esse, could not
flow into heaven with the angels, nor with men, except through the Divine Human, n. (1646). 1990, 2016, 2034. That in heaven no other Divine
is perceived but the Divine Human, n 6475, 9303, (9387), 10067. That
the Divine Human from eternity was the divine truth in heaven, and the
Divine passing through heaven, thus the Divine Existere, which afterwards, in the Lord, was made the Divine Esse by itself, from which is the
Divine Existere in heaven, n. 3061, 6280, 6880, 10579. What was the quality of the state of heaven before the coming of the Lord, n. 6371, 6372.
6373. That the Divine was not perceptible except when it had passed
through heaven, n. 6982, 6996, 7004.

That the inhabitants of all the earths adore the Divine under a human
form, thus the Lord, n. 6700, 8541 to 8547, 10736, 10737, 10738. That they
rejoice when they hear that God was actually made a Man, n. 9361.
That the Lord receives all who are in good, and who adore the Divine
under a human form, n. 9359. That God cannot be thought of except in
a human form, and that what is incomprehensible falls into no idea, and
therefore is no object of faith, n. 9359, 9972. That man is capable of wor-

cares only for worldly things, because they please the external
senses, and delight the carnal appetite ; and has no concern about

---

shiping what he has some idea of, but not what he has no idea of, n. 4733,
5110, 5633, 7211, 9356. 10067. That, therefore, by the generality in the
universal terrestrial globe, the Divine is worshiped under a human form,
and that this is the effect of influx from heaven, n. 10159. That all who
are in good as to life, when they think of the Lord, think of the Divine
Human, and not of the Human separate from the Divine. It is otherwise
with those who are not in good as to life, n. 2326, 4724, 4731, 4766, 8878,
9193, 9198. That in the church at this day, they who are in evil as to life,
and also they who are in faith separate from charity, think of the Human
of the Lord without the Divine, and likewise do not comprehend what the
Divine Human is; and the reasons therof, n. 3212, 3241, 4689, 4692, 4724,
4731, 5321, (6372), 8878, 9193, 9198. That the Human of the Lord is Divine. because from the Esse of the Father, which was His soul, illustrated
by the likeness of the father in the children, n. 10269, (10372), 10823; and
because it was from the divine love, which was the very Esse of His life
from conception, n. 6872. That every man is such as his love is, and that
he is his own love, n. 6872, 10177, 10284. That the Lord made all the
Human, both internal and external, Divine, n. 1603, 1815, 1902, 1926, 2093,
2803. That therefore He rose again as to the whole body, differently from
any man, n. 1729, 2083, 5078, 10825.

That the Human of the Lord is Divine, is acknowledged from His om-
nipresence in the Holy Supper, n. 2343, (2359); and from His transfiguration before His three disciples, n. 3212; and also from the Word of the
Old Testament, in that it is called God, n. 10154; and Jehovah, n. (1603),
1736, 1815, 1902, 2921, 3035, 5110, 6281, 6303, 8864, 9194, 9315. That a distinction is made in the sense of the letter between the Father and the
Son, or between Jehovah and the Lord, but not in the internal sense of
the Word, in which the angels of heaven are, n. 3035. That in the Christian world the Human of the Lord has been declared to be not Divine,
and that this was done in a council for the sake of the Pope, that he might
be acknowledged as His vicar, n. 4738.

That Christians were examined in the other life as to the idea they entertained concerning one God, and that it was found they had an idea of
three Gods, r.. 2329, 5256, 10736, 10737, 10738, 10821. That a Trinity, or
Divine Trine, may be conceived of in one person, and thus one God, but not
in three persons, n. 10738, 10821, 10824. That a Divine Trine in the Lord
is acknowledged in heaven, n. 14, 15, 1729, 2005, 5256, 9303. That the
Trine in the Lord is the Divine Itself, which is called the Father, the Divine Human, which is called the Son, and the Divine Proceeding which is
called the Holy Spirit, and that this Divine Trine is one, n. 2149, 2156,
2288, 2321, 2329, 2447, 3704, 6993, 7182, 10738, 10822, 10823. That the

spiritual things, because they please the internal senses, and
delight the rational mind ; wherefore such men reject spiritual
things, saying they are too high for their comprehension. It was
otherwise with the ancients. To them the science of correspondences was the chief of all sciences. By means of this they acquired intelligence and wisdom, and those who were of the
church had communication with heaven ; for the science of correspondences is an angelic science. The most ancient people,
who were celestial men, actually thought from correspondence

Lord Himself teaches that the Father and He are one, n. 1729, 2004, 2005,
2018, 2025, 2751, 3704, 3736, 4766 : and that the Holy Spirit proceeds from
Him, and is His, n. 3969, 4673, 6788, 6993, 7499, 8127, 8302, 9199, (9228),
9229, 9270, 9407, 9818, 9820, 10330.
That the Divine Human flows into heaven, and makes heaven, n. 3038.
That the Lord is the all in heaven, and that He is the life of heaven, n.
7211, (9128). That the Lord dwells in the angels in what is His own, n.
9338, 10125, 10151, 10157. That hence they who are in heaven are in the
Lord, n. 3637, 3638. That the conjunction of the Lord with the angels is
according to their reception of the good of love and of charity from Him,
n. 904, 4198, 4205, 4211, 4220, (6280), 6832, 7042, 8819, 9680, 9682, 9683,
(10106), (10811). That the universal heaven has reference to the Lord, n.
551, 552. That the Lord is the common centre of heaven, n. 3633. That
all in heaven turn themselves to the Lord, who is above the heavens, n.
9828, 10130, 10189. That, nevertheless, the angels do not turn themselves
to the Lord, but the Lord turns them to Himself, n. 10189. That the presence of the angels is not with the Lord, but the presence of the Lord with
the angels, n. 9415. That in heaven there is no conjunction with the Divine Itself, but with the Divine Human, n. 4211, 4724, (5633).
That heaven corresponds with the Divine Human of the Lord, and that
hence the universal heaven is as one man, and that on this account heaven is called the GRAND MAN. n. 2996, 2998, 3624 to 3649, 3741 to 3745,
4625. That the Lord is the only Man, and that they only are men who
receive what is Divine from Him, n. 1894. That so far as they receive,
so far they are men, and images of Him, n. 8547. That therefore the
angels are forms of love and charity in a human form, and that this is
from the Lord, n. 3804, 4735, 4797, 4985, 5199, 5530, 9879, 10177.
That the universal heaven is the Lord's, n. 2751, 7086. That He has all
power in the heavens and in the earths, n. 1607, 10089, 10827. That the
Lord rules the universal heaven, and that He also rules all things which
thence depend, thus all things in the world, n. 2026, 2027, 4523, 4524.
That the Lord alone has the power of removing the hells, of withholding
from evils, and of holding in good, thus of saving, n. 10019.

as do the angels; for this reason also they conversed with the angels; and for the same reason the Lord often appeared to them and instructed them. But that science is now so entirely lost, that it is not known what correspondence is.[1]

88. Without a knowledge of correspondence, no clear understanding can be had of the spiritual world; of its influx into the natural world; of the relation of the spiritual to the natural; of the spirit of man, which is called the soul; of the operation of the soul upon the body; and of the state of man after death; therefore it is necessary to explain the nature of correspondence, and thus prepare the way for what is to follow.

89. First, I will explain what correspondence is. The whole natural world corresponds to the spiritual world; not only the natural world in general, but also every particular part thereof. Wherefore, whatever exists in the natural world from the spiritual, is said to be the correspondent [of that from which it exists]. It is to be observed that the natural world exists and subsists from the spiritual world, precisely as an effect from its efficient cause. All that is called the natural world which lies beneath the sun, and receives therefrom heat and light; and the things of this world are all those which thence subsist. But the spiritual world is heaven; and the things of that world are all those which are in the heavens.

90. Since man is a heaven and also a world in the least form after the image of the greatest, (see above, n. 57), therefore there is both a spiritual and a natural world belonging to him. The interiors which belong to his mind, and have relation to understanding and will, constitute his spiritual world; but the exteriors which belong to his body, and have relation to its senses and actions, constitute his natural world. Whatever therefore in his natural world, that is, in his body and its senses and actions, exists from his spiritual world, that is, from his mind and its understanding and will, is called correspondent.

[1] How far the science of correspondences excels other sciences, n. 4280. That the chief science among the ancients was the science of correspondences, but that at this day it is obliterated, n. 3021, 3419, 4280, 4749, 4844, 4964, 4966, 6004, 7729, 10252. That with the orientals, and in Egypt, the science of correspondences flourished, n. 5702, 6692, 7097, 7779, 9391, 10407.

91. The nature of correspondence may be seen from the human face. In a face which has not been taught to dissemble, all the affections of the mind appear visibly in a natural form, as in their type; hence the face is called the index of the mind. Thus man's spiritual world is apparent in his natural world. In like manner the thoughts of his understanding are manifested in his speech, and the determinations of his will in the gestures of his body. Those things, therefore, which occur in the body, whether it be in the face, the speech, or the gestures, are called correspondences.

92. From these considerations may also be seen what the internal man is, and what the external; namely, that the internal is that which is called the spiritual man, and the external is that which is called the natural man; also that one is distinct from the other, as heaven from the world; and likewise, that all things which are done and exist in the external or natural man, are done and exist from the internal or spiritual man.

93. Thus far concerning the correspondence of the internal or spiritual man with the external or natural. I shall now treat of the correspondence of the whole heaven with every part of man.

94. It has been shown that the universal heaven resembles one man, that it is in the form of a man, and is therefore called the GRAND MAN. It has also been shown that the angelic societies, whereof heaven consists, are thence arranged like the members, organs, and viscera, in man; so that some are in the head, some in the breast, some in the arms, and some in every particular part of those members, (see above, n. 59 to 72). The societies, therefore, which are in any member in heaven, correspond to a like member in man. For instance, those which are in the head there, correspond to the head in man; those which are in the breast there, correspond to the breast in man: those which are in the arms there, correspond to the arms in man; and so with the rest. From this correspondence man subsists, for he subsists from heaven alone.

95. That heaven is distinguished into two kingdoms, one of which is called the celestial kingdom, the other the spiritual kingdom, may be seen above in its proper chapter. The celestial kingdom in general corresponds to the heart, and to all things

belonging to the heart in the whole body; and the spiritual kingdom to the lungs, and to all things belonging to them throughout the body. The heart and the lungs also form two kingdoms in man; the heart rules therein by the arteries and veins, the lungs by the nervous and moving fibres,—both, in every effort and action. In every man's spiritual world which is called his spiritual man, there are also two kingdoms, the kingdom of the will, and the kingdom of the understanding. The will rules by the affections of good, and the understanding by the affections of truth. These kingdoms also correspond to the kingdoms of the heart and lungs in the body. The case is similar in the heavens. The celestial kingdom is the will-principle of heaven, and the good of love there rules. The spiritual kingdom is the intellectual principle of heaven, and there truth rules. These are what correspond to the functions of the heart and lungs in man. It is from this correspondence that the heart, in the Word, signifies the will, and also the good of love; and the breath of the lungs, the understanding, and the truth of faith. Hence also the affections are ascribed to the heart, although they are not there, nor thence derived.[1]

96. The correspondence of the two kingdoms of heaven with the heart and lungs, is the general correspondence of heaven with man. But there is one less general with each member, organ, and viscus, which shall now be explained. In the GRAND MAN, which is heaven, they who are in the head excel all others in every good; for they are in love, peace, innocence, wisdom, intelligence, and thence in joy and happiness. These flow into

[1] Concerning the correspondence of the heart and lungs with the GRAND MAN, which is in heaven, from experience, n. 3883 to 3896. That the heart corresponds to those who are in the celestial kingdom, and the lungs to those who are in the spiritual kingdom, n. 3885, 3886, 3887. That in heaven there is a pulse like that of the heart, and a respiration like that of the lungs, but more interior, n. 3884, 3885, 3887. That the pulse of the heart is various there according to states of love, and the respiration according to the states of charity and faith, n. 3886, 3887, 3889. That the heart, in the Word, denotes the will, thus that what is from the heart is from the will, n. 2930, 7542, 8910, 9113, 10336. That the heart also, in the Word, signifies the love, thus that what is done from the heart is done from the love, n. 7542, 9050, 10336.

the head of man, and the things thereto belonging, and correspond to them.   They who are in the breast, in the GRAND MAN,
which is heaven, are in the good of charity and faith, and also
flow into the breast of man, to which they correspond.   But they
in the GRAND MAN or heaven, who are in the loins, and in the
organs dedicated to generation there, are in conjugial love.   They
who are in the feet, are in the ultimate good of heaven, which
is called spiritual-natural.   They who are in the arms and
hands, are in the power of truth derived from good.   They who
are in the eyes, excel in understanding ; they who are in the ears,
in attention and obedience ; they who are in the nostrils, in
perception ; and they who are in the mouth and tongue, in discourse from understanding and perception.   They who are in
the kidneys, excel in truth which examines, separates and cor-
rects ; and they who are in the liver, pancreas, and spleen, are
skilled in the various purifications of good and truth.   So with
those in other members and organs.   They all flow into similar
parts of man, and correspond to them.   The influx of heaven is
into the functions and uses of the members ; and uses, because
they are from the spiritual world, clothe themselves with a form
by means of things in the natural world, and thus appear in
the effect.   Hence comes correspondence.

97. Hence it is, that those same members, organs, and viscera,
denote similar things in the Word ; for all things in the Word
have a signification according to correspondences.   By the head,
therefore, is signified intelligence and wisdom ; by the breast,
charity ; by the loins, conjugial love ; by the arms and hands,
the power of truth ; by the feet, the natural [principle] ; by the
eyes, understanding : by the nostrils, perception ; by the ears,
obedience ; by the kidneys, the purification of truth ; and so
on.[1]   Hence also it is usual, in common discourse, to say of

---

[1] That the breast, in the Word, signifies charity, n. 3934, 10081, 10087.
That the loins and organs of generation signify conjugial love, n. 3021,
4280, 4462, 5050, 5051, 5052.   That the arms and hands signify the power
of truth, n. 878, 3091, 4933 to 4937, 6947, 7205, 10019.   That the feet signify the natural principle, n. 2162, 3147, 3761, 3986, 4280, 4938 to 4952
That the eye signifies the understanding, n. 2701, 4403 to 4421, 4523 to
4534, 6923, 9051, 10569.   That the nostrils signify perception, n. 3577,

an intelligent and wise man, that he has a head; of one who is
in charity, that he is a bosom friend; of one who excels in perception, that he is quick-scented; of one who excels in intelligence, that he is sharp-sighted; of one in power, that he has
long arms; and of one who purposes from love, that he does it
from the heart. These and many other sayings in common use,
are from correspondence; for such expressions are from the spiritual world, although man does not know it.

98. That there is such a correspondence of all things of heaven
with all things of man, has been shown me by much experience; by so much, indeed, that I am as sure of it as of any truth
that is clear beyond a doubt. But it is needless to adduce here
all this experience; nor can I, on account of its abundance. It
may be seen in the ARCANA CŒLESTIA, in the chapters which
treat of Correspondences, of Representations, of the Influx of
the Spiritual World into the Natural, and of the Intercourse between the Soul and the Body.[1]

99. But although all things of the human body correspond to
all things of heaven, still man is not an image of heaven as to
his external form, but as to his internal; for the interiors of man
receive heaven, and his exteriors receive the world. So far,
therefore, as his interiors receive heaven, man as to them is a
heaven in the least form after the image of the greatest; but so
far as his interiors do not receive, he is not a heaven nor an

---

4624, 4625, 4748, 5621, 8286, 10054, 10292. That the ears signify obedience,
n. 2542, 3869, 4523, 4653, 5017, 7216, 8361, 8990, 9311, 9397, 10061. That
the kidneys signify the examination and correction of truth, n. 5380 to
5386, 10032.

[1] Concerning the correspondence of all the members of the body with
the GRAND MAN or heaven, generally and specifically, from experience,
n. 3021, 3624 to 3649, 3741 to 3750, 3883 to 3896, 4039 to 4055, 4218 to 4228,
4318 to 4331, 4403 to 4421, 4523 to 4534, 4622 to 4633, 4652 to 4660, 4791 to
4805, 4931 to 4953, 5050 to 5061, 5171 to 5189, 5377 to 5396, 5552 to 5573,
5711 to 5727, 10030. Concerning the influx of the spiritual world into the
natural world, or of heaven into the world, and concerning the influx of
the soul into all things of the body, from experience, n. 6053 to 6058, 6189
to 6215, 6307 to 6327, 6466 to 6495, 6598 to 6626. Concerning the intercourse between the soul and the body; from experience, n. 6053 to 6058,
6189 to 6215, 6307 to 6327, 6466 to 6495; 6598 to 6626

9

image of the greatest. Nevertheless the exteriors, which receive the world, may be in a form according to the order of the world, and thence in various beauty; for external beauty, which is of the body, derives its cause from parents, and from the formation in the womb, and is afterwards preserved by a common influx from the world. Hence it is that the form of one's natural man may differ very much from the form of his spiritual man. I have occasionally seen the form of the spirit of particular persons. In some, who had beautiful and charming faces, the spirit was deformed, black, and monstrous, so that it might be called an image of hell, not of heaven; but in some, who were not beautiful in person, the spirit was beautiful, fair, and angelic. The spirit of man also appears after death such as it had been in the body which clothed it when living in the world.

100. Correspondence not only reaches to man, but extends still more widely; for the heavens correspond one with another. The second or middle heaven corresponds to the third or inmost; and the first or ultimate heaven corresponds to the second or middle. The first or ultimate heaven also corresponds to the corporeal forms in man, which are called his members, organs, and viscera. Thus the corporeal part of man is that in which heaven at last terminates, and on which it rests as on its base. But this arcanum will be more fully unfolded elsewhere.

101. It is, however, to be carefully noted, that all the correspondence which exists with heaven, is with the Divine Human of the Lord, because heaven is from Him, and He is heaven, as has been shown in preceding chapters; for unless the Divine Human flowed into all things of heaven, and according to correspondences into all things of the world, neither angel nor man would exist. Hence, again, it appears why the Lord became man, and clothed His Divine with the Human from first to last; it was, because the Divine Human from which heaven subsisted before the coming of the Lord, was no longer able to sustain all things, because man, who is the basis of the heavens, overthrew and destroyed order. What the nature and quality of the Divine Human was before the coming of the Lord, and what the state of heaven at that time, is described in the extracts [from the AR- CANA CŒLESTIA] at the close of the preceding chapter.

102. The angels are astonished when they hear that there are men who ascribe all things to nature, and nothing to the Divine; who also believe that their bodies, into which so many wonders of heaven are collated, were framed by nature; and still more, that the rational principle of man is from the same source; when yet, if they would elevate their minds a little, they would see that such things are from the Divine, and not from nature; and that nature was only created for the purpose of clothing what is spiritual, and of presenting it in a corresponding form in the ultimate of order. But they compare such men to owls, which see in darkness, but are blind in the light.

THERE IS A CORRESPONDENCE OF HEAVEN WITH ALL THINGS OF THE EARTH.

103. It was stated in the foregoing chapter what correspondence is; and it was also shown that all the parts and every single part of the animal body, are correspondences. The next step in order is, to show that all things of the earth, and in general all things of the world are correspondences.

104. All things which belong to the earth are distinguished into three great classes, called kingdoms; namely, the animal kingdom, the vegetable kingdom, and the mineral kingdom. The objects in the animal kingdom are correspondences in the first degree, because they live; those in the vegetable kingdom are correspondences in the second degree, because they only grow; those in the mineral kingdom are correspondences in the third degree, because they neither live nor grow. The correspondences in the animal kingdom are living creatures of various kinds, both those which walk and creep on the earth, and those which fly in the air. They are not specifically mentioned here, because they are well known. The correspondences in the vegetable kingdom are all things which grow and flourish in gardens, forests, fields, and plains,—which are not named, because they also are known.

The correspondences in the mineral kingdom are the metals, both noble and base,—precious stones, and those not precious, —earths of various kinds, and also waters. Besides these, whatever the industry of man prepares from them for his own use, are also correspondences,—such as food of every kind, garments, houses, temples and other things.

105. The things above the earth, as the sun, moon, and stars, likewise those in the atmospheres, as clouds, mists, rain, lightnings, and thunders, are also correspondences. Those, too, which result from the presence and absence of the sun, as light and shade, heat and cold, are correspondences; likewise those which thence follow in succession, as the seasons of the year, which are called spring, summer, autumn, and winter; and the times of the day, as morning, noon, evening, and night.

106. In a word, all things which exist in nature, from the least to the greatest, are correspondences.[1] They are correspondences, because the natural world, and all that belongs to it, exists and subsists from the spiritual world and both from the Divine. Subsists, I say, because everything subsists from that which gave it existence, for subsistence is perpetual existence; and because nothing can subsist from itself, but from a cause prior to itself, thus from the First; should it, therefore, be separated from the First, it would utterly perish and disappear.

107. Everything in nature which exists and subsists from divine order, is a correspondent. The divine good which proceeds from the Lord makes divine order. It commences from Him, proceeds from Him through the heavens successively into the world, and there terminates in ultimates. All things in the world which are according to order, are correspondences; and all things there are according to order, which are good and perfect

---

[1] That all things which are in the world, and in its three kingdoms correspond to celestial things which are in heaven, or that the things which are in the natural world correspond to those which are in the spiritual, n. 1632, 1881, 2758, 2760 to 2763, 2987 to 3003, 3213 to 3227. 3483, 3624 to 3639, 4044, 4053, 4115, 4366, 4939, 5116, 5377, 5428, 5477, 9280. That by correspondences the natural world is conjoined to the spiritual world, n. 8615. That hence universal nature is a theatre representative of the Lord's kingdom, n. 2758, 2999, 3000, 3483, 3518, 4939, (8848), 9280.

for use ; for every good is a good according to use. Form has
relation to truth, because truth is the form of good. Hence it is
that all things in the whole world, and partaking of the nature
of the world, which are in divine order, have relation to good
and truth.[1]

108. That all things in the world exist from the Divine, and
are appropriately clothed in nature, so as to exist there, to perform use, and thus to correspond, is manifest from everything
seen both in the animal and in the vegetable kingdom. In both
these kingdoms there are such things as every one, who thinks
interiorly, may see to be from heaven. To begin with some
examples by way of illustration, I will cite a few from among
innumerable instances from the *Animal Kingdom*.

The wonderful knowledge which is, as it were, implanted in
every animal, is generally known. The bees know how to gather
honey from flowers, to build cells of wax in which to store
their honey, and thus to provide food for themselves and theirs
against the coming winter. The queen-bee lays her eggs, and
the rest wait upon her and cover them up, that a new generation
may spring therefrom. They live under a certain form of government, with which all in the hive are instinctively acquainted.
They preserve the useful, and cast out the useless, depriving them
of their wings. Besides other wonderful things, which they receive from heaven on account of their use ; for their wax is used
for candles in all parts of the globe, and their honey for sweeten-
ing man's food. What wonderful creatures, too, are caterpillars,
which are among the vilest things in the animal kingdom !
They know how to nourish themselves with the juice of leaves
suited to their nature, and afterwards at the exact time, to wrap
themselves up in a covering, and deposit themselves, as it were,
in a womb, and thus bring forth a progeny of their own kind.
Some are first changed into nymphs and chrysalids, and spin out
threads ; and when their task is ended, they are adorned with other

---

[1] That all things in the universe, both in heaven and in the world which
are according to order, have relation to good and truth, n. 2452, 3166, 4390,
4409, 5232, 7256, 10122; and to the conjunction of both, that they may be
something, n. 10555.

bodies, decorated with wings, fly in the open air as in their heaven, celebrate marriages, lay eggs, and provide for themselves a
posterity. Besides these special instances, all the fowls of the air
in general know their proper food; and not only what is suitable
for their nourishment, but where it is to be found. They know
how to build their nests, every species in a manner peculiar to
itself; to lay their eggs in them, to sit upon them, to hatch their
young, to nourish them, and to drive them from their home as
soon as they are able to take care of themselves. They also
know their enemies whom they should shun, and their friends
with whom they may associate, and this from their earliest infancy; not to mention the wonders contained in their eggs themselves, wherein all things requisite for the formation and nourishment of the embryo-chick, lie prepared in their order; with innumerable other wonders. Who that thinks from any rational
wisdom, will ever say that these instincts are from any other
source than from the spiritual world?—for the natural world is
subservient to the spiritual for the purpose of clothing with a
body what is thence derived, or of presenting in effect that
which is spiritual in its cause. The reason why the animals of
the earth and the fowls of the air are born into all this knowledge, and man is not, though he is more excellent than they, is
because animals are in the order of their life, and have not been
able to destroy what is in them from the spiritual world, since
they have no rational faculty. It is otherwise with man, who
thinks from the spiritual world. Because he has perverted
what is in him from that world, by a life contrary to the order
which his rational faculty approves, he must, therefore, be born
entirely ignorant, and afterwards be brought back, by divine
means, to the order of heaven.

109. How the things which belong to the *Vegetable Kingdom*
correspond, may appear from many considerations; as that little
seeds grow into trees, which put forth leaves, produce blossoms,
and then fruit, in which, again, they deposit seeds; and that these
effects take place successively, and exist together in such wonderful order, that it is impossible to describe them in few words.
If volumes were written concerning them, there would still
remain interior arcana in more intimate connection with their

uses, which science could never exhaust. Since these things also are from the spiritual world or heaven, which is in the form of a man,—as was shown above in its proper chapter,—therefore every thing in the vegetable kingdom has a certain relation to something in man. This also is known to some in the learned world. That all the things in this kingdom are correspondences, has been made evident to me by much experience; for often, when I have been in gardens, and have noticed the trees, fruits, flowers, and vegetables, I have observed the correspondences in heaven, and have conversed with those near whom they were, and have been instructed concerning their origin and quality.

110. But no one at this day can know the spiritual things in heaven to which the natural things in the world correspond, except by revelation from heaven, because the science of correspondences is now lost. I will therefore illustrate by some examples, the nature of the correspondence of spiritual things with natural.

The animals of the earth in general correspond to affections; the gentle and useful ones, to good affections, the savage and useless, to evil affections. In particular, cows and oxen correspond to the affections of the natural mind; sheep and lambs, to the affections of the spiritual mind; but winged creatures, according to their species, correspond to the intellectual things of both minds.[1] Hence it is that various animals, as cows, oxen, rams, sheep, she-goats, he-goats, he-lambs, she-lambs, and also pigeons and turtle-doves, were devoted to a sacred use in the Israelitish church,—which was a representative church,—and sacrifices and

---

[1] That animals, from correspondence, signify affections; the tame and useful animals, good affections, and the savage and useless ones, evil affections, n. 45, 46, 142, 143, 246, 714, 715, 719, 2179, 2180, 3519, 9280: illustrated by experience from the spiritual world, n. 3218, 5198, 9090. Concerning the influx of the spiritual world into the lives of beasts, n. 1633, 3646. That oxen and bullocks, from correspondence, signify the affections of the natural mind, n. 2180, 2566, 9391, 10132, 10407. What sheep signify, n. 4169, 4809. What lambs, n. 3994, 10132. That winged animals signify things intellectual, n. 40, 745, 776, 778, 866, 988, 994, 5149, 7441, with a variety according to their genera and species, from experience in the spiritual world, n. 3219.

burnt-offerings were made of them; for in that use they corresponded to things spiritual, which were understood in heaven
according to correspondences.   Animals, also, according to their
genera and species, are affections, because they live; for everything has life from no other source than from affection and according to it.   Hence every animal has innate knowledge according
to the affection of its life.   Man, too, is similar to animals as to
his natural man, and therefore is compared to them in common
discourse.   If he be of a gentle disposition, he is called a sheep
or a lamb; if of a savage temper, he is called a bear or a wolf;
if cunning, he is called a fox or a serpent—and so forth.

111. There is a like correspondence with the things in the
vegetable kingdom.   A garden in general corresponds to heaven
as to intelligence and wisdom; on which account heaven is called
in the Word the garden of God, and paradise,[1] and also by man
the heavenly paradise.   Trees, according to their species, correspond to the perceptions and knowledges of good and truth, from
which come intelligence and wisdom; wherefore the ancients,
who were skilled in the science of correspondences, held their
sacred worship in groves;[2] and hence it is that in the Word trees
are so often mentioned, and that heaven, the church, and man,
are compared to them, as to the vine, the olive, the cedar, and
others; and the good works which they do, to fruits.   The food also
which they produce, especially that from grain, corresponds to
the affections of good and truth, because these nourish the spiritual life, as terrestrial food does the natural.[3]   Hence bread in general corresponds to the affection of all good, because it supports

----

[1] That a garden and a paradise, from correspondence, signify intelligence and wisdom, n. 100, 108; from experience, n. 3220.   That all things
which correspond, also signify the same things in the Word, n. 2896, 2987,
2989, 2990, 2991, 3002, 3225.

[2] That trees signify perceptions and knowledges, n. 103, 2163, 2682,
2722, 2972, 7692.   That therefore the ancients celebrated divine worship in
groves under trees, according to their correspondences, n. 2722, 4552.
Concerning the influx of heaven into the subjects of the vegetable kingdom, as into trees and plants, n. 3648.

[3] That meats, from correspondence, signify such things as nourish
spiritual life, n. 3114, 4459, 4792, 4976, 5147, 5293, 5340, 5342, 5410, 5426,
5576, 5582, 5588, 5655, 5915, 6277, 8562, 9003.

life better than other aliments, and because bread means all kinds
of food. On account of this correspondence, also, the Lord calls
Himself the bread of life; and for the same reason, too, bread
was applied to a sacred use in the Israelitish church; for it was
set upon the table in the tabernacle, and called the bread of faces
[or show-bread]; likewise all the divine worship, which was
performed by sacrifices and burnt-offerings, was called bread.
On account of this correspondence, also, the most holy solemnity
of worship in the Christian church is the Holy Supper, in which
are distributed bread and wine.[1] From these few examples the
nature of correspondence may be clearly seen.

112. In what manner the conjunction of heaven with the
world is effected by correspondences, shall also be briefly explained.

The kingdom of the Lord is a kingdom of ends, which are
uses; or,—what is the same,—it is a kingdom of uses, which are
ends. Therefore the universe was so created and formed by the
Divine, that uses might everywhere be clothed with coverings,
whereby they are embodied in act or in effect, first in heaven and
afterwards in the world, thus by degrees and successively even to
the ultimates of nature. Hence it is evident that the correspondence of natural with spiritual things, or of the world with
heaven, is effected by uses, and that uses conjoin them; and that
the forms with which uses are clothed, are correspondences and
mediums of conjunction, in proportion as they are forms of uses.
In the natural world and its three kingdoms, all things which exist according to order are forms of uses, or effects formed from
use for use; wherefore these things are correspondences. The
actions of man likewise are uses in form, and are correspondences,
whereby he is conjoined to heaven so far as he lives according to
divine order, or so far as he is in love to the Lord and in char-

---

[1] That bread signifies all the good which nourishes the spiritual life of
man, n. 2165, 2177, 3478, 3735, 3813, 4211, 4217, 4735, 4976, 9323, 9545,
10686. That the bread, which was on the table in the tabernacle, had a
like signification, n. 3478, 9545. That sacrifices in general were called
bread, n. 2165. That bread involves all food, n 2165. Thus that it signifies all food, celestial and spiritual, n. 276, 680, 2165, 2177, 3478, 6118,
8410

10   D

ity toward his neighbor. To love the Lord and the neighbor in general is to perform uses.[1] It is to be further observed, that the natural world is conjoined with the spiritual by means of man, or, that he is the medium of their conjunction; for both worlds exist in him, as may be seen above, n. 57. Wherefore so far as man is spiritual, so far he is a medium of conjunction; but so far as he is natural and not spiritual, so far he is not a medium of conjunction. Still, without man as a medium, the divine influx into the world continues, and also into those things which are of the world with man, but not into his rational faculty.

113. As all things which are according to divine order correspond to heaven, so all things which are contrary to divine order correspond to hell. All those which correspond to heaven, have relation to good and truth; and those which correspond to hell, have relation to the evil and the false.

114. Something shall now be said concerning the science of correspondences and its use. It was remarked above, that the spiritual world, which is heaven, is conjoined with the natural world by correspondences. Hence man has communication with heaven by correspondences, for the angels of heaven do not think from natural things as man does. Wherefore when man is in the science of correspondences, he may be consociated with the

---

[1] That all good has its quality and delight from, and according to, uses, and that hence, such as the use is, such is the good, n. 3049, 4984, 7038. That angelic life consists in the goods of love and charity, thus in performing uses, n. 454. That nothing is regarded by the Lord, and thence by the angels, but ends, which are uses appertaining to man, n. 1317, 1645, 5949. That the kingdom of the Lord is a kingdom of uses, thus of ends, n. 454, 696, 1103, 3645, 4054, 7038. That to serve the Lord is to perform uses, n. 7038. That all things in man, both general and particular, are formed for use, n. (3565), 4104, 5189, 9297; and that they are formed from use, thus that use is prior to the organical forms in man by which use is effected, because use is from the influx of the Lord through heaven, n. 4223, 4926. That the interiors of man also, which are of his mind, are formed as he grows up, from use and for use, n. 1964, 6815, 9297. That hence the quality of a man's uses is the quality of the man, n. 1568, 3570, 4054, 6571, 6935, 6938, 10284. That uses are the ends, for the sake of which man acts, n. 3565, 4054, 4104, 6815. That use is the first and last, thus the all of man, n. 1964.

angels as to the thoughts of his mind, and thus be conjoined with them as to his spiritual or internal man. The Word was written by pure correspondences, in order that man might be conjoined with heaven; for even the minutest parts of the Word, correspond to something spiritual.[1] Wherefore if man were skilled in the science of correspondences, he would understand its spiritual sense, and become acquainted with arcana whereof he perceives nothing in the sense of the letter. For in the Word there is both a literal and a spiritual sense. The literal sense consists of such things as are in the world, but the spiritual sense of such things as are in heaven; and since the conjunction of heaven with the world is by correspondences, therefore such a Word was given, that everything in it, even to an iota, corresponds.[2]

115. I have been informed from heaven, that the most ancient people on our earth, who were celestial men, thought from correspondences themselves, and that the natural things of the world, which were before their eyes, served them as mediums of such thought; and because they were of such a character, they were associated with the angels and conversed with them; and that thus heaven was conjoined to the world through them. On this account that time was called the golden age; concerning which it is also said by ancient writers, that the inhabitants of heaven dwelt with men, and held intercourse with them as friends with friends. After those times there arose another race, who did not think from correspondences themselves, but from the science of correspondences; and I was informed that there was conjunction of heaven with man even then, but not so intimate. That period was called the silver age. After them succeeded a race, who, indeed, were acquainted with correspondences, but did not think from the science of them, because they were in natural good, and not, like their predecessors, in spiritual good. That period was called the copper age. I was told that, after those times, man gradually be-

---

[1] That the Word was written by pure correspondences, n. 8615. That man has conjunction with heaven by the Word, n. 2899, 6943, 9396, 9400, 9401, 10375, 10452.

[2] Concerning the spiritual sense of the Word, see the small work ON THE WHITE HORSE MENTIONED IN THE APOCALYPSE.

came external, and at length corporeal; and that then the science
of correspondences was wholly lost, and with it the knowledge
of heaven and of nearly every thing relating to heaven. These
ages were named from gold, silver, and copper;[1] because gold
from correspondence signifies celestial good, in which the most
ancient people were principled; silver, spiritual good, which was
the characteristic of the ancients who succeeded them; and copper, natural good, in which the next succeeding race were principled; but iron, from which the last age was named, signifies
hard truth without good.

THE SUN IN HEAVEN.

116. THE sun of this world does not appear in heaven, nor
any thing which exists from that sun, because all that is natural;
for nature commences from that sun, and whatsoever is produced
by it is called natural. But the spiritual in which heaven is, is
above nature, and entirely distinct from the natural; nor do they
communicate with each other except by correspondences. The
nature of the distinction may be comprehended from what was
said above, n. 38, concerning degrees; and the nature of their
communication, from what was said in the two preceding chapters concerning correspondences.

117. But although the sun of the world does not appear in
heaven, nor any thing which exists from that sun, still there is a
sun there, and light, and heat, and all things which are in the
world, and a great many more, but not from a similar origin; for
the things which exist in heaven are spiritual, and those which exist in the world are natural. The sun of heaven is the Lord; the

[1] That gold, from correspondence, signifies celestial good, n. 113, 1551,
1552, 5658, 6914, 6917, 9510, 9874, 9881. That silver signifies spiritual
good, or truth from a celestial origin, n. 1551, 1552, 2954, 5658. That
copper signifies natural good, n. 425, 1551. That iron signifies truth in
the ultimate of order, n. 425, 426.

light there is divine truth, and the heat is divine good, both of which proceed from the Lord as a sun. From that origin are all things which exist and appear in the heavens. But concerning the light and heat, and the things which thence exist in the heavens, more will be said in the following chapters. At present we shall speak only of the sun there. The Lord appears in heaven as a sun, because He is the divine love from which all spiritual things exist, as all natural things exist by means of the sun of this world. It is that love which shines as a sun.

118. That the Lord actually appears in heaven as a sun, has not only been told me by the angels, but has also been given me occasionally to see. What, therefore, I have heard and seen concerning the Lord as a sun, I will here briefly record.

The Lord appears as a sun, not in heaven, but high above the heavens: nor does He appear above the head, or in the zenith, but before the faces of the angels at a middle altitude. He appears far distant, in two places; in one before the right eye, and in another before the left. Before the right eye He appears exactly like a sun, fiery and of the same magnitude as the sun of the world; but before the left eye He does not appear as a sun, but as a moon,* white like the moon of our earth and of similar magnitude, but more resplendent; nay, it appears encompassed with several, as it were, smaller moons, each of which is alike

---

* [It is not to be supposed, from what is here said, that the Lord appears both as a sun and moon to the same angels; still less that, as a moon, He appears not more bright than the moon in the world. The two appearances are described as those of a sun and moon respectively, because they bear the same relation to each other as do those two natural luminaries; but in reality, to those by whom the Lord is said to be seen as a moon, that moon is their sun, and is so denominated by the author in some of his other works. To the angels of the celestial kingdom, the Lord appears as a sun, of a glowing brightness, whereof no adequate conception can be formed by man; and it is seen by them rather toward the right, or before the right eye: and to the angels of the spiritual kingdom He also appears as a sun, far exceeding in radiance the sun of this world, though compared to the sun seen by the celestial angels, this sun is only as a moon; and it appears rather toward the left, or before the left eye of those who behold it. With this explanation in the mind, all that is said above, and in what follows, may be more easily understood.—TR.]

white and brilliant. The Lord appears thus differently, in two places, because he appears to every one according to the quality of his reception of Him; and therefore in one way to those who receive Him in the good of love, and in another to those who receive Him in the good of faith. To those who receive Him in the good of love, He appears as a sun, fiery and flaming according to reception. These are in His celestial kingdom. But to those who receive Him in the good of faith, He appears as a moon, white and shining according to reception. These are in His spiritual kingdom.[1] This difference in the Lord's appearance arises from correspondence; for the good of love corresponds to fire, and therefore fire in the spiritual sense is love; and the good of faith corresponds to light, and therefore light in the spiritual sense is faith[2]

The reason that he appears before the eyes is because the interiors, which belong to the mind, see through the eyes,—from the good of love through the right eye, and from the good of faith through the left eye:[3] for all the things on the right side, both in angels and men, correspond to good from which truth is

---

[1] That the Lord appears in heaven as a sun, and that He is the sun of heaven, n. 1053, 3636, 3643, 4060. That the Lord appears to those who are in the celestial kingdom, where love to Him is the ruling love, as a sun, and to those who are in the spiritual kingdom, where charity toward the neighbor and faith rule, as a moon, n. 1521, 1529, 1530, 1531, 1837, 4060. That the Lord as a sun appears at a middle altitude before the right eye, and as a moon before the left eye, n. 1053, 1521, 1529, 1530, 1531, 3636, 3643, 4321, 5097, 7078, 7083, 7173, 7270, 8812, 10809. That the Lord has been seen as a sun and as a moon by me, n. 1531, 7173. That the Essential Divine of the Lord is far above His Divine in heaven, n. 7270, 8760.

[2] That fire in the Word, both heavenly and infernal, signifies love, n. 934, 4906, 5215. That sacred or heavenly fire signifies divine love, n. 934, 6314, 6832. That infernal fire signifies the love of self and of the world, and every concupiscence which is of those loves, n. 1861, 5071, 6314, 6832, 7575, 10747. That love is the fire of life, and that life itself is actually thence derived, n. 4906, 5071, 6032, 6314. That light signifies the truth of faith, n. (3395), 3485, 3636, 3643, 3993, 4302, 4413, 4415, 9548, 9684.

[3] That the sight of the left eye corresponds to the truths of faith, and the sight of the right eye, to their goods, n. 4410, 6923.

derived; and those on the left, to truth derived from good.[1] The good of faith, in its essence, is truth derived from good.

119. Hence it is that in the Word, the Lord, as to love, is compared to the sun, and as to faith, to the moon; and also, that love from the Lord to the Lord is signified by the sun, and faith from the Lord in the Lord is signified by the moon; as in the following passages: "*The light of the moon shall be as the light of the sun, and the light of the sun shall be seven-fold, as the light of seven days.*" Isaiah xxx. 26. "*When I shall put thee out, I will cover the heavens, and I will darken the stars; I will cover the sun with a cloud, and the moon shall not make her light to shine; all the bright lights in the heavens I will make dark over thee, and I will give darkness upon thy land.*" Ezekiel xxxii. 7, 8. "*I will darken the sun in his rising, and the moon shall not cause her light to shine.*" Isaiah xiii. 10. "*The sun and the moon shall be darkened, and the stars shall withdraw their brightness. The sun shall be turned into darkness, and the moon into blood.*" Joel ii. 2, 10, 31; chap. iv. 15. "*The sun became black as sackcloth of hair, and the moon became as blood, and the stars fell to the earth.*" Apoc. vi. 12. "*Immediately after the tribulation of those days, the sun shall be darkened, and the moon shall not give her light, and the stars shall fall from heaven.*" Matt. xxiv. 29: and elsewhere. In these passages, by the sun is signified love, by the moon faith, and by the stars the knowledges of good and truth;[2] these are said to be darkened, to lose their light, and to fall from heaven, when they no longer exist [in the church]. That the Lord appears in heaven as a sun, is evident also from His transfiguration before Peter, James, and John; "*Then His face shone as the sun.*" Matt. xvii. 2. When the Lord was thus seen by those disciples, they were withdrawn from the body and in the light of heaven. Hence it was that the ancients, with whom the church was representative, turned their faces toward

---

[1] That the things which are on man's right side have reference to good from which truth is derived, and that the things on the left side have reference to truth derived from good, n. 9495, 9604.

[2] That constellations and stars, in the Word, signify the knowledges of good and truth, n. 2495, 2849, 4697.

the sun in the east when engaged in divine worship; and from them is derived the custom of building churches with an aspect toward the east.

120. The nature and intensity of the Divine Love may be manifest from comparison with the sun of the world, for—though it may appear incredible—the Divine Love is far more ardent than that sun. Therefore the Lord, as a sun, does not flow immediately into the heavens, but the ardency of His love is tempered by degrees in the way. The tempering mediums appear as radiant belts around the sun; and besides, the angels are veiled in a thin suitable cloud, lest they should suffer injury from the influx.[1] Therefore they are distant from the Lord according to their reception of His love. The superior heavens are nearest the Lord as a sun, because they are in the good of love; but the inferior heavens are more remote from Him, because they are in the good of faith; but they who are in no good, like the infernals, are most remote, and remote in proportion as they are opposed to good.[2]

121. But when the Lord appears in heaven, which often occurs, He does not appear clothed with the sun, but in an angelic form, distinguished from the angels by the Divine which is translucent from His face. For the Lord is not there in person, because in person He is always encompassed with the sun,—but

---

[1] The nature and intensity of the Divine Love of the Lord illustrated by comparison with the fire of the sun of the world, n. 6834, (6844), 6849. That the Divine Love of the Lord is love toward all the human race, desiring to save them, n. 1820, 1865, 2253, 6872. That the love proximately proceeding from the fire of the Lord's love does not enter heaven, but that it appears around the sun as radiant belts, n. 7270. That the angels, also, are veiled with a thin corresponding cloud, lest they should suffer injury from the influx of burning love, n. 6849.

[2] That the presence of the Lord with the angels is according to the reception of the good of love and of faith from Him, n. 904, 4198, 4320, 6280, 6832, 7042, 8819, 9680, 9682, 9683, 10106, 10811. That the Lord appears to every one according to his quality, n. 1861, 2235, 4198, 4206. That the hells are remote from the heavens, because evil spirits cannot bear the presence of Divine Love from the Lord, n. 4299, 7519, 7738, 7989, (8157), 8306, 9327. That hence the hells are most remote from the heavens, and that this remoteness is a great gulf, n. 9346, 10187.

He is present there by aspect. For it is common in heaven for persons to appear as present in the place where the view is fixed or terminated, although it is very far from the place where they actually are. This presence is called the presence of the internal sight, of which I shall speak hereafter. I have also seen the Lord out of the sun in an angelic form, a little beneath the sun on high ; and also near, in a similar form, with a resplendent countenance ; and once as a burning light in the midst of the angels.

122. The sun of the natural world appears to the angels as something very dark opposite to the sun of heaven, and the moon as something dark opposite to the moon of heaven, and this constantly. The reason is, because anything fiery belonging to the world, corresponds to the love of self, and the light thence derived corresponds to the falses derived from that love ; and the love of self is diametrically opposite to divine love, and the false derived from that love is diametrically opposite to divine truth ; and what is opposite to divine love and divine truth is thick darkness to the angels. Hence it is, that, to worship the sun and moon of the natural world, and to bow down to them, signifies, in the Word, to love one's self and the falses derived from that love ; and that such idolaters should be cut off, see Deut. iv. 19 ; chap. xviii. 3, 4, 5 ; Jer. viii. 1, 2 ; Ezek. viii. 15, 16, 18 ; Apoc. xvi. 8 ; Matt. xiii. 6.[1]

123. Since the Lord appears in heaven as a sun, from the divine love which is in Him and from Him, therefore all who are in the heavens turn themselves constantly to Him. They who are in the celestial kingdom turn themselves to Him as a sun, and they who are in the spiritual kingdom, as a moon. But they who are in hell turn themselves to the thick darkness and darkness which are opposite to the former, thus backward from the Lord. The reason is, because all who are in the hells are in

---

[1] That the sun of the world does not appear to the angels, but, in its place, something darkish at the back, opposite to the sun of heaven, or the Lord, n. 7078, 9755. That the sun, in the opposite sense, signifies the love of self, n. 2441 ; in which sense, by adoring the sun, is signified to worship those things which are contrary to heavenly love, or to the Lord, n. 2441, 10584. That to those who are in the hells, the sun of heaven is thick darkness, n. 2441.

the love of self and of the world, thus opposite to the Lord.
They who turn themselves to the thick darkness which is in
place of the sun of the world, are in the hells behind, and are
called genii; and they who turn themselves to the darkness
which is in place of the moon, are in the hells in front, and are
called spirits.   Hence it is that they who are in the hells are
said to be in darkness, and they who are in the heavens, in light.
Darkness signifies the false from evil, and light, the truth from
good.   They turn themselves thus, because all in the other life
look to those things which rule in their interiors, that is to their
loves, and the interiors fashion the countenance of an angel and
spirit; and in the spiritual world there are not determinate quarters, as in the natural world, but they are determined by the direction of the face.   Man also, as to his spirit, turns himself in like
manner,—away from the Lord, if he be in the love of self and
the world, and toward Him, if he be in love to the Lord and the
neighbor.   But man is ignorant of this, because he is in the natural world, where the quarters are determined according to the
rising and setting of the sun.   But this subject, because it is
hard for man to understand, shall be illustrated hereafter when
the Quarters, Space, and Time, in heaven, come to be treated of.

124. Since the Lord is the sun of heaven, and all things which
are derived from Him look to Him, therefore also He is the common centre from which is all direction and determination;[1] and
therefore all things which are beneath, both those in heaven and
those on earth, are in His presence and under His auspices.

125. From these considerations may be seen more clearly what
was said and shown in the preceding chapters concerning the
Lord; namely, *That He is the God of heaven*, n. 2 to 6.   *That
His Divine makes heaven*, n. 7 to 12.   *That the Divine of the
Lord in heaven is love to Him and charity toward the neighbor*, n. 13 to 19.   *That there is a correspondence of all things
of the world with heaven, and through heaven with the Lord*,
n. 87 to 115.   Also, *that the sun and moon of the world correspond*, n. 105.

---

[1] That the Lord is the common centre, to which all things of heaven
turn themselves, n. 3633.

LIGHT AND HEAT IN HEAVEN.

126. THAT there is light in the heavens cannot be comprehended by those who think only from nature ; when yet the light there is so great, as to exceed by many degrees the mid-day light of the world. I have often seen it, even in the evening and night. At first I wondered when I heard the angels say, that the light of the world is little more than shade in comparison with the light of heaven ; but since I have seen it, I can testify that it is so. Its whiteness and brilliancy surpass all description. The things seen by me in the heavens, were seen in that light ; thus more clearly and distinctly than things in the world.

127. The light of heaven is not natural, like that of the world, but spiritual ; for it proceeds from the Lord as a sun, and that sun is divine love, as shown in the preceding chapter. That which proceeds from the Lord as a sun, is called in the heavens divine truth, although in its essence it is divine good united to divine truth. Hence the angels have light and heat ; light from the divine truth, and heat from the divine good. From this consideration it is evident that the light and heat of heaven are not natural but spiritual from their origin.[1]

128. Divine truth is light to the angels, because they are spiritual, and not natural. Spiritual beings see from their sun, and natural beings from theirs. Divine truth is the source whence the angels have understanding, and understanding is their internal sight, which flows into and produces their external sight. Hence the things which appear in heaven from the Lord as a sun, appear in light.[2] Such being the origin of light in heaven, therefore it varies according to the reception of divine truth from the Lord, or—what is the same—according to the intelligence

---

[1] That all light in the heavens is from the Lord as a sun, n. 1053, 1521, 3195, 3341, 3636, 3643, 4415, 9548, 9684, 10809. That the divine truth proceeding from the Lord appears in heaven as light, and is all the light of heaven, n. 3195, 3223, 5400, 8644, 9399, 9548, 9684.

[2] That the light of heaven illuminates both the sight and the understanding of angels and spirits, n. 2776, 3138.

and wisdom of the angels. It is therefore different in the celestial kingdom from what it is in the spiritual, and different in each society. The light in the celestial kingdom appears flamy, because the angels of that kingdom receive light from the Lord as a sun; but the light in the spiritual kingdom is white, because the angels of that kingdom receive light from the Lord as a moon, (see above, n. 118). Moreover, the light is not the same in one society as in another. It differs also in each society; for those in the centre are in greater light, and those round about them in less, (see n. 43). In a word, in the same degree in which the angels are recipients of divine truth—that is, in intelligence and wisdom from the Lord—they have light;[1] hence they are called angels of light.

129. Since the Lord in the heavens is divine truth, and divine truth there is light, therefore the Lord in the Word is called the Light, and in like manner every truth which is from Him; as in the following passages: "*Jesus said, I am the light of the world; he that followeth Me shall not walk in darkness, but shall have the light of life.*" John viii. 12. "*As long as I am in the world, I am the light of the world.*" John ix. 5. "*Jesus said, Yet a little while is the light with you. Walk while ye have the light, lest darkness come upon you. While ye have the light, believe in the light, that ye may be the children of light. I have come a light into the world, that whosoever believeth in Me may not abide in darkness.*" John xii. 35, 36, 46. "*Light is come into the world, but men loved darkness rather than light.*" John iii. 19. John says concerning the Lord, "*This is the true light, which enlighteneth every man.*" John i. 4, 9. "*The people who sit in darkness have seen a great light; and to them who sat in the shadow of death, light has arisen.*" Matt. iv. 16. "*I will give thee for a covenant of the people, for a light of the nations.*" Isaiah xlii. 6. "*I have ordained thee for a light of the nations, that thou mayest be My*

[1] That light in heaven is according to the intelligence and wisdom of the angels, n. 1524, 1529, 1530, 3339. That the differences of light in the heavens are as many as are the angelic societies, since perpetual varieties as to good and truth, thus as to wisdom and intelligence, exist in the heavens, n. 684, 690, 3241, 3744, 3745, 4414, 5598, 7236, 7833, 7836.

salvation even to the end of the earth." Isaiah xlix. 6. *"The nations that are saved shall walk in His light."* Apoc. xxi. 24. *"Send Thy light and Thy truth, they shall lead me."* Psalm xliii. 3. In these and other passages, the Lord is called light from divine truth which is from Him; in like manner the truth itself is called light. Since light in the heavens proceeds from the Lord as a sun, therefore when He was transfigured before Peter, James, and John, *"His face appeared as the sun, and His raiment as the light, glittering and white as snow, so as no fuller on earth could whiten them."* Mark ix. 3; Matt. xvii. 2. The Lord's raiment appeared thus, because it represented the divine truth which is from Him in the heavens. Garments in the Word also signify truths;[1] whence it is said in David, *"Jehovah, Thou clothest Thyself with light as with a garment."* Psalm civ. 2.

130. That the light in the heavens is spiritual, and that spiritual light is divine truth, may also be inferred from this consideration, that man likewise enjoys spiritual light, and derives illustration therefrom so far as he is in intelligence and wisdom from divine truth. The spiritual light of man is the light of his understanding, and the objects of the understanding are truths, which he arranges analytically into classes, forms into reasons, and from them draws conclusions in a series.[2] The natural man is not aware that it is real light by which the understanding sees

---

[1] That garments in the Word signify truths, because they invest good, n. 1073, 2576, 5248, 5319, 5954, 9216, 9952, 10536. That the garments of the Lord, when He was transfigured, signified divine truth proceeding from His divine love, n. 9212, 9216.

[2] That the light of heaven illuminates the understanding of man, and that on this account man is rational, n. 1524, 3138, 3167, 4408, 6608, 8707, 9128, 9399, 10569. That the understanding is enlightened, because it is recipient of truth, n. 6222, 6608, 10661. That the understanding is enlightened so far as man receives truth in good from the Lord, n. 3619. That the understanding is of such a quality as are the truths derived from good, from which it is formed, n. 10064. That the understanding has light from heaven, as the sight has light from the world, n. 1524, 5114, 6608 9128. That the light of heaven from the Lord is always present with man, but that it flows-in only so far as man is in truth derived from good, n. 4060, 4214.

such things, because he does not see that light with his eyes, nor perceive it in thought; many, however, know that this light is real, and they also distinguish it from the natural light in which those are, who think naturally and not spiritually. They think naturally who look only to the world, and attribute all things to nature; but they think spiritually who look to heaven, and attribute all things to the Divine. It has been frequently granted me to perceive, and also to see, that the light which enlightens the mind is true light, altogether distinct from that which is called natural light [*lumen*]. I have been elevated into that light more and more interiorly, by degrees, and my understanding was enlightened in proportion to the elevation; until at length I perceived what I did not perceive before, and lastly such things as I could not even grasp in thought from natural light. I have sometimes been vexed at this dulness of the natural mind about things which were very distinctly perceived in heavenly light.[1] Since there is a light appropriate to the understanding, therefore we speak of the understanding in the same terms as of the eye; as, that it sees and is in light when it perceives, and that it is obscure and dark when it does not perceive; with many similar expressions.

131. Since the light of heaven is divine truth, therefore also that light is divine wisdom and intelligence; wherefore to be elevated into the light of heaven, means to be elevated into intelligence and wisdom, and to be enlightened. Hence it follows that the angels are in light exactly in proportion to their intelligence and wisdom. Again: because the light of heaven is divine wisdom, therefore the true character of all is manifest in that light; for the interiors of every one there are clearly revealed in the face, and his precise quality made known. Not the least thing is concealed. The interior angels even love to have all things within them made manifest, because they will nothing but good. They, on the other hand, who are beneath heaven, and

---

[1] That man, when he is elevating from the sensual principle, comes into a milder light, and at length into celestial light, n. 6313, 6315, 9407. That there is an actual elevation into the light of heaven, when man is elevated into intelligence, n. 3190. How great a light has been perceived, when I have been withdrawn from worldly ideas, n. 1526, 6608.

do not will what is good, are very much afraid of being seen in the light of heaven. And, what is wonderful, the infernals appear to each other as men, but in the light of heaven as monsters, with horrible faces and horrible bodies,—the exact forms of their own evil.[1] Man, as to his spirit, appears in a similar way, when he is looked at by the angels. If good, he appears as a man, beautiful according to his good; if evil, as a monster, deformed according to his evil. Hence it is evident that all things are made manifest in the light of heaven; they are made manifest, because the light of heaven is divine truth.

132. Inasmuch as divine truth is light in the heavens, therefore all truths, wheresoever they are,—whether within an angel or without him, in the heavens or out of them,—emit light; but truths without the heavens do not shine like truths within the heavens. Truths without the heavens shine with a cold light like snow, because they do not derive their essence from good like truths within the heavens; wherefore also that cold light, as soon as the light from heaven flows-in, disappears; and if evil be underneath, it is turned into darkness. This I have several times witnessed, and many other remarkable things concerning the lucidity of truths, which are here passed by.

133. Something shall now be said concerning the heat of heaven.—The heat of heaven in its essence is love. It proceeds from the Lord as a sun: and that this is the divine love in the Lord and from Him, has been shown in the preceding chapter. Hence it is evident that the heat of heaven is spiritual as well as its light; for it is from the same origin.[2] There are two things which proceed from the Lord as a sun, divine truth and divine good. Divine truth in the heavens is light, and divine good is heat; but divine truth and divine good are so united, that they

---

[1] That they who are in the hells, in their own light, which is like that of burning charcoal, appear to themselves as men, but in the light of heaven as monsters, n. 4531, 4533, 4674, 5057, 5058, 6605, 6626.

[2] That there are two origins of heat, and likewise two origins of light, namely, the sun of the world and the sun of heaven, n. 3338, 5215, 7324. That heat from the Lord as a sun is the affection which is of love, n. 3636, 3643. Hence that spiritual heat is, in its essence, love, n. 2146, 3338, 3339, 6314.

are not two, but one ; yet even with the angels they are separated,—for there are angels who receive the divine good more than
the divine truth, and others who receive the divine truth more
than the divine good.　They who receive more of the divine good,
are in the Lord's celestial kingdom ; and they who receive more
of the divine truth, are in His spiritual kingdom.　The most perfect angels are they who receive both in the same degree.

134.　The heat of heaven, like its light, is everywhere various.
That in the celestial kingdom differs from that in the spiritual ;
and it differs also in every society.　And not only does it differ
in degree, but even in kind.　It is more intense and pure in the
Lord's celestial kingdom, because the angels there are more receptive of the divine good ; it is less intense and pure in the
Lord's spiritual kingdom, because the angels there are more receptive of divine truth ; and it differs also in every society according to reception.　There is heat also in the hells, but it is unclean.[1]　The heat in heaven is what is meant by sacred and
celestial fire, and the heat of hell is what is meant by profane and
infernal fire ; and by both is meant love.　Celestial fire means
love to the Lord and love toward the neighbor, and every affection derived from those loves ; and infernal fire means the love
of self, and the love of the world, and every concupiscence derived from those loves.　That love is heat from a spiritual origin,
is evident from a man's growing warm according to the intensity
of his love ; for according to its strength and quality, he grows
hot, and is inflamed, and the ardor of his love becomes manifest
when it is assailed.　Hence also it is common to speak of being
inflamed, becoming heated, burning, boiling, taking fire, both in
reference to the affections which are of the love of good, and also
to the concupiscences which are of the love of evil.

135.　The love which proceeds from the Lord as a sun is felt in
heaven as heat, because the interiors of the angels receive love
from the divine good which is from the Lord, and their exteriors

---

[1] That there is heat in the hells, but that it is unclean, n. 1773, 2757,
3340 ; and that the odor arising from it is like the smell of dung and
excrement in the world, and in the worst hells is, as it were, cadaverous,
n. 814, 819, 820, 943, 954, 5394.

are warmed from the love in their interiors. Hence it is that
heat and love so perfectly correspond to each other in heaven,
that every one there enjoys a kind and degree of heat corresponding to the kind and degree of his love,—agreeably to what
was just stated. The heat of the world does not enter heaven
at all, because it is too gross, and is not spiritual but natural.
But it is otherwise with men, because they are in the spiritual
world as well as in the natural world. They, as to their spirit,
grow warm altogether according to their loves; but as to their
body they become warm both from the heat of the spirit and
from the heat of the world. The former flows into the latter,
because they correspond. The nature of the correspondence of
these two kinds of heat is manifest from animals; for their loves,
—the chief of which is the love of propagating their species,—
burst forth and operate according to the presence and afflux of
heat from the sun of the world, which heat prevails only in the
spring and summer seasons. They are much mistaken who imagine that the influent heat of the world excites loves; for the natural does not flow into the spiritual, but the spiritual into the
natural. The latter kind of influx is according to divine order,
but the former is contrary to divine order.[1]

136. Angels, like men, have understanding and will. The
light of heaven forms the life of their understanding, because the
light of heaven is divine truth, and thence divine wisdom; and
the heat of heaven forms the life of their will, because the heat
of heaven is divine good, and thence divine love. The very life
itself of the angels is from that heat; but not from the light,
except so far as it contains heat. That life is from heat is evident; for on the removal of heat, life perishes. The case is similar in regard to faith without love, or truth without good; for
truth, which is called the truth of faith, is light, and the good
which is of love is heat.[2] These truths appear more manifest

---

[1] That there is spiritual influx, and not physical; thus that there is influx from the spiritual world into the natural, and not from the natural
into the spiritual, n. 3219, 5119, 5259. 5427, 5428, 5477, 6322, 9110, 9111.

[2] That truths without good are not in themselves truths, because they
have not life; for truths have all their life from good, n. 9603. Thus that

12

[when illustrated by comparisons drawn] from the heat and light of the world, to which the heat and light of heaven correspond. From the heat of the world conjoined with light, all things which grow on the earth are vivified and flourish; this conjunction takes place in the seasons of spring and summer. But from light separate from heat nothing is vivified or flourishes, but all things become torpid and die; this separation takes place in winter-time, when heat is absent, though light continues. From this correspondence heaven is called paradise, because there truth is conjoined with good, or faith with love, as light is conjoined with heat in the spring-time on earth. From these considerations the truth is more clearly manifest which was stated in a previous chapter, (n. 13 to 19), that the Divine of the Lord in heaven is love to Him and charity toward the neighbor.

137. It is said in John, "*In the beginning was the Word, and the Word was with God, and the Word was God: all things were made by Him, and without Him was not any thing made that was made. In Him was life; and the life was the light of men; He was in the world and the world was made by Him.—And the Word was made flesh and dwelt among us, and we beheld His glory.*" i. 1, 3, 4, 10, 14. That it is the Lord who is meant by the Word, is plain; for it is said that the Word was made flesh. But what is specifically meant by the Word, has not yet been known, and shall therefore be declared. The Word in the above passage is divine truth, which is in the Lord and from the Lord;[1] wherefore also it is there called light; and that light is divine truth has been shown

they are as a body without a soul, n. 3180, 9154. That truths without good are not accepted of the Lord, n. 4368. What is the quality of truth without good, thus of faith without love, and what the quality of truth derived from good, or of faith derived from love, n. 1949, 1950, 1951, 1964, 5830, 5951. That it amounts to the same thing whether we speak of truth or of faith, and of good or of love, because truth is of faith and good is of love, n. (2839), (4353), 4997, 7178, 7623, 7624, 10367.

[1] That the term Word, in the Sacred Scripture, signifies various things; namely, discourse, the thought of the mind, every thing which really exists; also something; and, in the supreme sense, Divine Truth, and the Lord, n. 9987. That the Word signifies Divine Truth, n. 2803, 2894, 4692, 5075, 5272, (7830), 9987. That the Word signifies the Lord, n. 2533, 2859.

in previous portions of this chapter. That all things were made and created by the divine truth will now be explained.

Divine truth has all power in heaven, and without it there is absolutely none.[1] All the angels are called powers from divine truth, and actually are powers in proportion as they are recipients or receptacles thereof. By means of it they have power over the hells, and over all who set themselves in opposition to it. A thousand enemies cannot there endure one ray of the light of heaven, which is divine truth. Since the angels are angels by virtue of their reception of divine truth, it follows that the whole heaven is from no other source; for heaven consists of angels.

That such immense power is inherent in divine truth, cannot be believed by those who have no other idea of truth than they have of thought, or discourse, in which there is no inherent power, except so far as others obey it; but there is an inherent power in divine truth, and such power that heaven and earth and all things therein were created by it. That divine truth possesses such inherent power, may be illustrated by two comparisons, namely, by the power of truth and good in man, and by the power of light and heat from the sun in the world.

By the power of truth and good in man. Every thing which man does, he does from his understanding and will. He acts from his will by good, and from his understanding by truth; for all things in the will have relation to good, and all things in the understanding to truth.[2] From these, therefore, man puts his whole body in action, and thousands of things spontaneously and

[1] That the divine truth proceeding from the Lord has all power, n. 6948, 8200. That all power in heaven is of truth derived from good, n. 3091, 3563, 6344, 6423, 8304, 9643, 10019, 10182. That the angels are called "powers," and that they likewise are powers, by virtue of the reception of divine truth from the Lord, n. 9639. That the angels are recipients of divine truth from the Lord, and that, on this account, they are frequently called gods in the Word, n. 4295, 4402, 8301, 8192, 9160.

[2] That the understanding is recipient of truth, and the will recipient of good, n. 3623, 6125, 7503, 9300, (9930). That, therefore, all things which are in the understanding, have relation to truths, whether they really are truths, or are only thought to be so by man; and that all things which are in the will have reference to goods in like manner, n. 803, 10122.

at once rush in at their nod and pleasure. Hence it is evident
that the whole body was formed to be obsequious to good and
truth, and, consequently, was formed from good and truth.

By the power of heat and light from the sun in the world.
All things which grow in the world, as trees, cereals, flowers,
grasses, fruits, and seeds, exist from no other source than the
heat and light of the sun. Hence it may appear what a power
of production is inherent in those elements. What, then, must be
the power of divine light, which is divine truth, and of divine
heat, which is divine good! From these heaven exists, and consequently the world,—for the world exists through heaven, as was
shown above. From these considerations may be seen in what
manner it is to be understood, that by the Word all things were
made, and that without Him was not anything made that was
made; and also that the world was made by Him, namely, by
divine truth from the Lord.[1] Hence also it is, that in the book
of Genesis mention is first made of light, and afterwards of those
things which are from light. Gen. i. 3, 4. It is from the same
cause also, that all things in the universe, both in heaven and in
the world, have relation to good and truth and to their conjunc
tion, in order that they may be real existences.

139.* It is to be observed, that the divine good and divine truth
which are in the heavens from the Lord as a sun, are not in the
Lord, but from the Lord. In the Lord there is only divine love,
which is the esse from which those exist. To proceed, means to
exist from an esse. This, too, may be illustrated by comparison
with the sun of the natural world. The heat and light which
are in the world, are not in the sun, but from the sun. In the
sun there is nothing but fire, from which heat and light exist and
proceed.

140. Since the Lord as a sun is divine love, and divine love is
divine good itself, therefore the Divine which proceeds from Him,
and is His Divine in heaven, is called, for the sake of distinction,

---

[1] That the divine truth proceeding from the Lord, is the only real existence, n. 6880, 7004, 8200. That all things were made and created by
divine truth, n. 2803, 2884, 5272, 7678.

* [There is no n 138 in the original.—Tr.]

divine truth; although it is divine good united with divine truth. This divine truth is what is called the Holy [Spirit] proceeding from Him.

THE FOUR QUARTERS IN HEAVEN.

141. IN heaven as in the world, there are four quarters; the east, the south, the west, and the north. These are determined in both worlds by their respective suns; in heaven by the sun of heaven, which is the Lord; in the world by the sun of the world: but still there are great differences between them.

THE FIRST difference is, that, in the world, that quarter is called the south, where the sun is at its greatest altitude above the earth; the north, where he is at the opposite point beneath the earth; the east, where he rises at the equinoxes; and the west, where he then sets. Thus in the world, all the quarters are determined from the south. But in heaven, it is called the east where the Lord appears as a sun; opposite is the west; on the right is the south; and on the left is the north; and this in whatever direction the angels turn themselves. Thus in heaven, all the quarters are determined from the east. It is called the east (*oriens*) where the Lord appears as a sun, because all the *origin* of life is from Him as a sun; and also because in proportion as heat and light, or love and intelligence, are received from Him by the angels, the Lord is said to *arise* upon them.* Hence also it is, that the Lord in the Word is called the East.[1]

---

* [To enable the English reader to understand this sentence, he must be informed, that the Latin word for the east is *oriens*, derived from *orior*, to arise; whence also is formed *origo*, the exact meaning of which is retained in our word "*origin*." The sense of the above will be clear to the English reader, if, wherever the term "east" occurs, he substitutes in his mind "the rising" which is the literal signification of the Latin word.—TR.]

[1] That the Lord, in the supreme sense, is the east, because He is the sun of heaven, which is always in its rising, and never in its setting, n. 101, 5097, 9668.

142. ANOTHER difference is, that the east is always before the angels, the west behind them, the south on their right, and the north on their left; but since this cannot be easily understood in the world, because man turns his face to every quarter, therefore it shall be explained.

The whole heaven turns itself toward the Lord as to its common centre; hence all the angels turn themselves thither. That there is also a universal tendency on earth to a common centre, is well known: but the tendency in heaven differs from that in the world. In heaven the front parts [or anteriors] tend to the common centre, but in the world the lower parts. The tendency in the world is called the centripetal force, and also gravitation. The interiors of the angels are also actually turned forward; and because the interiors present themselves in the face, therefore the face is what determines the quarters.[1]

143. But that the angels have the east before them *whithersoever they turn their faces and bodies*, is something still harder to understand in the world, because man has every quarter before him according to the direction in which he turns himself. Therefore, this also shall be explained.

The angels turn and bend their faces and bodies in every direction like men; but still they have the east constantly before their eyes. But the changes of aspect with the angels are unlike those of men, and are from another origin. They appear similar, indeed, but still they are not, because all determinations of aspect both with angels and spirits result from the ruling love. For, as was said just above, their interiors are actually turned toward their common centre, thus in heaven toward the Lord as a sun. Wherefore since the love is continually before their interiors, and the face exists from the interiors,—for it is their external form,—therefore the ruling love is always before the face. Hence, in the heavens, the Lord as a sun is continually before them, be-

---

[1] That all in heaven turn themselves to the Lord, n. 9828, 10130, 10189, 10420. That, nevertheless, the angels do not turn themselves to the Lord, but the Lord turns them to Himself, n. 10189. That the presence of the angels is not with the Lord, but the Lord's presence is with the angels, n. 9415.

cause He is the source from which they derive their love ;[1] and since the Lord Himself is in His own love with the angels, therefore it is He who causes them to look to Him in whatever direction they turn. These things cannot as yet be further elucidated ; but in the following chapters,—those especially which treat of Representations and Appearances, and of Time and Space in heaven,—they will be made more intelligible.

That the angels have the Lord constantly before them, has been given me to know and also to perceive from much experience ; for whenever I have been in company with them, the Lord has been perceptibly present before my face ; not seen, indeed, but still clearly perceived. That this is the case, the angels also have often testified.

Because the Lord is constantly before the faces of the angels, therefore also it is usual in the world to say of those who believe in God, and love Him, that they set Him before their eyes, and before their face, and that they look to Him, and keep Him in view. Man derives this mode of speaking from the spiritual world ; for many expressions in human language are thence derived, although man is ignorant of their origin.

144. That there is such a turning to the Lord is one of the wonders of heaven ; for many may be together there in one place, and one may turn his face and body in one direction, and another in another ; and yet they all see the Lord before them, and every one has the south on his right hand, the north on his left, and the west behind. Another of the wonders of heaven is, that although the aspect of the angels is always toward the east, still they have an aspect also toward the other three quarters ; but their aspect toward these is from their interior sight, which is the sight of thought. Another wonder also is, that it is never permit-

---

[1] That all in the spiritual world constantly turn themselves to their own loves, and that the quarters commence, and are determined, in that world from the face, n. 10130, 10189, 10420, 10702. That the face is formed to correspondence with the interiors, n. 4791 to 4805, 5695. That hence the interiors shine forth from the face, n. 3527, 4066, 4796. That with angels the face makes one with the interiors, n. 4796, 4797, 4799, 5695, 8250. Concerning the influx of the interiors into the face and its muscles, n. 3631, 4800.

ted any one in heaven to stand behind another, and to look at the back of his head; and if he should, the influx of good and truth which is from the Lord would be thereby disturbed.

145. The angels do not see the Lord as He sees them. They see the Lord through the eyes; but the Lord sees them in the forehead, because the forehead corresponds to love, and the Lord by love flows into their wills, and makes Himself visible to their understandings, to which the eyes correspond.[1]

146. But the quarters in the heavens which constitute the Lord's celestial kingdom, differ from those which constitute His spiritual kingdom, by reason that the Lord appears to the angels in His celestial kingdom as a sun, but to those in His spiritual kingdom as a moon; and where the Lord appears is the east. The distance between the sun and the moon there is thirty degrees; hence there is a like difference between the quarters of the two kingdoms.—That heaven is distinguished into two kingdoms, called the celestial and the spiritual, may be seen in its proper chapter, n. 20 to 28: and that the Lord appears in the celestial kingdom as a sun, and in the spiritual as a moon, n. 118:—nevertheless the quarters in heaven are not thereby rendered indistinct, since the spiritual angels cannot ascend to the celestial angels, nor can the celestial descend to the spiritual; (see above, n. 35).

147. Hence it is evident what is the nature of the Lord's presence in the heavens,—that He is everywhere and with every one, in the good and truth which proceed from Him; consequently that He is with the angels in what is His own, as was said above, n. 12. The perception of the Lord's presence is in their interiors, from which the eyes see; and therefore they behold Him out of themselves, because there is continuity [between the Lord as existing within, and the Lord as existing without them]. Hence it is evident how it is to be understood, that the

---

[1] That the forehead corresponds to celestial love, and that, therefore, the forehead, in the Word, signifies that love, n. 9936. That the eye corresponds to the understanding, because the understanding is internal sight, n. 2701, 4410, 4526, 9051, 10569; wherefore, to lift up the eyes and see, signifies to understand, to perceive, and to observe, n. 2789, 2829, 3198, 3202, 4083, 4086, 4339, 5684.

Lord is in them, and they in the Lord, according to His own words, "*Abide in Me, and I in you.*" John xv. 4. "*He that eateth My flesh, and drinketh My blood, abideth in Me, and I in Him.*" John vi. 56. The Lord's flesh signifies divine good, and His blood, divine truth.[1]

148. All in the heavens dwell distinctly according to the quarters. They who are in the good of love dwell in the east and west · in the east they who are in clear perception of it, and in the west they who are in obscure perception of it They who are in wisdom derived from the good of love, dwell in the south and north; they who are in the clear light of wisdom, in the south, and they who are in the obscure light of wisdom, in the north. The angels in the Lord's spiritual kingdom dwell in like manner as those in His celestial kingdom, yet with a difference according to the good of love and the light of truth derived from good. For the love in the celestial kingdom is love to the Lord, and the light of truth thence derived is wisdom; but in the spiritual kingdom it is love toward the neighbor, which is called charity, and the light of truth thence derived is intelligence, which is likewise called faith: see above, n. 23. They differ also as to the quarters; for the quarters in the two kingdoms are distant thirty degrees from each other, as was said just above, n. 146.

149. In every society of heaven a similar arrangement prevails. They who are in a superior degree of love and charity are in the east, they who are in a lower degree are in the west; they who are in the greater light of wisdom and intelligence are in the south, and they who are in less light are in the north. The angels dwell thus distinctly because every society is an image of the whole heaven, and also is a heaven in miniature: see above, n. 51 to 58. The same order prevails in their assemblies. They are brought into this order as a consequence of the form of heaven. by virtue of which every one knows his own place. The

---

[1] That the flesh of the Lord signifies His Divine Human, and the divine good of His love, n. 3813, 7850, 9127, 10283; and that the blood of the Lord signifies divine truth, and the holy principle of faith, n. 4735, 6978, 7317, 7326, 7846, 7850, 7877, 9127, 9393, 10026, 10033, 10152, 10204.

13   E

Lord also provides that in every society there may be some of every class, to the intent that the form of heaven may be everywhere the same. Nevertheless the arrangement of the whole heaven differs from that of each society, as the whole differs from a part; for the societies which are in the east excel those in the west, and those in the south excel those in the north.

150. Hence it is that the quarters in the heavens signify the qualities which peculiarly characterize those who dwell theic; thus the east signifies love and its good in clear perception; the west, the same in obscure perception; the south, wisdom and intelligence in clear light; and the north, the same in obscure light. From this signification of the quarters in heaven, they have a similar signification in the internal or spiritual sense of the Word;[1] for the internal or spiritual sense of the word is in perfect agreement with the things which exist in heaven.

151. The order in hell is the reverse of that in heaven. The infernals do not look to the Lord as a sun or as a moon, but backward from the Lord to that thick darkness [*caliginosum*] which is in the place of the sun of the world, and to the darkness [*tenebrosum*] which is in the place of the moon of the earth. They who are called genii look to the thick darkness which is in the place of the sun of the world, and they who are called spirits look to the darkness which is in the place of the moon of the earth.[2]—That the sun of the world and the moon of the earth do not appear in the spiritual world, but in the place of that sun, a thick dark thing opposite to the sun of heaven, and in the place of that moon, a dark thing opposite to the moon of heaven, may be seen above, n. 122.—The quarters in hell are, therefore, opposite to those in heaven. The thick dark thing and the dark thing are in the east; the west is wheie the sun of heaven is; the south is on the right, and the north on the

---

[1] That the east, in the Word, signifies love in clear perception, n. 1250, 3708; the west, love in obscure perception. n. 3708, 9653; the south, a state of light, or of wisdom and intelligence, n. 1458, 3708, 5672; and the north, that state in obscurity, n. 3708.

[2] Who, and of what quality they are who are called genii, and who, and of what quality they are who are called spirits, n. 947, 5035, 5977, 8593, 8622, 8625.

left; and this, too, in whatever direction their bodies are turned; nor can it be otherwise, because every tendency of their interiors, and thence every determination inclines and struggles in that direction. That the direction of the interiors, and thence the actual determination of all in the other life, is according to their love, may be seen, n. 143. The love of those who are in the hells is the love of self and of the world; and these loves are signified by the sun of the natural world and the moon of the earth, see n. 122; and they are also the opposites of love to the Lord and love toward the neighbor.[1] Hence it is that evil spirits turn themselves toward those dark appearances [*caligines*], and backward from the Lord. Those in the hells also dwell according to their quarters; they who are in the evils which spring from self-love, from their east to their west; and they who are in the falses of evil, from their south to their north. But on this subject more will be said below, when the hells come to be treated of.

152. When any evil spirit comes among the good, the quarters are so confounded that the good scarcely know where their east is. I have several times perceived this to be the case, and have also been informed by spirits who complained of it.

153. Evil spirits sometimes appear to be turned to the quarters of heaven, and then they have intelligence and the perception of truth, but no affection of good; wherefore as soon as they turn themselves back to their own quarters, they cease to be in intelligence and in the perception of truth; and then they say that the truths which they had before heard and perceived are not truths, but falses. They also desire that falses may be truths. I have been informed concerning this turning, namely, that with the wicked the understanding can be so turned, but not the will; and that this is provided by the Lord, in order that every one may be able to see and acknowledge truths; but that no one may receive them unless he be in good, because it is good and never

---

[1] That they who are in the loves of self and of the world turn themselves backward from the Lord, n. 10130, 10189, 10420, 10702. That love to the Lord and charity toward the neighbor, make heaven, whilst the love of self and the love of the world make hell, because they are opposites, n. 2041, 3610, 4225, 4776, 6210, 7366, 7369, 7490, 8232, 8678, 10455, 10741 to 10745.

evil which receives truths. I have also been informed that the
case is similar with man, to the end that he may be amended by
truths, but that still he is not amended except in the degree that
he is in good; and that on this account man, in like manner, can
be turned to the Lord; but that, if he be in evil as to life, he
immediately turns himself back again, and confirms in himself
the falses of his evil in opposition to the truths which he understood and saw; and that this occurs when he thinks with himself
from his interior.

CHANGES OF STATE WITH THE ANGELS IN HEAVEN.

154. By changes of state with the angels, are meant their
changes as to love and faith, and thence as to wisdom and intelligence, thus as to the states of their life. States are predicated
of life, and of those things which belong to life; and since
angelic life is the life of love and faith, and thence of wisdom
and intelligence, therefore states are predicated of these, and are
called states of love and faith, and states of wisdom and intelligence. How these states with the angels are changed, shall now
be told.

155. The angels are not constantly in the same state as to love,
nor, consequently, as to wisdom; for all their wisdom is from
love and according to love. Sometimes they are in a state of
intense love, and sometimes in a state of love not so intense. It
decreases by degrees from its greatest to its least. When they
are in the greatest degree of love, they are in the light and heat
of their life, or in their bright and delightful state; but when
they are in the least degree, they are in shade and cold, or in
their state of obscurity and undelight. From the last state they
return again to the first; and so on. These states do not succeed
each other uniformly, but with variety, like the variations of the
state of light and shade, and of heat and cold; or like morning,
noon, evening, and night, every day in the world, with perpetual

variety throughout the year. They also correspond,—morning to a state of their love in brightness; noon to a state of their wisdom in brightness; evening to a state of their wisdom in obscurity; and night to a state of no love and wisdom. But it is to be observed that there is no correspondence of night with the states of life of those who are in heaven; but there is a correspondence of the twilight which precedes the morning; the correspondence of night is with those who are in hell.[1] From this correspondence days and years in the Word signify states of life in general; heat and light, love and wisdom; morning, the first and highest degree of love; noon, wisdom in its light; evening, wisdom in its shade; day-break, the obscurity which precedes the morning; and night, the deprivation of love and wisdom.[2]

156. The states of the various things without the angels, and which appear before their eyes, are also changed with the states of their interiors which are of their love and wisdom; for the things which are without them, assume an appearance according to those within them. What those things are, and what their quality, will be shown hereafter when representatives and appearances in heaven are treated of.

157. Every angel undergoes and passes through such changes of state, and so does each society as a whole,—but still with variety, because they differ in love and wisdom; for they who are in the midst are in a more perfect state than they who are around them. Perfection diminishes successively from the centre to the circumferences of each society, as may be seen above, n.

---

[1] That in heaven there is no state corresponding to night, but to the twilight which precedes morning, n. 6110. That twilight signifies a middle state between the last and the first, n. 10134.

[2] That the vicissitudes of states as to illustration and perception in heaven, are as the times of the days in the world, n. 5672, 5962, (6310), 8426, 9213, 10605. That a day, and a year, in the Word, signify all states in general, n. 23, 487, 488, 493, 893, 2788, 3462, 4850, 10656. That morning signifies the beginning of a new state, and a state of love, n. 7218, 8426, 8427, 10114, 10134. That evening signifies a state of closing light and love, n. 10134, 10135. That night signifies a state of no love and faith, n. 221, 709, 2352, 6000, 6110, 7870, 7947.

23 and 128. But it would be tedious to specify the differences, for every one undergoes changes according to the quality of his love and faith. Hence it is, that one is in his brightness and delight, when another is in his obscurity and undelight; and this at the same time and within the same society. The changes in one society also differ from those in another, and those in the societies of the celestial kingdom from those in the societies of the spiritual kingdom. These differences in their changes of state are, in general, like the variations of the state of days in different climates on earth; where it is morning with some when it is evening with others; and warm with some when it is cold with others; and *vice versa.*

158. I have been informed from heaven why such changes of state prevail there. The angels told me there were several reasons: *First,* that the delight of life and of heaven, which results from their love and wisdom derived from the Lord, would gradually lose its value if they were always in it; as is the case with those who are in the enjoyment of delights and pleasures without variety. *Another* reason is, that angels have a proprium* as well as men; that this consists in loving themselves; that all in heaven are withheld from their proprium, and are in love and wisdom so far as they are withheld from it by the Lord; but so far as they are not withheld, they are in the love of self; and because every one loves his proprium,[1] and this draws him down, therefore they have changes of state or successive alternations. A *third* reason is, that they are perfected by these

---

* [*Proprium* is the Latin word that occurs in this connection, and which it is thought best to leave untranslated. It means simply *the selfhood,* or *what is one's own.* This being known, it is believed that no inconvenience will result from the use of the Latin word. No doubt this term will, in time, become as thoroughly domesticated among us, as many others from the Latin have already, such as *medium, decorum, memorandum,* &c.; and then it will cause as little embarrassment to the English reader, as these terms now do.—TR.]

[1] That the proprium of man consists in loving himself, n. 694, 731, 4317, 5660. That the proprium must be separated, in order that the Lord may be present, n. 1023, 1044. That it is also actually separated, when any one is held in good by the Lord, n. 9334, 9335, 9336, 9447, 9452, 9453, 9454, 9938.

changes, for they are thus habitually held in love to the Lord, and withheld from the love of self. Their perception and sense of good is also rendered more exquisite by the alternations of delight and undelight.[1] The angels further said, that the Lord does not produce their changes of state,—because the Lord, as a sun, is always flowing in with heat and light, that is, with love and wisdom,—but that the cause is in themselves, because they love their proprium, which continually draws them away from the Lord. This they illustrated by a comparison with the sun of the world; for the changes of the state of heat and cold, of light and shade, every year and every day, do not originate in the sun, because it stands still, but they are occasioned by the motion of the earth.

159. It has been shown me how the Lord as a sun appears to the angels in the celestial kingdom in their first state, how in the second, and how in the third. I saw the Lord as a sun, at first fiery and glistening in such splendor as cannot be described; and I was told that the Lord as a sun appears thus to the angels in their first state. Afterwards there appeared a great dusky belt around the sun, in consequence of which its bright and dazzling splendor began to grow dim; and it was told me that the sun appears to them in this manner in their second state. Then the belt seemed to become gradually more dusky, and the sun, in consequence, less glowing, and this by degrees, until at length it became apparently white; and it was told me that the sun so appears to them in their third state. Afterwards that white orb seemed to advance to the left toward the moon of heaven, and to add itself to her light, in consequence of which the moon shone with more than its usual brightness; and it was told me that this was the fourth state with the angels of the celestial kingdom, and the first with those of the spiritual kingdom; that the changes of state in each kingdom are thus alternate, yet not in the whole kingdom at once, but in one society after another: and also that these vicissitudes do not return at stated periods, but occur to them

---

[1] That the angels are perfected to eternity, n. 4803, 6648. That in heaven one state is in no case exactly like another, and that hence is perpetual progress toward perfection, n. 10200.

earlier or later, without their knowledge. The angels said further, that the sun is not so changed in itself, nor does it really so advance, but still that it appears so according to the successive progressions of their states; because the Lord appears to every one according to the quality of his state; thus glowing to them when they are in intense love, less glowing and at length white as their love decreases; and that the quality of their state wɛs represented by the dusky belt, which occasioned in the sun those apparent variations in its flame and light.

160. When the angels are in their last state, which is when they are in their proprium, they begin to be sad. I have conversed with them when they were in that state. and have seen their sadness; but they said that they hoped soon to return to their former state, and thus as it were again into heaven; for it is heaven to them to be withheld from proprium.

161. There are also changes of state in the hells, but these will be spoken of below when hell comes to be treated of.

TIME IN HEAVEN.

162. ALTHOUGH all things in heaven have succession and progression as in the world, still the angels have no notion or idea of time and space, insomuch that they are altogether ignorant as to what time and space are. I shall now speak of time in heaven, and of space in its proper chapter.

163. The angels do not know what time is,—although all things with them are in successive progression as in the world, and that so completely that there is no difference,—because in heaven there are not years and days, but changes of state; and where years and days are, there are times, but where changes of state are, there are states.

164. There are times in the world, because the sun of the world appears to advance successively from one degree [in the heavens] to another, thus causing the times which are called the seasons

of the year; and moreover, he apparently revolves round the
earth, and thus causes the times which are called times of the
day. Both these changes occur at regular intervals. It is otherwise with the sun of heaven. That sun does not, by successive
progressions and circumgyrations, cause years and days, but, to
appearance, changes of state; and these not at regular intervals,
as was shown in the preceding chapter. Hence the angels cannot
have any idea of time, but in its place an idea of state. What
state is, may be seen above, n. 154.

165. Since the angels have no idea derived from time, like
men in the world, therefore they have no idea concerning time,
or anything relating to time. They do not even know what those
things are which are proper to time, as a year, a month, a week,
a day, an hour, to-day, to-morrow, yesterday. When the angels
hear them named by man, (for angels are always adjoined to man
by the Lord), they have, instead of them, a perception of states,
and of such things as relate to state; thus the natural idea of
man is turned into a spiritual idea with the angels. Hence it is
that times in the Word signify states; and that the things which
are proper to time, as those above mentioned, signify spiritual
things corresponding to them.[1]

166. The case is the same in regard to all things which exist
from time, such as the four seasons of the year called spring,
summer, autumn, and winter; the four times of the day, called
morning, noon, evening, and night; the four ages of man, called
infancy, youth, manhood, and old age; and all other things
which exist from time, or succeed according to time. In thinking
of them, man thinks from time, but an angel from state; wherefore what is derived from time in the thought of man, is turned
into the idea of state with an angel. Spring and morning are

---

[1] That times in the Word signify states, n. 2788, 2838, 3254, 3356, 4814,
4901, 4916, 7218, 8070, 10133, 10605. That the angels think without an
idea of time and space, n. 3404. The reasons why, n. 1274, 1382, 3356,
4882, 4901, 6110, 7218, 7381. What a year, in the Word, signifies, n. 487,
488, 493, 893, 2906, 7828, 10209. What a month, n. 3814. What a week,
n. 2044, 3845. What a day, n. 23, 487, 488, 6110, 7680, 8426, 9213, 10132,
10605. What to-day, n. 2838, 3998, 4304, 6165, 6984, 9939. What to-morrow, n. 3998, 10497. What yesterday, n. 6983, 7114, 7140.

turned into the idea of a state of love and wisdom such as they are with the angels in their first state : summer and noon, into an idea of love and wisdom such as they are in their second state ; autumn and evening, such as they are in their third state ; and night and winter, into the idea of such a state as exists in hell. Hence it is that similar things are signified in the Word by those times; see above, n. 155. It is plain from this how the natural ideas in man's thought become spiritual ideas with the angels attendant on him.

167. Since the angels have no idea of time, therefore they have a different idea of eternity from that entertained by men on earth. Eternity is perceived by them as infinite state, not as infinite time.[1] I was once thinking about eternity, and by the idea of time I could perceive what was [meant by the expression] *to eternity*, namely, time without end ; but I could form no conception what *from eternity* was, and therefore none of what God had done from eternity before creation. When anxiety arose in my mind on this account, I was elevated into the sphere of heaven, and thus into that perception of eternity in which the angels are ; and then I was enlightened to see that eternity must not be thought of from time, but from state, and that the meaning of *from* eternity may then be perceived ; which also was the case with me.

168. The angels who speak with men, never speak by natural ideas proper to man,—all of which are derived from time, space, materiality, and such things as are analogous thereto,—but by spiritual ideas, all of which are derived from states, and their various changes, within and without the angels ; nevertheless angelic ideas, which are spiritual, when they flow in with man, are turned in an instant, and of themselves, into the natural ideas proper to man, which exactly correspond to the spiritual. That this is the case is unknown both to angels and men ; but such is all influx of heaven into man. Certain angels were admitted more nearly than usual into my thoughts, and even into the natural ones, in which were many ideas derived from time and

---

[1] That men have an idea of eternity with time, but the angels without time, n. 1382, 3404, 8325.

space; but because they understood nothing, they quickly withdrew; and I afterwards heard them conversing and saying, that they had been in darkness. It has been granted me to know by experience how entirely ignorant the angels are of time. A certain one from heaven was of such a character, that he could be admitted into natural ideas, such as men have, and I therefore discoursed with him as man with man. At first he did not know what it was that I called time. Wherefore I was obliged to inform him precisely how the sun appears to be carried around our earth, causing years and days; and that hence the years are distinguished into four seasons, and also into months and weeks, and the days into twenty-four hours; and that these recur at regular intervals; and that such is the origin of times. On hearing this he was much surprised, and said that he knew nothing about such things, but what states were. In the course of our conversation I also observed, that it is known in the world that there is no time in heaven, or at least that men speak as if they knew it; for they say of those who die, that they leave the things of time, and that they pass out of time, by which they mean, out of the world. I remarked also that it is known by some that times in their origin are states, from this circumstance, that they are altogether according to the states of affection in which men are; short, to those who are in pleasant and joyous states; long, to those who are in unpleasant and sorrowful ones; and various in a state of hope and expectation; and that the learned, therefore, inquire what time and space are; and that some also know that time belongs to the natural man.

169. The natural man may imagine that he would be deprived of all thought, if the ideas of time, space, and material things, were taken away; for on these ideas are founded all the thought proper to man.[1] But he may rest assured that the thoughts are limited and confined in proportion as they partake of time, space, and materiality; and that they are unlimited and extended in proportion as they do not partake of these, because the mind is so far elevated above the things of the body and the world.

---

[1] That man does not think without an idea of time, otherwise than angels, n. 3404.

Hence the angels have wisdom, and their wisdom is called incomprehensible, because it does not fall into ideas which are derived merely from natural things.

REPRESENTATIVES AND APPEARANCES IN HEAVEN.

170. THE man who thinks only from natural light, cannot comprehend how anything in heaven can be similar to what exists in the world; the reason is, because from that light he has thought, and confirmed himself in the belief, that angels are only minds, and that minds are a sort of ethereal puffs of breath which, therefore, have no senses like a man, thus no eyes, and consequently no objects of sight; when yet angels have all the senses which men have, yea, much more exquisite. The light also by which they see, is much brighter than the light by which man sees. That angels are men in the most perfect form, and that they enjoy every sense, may be seen above, n. 73 to 77; and that the light in heaven is much brighter than the light in the world, n. 126 to 132.

171. The nature of the objects which appear to the angels in the heavens, cannot be described in a few words; for the most part they are like the things on the earth, but in form more perfect, and in number more abundant. That such things exist in the heavens, is evident from those seen by the prophets; as the things seen by Ezekiel, concerning the new temple and the new earth, which are described from chap. xl. to xlviii.; by Daniel from chap. vii. to xii.; by John from the first chapter of the Apocalypse to the last; and by others mentioned both in the historical and prophetical portions of the Word. They saw such things when heaven was opened to them; and heaven is said to be opened, when the interior sight, which is the sight of man's spirit, is opened. For the things which are in the heavens cannot be seen with the bodily eyes, but with the eyes of the spirit;

and these are opened when it pleases the Lord; and then man is withdrawn from the natural light in which he is by reason of the bodily senses, and is elevated into spiritual light in which he is by reason of his spirit. In that light I have seen the things which exist in heaven.

172. But although the objects which appear in the heavens are, for the most part, similar to those which exist on earth, still they are not similar as to essence; for the things which are in the heavens exist from the sun of heaven, and those which are on the earth, from the sun of the world. The things which exist from the sun of heaven are called spiritual, but those which exist from the sun of the world are called natural.

173. The things which exist in the heavens do not exist in the same manner as those which exist on earth. All things in the heavens exist from the Lord according to their correspondence with the interiors of the angels; for the angels have both interiors and exteriors. The things which are in their interiors all have relation to love and faith, thus to will and understanding,—for will and understanding are their receptacles; but the exterior things correspond to their interiors. That exteriors correspond to interiors may be seen above, n. 87 to 115. This may be illustrated by what was said above concerning the heat and light of heaven; that the angels have heat according to the quality of their love, and light according to the quality of their wisdom, may be seen n. 128 to 134. The case is similar with all other things which appear to the senses of the angels.

174. Whenever it has been granted me to be in company with angels, the things of heaven have appeared to me exactly like those in the world,—so perceptibly indeed, that I was not aware but that I was in the world, and in the palace of a king there. I also conversed with them as man with man.

175. Since all things which correspond to the interiors also represent them, therefore they are called REPRESENTATIVES; and since they vary according to the state of the interiors with the angels, therefore they are called APPEARANCES; although the objects which appear before the eyes of angels in the heavens, and which are perceived by their senses, appear and are perceived as much to the life as those on earth appear to man; yea,

much more clearly, distinctly, and perceptibly. The appearances thence existing in the heavens, are called *real appearances*, because they really exist. There are also appearances
not real, because, although they appear, it is true, they do not correspond to the interiors ;[1] but of these in what follows.

176. To illustrate the nature and quality of the objects which
appear to the angels according to correspondences, I will here
adduce a single instance. To those who are in intelligence, there
appear gardens and paradises full of trees and flowers of every
kind. The trees are planted in the most beautiful order, and so
interwoven as to form arbors, with entrances of verdant fret-work,
and walks around them,—all of such beauty as no language can
describe. They who are distinguished for intelligence also walk
there, and gather flowers, and weave garlands, with which they
adorn little children. There are also species of trees and flowers
there, such as were never seen and could not exist in the world.
On the trees also are fruits, according to the good of love in
which the intelligent are principled. Such things are seen by
them, because a garden and paradise, and also fruit trees and
flowers, correspond to intelligence and wisdom.[2] That such

---

[1] That all things which appear among the angels are representative,
n. 1971, 3213 to 3227, 3342, 3475, 3485, 9481, 9543, 9576, 9577. That the
heavens are full of representatives, n. 1521, 1532, 1619. That the representatives are more beautiful, as they are more interior in the heavens, n.
3475. That representatives in the heavens are real appearances, because
from the light of heaven, n. 3485. That the divine influx is turned into
representatives in the superior heavens, and thence also in the inferior
heavens, n. 2179, 3213, 9457, 9481, 9576, 9577. Things are called representative which appear before the eyes of the angels in such forms as are
in nature, that is, such as are in the world, n. 9577. That internal things
are thus turned into external, n. 1632, 2987 to 3002. The nature of representatives in the heavens illustrated by various examples, n. 1521, 1532,
1619 to 1628, 1807, 1973, 1974, 1977, 1980, 1981, 2299, 2601, 2761, 2762, 3217,
3219, 3220, 3348, 3350, 5198, 9090, 10278. That all the things which appear
in the heavens are according to correspondences, and are called representatives, n. 3213 to 3216, 3342, 3475, 3485, 9481, 9574, 9576, 9577. That all
correspondences are representative, and also significative, n. 2896, 2987 to
2989, 2990, 3002, 3225.

[2] That a garden and paradise signify intelligence and wisdom, n. 100,
108, 3220. What is meant by the garden of Eden and the garden of Jeho-

things are in the heavens is also known on earth, but only to those who are in good, and have not extinguished in themselves the light of heaven by natural light (*lumen*) and its fallacies ; for they think and say, when speaking of heaven, that such things **a** there *as the ear hath not heard, nor the eye seen.*

THE GARMENTS WITH WHICH THE ANGELS APPEAR CLOTHED.

177. SINCE angels are men, and live together in society like men on earth, therefore they have garments, habitations, and other things of a like nature,—yet with this difference, that all things with them are more perfect, because they are in a more perfect state ; for as angelic wisdom exceeds human wisdom in such a degree as to be called ineffable, so likewise do all things which are perceived by them and appear to them ; for all things which are perceived by the angels and appear to them correspond to their wisdom ; see above, n. 173.

178. The garments with which the angels are clothed, like all other things, correspond ; and because they correspond, they also really exist : see above, n. 175. Their garments correspond to their intelligence ; therefore all in the heavens appear clothed according to their intelligence ; and because some excel others in intelligence, (n. 43, 128), therefore they have more excellent garments. The most intelligent have garments that glitter as from flame, some those that shine as from light ; the less intelligent have bright and white garments without splendor ; and the

vah, n. 99, 100, 1588. Concerning paradisiacal scenes and their magnificence in the other life, n. 1122, 1622, 2296, 4528, 4529. That trees signify perceptions and knowledges, from which wisdom and intelligence are derived, n. 103, 2163, 2682, 2722, 2972, 7692. That fruits signify the goods of love and charity, n. 3146, 3690, 9337.

still less intelligent have garments of different colors. But the
angels of the inmost heaven are naked.

179. Since the garments of the angels correspond to their in
telligence, therefore they correspond also to truth, because all in
telligence is from divine truth ; wherefore, whether we say that
angels are clothed according to intelligence, or according to divine truth, it is the same thing. The garments of some glitter
as from flame, and those of others shine as from light, because
flame corresponds to good, and light to truth derived from good.[1]
The garments of some are bright and white without splendor,
and those of others are of diverse colors, because the divine good
and truth are less refulgent, and also variously received, with the
less intelligent ;[2] brightness also, and whiteness, correspond to
truth,[3] and colors to its varieties.[4] Those in the inmost heaven
are naked, because they are in innocence, and innocence corresponds to nakedness.[5]

---

[1] That garments, in the Word, signify truths, from correspondence, n.
1073, 2576, 5319, 5554, 9212, 9216, 9952, 10536; because truth invests good,
n. 5248. That a veil or covering signifies the intellectual principle, because
the intellect is the recipient of truth, n. 6378. That bright garments of
fine linen signify truths derived from the Divine, n. 5319, 9469. That
flame signifies spiritual good, and the light thence issuing, truth from that
good, n. 3222, 6832.

[2] That angels and spirits appear clothed with garments according to
their truths, thus according to their intelligence, n. 165, 5248, 5954, 9212,
9216, 9814, 9952, 10536. That the garments of the angels are sometimes
splendid, and sometimes not so, n. 5248.

[3] That brightness and whiteness, in the Word, signify truth, because
they are derived from the light of heaven, n. 3301, 3993, 4007.

[4] That colors in heaven are variegations of the light there, n. 1042, 1043,
1053, 1624, 3993, 4530, 4742, 4922. That colors signify various things
which relate to intelligence and wisdom, n. 4530, 4922, 9466. That the
precious stones in the Urim and the Thummim, according to their colors,
signified all things of truth derived from good in the heavens, n. 9865,
9868, 9905. That colors, so far as they partake of redness, signify good,
and so far as they partake of white, signify truth, n. 9476.

[5] That all in the inmost heaven are innocences, and that therefore they
appear naked, n. 154, 165, 297, 2736, 3887, 8375, 9960. That innocence, is
represented in the heavens by nakedness, n. 165, 8375, 9960. That to the
innocent and the chaste, nakedness is no shame, because without offense,
n. 165, 213, 8375.

180. Since the angels are clothed in heaven, therefore they have appeared clothed when seen in the world; as those seen by the prophets, and also at the Lord's sepulchre, "*whose appearance was like lightning,*" and "*their raiment glittering and white,*" Matt. xxviii. 3; Mark xvi. 5; Luke xxiv. 4; John xx. 12, 13; and those seen in heaven by John, "*whose garments were of fine linen and white,*" Apoc. iv. 4; chap. xix. 14. And because intelligence is from divine truth, therefore the garments of the Lord when He was transfigured, were "*glittering and white as the light.*" Matt. xvii. 2; Mark ix. 3; Luke ix. 29. That light is divine truth proceeding from the Lord may be seen above, n. 129. Hence it is that garments in the Word signify truths, and intelligence derived from truths; as in the Apocalypse: "*They who have not defiled their garments, shall walk with Me in white, for they are worthy. He that overcometh, the same shall be clothed in white raiment,*" chap. iii. 4, 5. "*Blessed is he that watcheth, and keepeth his garments,*" chap. xvi. 15: and concerning Jerusalem, by which is meant the church that is in truth,[1] it is thus written in Isaiah: "*Awake, put on strength, O Zion, put on thy beautiful garments, O Jerusalem,*" lii. 1; and in Ezekiel: "*O Jerusalem, I girded thee with fine linen, and covered thee with silk.—Thy raiment was of fine linen and silk,*" xvi. 10, 13; besides many other passages. But he who is not in truths, is said not to be clothed with a wedding garment; as in Matthew, "*When the king came in,—he saw there a man that had not on a wedding-garment; and he said unto him, Friend, how camest thou in hither not having a wedding-garment?—Wherefore he was cast into outer darkness.*" xxii. 12, 13. The house where the marriage was celebrated signifies heaven and the church, on account of the Lord's conjunction with them by His divine truth; wherefore the Lord in the Word is called the Bridegroom and Husband, and heaven with the church, the bride and wife.

181. That the garments of the angels do not merely appear as garments, but that they really are garments, is manifest from

---

[1] That Jerusalem signifies the church in which there is genuine doctrine n. 402, 3654, 9166.

tl ese considerations : that they not only see them, but also feel them ; that they have many garments ; that they take them off and put them on ; that they lay aside those which are not in use, and when they come into use again they resume them. That they are clothed with a variety of garments I have witnessed a thousand times. I inquired whence they obtained them, and they told me from the Lord ; that they received them as gifts, and that they are sometimes clothed without knowing how. They also said that their garments are changed according to the changes of their state ; that in the first and second states they are bright and shining, and in the third and fourth states rather more dim ; and that this also is from correspondence, because their changes of state are changes as to intelligence and wisdom, concerning which see above, n. 154 to 161.

182. Since every one in the spiritual world is clothed according to his intelligence, thus according to the truths from which his intelligence is derived, therefore those in the hells, being without truths, appear only in torn, squalid, and miserable garments, each one according to his insanity ; nor can they wear any others. The Lord permits them to be clothed in this manner, that they may not appear naked.

————————

THE HABITATIONS AND MANSIONS OF THE ANGELS.

183. SINCE there are societies in heaven, and the angels live as men, therefore also they have habitations, and these likewise various according to every one's state of life ; magnificent for those in a state of superior dignity, and less magnificent for those in an inferior condition. I have occasionally conversed with the angels concerning the habitations in heaven, and I told them that scarcely any one at this day will believe that angels have habitations and mansions ; some, because they do not see them ; others because they do not know that angels are men ; and others, because they believe that the angelic heaven is the heaven which

they see around them; and because this appears empty, and they suppose the angels to be ethereal forms, they conclude that they live in the ether. Besides, they do not comprehend how there can be such things in the spiritual world as exist in the natural world, because they know nothing concerning what is spiritual. The angels replied, that they know such ignorance prevails in the world at this day; and, to their surprise, chiefly within the church, and more among the intelligent there, than among those whom they call the simple. They said further, that they who are so ignorant might know from the Word that angels are men, because those who have been seen have been seen as men; in like manner the Lord, who took with Him all His Human; and because they are men, that they have mansions and habitations; and that, although they are called spirits, they are not mere ethereal forms which fly about in the air, as some ignorantly suppose. Such ignorance they call insanity. They also said that men might know the truth, if they would think of angels and spirits apart from their preconceived notions; and that they do so when the question, *whether it be so*, is not the immediate subject of inquiry; for every one has a general idea that angels are in the human form; and that they have dwellings, which they call the habitations of heaven, surpassing in magnificence the habitations of earth; but that this general idea, which flows-in from heaven, is instantly annihilated when the question *whether it be so*, is made the central subject of thought,—which occurs chiefly with the learned, who, by their own intelligence, have closed heaven against themselves, and the way of light thence. Similar is the case in regard to a belief in the life of man after death. He who speaks about it, and does not at the same time think from erudition concerning the soul, or from the doctrine of its re-union with the body, believes that he shall live a man after death; that he shall dwell among angels if he has lived well, and that then he will see magnificent objects, and feel transporting joys; but as soon as he reverts to the doctrine of the soul's re-union with the body, or to the common theory concerning the soul, and the thought occurs whether the soul be of such a nature, and thus, *whether it be so*, his former idea is dissipated.

184. But it is better to adduce the evidence of experience.

Whenever I have conversed with the angels mouth to mouth, I have been present with them in their habitations, which are exactly like the habitations on earth called houses, but more beautiful. They contain halls, inner-rooms, and bed-chambers, in great numbers; courts also, and round about them, gardens, shrubberies, and fields. Where the angels live in societies, their habitations are contiguous, close to each other, and arranged in the form of a city, with streets, ways, and public squares, exactly like the cities on our earth. I have also been permitted to walk through them, and to look around on every side, and occasionally to enter the houses. This occurred in a state of full wakefulness, when my interior sight was opened.[1]

185. I have seen the palaces of heaven, which were magnificent beyond description. Their upper parts shone refulgent as if of pure gold, and their lower parts as if of precious stones. Some were more splendid than others; and the splendor without was equaled by the magnificence within. The apartments were ornamented with decorations, which neither language nor science can adequately describe. On the side that looked to the south were paradises, where all things were equally resplendent. In some places the leaves of the trees were like silver, and the fruits like gold; and the flowers arranged in their beds presented, by their colors, the appearance of rainbows. Near the boundaries, again, appeared other palaces, which terminated the view. Such is the architecture of heaven, that one might say it is the very art itself; and no wonder, for that art itself is from heaven. The angels said that such things, and innumerable others still more perfect, are presented before their eyes by the Lord; but that, nevertheless, they delight their minds more than their eyes, because in everything they see correspondences, and by means of the correspondences, things divine.

186. Concerning correspondences I have also been informed, that not only the palaces and houses, but the minutest particulars both within and without them, correspond to interior things which are in the angels from the Lord; that the house itself in

---

[1] That angels have cities, palaces, and houses, n. 940, 941, 942, 1116, 1626, 1627, 1628, 1630, 1631, 4622.

general corresponds to their good, and the various things within
it to the various particulars of which their good is composed;[1]
and the things out of the houses correspond to their truths which
are derived from good, and also to their perceptions and knowledges ; and that, because they correspond to the goods and truths
appertaining to the angels from the Lord, they correspond to
their love and thence to their wisdom and intelligence, because
love is of good, wisdom is of good and at the same time of truth,
and intelligence is of truth derived from good; and that these
interior things are perceived by the angels when they look at
those objects, and that on this account they delight and affect
their minds more than their eyes.

187. Hence it is evident why the Lord called Himself the
temple which is in Jerusalem, John ii. 19, 21 ;[2] and why the New
Jerusalem appeared of pure gold, its gates of pearl, and its foundations of precious stones, Apoc. xxi.: namely, because the
temple represented the Divine Human of the Lord; the New
Jerusalem signifies the church which is to be established hereafter ; its twelve gates denote the truths which lead to good ; and
its foundations the truths on which it is built.[3]

188. The angels who constitute the Lord's celestial kingdom
dwell for the most part in elevated places, which appear like

---

[1] That houses and the things which they contain signify those things in
man which are of his mind, that is, his interiors, n. 710, 2233, 2331, 2559,
3128, 3538, 4973, 5023, 6106, 6690, 7353, 7848, 7910, 7929, 9150; consequently which relate to good and truth, n. 2233, 2331, 2559, 4982, 7848,
7929. That inner rooms and bed-chambers signify interior things, n.
3900, 5694, 7353. That the roof of a house signifies what is inmost, n.
3652, 10184. That a house of wood signifies what is of good, and a house
of stone what is of truth, n. 3720.

[2] That the house of God, in the supreme sense, signifies the Divine
Human of the Lord, as to divine good, but the temple, as to divine truth;
and, in the respective sense, heaven and the church as to good and truth,
n 3720.

[3] That Jerusalem signifies the church in which there is genuine doctrine, n. 402, 3654, 9166. That gates signify introduction to the doctrine
of the church, and by doctrine into the church, n. 2943, 4777. That foundation signifies truth on which heaven, the church, and doctrine are
founded, n. 9643.

mountains rising out of the earth. The angels who constitute the Lord's spiritual kingdom, dwell in less elevated places, which appear like hills. But the angels who are in the lowest parts of heaven dwell in places which appear like rocks of stone. These things also exist from correspondence; for interior things correspond to superior, and exterior things to inferior.[1] Hence it is that mountains in the Word signify celestial love; hills, spiritual love; and rocks, faith.[2]

189. There are also angels who do not live in societies, but in separate houses. These dwell in the midst of heaven, because they are the best of the angels.

190. The houses in which the angels dwell are not built like houses in the world, but are given to them gratis by the Lord,— to each one according to his reception of good and truth. They also vary a little according to the changes of the state of their interiors, spoken of above, n. 154 to 160. All things whatsoever which the angels possess, they hold as gifts from the Lord, and they are supplied with every thing they need.

---

[1] That in the Word interior things are expressed by superior, and that superior things signify things interior, n. 2148, 3084, 4599, 5146, 8325. That high signifies what is internal, and likewise heaven, n. 1735, 2148, 4210, 4599, 8153.

[2] That in heaven there appear mountains, hills, rocks, valleys, and countries, exactly as in the world, n. 10608. That angels who are in the good of love dwell on mountains; they who are in the good of charity on hills, and they who are in the good of faith on rocks, n. 10438. That, therefore, by mountains, in the Word, is signified the good of love, n. 795, 4210, 6435, 8327, 8758, 10438, 10608; by hills, the good of charity, n. 6435, 10438; and by rocks, the good and truth of faith, n. 8581, 10580. That stone, of which a rock consists, in like manner signifies the truth of faith, n. 114, 643, 1298, 3720, 6426, 8609, 10376. Hence it is, that by mountains is signified heaven, n. 8327, 8805, 9420; and by the top of a mountain, the supreme of heaven, n. 9422, 9434, 10608. That therefore the ancients celebrated holy worship on mountains, n. 796, 2722.

SPACE IN HEAVEN.

191. ALTHOUGH all things in heaven appear to be in place
and in space exactly as they do in the world, still the angels have
no notion or idea of place and space. This must necessarily appear paradoxical; and since the subject is one of great importance, I will endeavor to explain it clearly.

192. All progressions in the spiritual world are made by
changes of the state of the interiors, so that they are nothing but
changes of state.[1] By such changes have I also been conducted
by the Lord into the heavens, and likewise to the earths in the
universe. I was carried there as to the spirit only, my body
meanwhile remaining in the same place.[2] Thus do all the angels
journey. Hence they have no distances; and since they have no
distances, they have no spaces, but instead of spaces they have
states and their changes.

193. Change of place being only change of state, it is evident
that approximations are similitudes as to the state of the interiors,
and that removals are dissimilitudes. Hence it is that those are
near together who are in a similar state, and those distant who
are in a dissimilar state; and that spaces in heaven are merely
external states corresponding to internal. From this cause alone
the heavens are distinct from each other, also the societies of
each heaven, and every individual in a society. Hence, too, the

---

[1] That, in the Word, places and spaces signify states, n. 2625, 2837, 3356,
3387, 7381, 10580; from experience, n. 1274, 1277, 1376 to 1381, 4321, 4882,
10146, 10580. That distance signifies the difference of the state of life, n.
9104, 9967. That motion and changes of place in the spiritual world, are
changes of the state of life, because they originate in them, n. 1273, 1274,
1275, 1377, 3356, 9440. In like manner journeyings, n. 9440, 10734; illustrated by experience, n. 1273 to 1277, 5605. That hence, in the Word, to
journey, signifies to live, and likewise a progression of life; in like manner to sojourn, n. 3335, 4554, 4585, 4882, 5493, 5605, 5996, 8345, 8397, 8417,
8120, 8557. That to walk with the Lord, is to live with Him, n. 10567.

[2] That man, as to his spirit, may be led to a distance afar off by changes
of state, whilst his body remains in its place, also from experience, n.
9440, 9967, 10734. What it is to be led by the spirit into another place, n.
1884.

hells are altogether separated from the heavens, for they are in an opposite state.

194. From this cause also it is, that in the spiritual world one becomes manifestly present to another, if that other intensely desires his presence; for thus he sees him in thought, and puts himself in his state. On the other hand, one is removed from another in proportion as he holds him in aversion. All aversion is from contrariety of the affections and disagreement of the thoughts; hence it happens that many who are together in one place in the spiritual world, appear to each other so long as they agree, but disappear as soon as they disagree.

195. Further: when any one goes from one place to another, whether it be in his own city, or in the courts, or in the gardens, or to others out of his own society, he arrives sooner when he desires, and later when he does not,—the distance itself being lengthened or shortened according to the desire, although it is the same. I have often observed this, and wondered at it. Hence again it is evident that distances, consequently spaces, are altogether according to the states of their interiors with the angels; and that on this account no notion or idea of space can enter their thoughts, although there are spaces with them just the same as in the world.[1]

196. This may be illustrated by the thoughts of man, which have nothing in common with space; for whatever a man looks at intently in thought, is set before him as present. Whoever reflects upon it knows also that his sight takes no cognizance of distances, except from the intermediate objects on the earth, which he sees at the same time; or from his previous knowledge of the extent of the distances. This occurs because space is continuous; and in what is continuous, distance does not appear except as it is estimated by things not continuous. This is especially the case with the angels, because their sight acts in unity with their thought, and their thought in unity with their affection; and because things appear near and remote, and are also varied, according to the states of their interiors, as was said above.

---

[1] That places and spaces appear visible according to the states of the interiors of angels and spirits, n. 5605, 9440, 10146.

197. Hence it is that, in the Word, by places and spaces and all things which relate to space, are signified such things as belong to state; as by distances, nearness, remoteness, ways, marches and journeyings; by miles and furlongs; by plains, fields, gardens, cities and streets; by motions; by measures of various kinds; by length, breadth, hight and depth; and by innumerable other things: for most things which are in the thought of man in the world, derive something from space and time. I shall only declare what is signified in the Word by length, breadth, and hight. In the world, length and breadth are predicated of things which are long and broad as to space; the same is the case with hight. But in heaven, where space is not an object of thought, by length is understood a state of good, by breadth a state of truth, and by hight, their discrimination according to degrees; concerning which, see n. 38. Such things are understood by those three dimensions, because length in heaven is from east to west, and they dwell there who are in the good of love; and breadth in heaven is from south to north, and they dwell there who are in truth derived from good, see above, n. 148; and hight in heaven is both, according to degrees. Hence it is that such things are signified in the Word by length, breadth, and hight; as in Ezekiel, from chap. xl. to xlviii., where the new temple and new earth, with the courts, chambers, doors, gates, windows, and suburbs, are described by measures of length, breadth, and hight. These things signify a New Church, and the goods and truths which belong to it; otherwise, to what purpose were all those measures? So the New Jerusalem is described in the Apocalypse in these words: "*The city lieth four square, and the length is as large as the breadth. And he measured the city with the reed, twelve thousand furlongs. The length and the breadth and the hight of it are equal,*" xxi. 16. Here, by the New Jerusalem is signified a New Church; therefore its dimensions signify the things which belong to the church; by length, the good of its love; by breadth, the truth derived from that good; by hight, good and truth as to their degrees; by twelve thousand furlongs, all good and truth in the complex. What else could be meant by the hight of the city being twelve thousand furlongs, and the length and breadth the same as the

hight?   That breadth in the Word signifies truth, is evident in David: "*Jehovah, Thou hast not shut me up into the hand of the enemy.   Thou hast set my feet in a large room,*" [literally, *in a broad place*].   Psalm xxxi. 8.   Again: "*I called upon Jehovah in distress*" [literally, "*out of a narrow place*"].   "*Jehovah answered me and set me in a large place*" [literally, "*in a broad place*"].   Psalm cxviii. 5. besides other passages, as in Isaiah viii. 8 ; and in Habakkuk, i. 6.   And so in all other cases.

198. From these things it may be seen, that in heaven, although there are spaces as in the world, still nothing there is estimated by spaces, but by states : consequently that spaces cannot be measured there as in the world, but only can be seen from the state and according to the state of the interiors of the angels.[1]

199. The first and veriest cause of this is, that the Lord is present with every one according to his love and faith,[2] and that all things appear near and distant according to His presence ; for thence all things in the heavens are determined.   By His presence also the angels have wisdom, for by it they have extension of the thoughts, and by it there is communication of all things which are in the heavens ; in short, by His presence they have the ability to think spiritually, and not naturally like men.

THE FORM OF HEAVEN ACCORDING TO WHICH ARE CONSOCIATIONS AND COMMUNICATIONS THERE.

200. WHAT the form of heaven is, may in some measure appear from what has been shown in the preceding chapters ; as, that heaven is like itself in its greatest and in its least forms,

---

[1] That, in the Word, length signifies good, n. 1613, 9487 ; that breadth signifies truth, n. 1613, 3433, 3434, 4482, 9487, 10179 ; and that hight signifies good and truth as to degrees, n. 9489, 9773, 10181.

[2] That the conjunction and presence of the Lord with the angels is according to their reception of love and charity from Him, n. 290, 681, 1954, 2658, 2886, 2888, 2889, 3001, 3741, 3742, 3743, 4318, 4319, 4524, 7211, 9128

n. 72; hence, that every society is a heaven in a less form, and every angel in the least, n. 51 to 58; that, as the whole heaven resembles one man, so every society of heaven resembles a man in a less form, and every angel in the least, n. 59 to 77; that the wisest are in the midst, and that around them even to the borders are the less wise; and that this is the case also in every society, n. 43; that they who are in the good of love dwell from the east to the west in heaven, and from the south to the north, they who are in truths derived from good; in like manner in every society, n. 148, 149. All these things are according to the form of heaven; and from them its form in general may be inferred.[1]

201. It is important to understand the form of heaven, since not only are all consociated according to that form, but all communication also is according to it, and therefore all extension of thoughts and affections, hence all the intelligence and wisdom of the angels. Therefore as far as any one is in the form of heaven, or is a form of heaven, so far he is wise. Whether we speak of being in the form of heaven, or in the order of heaven, it amounts to the same; since the form of everything is from order and according to it.[2]

202. First, something shall here be said in explanation of what is meant by being in the form of heaven. Man was created after the image of heaven and the world; his internal after the image of heaven, and his external after that of the world, see above, n. 57; whether we say after the image, or according to the form, it is the same thing. But because man, by evils of the will, and falses of thought thence derived, has destroyed in himself the image, and thus the form, of heaven, and introduced in its place the image and form of hell, therefore his internal is closed from his birth. This is the reason why man, differently

---

[1] That the universal heaven, as to all the angelic societies, is arranged by the Lord according to His divine order, because the Divine of the Lord with the angels makes heaven, n. 3038, 7211, 9128, 9338, 10125, 10151, 10157. Concerning the heavenly form, n. 4040, 4041, 4042, 4043, 6607, 9877.

[2] That the form of heaven is according to divine order, n. 4040 to 4043, 6607, 9877.

from every kind of animal, is born into mere ignorance. In order, therefore, that the image or form of heaven may be restored to him, he must be instructed in the things relating to order; for, as remarked above, the form is according to order. The Word contains all the laws of divine order, for the laws of divine order are the precepts of the Word. In proportion, therefore, as man becomes acquainted with these, and lives according to them, his internal is opened, and there the order or image of heaven is formed anew. Hence it is evident what is meant by being in the form of heaven, namely, living according to the truths of the Word.[1]

203. As far as any one is in the form of heaven, so far he is in heaven, yea, is a heaven in the least form, n. 57; consequently he is so far in intelligence and wisdom: for, as was said above, all the thoughts of his understanding, and all the affections of his will extend themselves into heaven in every direction according to its form, and communicate in a wonderful manner with the societies there, and these in turn with him.[2] Some think that their thoughts and affections do not actually extend themselves around them, but that they are within them, because they see the things which they think inwardly in themselves, and not as distant. But they are much mistaken; for as the sight of the

---

[1] That divine truths are the laws of order, n. 2447, 7995. That man, so far as he lives according to order, that is, so far as he is principled in good according to divine truths, becomes a man, n. 4839, 6605, 6626. That man is the being into whom are collated all things of divine order, and that, from creation, he is divine order in form, n. 4219, 4220, 4223, 4523, 4524, 5114, 5368, 6013, 6057, 6605, 6626, 9706, 10156, 10472. That man is not born into good and truth, but into evil and the false, thus into what is contrary to divine order; that hence he is born into mere ignorance; that, therefore, it is necessary he should be born anew, that is, regenerated; and that regeneration is effected by divine truths from the Lord, that man may be inaugurated into order, n. 1047, 2307, 2308, 3518, 3812, 8480, 8550, 10283, 10284, 10286, 10731. That the Lord, when He forms man anew, that is, regenerates him, arranges all things in him according to order, that is into the form of heaven, n. 5700, 6690, 9931, 10303.

[2] That every one in heaven has communication of life, which may be called an extension into the angelic societies around him, according to the quantity and quality of his good, n. 8794, 8797. That thoughts and affections have such extension, n. 2475, 6598 to 6613. That they are conjoined and disjoined according to the ruling affections, n. 4111.

eye has extension to remote objects, and is affected according to the order of the things which it sees in that extension, so likewise the interior sight, which is that of the understanding, has extension into the spiritual world, although man is not sensible of it, for the reason above mentioned, n. 196. The only difference is, that the sight of the eye is affected naturally, because by things in the natural world, while the sight of the understanding is affected spiritually, because by those in the spiritual world, all of which have relation to good and truth. Man does not know that this is the case, because he is not aware that there is a light which enlightens the understanding, when yet, without that light, he would be unable to think at all. Concerning that light, see above, n. 126 to 132. There was a certain spirit who likewise imagined that he thought from himself, thus without any extension out of himself, or any consequent communication with societies existing without himself. To convince him of his error, all communication with the neighboring societies was taken away, in consequence of which he was not only deprived of thought, but fell down as if dead,—yet he threw his arms about like a new-born infant. After a while the communication was restored ; and according to the degree in which it was restored, he returned into the state of his own thought. Other spirits, who witnessed this, thereupon confessed that all thought and affection flows-in according to communication, and—since all thought and affection —-therefore also the all of life ; since all of man's life consists in this, that he can think and be affected, or, what is the same, can understand and will.[1]

---

[1] That there is only one single Life, from which all live both in heaven and in the world, n. 1954, 2021, 2536, 2658, 2886 to 2889, 3001, 3484, 3742, 5847, 6467. That that life is from the Lord alone, n. 2886 to 2889, 3344, 3484, 4319, 4320, 4524, 4882, 5986, 6325, 6468, 6469, 6470, 9276, 10196. That it flows into angels, spirits, and men, in a wonderful manner, n. 2886 to 2889, 3337, 3338, 3484, 3742. That the Lord flows-in from His divine love, which is of such a nature, that what is His own He wills should be another's, 3742, 4320. That, for this reason, life appears as if it were in man, and not influent, n. 3742, 4320. Concerning the joy of the angels, perceived and confirmed by what they told me, that they do not live from themselves, but from the Lord, n. 6469. That the wicked are not willing

204. It is, however, to be observed, that intelligence and wisdom vary with every one according to communication. They whose intelligence and wisdom are formed from genuine truths and goods, communicate with societies according to the form of heaven; but they whose intelligence and wisdom are not formed from genuine truths and goods, but still from things which agree with them, have a broken and rather incoherent communication, because it does not take place with societies in a series agreeable to the form of heaven; but they who are not intelligent and wise, because they are in falses derived from evil, communicate with societies in hell. The extent of their communication is according to the degree of their confirmation. It is further to be noted, that this communication with societies is not a communication which comes to the manifest perception of those there, but it is a communication with the quality [as to good or evil] in which they are principled, and which flows from them.[1]

205. All in heaven are consociated according to spiritual affinities, which are those of good and truth in their order. So is it in the whole heaven, so in every society, and so in every house. Hence it is that the angels who are in similar good and truth, know each other like those related by consanguinity and affinity on earth, just as if they had been acquainted from infancy. In like manner are consociated the goods and truths which constitute wisdom and intelligence with every angel; they know each other in like manner, and as they know each other so likewise they join themselves together.[2] Wherefore they with whom truths and goods are conjoined according to the form of heaven,

---

to be convinced that life flows-in, n. 3743. That life from the Lord flows also into the wicked, n. 2706, 3743, 4417, 10196; but that they turn good into evil and truth into falsity, for according to man's quality, such is his reception of life; illustrated, n. 4319, 4320, 4417.

[1] That thought diffuses itself into the societies of spirits and angels round about, n. 6600 to 6605; but that still it does not move and disturb the thoughts of those societies, n. 6601, 6603.

[2] That good acknowledges its truth, and truth its good, n. 2429, 3101, 3102. 3161, 3179, 3180, 4358, 5407, 5835, 9637. That hence is the conjunction of good and of truth, n. 3834, 4096, 4097, 4301, 4345, 4353, 4364, 4368, 5365, 7623 to 7627, 7752 to 7762, 8530, 9258, 10555; and that this is from the influx of heaven, n. 9079.

see the things which follow in a series, and have an extended view of the manner of their coherence in all directions. It is otherwise with those with whom goods and truths·are not conjoined according to the form of heaven.

206. Such is the form in each heaven, according to which the angels have communication and extension of thoughts and affections, thus according to which they have intelligence and wisdom. But the communication of one heaven with another, as of the third or inmost with the second or middle, and of both these with the first or ultimate, is of a different nature; and, indeed, ought not to be called communication, but influx,—of which something shall now be said. That there are three heavens, and these distinct from each other, may be seen above in its proper chapter, n. 29 to 40.

207. That there is not communication of one heaven with another, but influx, may be manifest from their relative situation. The third or inmost heaven is above; the second or middle heaven is beneath; and the first or ultimate heaven is still lower. All the societies of each heaven are arranged in a similar manner. Some are in elevated places, which appear as mountains, (n. 188), upon whose summits dwell those of the inmost heaven; beneath them are the societies of the second heaven; beneath these, again, the societies of the ultimate heaven; and so throughout, whether it be in elevated places or not. A society of a superior heaven has no communication with a society of an inferior heaven except by correspondences (see above, n. 100); and communication by correspondences is called influx.

208. One heaven is conjoined with another, or a society of one heaven with a society of another, by the Lord alone, by influx both immediate and mediate,—immediate from Himself, and mediate through the superior heavens in order into the inferior.[1] Since the conjunction of the heavens by influx is from the Lord alone, therefore it is most carefully provided that no angel of a

---

[1] That influx is immediate from the Lord, and mediate through heaven, n. 6163, 6307, 6472, 9682, 9683. That the Lord's influx is immediate into the minutest parts of all things, n. 6058, 6474 to 6478, 8717. 8728. Concerning the Lord's mediate influx through the heavens, n. 4067, 6982, 6985, 6996.

superior heaven look down into a society of an inferior, and converse with any one there; the moment this occurs, the angel is
deprived of his intelligence and wisdom. The reason is this:
Every angel has three degrees of life, corresponding with the
three degrees of heaven. Those in the inmost heaven have the
third or inmost degree open, and the second and first closed;
those in the middle heaven have the second degree open, and the
first and third closed; and those in the ultimate heaven have the
first degree open, and the second and third closed. As soon.
therefore, as an angel of the third heaven looks down into a
society of the second, and converses with any one there, his third
degree is closed, and he is deprived of his wisdom; for his wisdom resides in the third degree, and he has none in the second
and first. This is meant by the Lord's words in Matthew: "*He
that is on the housetop, let him not go down to take what is in
his house; and he that is in the field, let him not return back
to take his garment.*" xxiv. 18, 19. And in Luke: "*In that
day, he that shall be upon the housetop, and his vessels in the
house, let him not go down to take them away; and he that is
in the field, let him likewise not return back. Remember
Lot's wife.*" xvii. 31, 32.

209. There is no influx from the inferior heavens into the superior, because this is contrary to order,—but from the superior heavens into the inferior. The wisdom, too, of the angels of a
superior heaven exceeds that of the angels of an inferior heaven,
as a myriad to one. This also is the reason that the angels of an
inferior heaven cannot converse with those of a superior one,—
yea, when they look in that direction, they do not see them: their
heaven appears as something cloudy above their heads. But the
angels of a superior heaven can see those in an inferior one; yet
they are not allowed to converse with them, except with the loss
of their wisdom, as was said above.

210. The thoughts and affections, and also the discourse, of the
angels of the inmost heaven, are never perceived in the middle
heaven, because they transcend [the perceptions of the angels of
that heaven]; but when it pleases the Lord, there is an appearance thence in the inferior heavens as of something flamy; and
the thoughts, affections, and discourse of those in the middle hea-

ven appear as something lucid in the ultimate heaven, and sometimes as a bright and variously colored cloud; and from the
ascent, descent, and form of that cloud, the subject of their conversation is in some measure known.

211. From these observations it may be evident what the form
of heaven is, namely, that in the inmost heaven it is most perfect; in the middle heaven also perfect, but in an inferior degree;
and in the ultimate heaven in a degree still lower; and that the
form of one heaven subsists from another by influx from the
Lord. But the nature of communication by influx cannot be
comprehended without knowing what degrees of altitude are,
and what is the difference between these degrees and degrees of
longitude and latitude. The nature of both these kinds of degrees
may be seen, n. 38.

212. With respect to the form of heaven specifically, and the
manner in which its motions and fluxions proceed (*vadit et
fluit*), this is incomprehensible even to the angels. Some idea
of it may be conceived from the form of all things in the human
body, when examined and explored by a sagacious and wise observer; for it was shown above in their proper chapters, that
the whole heaven resembles one man, (see n. 59 to 72), and that
all things in man correspond to the heavens, (n. 87 to 102).
How incomprehensible and unsearchable that form is, may appear in some general way from the nervous fibres, whereby each
and all of the parts are woven together. What is the nature of
those fibres, and in what manner they perform their motions and
fluxions (*vadunt et fluunt*) in the brain, cannot be discerned by
the eye; for innumerable fibres are there so folded together, that,
taken in the gross, they appear as a soft, continuous mass; and
yet all and each of the things belonging to the will and understanding flow most distinctly into acts, along those innumerable
complicated fibres. How these fibres, again, wreathe themselves
together in the body, appears from the various collections of
them called plexuses,—such as the cardiac plexus, the mesenteric
plexus, and others; and also from the knots of them which are
called ganglions, into which many fibres from every province enter,
and therein mingle together, and again go forth in new combina-
tions to the performance of their functions,—and this repeated

17   F*

again and again ; besides similar things in every viscus, member, organ, and muscle. Whoever examines these fibres with the eye of wisdom, and the many wonderful things pertaining to them, will be utterly astonished. And yet the things which the eye sees are few ; those which it does not see are yet more wonderful because tl ey belong to an interior realm. That this form corresponds to the form of heaven, is very plain from the operation of all things of the understanding and will in it and according to it ; for whatever a man wills, descends spontaneously into act according to that form ; and whatever he thinks, pervades those fibres from their beginnings even to their terminations,—whence comes sensation ; and because it is the form of thought and will, it is the form of intelligence and wisdom. It is this form which corresponds to the form of heaven. Hence it may be known, that every affection and every thought of the angels extends itself according to that form, and that so far as they are in it they are intelligent and wise. That this form of heaven is from the Divine Human of the Lord, may be seen above, n. 78 to 86. These facts are adduced, that it may also be known that the heavenly form is of such a nature that it can never be exhausted, even as to its general principles, and thus that it is incomprehensible even to the angels, as was said above.

GOVERNMENTS IN HEAVEN.

213. Since heaven is distinguished into societies, and the larger societies consist of some hundreds of thousands of angels, (n. 50), and since all the members of one society are indeed, in similar good, but not in similar wisdom, (n. 43), it necessarily follows, that there are governments in heaven. For order must be observed, and all things of order are to be kept inviolable. But the governments in the heavens are various ; of one sort in the societies which constitute the Lord's celestial kingdom, and of another in the societies which constitute His spiritual king-

dom. They differ also according to the ministries performed by each society. But the government of mutual love is the only government in the heavens, and the government of mutual love is heavenly government.

214. The government in the Lord's celestial kingdom is called JUSTICE, because all who belong to that kingdom are in the good of love to the Lord derived from the Lord ; and whatever is done from that good is called just. The government there is of the Lord alone : He leads them and teaches them in the affairs of life. The truths, which are called truths of judgment, are inscribed on their hearts. Every one knows, perceives, and sees them ;[1] wherefore matters of judgment never come into dispute there, but matters of justice, which relate to life. The less wise interrogate the more wise on these points, and the latter the Lord, and receive answers. Their heaven or inmost joy is to live justly from the Lord.

215. The government in the Lord's spiritual kingdom is called JUDGMENT, because the inhabitants of that kingdom are in spiritual good, which is the good of charity toward the neighbor; and this good, in its essence, is truth.[2] Truth is of judgment, and good is of justice.[3] The spiritual angels also are led by the Lord, but mediately, (n. 208) ; wherefore they have governors,

---

[1] That the celestial angels do not think and speak from truths, like the spiritual angels, because they are in the perception of all things relating to truths from the Lord, n. 202, 597, 607, 784, 1121, 1387, 1398, 1442, 1919, 7680, 7877, 8780, 9277, 10336. That the celestial angels say of truths, " yea, yea; nay, nay," but that the spiritual angels reason about them, whether it be so, or not so, n. 2715, 3246, 4446, 9166, 10786; where the Lord's words are explained, "*Let your discourse be yea, yea; nay, nay. What is beyond this is from evil.*" Matt. v. 37.

[2] That they who are in the Lord's spiritual kingdom, are in truths, and they who are in the celestial kingdom, in good, n. 863, 875, 927, 1023, 1043, 1044, 1555, 2256, 4328, 4493, 5113, 9596. That the good of the spiritual kingdom is the good of charity toward the neighbor, and that this good in its essence is truth, n. 8042, 10296.

[3] That justice, in the Word, is predicated of good, and judgment of truth, and that hence to do justice and judgment denotes good and truth, n. 2235, 9857. That great judgments denote laws of the divine order, thus divine truths, n. 7206.

few or more, according to the need of the society in which they are. They also have laws, according to which they live together. The governors administer all things according to the laws. They understand them because they are wise; and in doubtful cases they are enlightened by the Lord.

2:6. Since government from good, like that which prevails in the Lord's celestial kingdom, is called justice, and government from truth, like that which prevails in His spiritual kingdom, is called judgment, therefore in the Word justice and judgment are mentioned, where heaven and the church are treated of; and by justice is signified celestial good, and by judgment spiritual good, which, in its essence is truth, as was said above; as in the following passages: "*To peace there shall be no end upon the throne of David, and upon his kingdom, to order it and to establish it, with* JUDGMENT *and with* JUSTICE, *from henceforth even forever.*" Isaiah ix. 6. By David is here meant the Lord,[1] and by his kingdom heaven, as is evident from the following passage: "*I will raise unto David a righteous branch, a king shall reign and prosper, and shall execute* JUDGMENT *and* JUSTICE *in the earth,*" Jer. xxiii. 5: "*Let Jehovah be exalted; for He dwelleth on high; He hath filled Sion with* JUDGMENT *and* JUSTICE." Isaiah xxxiii. 5. By Sion also is meant heaven and the church.[2] "*I am Jehovah, doing* JUDGMENT *and* JUSTICE *in the earth, for in these things I delight.*" Jer. ix. 24. "*I will betroth thee unto Me forever, yea, I will betroth thee unto Me in* JUSTICE *and* JUDGMENT." Hosea ii. 19: "*O Jehovah—in the heavens Thy* JUSTICE *is as the mountains of God, and Thy* JUDGMENTS *as a great deep.*" Psalm xxxvi. 5, 6. "*They ask of me the* JUDGMENTS *of* JUSTICE, *they desire the approach of God.*" Isaiah lviii. 2: and in other passages.

217. In the spiritual kingdom of the Lord there are various forms of government, differing in different societies. Their variety is according to the ministries which the societies perform;

---

[1] That by David, in the prophetical parts of the Word, is meant the Lord, n. 1888, 9954.

[2] That by Zion, in the Word, is meant the church, and, specifically, the celestial church, n. 2362, 9055.

and these are similar to the functions of all the parts in man to which they correspond. That these are various is well known; for the heart has one function, the lungs another, the liver another, the pancreas and spleen another, and every organ of sense also another. As the functions of these members are various in the body, so likewise are those of the societies in the GRAND MAN, which is heaven; for there are societies which correspond to those organs. That there is a correspondence of all things of heaven with all things of man, has been shown in its proper chapter above, n. 87 to 101. But all the forms of government agree in this, that they regard the general good as their end, and in that, the good of every individual.[1] And this results from the fact, that all in the universal heaven are under the auspices of the Lord, who loves all, and from divine love ordains that the common good shall be the source of good to every individual, and that every individual shall receive good in proportion as he loves the common good. For so far as any one loves the community, he loves all the individuals who compose it; and since that love is the love of the Lord, therefore he is so far loved by the Lord, and good results to him.

218. From these observations it may appear what is the character of the governors, namely, that they are in love and wisdom more than others, and that they will well to all from love, and from wisdom know how to provide that the good they desire may be realized. They who are of this character, do not domineer and command imperiously, but minister and serve; for to do good to others from the love of good, is to serve; and to provide

---

[1] That every man and society, also a man's country and the church, and in a universal sense, the kingdom of the Lord, is the neighbor; and that to do good to them from the love of good, according to the quality of their state, is to love the neighbor; thus that their good, which also is the general good, and ought to be consulted, is the neighbor, n. 6818 to 6824, 8123. That civil good also, consisting in what is just, is the neighbor, n. 2915, 4730, 8120, 8123. Hence, that charity toward the neighbor extends itself to all and everything of the life of man, and that to love good and to do good from the love of what is good and true, and also to do what is just from the love of what is just, in every office and in every act, is to love the neighbor, n. 2417, 8121, 8124.

that the intended good be realized, is to minister. Nor do they account themselves greater than others, but less; for they esteem the good of society and of their neighbor in the first place, but their own in the last; and what is in the first place is the greater, and what is in the last, the less. Nevertheless they enjoy honor and glory. They dwell in the midst of the society, in a more elevated situation than others, and inhabit magnificent palaces. They also accept glory and honor, not for the sake of themselves, but for the sake of obedience; for all in heaven know that honor and glory are from the Lord, and that for this reason they ought to be obeyed. These are the things which are meant by the Lord's words to his disciples: " *Whosoever would be great among you, let him be your minister; and whosoever would be chief among you, let him be your servant; even as the Son of Man came not to be ministered unto, but to minister—*" Matt. xx. 27, 28: " *He that is the greatest among you, let him be as the least, and he that is chief, as he that doth service.*" Luke xxii. 26.

219. A similar government in its least form prevails also in every house; for in every house there is a master, and there are servants; the master loves the servants, and the servants love the master, so that they serve each other from love. The master teaches how they should live, and directs what they should do; and the servants obey and perform their duties. To perform use is the delight of the life of all. Hence it is evident that the kingdom of the Lord is a kingdom of uses.

220. There are also governments in the hells, for unless there were governments, the infernals could not be kept under any restraint. But the governments there are the opposite of those in heaven. They are all founded in self-love; for every one there desires to rule over others and to be the greatest. They hate those who do not favor them, and pursue them with vindictiveness and cruelty,—for such is the very nature of self-love. Wherefore the most malignant are set over them as governors, whom they obey from fear.[1] But more will be said on this subject, when treating of the hells.

---

[1] That there are two kinds of rule, one from love to the neighbor, and

DIVINE WORSHIP IN HEAVEN.

221. DIVINE worship in the heavens is not unlike that on earth as to externals, but it differs as to internals. In the heavens, as on earth, there are doctrines, preachings, and temples. The *doctrines* agree as to essentials, but are of more interior wisdom in the superior than in the inferior heavens. The *preaching* is according to the doctrines; and as they have houses and palaces (n. 183 to 190), so also they have *temples*, in which preaching is performed. Such things exist in heaven, because the angels are continually being perfected in wisdom and love; for they have understanding and will like men, and are capable of advancing for ever toward perfection. The understanding is perfected by the truths which are of intelligence, and the will by the goods which are of love.[1]

222. But real divine worship in the heavens does not consist in frequenting temples and listening to sermons, but in a life of love, charity, and faith, according to doctrine. Sermons in the temples serve only as means of instruction in the conduct of life. I have conversed with angels on this subject, and have told them that it is believed in the world that divine worship consists merely in going to church, hearing sermons, attending the sacrament of the holy supper three or four times a year, and in other forms of worship prescribed by the church; to which may be

---

the other from the love of self, n. 10814. That all things good and happy result from the rule which springs from neighborly love, n. 10160, 10614. That in heaven no one can rule from the love of self, but all are willing to minister; that to minister is to rule from neighborly love, and that hence they possess such great power, n. 5732. That all evils result from rule grounded in the love of self, n. 10038. That when the loves of self and of the world began to prevail, men were compelled for security to subject themselves to governments, n. 7364, 10160, 10814.

[1] That the understanding is recipient of truth, and the will of good, n. 3623, 6125, 7503, 9300, 9930. That as all things have relation to truth and good, so the all of man's life has relation to understanding and will, n. 803, 10122. That the angels advance in perfection to eternity, n. 4803, 6648.

added, the setting apart of particular times for prayer, and a devout manner while engaged in it. The angels replied, that these are externals which ought to be observed, but that they are of no avail unless there be an internal from which they proceed ; and that this internal is a life according to the precepts which doctrine teaches.

223. In order that I might become acquainted with their meetings in the temples, I have several times been permitted to go in and listen to the discourses. The preacher stands in a pulpit on the east. Before his face sit those who are in the light of wisdom more than others, and on their right and left those who are in less light. The seats are arranged in a semi-circular manner, so that all are in view of the preacher. No one sits on either side of him, so as to be out of his sight. The novitiates stand at the door, on the east of the temple, and on the left of the pulpit. No one is allowed to stand behind the pulpit, because the preacher is thereby confused. The same thing occurs if any one in the congregation dissents from what is said ; wherefore the dissentient must turn away his face. The sermons are fraught with such wisdom, that none in the world can be compared with them ; for the preachers in the heavens are in interior light. The temples in the spiritual kingdom appear as of stone, and in the celestial kingdom as of wood ; because stone corresponds to truth, in which they are principled who are in the spiritual kingdom, and wood corresponds to good, in which they are principled who are in the celestial kingdom.[1] The sacred edifices in the latter kingdom are not called temples, but houses of God, and are not magnificent ; but in the spiritual kingdom they are more or less magnificent.

224. I have also conversed with one of the preachers concerning the holy state in which they are who hear the sermons in the temples ; and he said that every one is in a pious, devout, and holy state according to his interiors which are of love and faith, because in these is holiness itself from the Divine of the Lord ;

---

[1] That stone signifies truth, n. 114, 643, 1298, 3720, 6426, 8609, 10376. That wood signifies good, n. 643, 3720, 8354. That on this account the most ancient people, who were in celestial good, had sacred temples of wood, n. 3720.

and that he had no conception of external holiness separate from love and faith. When he thought of external holiness separate from these, he said that possibly it might be something artificial or hypocritical, which simulates the outward appearance of holiness ; and that some spurious fire, kindled by the love of self and the world, might awaken such holiness and give it form.

225. All the preachers belong to the Lord's spiritual kingdom, and none to the celestial kingdom, because the inhabitants of the spiritual kingdom are in truths derived from good, and all preaching is from truths. None of the preachers belong to the celestial kingdom, because the inhabitants of that kingdom are in the good of love, and from that good they see and perceive truths, but they do not speak of them. Although the angels in the celestial kingdom perceive and see truths, still they have preaching there, because by means of it they are enlightened in regard to truths which they already know, and are perfected by many which they did not know before. As soon as they hear them, they also acknowledge them, and thus perceive. The truths which they perceive, they also love ; and by living according to them, they incorporate them into their life. To live according to truths, they say, is to love the Lord.[1]

226. All the preachers are appointed by the Lord, and thence derive the gift of preaching ; nor are any others allowed to teach in the temples of heaven. They are called preachers but not priests, because the celestial kingdom is the priesthood of heaven ; for the priesthood signifies the good of love to the Lord, in which all in that kingdom are principled. But the royalty of heaven is the spiritual kingdom ; for royalty signifies truth derived from good, in which all in that kingdom are principled ; see above, n. 24.[2]

---

[1] That to love the Lord and the neighbor is to live according to the Lord's precepts, n. 10143, 10153, 10310, 10578, 10645, 10648.

[2] That priests represent the Lord as to divine good, and kings as to divine truth, n. 2015, 6148. That hence a priest, in the Word, signifies those who are in the good of love to the Lord, thus the priesthood signifies that good, n. 9806, 9809. That a king, in the Word, signifies those who are in divine truth, and royalty truth derived from good, n. 1672, 2015, 2069, 4575, 4581, 4966, 5044.

18

227. The doctrines preached in the temples of heaven all regard life as their end, and none of them faith without life. The doctrine of the inmost heaven is fuller of wisdom than that of the middle heaven; and the doctrine of the middle heaven is fuller of intelligence than that of the ultimate heaven; for the doctrines are adapted to the perception of the angels in each heaven. The essential of all the doctrines is, to acknowledge the Divine Human of the Lord.

THE POWER OF THE ANGELS OF HEAVEN.

228. THAT angels possess power, cannot be conceived by those who know nothing of the spiritual world, and its influx into the natural world. They suppose that the angels cannot have any power because they are spiritual beings, and of so pure and unsubstantial a nature that they cannot even be seen by the eyes. But they who look more interiorly into the causes of things, think differently: for they know that all the power of man is derived from his understanding and will, since he cannot move a particle of his body without them. The understanding and will are his spiritual man. This sets in motion the body and its members at pleasure; for what this thinks, the mouth and tongue speak; and what this wills, the body executes,—to which also it gives strength at pleasure. The will and understanding of man are ruled by the Lord through the instrumentality of angels and spirits; and therefore all things of the body are ruled in like manner, since these are from the will and understanding; and, incredible though it may seem, man cannot stir a single step without the influx of heaven. That this is the case, has been proved to me by much experience; for angels have been permitted to move my steps, actions, tongue, and speech, at their pleasure, by influx into my will and thought; and so I have learned by experience that of myself I could do nothing. They after-

wards said that every man is ruled in the same way, and that he might know it from the doctrine of the church and from the Word; for he prays that God will send His angels to lead him, to direct his steps, to teach him, and to inspire what he should think, and what he should speak,—and many things of the same kind; although when he thinks within himself without regard to doctrine, he says and believes otherwise. These observations are made that it may be known what power the angels exercise over man.

229. But the power of the angels in the spiritual world is so great, that were I to adduce all the examples of it which I have witnessed, they would exceed belief. If anything there offers resistance, and ought to be removed because it is contrary to divine order, they cast it down and overturn it by a mere effort of the will and by a look. Thus have I seen mountains, which were occupied by the wicked, cast down and overthrown, and sometimes shaken from one end to the other, as occurs in earthquakes; rocks also cleft in sunder down to the deep, and the wicked who were upon them swallowed up. I have likewise seen some hundreds of thousands of evil spirits dispersed by them and cast into hell. Numbers are of no avail against them, nor arts, nor cunning, nor confederacies; for they see through all subtle contrivances, and in a moment bring them to naught. But more may be seen on this subject in the relation concerning the destruction of Babylon. Such power have the angels in the spiritual world. That they have a like power in the natural world, when it is granted them to exercise it, is manifest from the Word, wherein we read that they destroyed whole armies, and caused a pestilence of which seventy thousand men died. Of the angel that caused the pestilence it is written: "*The angel stretched out his hand against Jerusalem to destroy it, but Jehovah repented of the evil, and said to the angel that destroyed the people, It is enough: stay now thy hand.—And David—saw the angel that smote the people.*" 2 Samuel xxiv. 15, 16, 17; besides other passages. Because the angels possess such power, they are therefore called powers; and in David it is said: "*Bless Jehovah, ye His angels most powerful in strength.*" Psalm ciii. 20.

230. It ought, however, to be known that the angels have no power at all of themselves, but that all their power is from the Lord; and that they are only so far powers as they acknowledge this. If any angel believes that he has power of himself, he instantly becomes so weak that he cannot even resist one evil spirit; therefore the angels attribute no merit to themselves, and are averse to all praise and glory on account of anything they do, ascribing it all to the Lord.

231. It is the divine truth proceeding from the Lord to which all power in the heavens belongs; for the Lord in heaven is divine truth united to divine good (see n. 126 to 140), and the angels are powers so far as they receive it.[1] Every one also is his own truth and his own good, because he is such as his understanding and will are; and the understanding is of truth, because all that belongs to it consists of truths; and the will is of good, because all that belongs to it consists of goods; for whatever a man understands he calls truth, and whatever he wills he calls good. Hence it is that every one is his own truth and his own good.[2] As far, therefore, as an angel is truth from the Divine and good from the Divine, so far he is a power, because so far the Lord is with him. And since no one is in similar or precisely the same good and truth as another,—for in heaven as in the world there is endless variety, see n. 20,—therefore one angel has not the same power as another. Those possess the greatest power, who constitute the arms in the GRAND MAN or heaven, because those belonging to that province are in truths more than others, and there is an influx of good into their truths from the universal heaven. Moreover, the power of the whole man transfers itself into the arms, and by them the whole body exercises its force.

---

[1] That angels are called powers, and that they are powers, by virtue of the reception of divine truth from the Lord, n. 9369. That angels are recipients of divine truth from the Lord, and that on this account they are called "gods" in the Word throughout, n. 4295, 4402, 8301, 9160.

[2] That a man and an angel is his own good and his own truth, thus his own love and his own faith, n. 10298, 10367. That he is his own understanding and his own will, since the all of life is thence derived, the life of good being of the will, and the life of truth being of the understanding, n. 10076, 10177, 10264, 10284.

Hence it is th..t the arms and hands in the Word denote power.[1] In heaven there sometimes appears stretched forth a naked arm of such stupendous power, as to be able to break in pieces whatever comes in its way, even if it were a great rock on earth. Once also it was brought near to me, and I perceived that it was able to crush my bones to atoms.

232. That the divine truth which proceeds from the Lord has all power, and that the angels have power in proportion as they receive divine truth from the Lord, may be seen above, n. 137. But the angels receive divine truth only so far as they receive divine good, for truths have all their power from good, and none without good; and on the other hand, good has all its power by truths, and none without truths. Power results from the conjunction of both. It is similar with faith and love; for whether we speak of truth or faith it is the same, since the all of faith is truth; and whether we speak of good or love it is the same, since the all of love is good.[2] How great power the angels have by means of truths derived from good, was also made manifest by this circumstance, that an evil spirit, when only looked at by the angels, would fall into a swoon, and lose the appearance of a man,—and this until the angel turned away his eyes. Such an effect is produced by a look of the angels, because their sight is from the light of heaven, and the light of heaven is divine truth: see above, n. 126 to 132. The eyes also correspond to truths derived from good.[3]

---

[1] Concerning the correspondence of the hands, the arms, and shoulders, with the GRAND MAN, or heaven, n. 4931 to 4937. That by arms and hands, in the Word, is signified power, n. 878, 3091, 4931, 4932, 6947, 10019.

[2] That all power in the heavens is from truth derived from good, thus from faith grounded in love, n. 3091, 3563, 6423, 8304, 9643, 10019, 10182. That all power is from the Lord, because from Him is all the truth which is of faith, and all the good which is of love, n. 9327, 9410. That this power is meant by the keys given to Peter, n. 6344. That the divine truth proceeding from the Lord has all power, n. 6948, 8200. That this power of the Lord is what is understood by sitting at the right hand of Jehovah, n. 3387, 4592, 4933, 7518, 7673, 8281, 9133. That the right hand denotes power, n. 10019.

[3] That the eyes correspond to truths derived from good, n. 4403 to 4421, 4523 tr 4534, 6923.

233. Since truths derived from good have all power, therefore no power at all belongs to falses derived from evil.[1] All in hell are in falses from evil, and therefore they have no power against truth and good. But what their power is among themselves, and what the power of evil spirits before they are cast into hell, will be shown hereafter.

THE SPEECH OF ANGELS.

234. THE angels converse together just as men do in the world, and talk, like them, on various subjects, such as domestic affairs, social affairs, and matters pertaining to moral and spiritual life. Nor is there any difference, except that they converse more intelligently than men, because from more interior thought. I have often been permitted to associate with them, and to converse with them as friend with friend, and sometimes as stranger with stranger ; and because I was then in a state similar to the'rs, I knew not but that I was conversing with men on earth.

235. Angelic speech consists of distinct words like human speech, and is equally sonorous ; for angels have a mouth, a tongue, and ears ; also an atmosphere in which the sound of their speech is articulated ; but it is a spiritual atmosphere accommodated to the angels, who are spiritual beings. The angels also breathe in their atmosphere, and pronounce their words by means of their breath, as men do in theirs.[2]

236. All in the whole heaven have one language, and all understand each other, whatever society they belong to, whether

---

[1] That falses derived from evil have no power, because truth derived from good has all power, n. 6784, 10481.

[2] That there is respiration in the heavens, but of an interior kind, n. 3884. 3885 : from experience, n. 3884, 3885, 3891, 3893. That respirations are dissimilar there, and various, according to their states, n. 1119, 3886, 3887, 3889, 3892, 3893. That the wicked cannot breathe in heaven, and that if they enter heaven they are suffocated, n. 3894.

neighboring or remote. The language is not learned there, but is implanted in every one; for it flows from his very affection and thought. The sound of their speech corresponds to their affection, and the articulations of sound, which are words, correspond to the ideas of thought derived from affection ; and because their language corresponds to these, that also is spiritual, for it is affection sounding and thought speaking. Every attentive observer may know, that all thought is from affection which is of love, and that the ideas of thought are various forms into which the common affection is distributed ; for no thought or idea can possibly exist without affection,—its soul and life being thence. Hence the angels know the quality of any one merely from his speech,—from its sound the quality of his affection, and from the articulations of the sound, or from the words, the quality of his mind. The wiser angels, from a single series of words, know what the ruling affection is, for they attend chiefly to that. That every one has various affections, is well known ; one kind in a state of gladness, another in a state of grief, another in a state of mildness and mercy, another in a state of sincerity and truth, another in a state of love and charity, another in a state of zeal or anger, another in a state of simulation and deceit, another in the pursuit of honor and glory, and so on ; but the ruling affection or love is in them all. Wherefore the wiser angels, who attend chiefly to this, discover from the speech the whole character of the speaker. This has been proved to me by much experience. I have heard angels revealing the life of another merely from hearing him speak. They have also told me that they know the whole of another's life from a few ideas of his thought, because they learn from them his ruling love, wherein are inscribed all the particulars of his life in their order ; and that man's book of life is nothing else.

237. Angelic language has nothing in common with human languages, except with certain words which derive their sound from a peculiar affection ; yet not with the words themselves, but with their sound,—concerning which something will be said hereafter. That angelic language has nothing in common with human languages, is evident from this, that it is impossible for angels to utter a single word of human language. They have

tried, but were unable ; for they cannot utter anything but what is in perfect agreement with their affection. Whatever is not in agreement with their affection, is repugnant to their very life ; for their life is that of affection, and from this comes their speech. I have been told that the first language of men on our earth was in agreement with that of the angels, because they derived it from heaven ; and that the Hebrew tongue agrees with it in some particulars.

238. Because the speech of angels corresponds to their affection which is of love, and the love of heaven is love to the Lord and love toward the neighbor, (see above, n. 13 to 19), it is obvious how elegant and delightful must be their discourse. It affects not only the ears of the listeners, but even the interiors of their minds. An angel once conversed with a certain hardhearted spirit, who was at length so affected by his discourse that he burst into tears, saying that he could not help it, for it was love speaking ; and that he had never wept before.

239. The speech of angels is also full of wisdom, because it proceeds from their interior thought, and their interior thought is wisdom, as their interior affection is love. Love and wisdom are united in their discourse ; hence it is so full of wisdom, that they can express by one word what man cannot express by a thousand. The ideas of their thought also comprehend things which man cannot conceive, much less utter. Hence it is that the things which have been heard and seen in heaven are said to be ineffable, and such as ear hath not heard nor eye seen. It has also been my privilege to know by experience that this is so. I have sometimes been let into the state in which the angels are, and have conversed with them ; and in that state I understood everything they said ; but when I was brought back into my former state, and thus into the natural thought proper to man, and wished to recall what I had heard, I was unable ; for there were a thousand things which could not be brought down to the ideas of natural thought, and therefore could not be at all expressed in human language, but only by variegations of heavenly light. The angels' ideas of the thought from which their words proceed, are likewise variegations of the light of heaven ; and their affections, from which proceeds the sound of the words,

are variations of the heat of heaven ; because the light of heaven is divine truth or wisdom, and the heat of heaven is divine good or love, (see above, n. 126 to 140) ; and the angels derive their affection from the divine love, and their thoughts from the divine wisdom.[1]

240. The ideas of thought are various forms into which the general affection is distributed, as was said above, n. 236 ; and since the speech of angels proceeds immediately from their affection, they are therefore able to express in a minute what man cannot express in half an hour ; they can also convey in a few words what, if written, would fill several pages. This, too, has been proved to me by much experience.[2] Thus the angels' ideas of thought and the words of their speech form a one, like the efficient cause and its effect ; for their words present in effect what exists in their ideas of thought as a cause ; hence it is that every word comprehends in itself so many things. All the particulars of the thought and thence of the speech of angels, when visibly presented, appear like a thin wave, or circumfluent atmosphere, wherein are things innumerable derived from angelic wisdom and arranged in their order, and which enter the thoughts of another and affect him. The ideas of the thought of every one, whether angel or man, are presented visibly in the light of heaven, whenever it pleases the Lord.[3]

---

[1] That the ideas from which angels speak, are formed by wonderful variegations of the light of heaven, n. 1646, 3343, 3963.

[2] That angels can express by their speech, in a moment, more than man can express by his in half an hour, and that they can also express such things as do not fall into the words of human speech, n. 1641, 1642, 1643, 1645, 4609, 7089.

[3] That there are innumerable things contained in one idea of thought, n. 1008, 1869, 4946, 6613, 6614, 6615, 6617, 6618. That the ideas of the thought of man are opened in the other life, and their quality openly revealed by a visible living image, n. 1869, 3310, 5510. What is the quality of their appearance, n. 6201, 8885. That the ideas of the angels of the inmost heaven appear like flaming light, n. 6615. That the ideas of the angels of the ultimate heaven appear like thin bright clouds, n. 6614. The idea of an angel seen, from which issued radiation to the Lord, n. 6620. That the ideas of thought extend themselves at large into angelic societies round about, n. 6598 to 6613.

241. The angels who belong to the Lord's celestial kingdom, converse in like manner as those of His spiritual kingdom, but from more interior thought than the spiritual angels. The celestial angels, being in the good of love to the Lord, speak from wisdom ; and the spiritual angels, being in the good of charity toward the neighbor, which in its essence is truth (n. 215), speak from intelligence ; for wisdom is from good, and intelligence from truth. Hence the speech of the celestial angels is like a gentle stream, soft, and, as it were, continuous ; but the speech of the spiritual angels is somewhat vibratory and discrete. The speech of the celestial angels partakes greatly of the sound of the vowels *u* and *o;* but the speech of the spiritual angels of the vowels *e* and *i;* for vowels are signs of sounds, and affection dwells in sound. It was shown above, n. 236, that the sound of angelic speech corresponds to affection, and the articulations of sound, which are words, to the ideas of thought derived from affection. Since the vowels do not belong to a language, but to the elevations of its words by sound to express various affections according to each one's state, therefore they are not written in the Hebrew language, and are also variously pronounced. Thence the angels know the quality of a man as to his affection and love. The speech of the celestial angels is also without hard consonants, and seldom glides from one consonant to another without the interposition of a word beginning with a vowel. Hence it is that, in the Word, the particle *and* so often occurs, as may be evident to those who read the Word in the Hebrew language, in which that particle has a soft expression, and always takes a vowel sound before and after it. In the Word in that language, it may also be known in some measure from the words themselves whether they belong to the celestial or to the spiritual class ; that is, whether they involve good or truth. Those which involve good partake largely of the sounds of *u* and *o*, and somewhat also of the sound of *a;* while those which involve truth partake of the sounds of *e* and *i.* Since affections are expressed for the most part by sounds, therefore, when great subjects are treated of in human language, such as heaven and God, those words are preferred wherein the sounds of *u* and *o* predominate. Musical sounds, also, swell to the fullness of the *u* and *o* when employed

on such themes; but when the subject is less imposing, othei sounds are preferred. Hence the ability of music to express various kinds of affection.

242. There is a kind of musical concord in the speech of angels which cannot be described.[1] This concord arises from the circumstance, that the thoughts and affections, which give birth to speech, pour themselves forth and diffuse themselves according to the form of heaven; and all consociation and communication there, are according to that form. That the angels are consociated according to the form of heaven, and that their thoughts and affections flow according to that form, may be seen above, n. 200 to 212.

243. Speech similar to that in the spiritual world is inherent in every man, but in his interior intellectual part. But man does not know this, because it does not fall into words analogous to his affection, as it does with the angels. Yet it is from this cause that man, when he comes into the other life, speaks the language of spirits and angels without effort or instruction. But on this subject more will be said below.

244. All in heaven speak the same language, as was said above; but it varies in this respect, that the speech of the wise is more interior, and fuller of the variations of affection and of the ideas of thoughts;[2] the speech of the less wise is more exterior, and less full; and the speech of the simple is still more exterior, and thence consisting of words, the sense of which is to be gathered in the same way as in the conversation of men. There is also a kind of speech by the face, terminating in somewhat sonorous modified by ideas; another kind in which representatives of heaven are mixed with the ideas, and consisting also of ideas made visible; another by gestures corresponding to the affections,

---

[1] That in angelic speech there is concord with harmonious cadence, n. 1648, 1649, 7191.

[2] That spiritual or angelic speech is latent in man, although he is ignorant of it, n. 4104. That the ideas of the internal man are spiritual, but that man, during his life in the world, perceives them naturally, because he then thinks in the natural principle, n. 10236, 10237, 10550. That man after death comes into his interior ideas, n. 3226, 3342, 3343, 10568, 10604. That those ideas then form his speech, n. 2470, 2478, 2479.

and representing things similar to those represented by their words; another by the generals of affections and thoughts; another that resembles thunder; and others besides.

245. The speech of wicked and infernal spirits is in like manner natural, because derived from their affections, but from evil affections, and the filthy ideas thence resulting, which the angels hold in the utmost aversion. The language of hell is therefore the opposite to that of heaven; wherefore the wicked cannot endure angelic speech, nor can the angels endure infernal speech. Infernal speech affects them as a bad odor does the nostrils. The speech of hypocrites, who are able to assume the appearance of angels of light, is like that of angels as to words, but as to affections and consequent ideas of thought, it is diametrically opposite; wherefore their speech, when its interior quality is perceived by the wise angels, is heard as the gnashing of teeth, and strikes the listener with horror.

THE SPEECH OF ANGELS WITH MAN.

246. WHEN angels converse with man, they do not speak in their own, but in the man's language, and also in others with which he is acquainted, but not in a language unknown to him. The reason is, because when angels speak with man, they turn themselves to him and conjoin themselves with him, and this conjunction causes them to be in similar thought; and because man's thought coheres with his memory, and from it flows his speech, therefore each is in the same language. Besides, when an angel or spirit comes to a man, and by turning to him is conjoined with him, he comes into all the man's memory so perfectly, that he is almost led to believe that he knows of himself what the man knows, even the languages which he has learned. I have conversed with the angels on this subject, and said to them, that possibly they supposed they were speaking with me in my

mother tongue, because it so appeared to them; when yet it was not they who spoke, but I; and that this was plain from the fact that angels are unable to utter a single word of human language, (n. 237); and besides, human language is natural, and they are spiritual, and spiritual beings cannot utter anything in a natural way. The angels replied, that they were aware that their conjunction with man, when conversing with him, is with his spiritual thought; but because that flows into his natural thought, and his natural thought coheres with his memory, therefore the language of the man appears to them as their own,—in like manner all his knowledge; and that this results from the Lord's good pleasure that such a conjunction, and as it were insertion of heaven into man, should take place; but that the state of man at this day is so altered, that he no longer has such conjunction with angels, but with spirits who are not in heaven. I have also conversed with spirits on this same subject; but they were unwilling to believe that it is the man who speaks, but insisted that they speak in the man; also that the man does not know what he knows, but they themselves; and thus that all things which the man knows are derived from them. I endeavored by many arguments to convince them that they were mistaken; but in vain. Who are meant by spirits, and who by angels, will be explained hereafter when the world of spirits is treated of.

247. Another reason why angels and spirits conjoin themselves so closely with man as not to know but that everything belonging to him is theirs, is, because the conjunction between the spiritual and the natural world with man is such, that they are as it were one. But since man had separated himself from heaven, it was provided by the Lord that there should be angels and spirits with every man, and that he should be governed by them from the Lord. It is on this account that there is so close a conjunction between them. It would have been otherwise if man had not separated himself from heaven; for then he might have been governed by the Lord by means of a common influx from heaven, without spirits and angels adjoined to him. But this subject will be particularly considered in a subsequent part of the work when treating of the conjunction of heaven with man.

248. The speech of an angel or spirit with man is heard as

sonorously as the speech of one man with another; it is not, however, heard by others who are present, but by himself alone, because the speech of an angel or spirit flows-in first into man's thought, and by an internal way into his organ of hearing, and thus actuates it from within; whereas the speech of man with man flows first into the air, and by an external way into his organ of hearing, which it actuates from without. Hence it is evident that the speech of an angel or spirit with man is heard in the man; and, since it affects the organs of hearing as much as speech from without, that it is also equally sonorous. That the speech of an angel or spirit flows down from within even into the ear, was proved to me by its effect upon the tongue, into which it also flows, producing therein a slight vibration, but not such motion as takes place when the sound of speech is articulated into words by the man himself.

249. But to speak with spirits at this day is rarely permitted, because it is dangerous;[1] for the spirits then know that they are present with man, which they otherwise do not; and evil spirits are of such a nature that they regard man with deadly hatred; and desire nothing more than to destroy him, both soul and body. This also they accomplish with those who have indulged much in fantasies, so as to remove from themselves the delights suitable to the natural man. Yet some who lead a solitary life occasionally hear spirits speaking with them, and without danger; but the spirits present with them are removed at intervals by the Lord, lest they should know that they are with man; for most spirits are not aware that there is any other world than the one wherein they dwell, and therefore do not know that there are men elsewhere. Wherefore a man is not allowed to speak with them in return, for in that case they would know it. Persons who think much upon religious subjects, and are so intent upon them as to see them as it were inwardly in themselves, also begin

---

[1] That man is able to converse with spirits and angels, and that the ancients frequently did so, n. 67, 68, 69, 784, 1634, 1636, 7802. That in some earths angels and spirits appear in a human form and speak with the inhabitants, n. 10751, 10752; but that in this earth it is dangerous to discourse with spirits now, unless man be principled in a true faith, and be led by the Lord, n. 784, 9438, 10751.

to hear spirits speaking with them; for religious subjects of whatever kind,—when a man of his own accord dwells upon them, and does not interrupt the current of his thoughts by various uses in the world,—penetrate interiorly, become fixed there, occupy the whole spirit of the man, and in fact enter into the spiritual world and act upon the spirits who dwell there. But such persons are visionaries and enthusiasts, and believe whatever spirit they hear to be the Holy Spirit, when yet they are enthusiastic spirits. Such spirits see falses as truths, and because they see them, they persuade themselves that they are truths, and infuse the same persuasion into those who are receptive of their influx. And because those spirits began also to persuade to the commission of evils, and were even obeyed, therefore they were gradually removed. Enthusiastic spirits are distinguished from other spirits by this peculiarity, that they believe themselves to be the Holy Spirit, and their sayings divine. They do not hurt the man with whom they communicate, because he honors them with divine worship. I have also several times conversed with these spirits; and on such occasions the wicked principles and motives which they infused into their worshipers were discovered. They dwell together at the left in a desert place.

250. But to speak with the angels of heaven is granted only to those who are in truths derived from good, and especially to those who are in the acknowledgment of the Lord, and of the Divine in His Human, because this is the truth wherein the heavens are established. For, as was shown above, the Lord is the God of heaven, n. 2 to 6; the Divine of the Lord makes heaven, n. 7 to 12: the Divine of the Lord in heaven is love to Him and charity toward the neighbor derived from Him, n. 13 to 19: the universal heaven in one complex resembles one man; in like manner every society of heaven and every angel is in a perfect human form, derived from the Divine Human of the Lord, n. 59 to 86. From which it is evident, that to speak with the angels of heaven is not granted to any but those whose interiors are opened by divine truths even to the Lord; for the Lord flows into these with man, and heaven also flows-in with the Lord. Divine truths open the interiors of man, because he was so created, that he may be an image of heaven as to his internal man, and an

image of the world as to his external (n. 57) ; and the internal man is not opened except by divine truth proceeding from the Lord, because that is the light and life of heaven, (n. 126 to 140).

251. The influx of the Lord Himself with man is into his forehead, and thence into the whole face, because the forehead of man corresponds to his love, and the face to all his interiors.[1] The influx of the spiritual angels with man is into his head in every direction, from the forehead and temples to every part which covers the cerebrum,—because that region of the head corresponds to intelligence. But the influx of the celestial angels is into that part of the head which covers the cerebellum, and which is called the occiput, extending from the ears in all directions even to the back of the neck,—for that region corresponds to wisdom. The speech of angels with man always enters by those ways into his thoughts ; by noting which, I have perceived what angels they were who discoursed with me.

252. They who converse with the angels of heaven, see also the objects which exist in heaven, because they see by the light of heaven in which their interiors are. The angels also see through them the things which are on earth ;[2] for with them heaven is conjoined to the world, and the world to heaven. For, as was said above, n. 246, when angels turn themselves to man, they conjoin themselves to him in such a manner that they know no other than that the things which belong to the man are their own,—not only those which belong to his speech, but also those which belong to his sight and hearing. Man also, in his turn, knows no other than that the things which flow-in through the angels are his own. Such was the conjunction which existed between the angels of heaven and the most ancient people on this earth, whose times therefore were called the golden age. Be

---

[1] That the forehead corresponds to celestial love, and thence, in the Word, signifies that love, n. 9936. That the face corresponds to the interiors of man, which are of the thought and affection, n. 1568, 2988, 2989, 3631, 4796, 4797, 4800, 5165, 5168, 5695, 9306. That the face also is formed to correspondence with the interiors, n. 4791 to 4805, 5695. That hence the face, in the Word, signifies the interiors, n. 1999, 2434, 35.7, 4066, 4796.

[2] That spirits can see nothing through man which is in this solar world, but that they have seen through my eyes, and the reason why, n. 1880.

cause they acknowledged the Divine under a human form, that is, the Lord, they conversed with the angels of heaven as with their kindred, and the angels in turn conversed with them as with theirs; and in them heaven and the world formed a one. But after those times, man removed himself further and further from heaven, by loving himself more than the Lord, and the world more than heaven; in consequence of which he began to be sensible of the delights of self-love and the love of the world separate from the delights of heaven, and at last to such a degree that he became ignorant of any other delight. Then his interiors, which had been open to heaven, were closed, and his exteriors were opened to the world. And whenever this takes place, man is in light as to all things belonging to the world, but in thick darkness as to all things belonging to heaven.

253. Since those times it has rarely happened that any one has conversed with the angels of heaven; but some have conversed with spirits who were not in heaven. For the interiors and exteriors of man are either turned to the Lord as their common centre (n. 124), or to self, that is, backward from the Lord. Those which are turned to the Lord, are also turned to heaven, but those which are turned to self, are also turned to the world; those which are turned to the world, can with difficulty be elevated; nevertheless they are elevated by the Lord as far as possible, through a change of the love, which is effected by means of truths from the Word.

254. I have been informed in what manner the Lord spoke with the prophets, through whom the Word was given. He did not speak with them as with the ancients, by an influx into their interiors, but by spirits sent to them, whom the Lord filled with His aspect, and thus inspired with words which they dictated to the prophets; so that it was not influx, but dictation. And since the words came forth immediately from the Lord, therefore every one of them is filled with the Divine, and contains in it an internal sense of such a nature, that the angels in heaven understand the words in a celestial and spiritual sense, while men understand them in a natural sense. Thus the Lord has conjoined heaven and the world by means of the Word. In what manner spirits are filled with the Divine from the Lord by aspect, has also been

shown me. The spirit filled with the Divine from the Lord,
does not know but that he is the Lord, and that the Divine is
what speaks,—which state continues until he has delivered his
communication; afterward he perceives and acknowledges that
he is a spirit, and that he did not speak from himself but from
the Lord. Such being the state of the spirits who spoke with
the prophets, therefore it is said by them, that Jehovah spoke.
The spirits also called themselves Jehovah, as may be manifest,
not only from the prophetical, but also from the historical parts
of the Word.

255. That the nature of the conjunction of angels and spirits
with man may be known, it is permitted to relate some particulars worthy of being mentioned, which may tend to illustrate and
confirm the subject. When angels and spirits turn themselves to
a man, it appears to them that his language is their own, and that
they have no other language; because they are then in the man's
language, and not in their own, which they do not even remember. But as soon as they turn themselves away from the man,
they are in their own angelic and spiritual language again, and
know nothing whatever of the man's. The like has occurred to
myself. When I have been in company with angels, and in a
state similar to theirs, I have conversed with them in their language, and neither knew nor remembered anything of my own;
but as soon as I left them, I was in my own language. It is also
worthy of mention, that when angels and spirits turn themselves
to a man, they can converse with him at any distance. They have
conversed with me when they were afar off, and their speech
sounded as loud as when they were near; but when they turn
themselves from the man, and speak one with another, not a
syllable of what they say is heard by him, even though it be
spoken close to his ear. Hence it was made manifest to me that
all conjunction in the spiritual world is according to the degree
in which individuals turn toward each other. It deserves further
to be mentioned, that many spirits can converse with a man at
the same time, and the man with them; for they send one of
their number to the man with whom they wish to converse, and
this emissary spirit turns himself to the man, and the other spirits turn to their emissary, and in this way they concentrate their

thoughts, which the emissary spirit utters. That spirit knows not, at the time, but that he speaks from himself; neither do they know but that they speak from themselves. Thus the conjunction of many with one, is effected by the turning of the parties toward each other.[1] But concerning these emissary spirits who are also called subjects, and the communication effected through them, more will be said in what follows.

256. It is not allowed any angel or spirit to speak with man from his own memory, but only from the man's; for angels and spirits have memory as well as men. If a spirit should speak with a man from his own memory, the man would not then know but that the spirit's thoughts were his own, when yet they are not. It would be like the seeming recollection of a thing which the man never heard or saw. That such is the case, has been given me to know from experience. Hence the opinion held by some of the ancients, that after some thousands of years they should return into their former life, and into all its acts, and that indeed they actually had so returned. They believed so, because occasionally there occurred to them, as it were, a recollection of things which yet they never saw or heard. This appearance was produced by an influx of spirits from their own memory into the ideas of men's thought.

257. There are also certain spirits, called natural and corporeal spirits, who, when they come to a man, do not conjoin themselves with his thought like other spirits, but enter into his body, and take possession of all his senses, and speak through his mouth, and act by his members,—not knowing at the time but that all things belonging to the man are their own. These are the spirits that obsess man. But they have been cast into hell by the Lord, and thus altogether removed; so that there are no such obsessions at the present day.[2]

---

[1] That the spirits sent from societies of spirits to other societies are called subjects, n. 4403, 5856. That communications in the spiritual world are effected by such emissary spirits, n. 4403, 5846, 5983. That a spirit, when he is sent out and acts as a subject, does not think from himself, but from those who sent him, n. 5985, 5986, 5987.

[2] That external obsessions, or those of the body, do not exist at this day, as formerly, n. 1983; but that at this day internal obsessions, which are of

WRITINGS IN HEAVEN.

258. SINCE the angels have speech, and their speech consists of words, it follows that they have writings also, and that they express their sentiments by writing as well as by speaking. Sometimes sheets of paper have been sent me covered with writing, some of which were exactly like manuscripts, and others like printed sheets in the world. I could also read them in like manner; but it was not allowed me to draw from them more than one or two ideas, because it is not according to divine order for a man to be instructed from heaven by writings, but by the Word, since communication and conjunction of heaven with the world, and thus of the Lord with man, is effected by means of the Word alone. That papers written in heaven appeared also to the prophets, is evident from Ezekiel: "*When I looked, behold a hand put forth by a spirit unto me; and a roll of a book was therein; and he spread it before me: it was written on the front and on the back,*" chap. ii. 9, 10; and in the Apocalypse: "*I saw at the right hand of Him who sat on the throne, a book written within and on the back side, sealed with seven seals.*" Rev. v. 1.

259. That there should be writings in heaven was provided by the Lord for the sake of the Word; for the Word in its essence is divine truth, from which both men and angels derive all heavenly wisdom; for it was dictated by the Lord, and what is dictated by the Lord passes through all the heavens in order, and terminates with man. Hence it is accommodated both to the wisdom of angels and the intelligence of men. Therefore the

---

the mind, are more numerous than formerly, n. 1983, 4793. That man is obsessed interiorly, when he has filthy and scandalous thoughts concerning God and his neighbor, and when he is only withheld from publishing them by external bonds, which relate to the fear of the loss of reputation, of honor, of gain, to the dread of the law, and to the loss of life, n. 5990. Concerning the diabolical spirits who chiefly obsess the interiors of man, n. 4793. Concerning the diabolical spirits who are desirous to obsess the exteriors of man, but are shut up in hell, n. 2752, 5990.

angels have the Word, and read it just as men do on earth.
They also preach from it, and derive their doctrinals thence, (n.
221). The Word is the same in heaven as on earth; only its
natural sense, which is that of the letter with us, is not in heaven,
but the spiritual which is its internal sense. What this sense is,
may be seen in the small work on the White Horse mentioned
in the Apocalypse.

260. A bit of paper was once sent me from heaven, on which
were written only a few words in the Hebrew character; and I
was told that every letter involved arcana of wisdom, and that
those arcana were contained in the inflexions and curvatures of
the letters, and thence likewise in the sounds. From this was
made plain to me the meaning of the Lord's words: "*Verily I
say unto you, till heaven and earth pass, one iota or little horn
shall not pass from the law,*" Matt. v. 18. That the Word
is divine as to every tittle thereof, is also known in the church.
But where the Divine lies concealed in every tittle, is not yet
known; wherefore it shall be declared. The writing in the
inmost heaven consists of various inflected and circumflected
forms; and the inflexions and circumflexions are according to the
form of heaven. By these the angels express the arcana of their
wisdom, many of which cannot be expressed in words; and,
what is wonderful, the angels are skilled in such writing without
being taught. It is implanted in them like their speech, (concerning which see n. 236); wherefore this writing is heavenly
writing. The reason that it is inherent in the angels, is, because
all extension of their thoughts and affections, and thence all communication of their intelligence and wisdom, proceeds according
to the form of heaven, (n. 201); hence their writing flows into
that form. I was told that the most ancient people on this earth
wrote in the same manner before the invention of letters; and
that it was transferred into the letters of the Hebrew language,
which, in ancient times, were all inflected. Not one of them
had the square form in use at this day. Hence it is that things
divine and the arcana of heaven are contained even in the iotas,
apexes, and tittles of the Word.

261. This kind of writing, by means of characters of a heavenly form, is in use in the inmost heaven where they excel all

others in wisdom.　By those characters they express the affections
from which their thoughts flow and follow in order according to
the subject treated of.　Hence those writings involve arcana
which no thought can exhaust.　I have also been permitted to
see them.　But there are no such writings in the inferior heavens
The writings there are like those in the world, in similar letters,
yet not intelligible to man because they are in angelic language,
which has nothing in common with human languages, (n. 237) ;
for by the vowels they express affections, by the consonants, the
ideas of thought proceeding from those affections, and by the words
composed of both, the meaning they wish to convey, (see above,
n. 234, 241).　This kind of writing also involves in a few words
more than a man can record in several pages.　I have seen writings
of this kind also.　In this manner they have the Word written
in the inferior heavens ; and in the inmost heaven they have it
written in heavenly characters.

262. It is worthy of remark, that writings in the heavens flow
naturally from the very thoughts of the angels, and are executed
so easily, that it is as if thought threw itself upon paper.　The
hand does not hesitate in the choice of any word, because the
words they speak as well as those they write, correspond to the
ideas of their thought ; and all correspondence is natural and
spontaneous.　There are also writings in the heavens without the
assistance of the hand, from mere correspondence of the thoughts ;
but these are not permanent.

263. I have also seen writings from heaven consisting merely of
numbers written in order and in a series, exactly like writings composed of letters and words ; and I was informed that this writing
is from the inmost heaven, and that their heavenly writing,
treated of above, (n. 260, 261), takes the form of numbers before
the angels of an inferior heaven, when the thought from it flows
down thither ; and that this numerical writing in like manner
involves arcana, some of which can neither be comprehended by
thought nor expressed by words.　For all numbers have their
correspondence, and a signification according to their correspondence, the same as words ;[1] yet with this difference, that numbers

[1] That all numbers, in the Word, signify things, n. 482, 487, 647, 648,
755, 813, 1963, 1988, 2075, 2252, 3252, 4264, 4670, 6175, 9488. 9659, 10217,

ınvolve general ideas, and words particular ones; and since one general idea involves innumerable particulars, it follows that numerical writing involves more arcana than alphabetical. From these things it was made evident to me that numbers in the Word, as well as words, signify things. What the simple numbers signify, as 2, 3, 4, 5, 6, 7, 8, 9, 10, 12; and what the compound, as 20, 30, 50, 70, 100, 144, 1000, 10000, 12000, and others, may be seen in the ARCANA CŒLESTIA, where they are treated of. In the numerical writing in heaven, that number is always placed first, on which the following numbers depend as on their subject; for that number is as it were the index of the subject treated of, and from that number those which follow derive their specific determination to the subject.

264. They who know nothing about heaven, and do not wish to have any other idea concerning it than as of a purely atmospherical region, in which the angels fly about as intellectual minds destitute of the sense of hearing and sight, are unable to conceive that they have speech and writing; for they place the existence of everything real in material nature. Nevertheless, the things which exist in heaven are as real as those in the world; and the angels who are there possess everything useful for life, and conducive to wisdom.

THE WISDOM OF THE ANGELS OF HEAVEN.

265. THE nature of angelic wisdom can scarcely be comprehended, because it so far transcends human wisdom as to preclude all comparison; and what is thus transcendent appears to

---

10253. Shown from heaven, n. 4495, 5265. That numbers multiplied signify similar things with the simple numbers from which they result by multiplication. n. 5291, 5335, 5708, 7973. That the most ancient people had heavenly arcana in numbers, forming a kind of computation of things relating to the church, n. 575.

be nothing. Besides, some of the truths that must be employed in describing it, are as yet unknown ; and truths before they are known, are like shadows in the understanding, which render obscure the real nature of the subject thought of. Nevertheless, these unknown truths may be known and comprehended, provided the mind take delight in such knowledge ; for delight carries light with it, because it proceeds from love ; and light from heaven shines on those who love the things pertaining to divine and heavenly wisdom, and they receive illustration.

266. What the wisdom of the angels is may be concluded from the fact that they dwell in the light of heaven, and the light of heaven in its essence is divine truth, or divine wisdom ; and this light enlightens at the same time their internal sight, which is that of the mind, and their external sight which is that of the eyes. (That the light of heaven is divine truth, or divine wisdom, may be seen above, n. 126 to 133). The angels also dwell in the heat of heaven, which in its essence is divine good, or divine love, from which they derive the affection and desire of becoming wise. (That the heat of heaven is divine good, or divine love, may be seen above, n. 133 to 140). That the angels are in wisdom to such a degree that they may be called wisdoms, may be concluded from the fact that all their thoughts and affections flow according to the heavenly form, which is the form of divine wisdom ; and that their interiors which receive wisdom, are arranged in that form. (That the thoughts and affections of the angels flow according to the form of heaven, and consequently also their intelligence and wisdom, may be seen above, n. 201 to 212). That the angels possess superior wisdom, is further evident from this circumstance, that their speech is the speech of wisdom, for it flows immediately and spontaneously from thought, as thought flows from affection ; so that their speech is thought and affection in an external form. Hence nothing withdraws them from the divine influx, and no extraneous ideas enter their thoughts, as is the case with man while he is speaking. (That the speech of angels is that of their thought and affection, may be seen, n. 234 to 245). Another circumstance also conspires to exalt the wisdom of the angels, and that is, that all things which they see with their eyes and perceive by

their senses, are in agreement with their wisdom, because they are correspondences, and thence forms representative of such things as belong to wisdom. (That all things which appear in the heavens correspond with the interiors of the angels, and are representations of their wisdom, may be seen above, n. 170 to 182). Besides, the thoughts of the angels are not bounded and confined by ideas derived from space and time, like human thoughts ; for spaces and times belong to nature, and the things proper to nature withdraw the mind from spiritual things, and hinder the extension of intellectual vision. (That the ideas of angels derive nothing from time and space, and thus are not limited like those of men, may be seen above, n. 162 to 169, and 191 to 199). Neither are the thoughts of the angels drawn downward to things terrestrial and material, nor interrupted by cares about the necessaries of life ; consequently they are not withdrawn by them from the delights of wisdom, like the thoughts of men in the world. For all things are given them gratis by the Lord ; they are clothed gratis, they are fed gratis, they have habitations gratis, (n. 181 to 190) ; and moreover they are gifted with delights and pleasures according to their reception of wisdom from the Lord. These observations are made, that it may be known whence the angels have such exalted wisdom.[1]

267. The reason that angels are capable of receiving such wisdom, is because their interiors are open ; and wisdom, like every perfection, increases toward the interiors, thus according to the degree in which they are opened.[2] There are three de-

---

[1] That the wisdom of angels is incomprehensible and ineffable, n. 2795, 2796, 2802, 3314, 3404, 3405, 9094, 9176.

[2] That so far as man is elevated from things external toward interior things, so far he comes into light and intelligence, n. 6183, 6313. That there is an actual elevation, n. 7816, 10330. That elevation from things external to things interior is like elevation out of a mist into light, n. 4598. That exterior things are more remote from the Divine in man, and are therefore respectively obscure, n. 6451 ; and also respectively confused, n. 996, 3855. That interior things are more perfect, because nearer to the Divine, n. 5146, 5147. That in what is internal there are thousands and thousands of things which appear externally as one general thing, n. 5707. That hence thought and perception are clearer in proportion as they are interior, n. 5920.

grees of life with every angel, which correspond to the three heavens, (see n. 29 to 40). They with whom the first degree is open, are in the first or ultimate heaven; they with whom the second degree is open, are in the second or middle heaven; but they with whom the third degree is open, are in the third or inmost heaven. The wisdom of the angels in the heavens is according to these degrees. Hence the wisdom of the angels of the inmost heaven immensely transcends the wisdom of those of the middle heaven, and the wisdom of these immensely transcends that of the angels of the ultimate heaven. (See above, n. 209, 210; and on the nature of degrees, n. 38). Such distinction exists, because the things which are in a superior degree are particulars, and those in an inferior degree are generals, and generals include particulars. Particulars, in respect to generals, are as thousands or myriads to one; and so is the wisdom of the angels of a superior heaven, compared with that of the angels of an inferior heaven. But still the wisdom of these latter transcends the wisdom of man in the same proportion; for man is in a body and its sensuals, and the corporeal sensual things of man are in the lowest degree. Hence it is evident what kind of wisdom they possess, who think from things sensual, and are called sensual men; in truth they have no wisdom at all, but only science.[1] It is quite

---

[1] That the sensual principle is the ultimate of the life of man, and that it adheres to, and inheres in, his corporeal principle, n. 5077, 5767, 9212, 9216, 9331, 9730. That he is called a sensual man who judges and concludes about all things from the senses of the body, and who believes nothing but what he can see with his eyes and touch with his hands, n. 5094, 7693. That such a man thinks in externals, and not interiorly in himself, n. 5089, 5094, 6564, 7693. That his interiors are closed, so that he sees nothing therein of spiritual truth, n. 6564, 6844, 6845. In a word, that he is in gross natural light, and therefore perceives nothing which is from the light of heaven, n. 6201, 6310, 6564, 6844, 6845, 6598, 6612, 6614, 6622, 6624. That interiorly he is in contrariety to those things which relate to heaven and the church, n. 6201, 6316, 6844, 6845, 6948, 6949. That the learned, who have confirmed themselves against the truths of the church, become of such a character, n. 6316. That sensual men are more cunning and malicious than others, n. 7693, 10236. That they reason sharply and cunningly, but from the corporeal memory, in which they place all intelligence, n. 195, 196, 5700, 10236; and that they reason from the fallacies of the senses, n. 5084, 6948, 6949, 7693.

otherwise with those who elevate their thoughts above the things of sense, and especially with those whose interiors are open even into the light of heaven.

268. How great the wisdom of the angels is, may be further evident from the fact, that in the heavens there is a communication of all things,—the intelligence and wisdom of one being communicated to another. Heaven is a communion of all good things, because heavenly love wills that what is its own should be another's; consequently no one in heaven perceives his own good in himself as good, unless it be also in another. Thence also is the happiness of heaven. The angels derive from the Lord this disposition to communicate, for such is the nature of the Divine Love. That there is such communication in the heavens, has also been given me to know by experience. Certain simple spirits were once taken up into heaven; and when there, they came also into angelic wisdom, and then understood things which they could not comprehend before, and spoke such things as they were unable to utter in their former state.

269. The wisdom of angels is such as cannot be described in words, but can only be illustrated by some general observations. Angels can express by a single word, what man cannot express by a thousand. And besides, there are innumerable things in one angelic word, which cannot be expressed at all by the words of human language; for in every single word spoken by angels, there are contained arcana of wisdom in continuous connection, which human knowledge can never reach. The angels supply, by the tone of the voice, what they do not fully express by words, and in that tone there is contained the affection of the things spoken of in their proper order; for,—as was said above, n. 236, 241,—they express affections by sounds, and the ideas of thought derived from affections, by words. Hence it is that the things heard in heaven are said to be ineffable. The angels can like-wise relate in a few words the entire contents of any book, and infuse into every word such things as elevate to interior wisdom; for their speech is such that its sounds harmonize with their affections, and every word, with their ideas. Their words, too, are varied. by an infinity of methods, according to the series of things embraced within the compass of their thought. The in-

terior angels can also discover the whole life of a speaker from the tone of his voice coupled with a few expressions; for from the sound, variegated by the ideas expressed in words, they perceive his ruling love, on which is inscribed, as it were, every particular of his life.[1] From these considerations it is evident what the wisdom of the angels is. Their wisdom, in comparison with human wisdom, is as a myriad to one,—comparatively as the moving forces of the whole body, which are innumerable, are to the action resulting from them, wherein to human sense they appear as one; or as the thousand things pertaining to an object as seen through a perfect microscope, to the one obscure thing which it appears to the naked eye. To illustrate the subject by an example: An angel from his wisdom explained regeneration, and made known arcana concerning it in their order even to some hundreds, filling each one with ideas which contained arcana still more interior,—and this from beginning to end; for he explained how the spiritual man is conceived anew, is carried as it were in the womb, is born, grows up, and is successively perfected. He said that he could increase the number of arcana even to some thousands; and that he had only mentioned those concerning the regeneration of the external man, and that there were innumerably more concerning the regeneration of the internal. From this and other similar examples which I have heard from the angels, it was made manifest to me how great is their wisdom, and how great, respectively, the ignorance of man; for he scarcely knows what regeneration is, and is unacquainted with a single step of its progression while being regenerated.

---

[1] That what rules, or has universal dominion with man, is in every particular of his life, and thus in all and everything of his affection and thought, n. 4459, 5949, 6159, 6571, 7648, 8067, 8853 to 8858. That the quality of man is such as his ruling love is, n. 918, 1040, 8858; illustrated by examples, n. 8854, 8857. That what reigns universally constitutes the life of the spirit of man, n. 7648. That it is his very will, his very love, and the end of his life; for what a man wills, he loves, and what he loves, he regards as an end, n. 1317, 1568, 1571, 1909, 3796, 5949, 6936. That therefore man is of such a quality as his will is; or of such a quality as his ruling love is; or of such a quality as the end of his life is, n. 1568, 1571, 3570, 4054, 6571, 6934, 6938, 8856, 10076, 10109, 10110, 10284.

270. Something shall now be said concerning the wisdom of the angels of the third or inmost heaven, and how much it exceeds the wisdom of the angels of the first or ultimate heaven. The wisdom of the angels of the third or inmost heaven is incomprehensible, even to those who are in the ultimate heaven; because the interiors of the angels of the third heaven are open to the third degree, but those of the angels of the first heaven only to the first degree; and all wisdom increases toward the interiors, and is perfected according to the degree in which they are opened, (n. 208, 267). Since the interiors of the angels of the third or inmost heaven are opened to the third degree, therefore divine truths are, as it were, inscribed on them; for the interiors of the third degree are in the form of heaven more than the interiors of the second and first degrees; and the form of heaven is from divine truth, thus according to divine wisdom. Hence it is that divine truths appear, as it were, inscribed on those angels, or as if they were inherent and innate. Wherefore as soon as they hear genuine divine truths, they immediately acknowledge and perceive them, and afterwards see them, as it were, inwardly in themselves. Since the angels of this heaven are of such a character, therefore they never reason about divine truths, still less do they dispute about any truth, whether it be so or not so; nor do they know what it is to believe or have faith; for they say, What is faith? for I perceive and see that it is so. This they illustrate by comparisons, saying, that, to urge a man to have faith, who sees the truth in himself, is like saying to one who sees a house and the various things in and around it, that he ought to have faith in them, and believe that they are just as he sees; or it is like telling a man who sees a garden with its trees and fruits, that he ought to have faith that it is a garden, and that the trees and fruits are trees and fruits, when yet he sees them plainly with his own eyes. Hence it is that the angels of the third heaven never name faith, nor have they any idea of it; therefore they do not reason about divine truths, still less do they dispute concerning any truth whether it be so or not so.[1] But

---

[1] That the celestial angels are acquainted with innumerable things, and are immensely wiser than the spiritual angels, n. 2718. That the celestial

the angels of the first or ultimate heaven have not divine truths thus inscribed on their interiors, because only the first degree of life is open with them; therefore they reason about truths; and they who reason scarcely see anything beyond the immediate object about which they reason, or go beyond the subject except only to confirm it by certain arguments; and when they have confirmed it, they say it shall be a matter of faith, and is to be believed. I have conversed with the angels on these subjects, and they told me, that the distinction between the wisdom of the angels of the third heaven and that of the angels of the first heaven, is like the distinction between what is lucid and what is obscure. They also compared the wisdom of the angels of the third heaven to a magnificent palace full of all things for use, around which are extensive paradises [or gardens] and around these magnificent objects of various kinds; and they said that, because those angels are in the truths of wisdom, they can enter into the palace, and look upon every thing there, and also ramble in the paradises in every direction, and gather delight from all they behold. But it is otherwise with those who reason concerning truths, and especially with those who dispute about them. These do not see truths from the light of truth, but either imbibe them from others, or from the literal sense of the Word not interiorly understood; and therefore they say that they are to be believed, or that faith is to be had in these truths, into which they are afterwards unwilling that any interior sight should enter. Concerning these they said, that they cannot approach the first threshold of the palace of wisdom, much less can they enter it and ramble about in its paradises, because they stop at the first step that conducts thither. It is otherwise with those who are in the truths themselves. Nothing hinders them from being borne on and making unlimited progress; for the truths seen lead them

---

angels do not think and speak from a principle of faith, like the spiritual angels, because they are in perception from the Lord of all things relating to faith, n. 202, 597, 667, 784, 1121, 1387, 1398, 1442, 1919, 7680, 7877, 8780, 9277, 10336. That in regard to the truths of faith, they only say, Yea, yea, or Nay, nay, but that the spiritual angels reason whether it be so, n. 2715, 3246, 4448, 9166, 10786; where the Lord's words are explained, "*Let your discourse be Yea, yea, Nay, nay,*" Matt. v. 36.

whithersoever they go, and into wide fields; for every truth is of infinite extent, and is in connection with many others. They said further, that the wisdom of the angels of the inmost heaven consists principally in this, that they see divine and heavenly things in every single object, and things wonderful in a series of many objects. For all things which appear before their eyes correspond; as when they see palaces and gardens, their view does not linger in the objects before their eyes, but they see also the interior things from which they originate, and to which they correspond; and this with all possible variety, according to the appearance of the objects,—thus beholding innumerable things at once in order and connection, which then so delight their minds that they seem to be carried out of themselves. That all things which appear in the heavens correspond to the divine things from the Lord with the angels, may be seen above, n. 170 to 176.

271. The angels of the third heaven are such, because they are in love to the Lord; and this love opens the interiors of the mind to the third degree, and is the receptacle of all things of wisdom. It is further to be known, that the angels of the inmost heaven are still continually perfecting in wisdom, and this, too, in a manner different from those of the ultimate heaven. The angels of the inmost heaven do not store up divine truths in the memory; thus they do not make anything like a science of them, but as soon as they hear them they perceive them to be truths, and commit them to life. Divine truths therefore remain with them as if inscribed on their interiors; for what is committed to the life thus abides internally. But it is otherwise with the angels of the ultimate heaven. These first store up divine truths in the memory, and reduce them to a science, and thence call them forth and perfect their understanding by them; and, without any interior perception whether they be truths, will them, and commit them to life. Hence they are respectively in obscurity. It is worthy of remark, that the angels of the third heaven are perfected in wisdom by hearing, and not by sight. The truths which they hear from preaching do not enter into their memory, but immediately into their perception and will, and become of their life; but the objects which they see with their eyes enter into

their memory, and they reason and converse about these ; whence
it was made manifest to me, that with them the way of hearing
is the way of wisdom.   This, too, is from correspondence ; for
the ear corresponds to obedience, and obedience has relation to
life ; but the eye corresponds to intelligence, and intelligence has
relation to doctrine.[1]   The state of these angels is also described in
many parts of the Word, as in Jeremiah : "*I will put My law
in their mind, and will write it on their heart.   They shall no
more teach every one his friend, and every one his brother,
saying, Know ye Jehovah; for they shall all know Me, from
the least of them to the greatest of them.*" xxxi. 33, 34.   And
in Matthew : "*Your discourse shall be Yea, yea, Nay, nay;
whatsoever is more than these is from evil.*" v. 37.   What is
more than these is from evil, because it is not from the Lord ; for
the truths which are in the angels of the third heaven are from
the Lord, because those angels are in love to Him.   Love to the
Lord in that heaven consists in willing and doing divine truth,
for divine truth is the Lord in heaven.

272. An additional reason—which also is the primary one in
heaven—why the angels are capable of receiving such exalted
wisdom, is, because they are free from self-love ; for in proportion
as any one is free from that love, he is capable of becoming wise
in things divine.   It is that love which closes the interiors against
the Lord and heaven, and opens the exteriors and turns them
toward self.   Wherefore all those with whom that love predominates are in thick darkness as to the things of heaven, however
enlightened they may be as to those of the world.   But angels
on the other hand, because they are free from self-love, are in the
light of wisdom ; for the heavenly loves in which they are,
which are love to the Lord and love toward the neighbor, open

---

[1] Concerning the correspondence of the ear and of hearing, n. 4652 to
4660.   That the ear corresponds to perception and obedience, and that
hence it signifies those principles, n. 2542, 3869, 4653, 5017, 7216, 8361,
9311, 9397, 10065.   That it signifies the reception of truths, n. 5471, 5475,
9926.   Concerning the correspondence of the eye and its sight, n. 4403 to
4421, 4523 to 4534.   That hence the sight of the eye signifies the intelligence which is of faith, and also faith itself, n. 2701, 4410, 4526, 6923, 9051,
10569

the interiors, because those loves are from the Lord, and the Lord Himself is in them. That those loves make heaven in general, and form heaven with every one in particular, may be seen above, n. 13 to 19. Since heavenly loves open the interiors to the Lord, therefore also all the angels turn their faces toward the Lord, (n. 142). For in the spiritual world the love turns the interiors of every one toward itself, and in whatever direction it turns the interiors, it also turns the face ; for the face there acts in unison with the interiors, of which it is indeed the external form. Since the love turns the interiors and the face toward itself, therefore it also conjoins itself with them,—for love is spiritual conjunction,—and communicates to them all its own. From this turning and consequent conjunction and communication, the angels derive their wisdom. That all conjunction in the spiritual world is according to the turning [or aspect], may be seen above, n. 255.

273. The angels are continually perfecting in wisdom ;[1] but still they cannot to eternity be so far perfected, that there can be any ratio between their wisdom and the divine wisdom of the Lord ; for the divine wisdom of the Lord is infinite, and between the infinite and the finite there is no ratio.

274. Because wisdom perfects the angels and constitutes their life, and because heaven with its goods flows into every one according to his wisdom, therefore all in heaven desire wisdom, and long for it scarcely otherwise than as a hungry man longs for food. Knowledge, intelligence, and wisdom are also spiritual nourishment, as food is natural nourishment ; besides, they mutually correspond to each other.

275. The angels in one heaven and those in one society of heaven, are not in the same but in different degrees of wisdom. Those in the midst are in the greatest wisdom, and those round about them are in less and less in proportion as they are distant from the centre. The decrease of wisdom according to distance from the centre, is like the decrease of light verging to shade ; (see above, n. 43 and 128). They also have light in a degree corresponding to their wisdom ; for the light of heaven is divine

---

[1] That the angels advance in perfection to eternity, n. 4803, 6648.

22   H

wisdom, and every one is in light according to his reception of that wisdom. Concerning the light of heaven and its various reception, see above, n. 126 to 132.

THE STATE OF INNOCENCE OF THE ANGELS IN HEAVEN.

276. WHAT innocence is, and what its quality, is known to few in the world, and is altogether unknown to those who are in evil. It appears, indeed, before the eyes, displaying itself in the face, the speech, and the gestures, especially of little children; but yet its nature is not known, still less is it known that it is that in which heaven stores itself up with man. In order, therefore, that it may be known, I shall proceed in order, and speak first of the innocence of infancy, next of the innocence of wisdom, and lastly of the state of heaven in regard to innocence.

277. The innocence of infancy, or of little children, is not genuine innocence, for it exists only in the external form, and not in the internal. Nevertheless we may learn from that what innocence is, for it shines forth from their faces, from some of their gestures, and from their earliest speech, and affects those around them. The reason is, because they have no internal thought; for they do not yet know what is good and evil, nor what is true and false,—and from these, thought is derived. Hence they have no prudence derived from proprium, no determined and deliberate purpose, consequently no end of an evil nature. They have no proprium acquired from the love of self and the world; they attribute nothing to themselves,—regarding all that they have, as received from their parents; they are content and pleased with the few and little things which are given them; they have no anxiety about food and raiment, and none about the future; they do not look to the world, and covet many of its possessions; they love their parents, their nurses, and their little companions, with whom they play innocently; they suffer themselves to be led; they hearken and obey. And because they are in this state, they

receive all they are taught into the life; hence they have becoming manners, without knowing whence they came; hence they have speech, and the rudiment of memory and thought, for the receiving and implanting of which their state of innocence serves as a medium. But this innocence, as was said above, is external, because of the body only, not of the mind;[1] for their mind is not yet formed, because mind is understanding and will, and thought and affection thence derived. I have been told from heaven that infants are especially under the auspices of the Lord, and receive influx from the inmost heaven, where there is a state of innocence; and that the influx passes through their interiors, and in passing, affects them with nothing but innocence; and that hence innocence is exhibited visibly in their faces and some of their gestures, and becomes manifest; and that it is this innocence whereby parents are inmostly affected, and which produces the love that is called storge.

278. The innocence of wisdom is genuine innocence, because it is internal; for it belongs to the mind itself, thus to the will itself and thence to the understanding; and when innocence is in these, there is also wisdom, for wisdom pertains to the will and understanding. Hence it is said in heaven that innocence dwells in wisdom, and that an angel has as much of wisdom as he has of innocence. That such is the case, they confirm by this, that those who are in a state of innocence attribute nothing of good to themselves, but regard all their goods as gifts received, and ascribe them to the Lord; that they wish to be led by Him, and not by themselves; that they love everything which is good, and are delighted with everything which is true, because they know and perceive that to love what is good, thus to will and to do it, is to love the Lord; and to love what is true, is to love their neigh-

---

[1] That the innocence of infants is not true innocence, but that true nnocence dwells in wisdom, n. 1616, 2305, 2306, 3495, 4563, 4797, 5608, 301, 10021. That the good of infancy is not spiritual good, but that it ~ecomes so by the implantation of truth, n. 3504. That nevertheless the good of infancy is a medium by which intelligence is implanted, n. 1616, 3183, 9301, 10110. That man, without the good of innocence infused in infancy, would be a wild beast, n. 3494. That whatever is imbibed in infancy, appears natural, n. 3494.

bor; that they live contented with their own, whether it be little or much, because they know that they receive as much as is profitable for them; little, if little be profitable, and much, if much be profitable; and that they do not themselves know what is best for them, this being known only to the Lord, whose providence in all things contemplates eternal ends. Hence they are not anxious about the future. They call solicitude about the future, care for the morrow, which they say is grief for the loss or non-reception of things which are not necessary for the uses of life. In their intercourse with others they never act from an evil end, but from what is good, just, and sincere. To act from an evil end, they call cunning, which they shun as the poison of a serpent, since it is altogether contrary to innocence. Because they love nothing more than to be led of the Lord, and acknowledge their indebtedness to Him for everything they receive, therefore they are removed from their proprium; and in the degree that they are removed from their proprium, in the same degree the Lord flows-in. Hence it is, that whatever they hear from Him, whether through the medium of the Word or of preaching, they do not store up in the memory, but immediately obey; that is, they will and do it,—the will itself being their memory. These, for the most part, appear simple in the external form, but interiorly they are wise and prudent. These are they who are meant by the Lord when He says, "*Be ye prudent as serpents, and guileless as doves;*" Matt. x. 16. Such is the innocence which is called the innocence of wisdom. Because innocence attributes nothing of good to self, but ascribes all good to the Lord, and because it thus loves to be led by the Lord, and thence is the reception of all good and truth from which wisdom is derived, therefore man was so created, that when an infant he may be in external innocence, and when he becomes old he may be in internal innocence: that by means of the former he may come into the latter, and from the latter return into the former. Wherefore also when man becomes old, he even shrinks in body, and becomes, as it were, an infant again, but a wise infant, thus an angel; for an angel is a wise infant in an eminent sense. Hence it is that, in the Word, an infant signifies one who

is innocent; and an old man, a wise man in whom is innocence.[1]

279. The case is similar with every one who is regenerated,—
regeneration being a re-birth as to the spiritual man. He is first
introduced into the innocence of infancy, which consists in this,
that he knows nothing of truth, and can do nothing of good,
from himself, but only from the Lord; and that he desires and
longs after them, for no other reason than because truth is truth,
and good is good. They are also given him by the Lord, as he
advances in age. He is first led into the knowledge of them,
then from knowledge into intelligence, and finally from intelligence into wisdom,—innocence always accompanying, which
consists, as was said, in the acknowledgment that he knows nothing of truth and can do nothing of good from himself, but
from the Lord. Without this faith and the perception which it
gives, no one can receive anything of heaven. In this principally
consists the innocence of wisdom.

280. Because innocence consists in being led by the Lord and
not by self, therefore all who are in heaven are in innocence; for
all who are there love to be led by the Lord. They know, indeed, that to lead themselves, is to be led by the proprium, and
the proprium consists in loving one's self; and he who loves himself, does not permit another to lead him. Hence it is, that as
far as an angel is in innocence, so far he is in heaven, that is, so
far he is in divine good and divine truth; for to be in these is to be
in heaven. The heavens, therefore, are distinguished according
to innocence. They who are in the ultimate or first heaven, are
in innocence of the first or ultimate degree; they who are in the
middle or second heaven, are in innocence of the second or middle degree; but they who are in the inmost or third heaven, are
in innocence of the third or inmost degree. These last, therefore, are the very innocences of heaven, for they above the rest

[1] That innocence, in the Word, is signified by infants, n. 5608; and also
by sucklings, n. 3183. That an old man signifies a wise man, and, in the
abstract sense, wisdom, n. 3183, 6523. That man is so created, that in
proportion as he verges to old age, he may become as an infant; that
innocence may then be in wisdom, and that he may thus pass into heaven,
and become an angel, n. 3183, 5608.

love to be led by the Lord as little children by their father. Wherefore also they receive the divine truth,—which they hear, either immediately from the Lord or mediately through the Word and preaching,—directly into the will, and do it, and so commit it to life. Hence their wisdom so far exceeds that of the angels of the inferior heavens; (see n. 270, 271). Because these angels are of such a character, therefore they are nearest the Lord, from whom they derive their innocence; and they are also separated from the proprium, so that they live as it were in the Lord. They appear simple in the external form, and to the eyes of the angels of the inferior heavens, as infants, thus very small. And they also appear like those who are not very wise, although they are the wisest of the angels of heaven; for they know that they have nothing of wisdom from themselves, and that to be wise is to acknowledge this; and also, that what they know is as nothing in comparison with what they do not know. To know, acknowledge, and perceive this, they say, is the first step in wisdom. These angels are also naked, because nakedness corresponds to innocence.[1]

281. I have conversed much with the angels concerning innocence, and have been informed that it is the esse of all good, and therefore that good is only so far good as there is innocence in it; consequently that wisdom is only so far wisdom as it partakes of innocence; that it is the same with love, charity, and faith; and hence it is, that no one can enter heaven without innocence; and that this is what is meant by the Lord where He says, "*Suffer the little children to come unto Me, and forbid them not, for of such is the kingdom of the heavens. Verily, I say unto you, whosoever shall not receive the kingdom of the heavens as a little child, shall not enter therein.*" Mark x. 14, 15; Luke xviii. 16, 17. By little children in this passage, and also in other parts of the Word, are meant those who are inno-

---

[1] That all in the inmost heaven are forms of innocence, n. 154, 2736, 3887; and that, therefore, they appear to others as infants, n. 154. That they are also naked, n. 165, 8375, 9960. That nakedness is a sign of innocence, n. 165, 8375. That spirits have a custom of testifying their innocence by putting off their clothes, and presenting themselves naked, n 8375, 9960.

cent.[1] The state of innocence is also described by the Lord in
Matt. vi. 25 to 34, but by pure correspondences. Good is good
only so far as innocence is in it, because all good is from the
Lord, and because innocence consists in the desire to be led by
the Lord. I have also been informed that truth cannot be con
joined with good, and good with truth, except by means of in
nocence. Hence also it is, that an angel is not an angel of heaven unless innocence be in him; for heaven is not in any one
until truth be conjoined with good in him; whence the conjunction of truth and good is called the heavenly marriage, and the
heavenly marriage is heaven. I have been further informed,
that truly conjugial love derives its existence from innocence, because from the conjunction of good and truth in which two
minds,—namely, of husband and wife,—are established; and
that this conjunction, when it descends into a lower sphere, is
exhibited under the form of conjugial love; for conjugial partners,
like their minds, mutually love each other. Hence there is a
playfulness as of infancy and innocence in conjugial love.[2]

282. Because innocence is the very esse of good with the
angels of heaven, it is evident that the divine good proceeding
from the Lord is innocence itself; for it is this good which flows-

---

[1] That every good of love and truth of faith ought to have innocence in
it, that it may be good and true, n. 2526, 2780, 3111, 3994, 6013, 7840, 9262,
10134. That innocence is the essential of what is good and true, n. 2780,
7840. That no one is admitted into heaven unless he has something of
innocence, n. 4797.

[2] That love truly conjugial is innocence, n. 2736. That conjugial love
consists in willing what the other wills, thus mutually and reciprocally, n.
2731. That they who are in conjugial love cohabit together in the inmost
principles of life, n. 2732. That there is a union of two minds, and thus
that from love they are one, n. 10168, 10169. That love truly conjugial
derives its origin and essence from the marriage of good and truth, n.
2728, 2729. Of certain angelic spirits who have a perception whether
there be a conjugial principle, from the idea of the conjunction of good
and of truth, n. 10756. That conjugial love is altogether like the conjunction of good and of truth, n. 1094, 2173, 2429, 2503, 3103, 3132, 3155, 3179,
3180, 4358, 5407, 5835, 9206, 9207, 9495, 9637. That therefore, in the Word,
by marriage is understood the marriage of good and truth, such as is in
heaven, and such as should be in the church, n. 3132, 4434, 4835.

in with the angels, and affects their inmosts, and disposes and fits them to receive all the good of heaven. The case is similar with little children, whose interiors are not only formed by the transflux of innocence from the Lord, but are also continually adapted and disposed to receive the good of heavenly love ; since the good of innocence acts from the inmost, for it is, as was said, the esse of all good. From these considerations it is manifest that all innocence is from the Lord. Hence it is that the Lord in the Word, is called a lamb, for a lamb signifies innocence.[1] Because innocence is the inmost in every good of heaven, therefore also it so affects the mind, that he who has sensible perception of it,—which happens when an angel of the inmost heaven approaches,—seems unable to control himself, and to be affected and as it were transported with such delight, that every delight of the world appears comparatively as nothing. I speak this from experience.

283. All who are in the good of innocence, are affected by innocence ; and affected according to the degree in which they are in that good. But they who are not in the good of innocence, are not affected by it. Wherefore all who are in hell are altogether opposed to innocence. They do not even know what innocence is. Yea, they are of such a nature, that in proportion as any one is innocent, they burn to do him injury. Hence it is that they cannot bear the sight of little children ; as soon as they see them, they are inflamed with a cruel desire to hurt them. From this it was made evident that the proprium of man, and thence the love of self, is opposed to innocence ; for all who are in hell are in the proprium, and thence in the love of self.[2]

---

[1] That a lamb, in the Word, signifies innocence and its good, n. 3994, 10132.

[2] That the proprium of man consists in loving himself more than God, and the world more than heaven, and in making his neighbor of no account in respect to himself; thus that it consists in the love of self and of the world, n. 694, 731, 4317, 5660. That the wicked are altogether opposed to innocence, so that they cannot endure its presence, n. 2126.

THE STATE OF PEACE IN HEAVEN.

284. HE who has not experienced the peace of heaven, can have no conception of the peace which the angels enjoy. Nay, a man, so long as he is in the body, cannot receive the peace of heaven, consequently cannot perceive it, because man's perception is in the natural [degree]. In order to perceive it, he should be of such a character, that as to his thought, he can be elevated and withdrawn from the body, and be kept in the spirit, and then be with the angels. Because the peace of heaven has thus been perceived by me, I am able to describe it; not indeed by words, such as it is absolutely,—because human words are inadequate,—- but only by words such as it is relatively, as compared with that mental repose which those enjoy who are content in God.

285. There are two inmost things of heaven, namely, innocence and peace. They are called the inmost, because they proceed immediately from the Lord. Innocence is that from which every good of heaven is derived, and peace is that from which is derived all the delight of good. Every good has its delight; and both the good and the delight pertain to love; for what is loved is called good, and perceived as delightful. Hence it follows, that those two inmost things, which are innocence and peace, proceed from the Lord's divine love, and affect the angels from the inmost. That innocence is the inmost [principle] of good, may be seen in the chapter immediately preceding, which treats of the state of innocence of the angels of heaven; but that peace is the inmost [principle] of delight derived from the good of innocence, shall now be explained.

286. The origin of peace shall first be declared. Divine peace is in the Lord, existing from the union of the Divine Itself and the Divine Human in Him. The Divine of peace in heaven is from the Lord, existing from the conjunction of Himself with the angels of heaven, and in particular from the conjunction of good and truth in every angel. These are the origins of peace. Whence it may be manifest, that peace in the heavens is the Divine inmostly affecting with blessedness every good there,—yea,

is the source of all the joy of heaven; and that, in its essence, it is the Divine joy of the Lord's divine love, resulting from the conjunction of Himself with heaven and with every one there. This joy—perceived by the Lord in angels, and by angels from the Lord—is peace. Hence by derivation, the angels have all that is blessed, delightful, and happy, or that which is called heavenly joy.[1]

287. Because the origins of peace are from this source, therefore the Lord is called the Prince of peace, and says that peace is from Him, and that in Him is peace. The angels also are called angels of peace, and heaven the habitation of peace; as in the following passages: "*Unto us a child is born, unto us a Son is given, and the government shall be upon his shoulder; and his name shall be called Wonderful, Counsellor, God, Hero, Father of Eternity,* PRINCE OF PEACE; *of the increase of his government and peace there shall be no end.*" Isaiah ix. 5, 6. Jesus said, "PEACE *I leave with you, My* PEACE *I give unto you; not as the world giveth give I unto you.*" John xiv. 27. "*These things have I spoken unto you, that in Me ye may have* PEACE." John xvi. 33. "*Jehovah shall lift up His faces unto thee, and give thee* PEACE." Numb. vi. 26. " THE ANGELS OF PEACE *weep bitterly. The pathways are laid waste.*" Isaiah xxxiii. 7, 8. "*The work of justice shall be* PEACE, *and My people shall dwell in* THE HABITATION OF PEACE." Isaiah xxxii. 17, 18. That Divine and heavenly peace is the peace which is meant in the Word, is also evident from other passages where it is named; as in Isaiah lii. 7; chap. liv. 10; chap. lix. 8; Jerem. xvi. 5; chap. xxv. 37; chap. xxix. 11; Haggai ii. 9; Zech. viii. 12; Psalm xxxvii. 37; and elsewhere. Because peace signifies the Lord and heaven, and also heavenly joy and the delight of good, therefore the salutation in ancient times was, PEACE BE

---

[1] That by peace, in the supreme sense, is meant the Lord,—because peace exists from Him;—and, in the internal sense, heaven, because its inhabitants are in a state of peace, n. 3780, 4681. That peace in the heavens is the Divine inmostly affecting with blessedness every good and truth there, and that it is incomprehensible to man, n. 92, 3780, 5662, 8455, 8665. That divine peace is in good, but not in truth without good, n. 8722.

UNTO YOU. This form has descended to the present day, and was also ratified by the Lord when He said to the disciples whom He sent forth, "*Into whatsoever house ye enter, first say, Peace be to this house; and if the son of peace be there, your peace shall rest upon it.*" Luke x. 5, 6. And the Lord Himself also, when He appeared to the apostles, said, "*Peace be with you.*" John xx. 19, 21, 26. A state of peace is also understood in the Word, wherein Jehovah is said to have *smelled an odor of rest*, as in [the original of] Exod. xxix. 18, 25, 41 ; Levit. i. 9, 13, 17 ; chap. ii. 2, 9 ; chap. vi. 8, 14 ; chap. xxiii. 12, 13, 18 ; Numb. xv. 3, 7, 13 ; chap. xxviii. 6, 8, 13 ; chap. xxix. 2, 6, 8, 13, 36 ; an odor of rest, in the celestial sense, signifies the perception of peace.[1] Since peace signifies the union of the Divine Itself and the Divine Human in the Lord, and the conjunction of the Lord with heaven and the church, and with all in heaven, and also with those in the church who receive Him, therefore the Sabbath was instituted in remembrance of these things, and was named from rest or peace, and was the most holy representative of the church. And therefore the Lord called Himself the Lord of the Sabbath, Matt. xii. 8 ; Mark ii. 27, 28 ; Luke vi. 5.[2]

288. Because the peace of heaven is the Divine inmostly affecting with blessedness the good itself which is with the angels, therefore it does not come to their manifest perception, except by

---

[1] That odor, in the Word, signifies the perceptivity of what is agreeable or disagreeable, according to the quality of the love and the faith, of which it is predicated, n. 3577, 4626, 4628, 4748, 5621, 10292. That an odor of rest, when applied to Jehovah, denotes the perceptivity of peace, n. 925, 10054. That on this account, frankincense, incense, odors in oils and ointments, were made representative, n. 925, 4748, 5621, 10177.

[2] That the sabbath, in the supreme sense, signifies the union of the essential Divine with the Divine Human in the Lord; in the internal sense, the conjunction of the Divine Human of the Lord with heaven and the church; and in general, the conjunction of good and truth, thus the heavenly marriage, n. 8495, 10356, 10730. Hence that to rest on the sabbath day signified a state of that union, because then the Lord had rest, and by it there is peace and salvation in the heavens and on earth ; and, in the respective sense, the conjunction of the Lord with man, because then he has peace and salvation, n. 8494, 8510, 10360, 10367, 10370, 10374, 10668, 10730.

a delight of heart when they are in the good of their life, by a pleasantness when they hear truth which is in agreement with their good, and by a cheerfulness of mind when they perceive their conjunction; nevertheless it flows thence into all the acts and thoughts of their life, and there presents itself as joy even in an external form. But peace as to quality and quantity differs in the heavens according to the innocence of those who are there, because innocence and peace go hand in hand; for, as was said above, innocence is that from which is all the good of heaven, and peace is that from which is all the delight of that good. Hence it is evident that the like things may here be said concerning a state of peace, as were said in the foregoing chapter concerning a state of innocence in the heavens, because innocence and peace are conjoined like good and its delight; for good is perceived by its delight, and delight is known from its good. Such being the case, it is evident that the angels of the inmost or third heaven are in the third or inmost degree of peace, because they are in the third or inmost degree of innocence; and that the angels of the inferior heavens are in a less degree of peace, because in a less degree of innocence; (see above, n. 280). That innocence and peace dwell together like good and its delight, may be seen in the case of little children, who, because they are in innocence, are also in peace; and because they are in peace, therefore they are full of playfulness; but their peace is external, for internal peace, like internal innocence, is not given except in wisdom, and therefore in the conjunction of good and truth,—for this is the origin of wisdom. Heavenly or angelic peace exists also with men who are in wisdom from the conjunction of good and truth, and are thence conscious of content in God; yet while they live in the world, that peace lies stored up in their interiors, but is revealed when they leave the body and enter heaven, for then the interiors are opened.

289. Because divine peace exists from the conjunction of the Lord with heaven, and specifically with every angel from the conjunction of good and truth, therefore when the angels are in a state of love, they are in a state of peace; for then good is conjoined to truth with them. That the states of the angels undergo regular changes may be seen above, n. 154 to 160. The

case is similar with a man while becoming regenerated. When the conjunction of good and truth exists with him, as is the case especially after temptations, he then comes into a state of delight from heavenly peace.[1] This peace may be compared to the morning or dawn in time of spring, when, the night being past, all things of the earth begin to live anew from the rising of the sun, which causes vegetation, refreshed by the dew that descends from heaven, to diffuse its fragrance around,—while the vernal temperature imparts fertility to the ground, and inspires pleasantness into human minds; and this, too, because the morning or dawn in time of spring, corresponds to the state of peace of the angels in heaven; see n. 155.[2]

290. I have also conversed with the angels about peace; and I remarked that it is called peace in the world, when wars and hostilities cease between kingdoms, and when enmity and discord cease among men; and that internal peace is believed to consist in a repose of mind arising from the removal of cares, and especially in tranquility and delight from success in business. But the angels said, that repose of mind, and tranquility and delight, arising from the removal of cares and from success in business, appear to be the constituents of peace, but are not so, except with those who are in heavenly good, since there is no peace except in that good; for peace flows-in from the Lord into the inmost degree of their minds, and from their inmost it descends and flows down into the lower degrees, and produces repose of the rational mind [*mens*], tranquility of the natural mind [*animus*] and joy thence. But they who are in evil have no peace.[3] There appears, indeed, something like rest, tranquility, and delight, when things succeed according to their wishes, but it is external

---

[1] That the conjunction of good and truth with man who is regenerating, is effected in a state of peace, n. 3696, 8517.

[2] That the state of peace in the heavens is like the state of day-dawn and of spring on earth, n. 1726, 2780, 5662.

[3] That the cupidities which originate in the love of self and of the world, entirely take away peace, n. 3170, 5662. That some make peace to consist in restlessness and in such things as are contrary to peace, n. 5662. That there can be no peace, unless the cupidities of evil are removed, n. 5662.

and not internal; for internally they burn with enmity, hatred, revenge, cruelty, and many other evil lusts, into which their external mind also rushes,—bursting forth into violence if unrestrained by fear,—the moment they see any one who is not favorable to them. And hence it is that their delight dwells in insanity, but the delight of those who are in good dwells in wisdom. The difference is like that between hell and heaven.

THE CONJUNCTION OF HEAVEN WITH THE HUMAN RACE.

291. It is known in the church that all good is from God, and none from man, and that no one therefore ought to ascribe any good to himself; and it is also known that evil is from the devil. Hence it is that they who speak from the doctrine of the church, say of those who act well, and also of those who speak and preach piously, that they are led of God; but the contrary of those who do evil and speak impiously. This would not be so, unless man had conjunction with heaven and conjunction with hell; and unless those conjunctions were with his will and understanding,—for from these the body acts and the mouth speaks. What that conjunction is shall now be told.

292. With every man there are good spirits and evil spirits. By means of the good spirits man has conjunction with heaven, and by means of the evil spirits, with hell. Those spirits are in the world of spirits, which is in the midst between heaven and hell,—which world will be particularly treated of hereafter. When those spirits come to a man, they enter into all his memory, and thence into all his thought; evil spirits, into those things of the memory and thought which are evil, but good spirits, into those things of the memory and thought which are good. The spirits are not at all aware that they are with the man; but when they are with him, they believe that all the things which belong to the man's memory and thought are their own; neither do they see the man, because the things in our solar world do not fall

within the compass of their vision.[1] The greatest care is exercised by the Lord to prevent spirits from knowing that they are with man; for if they knew it, they would speak with him, and then evil spirits would destroy him; for evil spirits, because they are conjoined with hell, desire nothing more than to destroy man, not only as to his soul, that is, as to his faith and love, but even as to his body. It is otherwise when they do not speak with man; then they are not aware that what they think, and also what they speak among themselves, is from him,—for they even speak from man, when conversing among themselves,—but believe that the things which they speak are their own, and every one esteems and loves his own. Thus spirits are obliged to love and esteem man, although they are not aware of it. That there is such conjunction of spirits with man, has been made so thoroughly known to me by the continual experience of many years, that there is nothing of which I am more certain.

293. Spirits who communicate with hell are also adjoined to man, because man is born into evils of every kind, and hence his first life is altogether from them; wherefore, unless spirits of a quality similar to his own were adjoined to him, he could not live, yea, could not be withdrawn from his evils and be reformed. Wherefore he is held in his own life by evil spirits, and withheld from it by good spirits. By means of both, he is also in equilibrium; and because he is in equilibrium he is in his freedom, and can be withdrawn from evils and inclined to good; and good can also be implanted in him, which could by no means be done unless he were in freedom; nor could he be endowed with freedom unless spirits from hell acted on one side, and spirits from heaven on the other, and man were in the midst. It has also been shown me that man, so far as he partakes of what is hereditary,

---

[1] That angels and spirits are attendant on every man, and that by them man has communication with the spiritual world, n. 697, 2796, 2886, 2887, 4047, 4048, 5846 to 5866, 5976 to 5993. That man without spirits attendant on him cannot live, n. 5993. That man does not appear to spirits, neither do spirits appear to man, n. 5862. That spirits can see nothing which is in our solar world belonging to man, except what belongs to him with whom they speak, n. 1880

and thence of self, would have no life if he were not permitted to be in evil ; and none also if he were not in freedom ; and moreover, that he cannot be compelled to good ; that what is induced by compulsion does not adhere ; as also that the good which man receives in freedom is implanted in his will, and becomes as it were his own ;[1] and that hence man has communication with hell, and also with heaven.

294. The nature of the communication of heaven with good spirits, and of hell with evil spirits, and thence of the conjunction of heaven and hell with man, shall also be made known. All the spirits who are in the world of spirits, have communication with heaven or with hell ; the evil with hell, and the good with heaven. Heaven is distinguished into societies ; and so is hell. Every spirit belongs to some society, and subsists by influx thence ; thus he acts as one with it. Hence it is, that as man is conjoined with spirits, so he is conjoined with heaven or with hell, and indeed with that society there in which he is as to his affection or as to his love : for all the societies of heaven are distinct, according to the affections of good and truth ; and all the societies of hell, according to the affections of evil and the false. Concerning the societies of heaven, see above, n. 41 to 45, also n. 148 to 151.

295. The spirits adjoined to a man are of a like quality with the man himself, as to affection or as to love. But good spirits are adjoined to him by the Lord, whereas evil spirits are invited by the man himself. His attendant spirits, however, are changed according to the changes of his affections. Hence one class attend him in infancy, another in childhood, another in youth

---

That all freedom is of love and affection, since what a man loves that he does freely, n. 2870, 3158, 8907, 8990, 9585, 9591. Since freedom is of love, it is therefore of man's life, n. 2873. That nothing appears as man's own but what is from freedom, n. 2880. That man ought to have freedom, to be capable of being reformed, n. 1937, 1947, 2876, 2881, 3145, 3146, 3158, 4031, 8700. That otherwise the love of good and of truth cannot be implanted in man, and be appropriated apparently as his own, n. 2877, 2879, 2880, 2888, 8700. That nothing is conjoined to man which is of compulsion, n. 2875, 8700. That if man could be reformed by compulsion, all would be reformed, n. 2881. That what is of compulsion in reformation is hurtful, n. 4031. What states of compulsion are, n. 8392.

and manhood, and another in old age. Spirits are present in infancy, who are characterized by innocence, and therefore communicate with the heaven of innocence, which is the inmost or third heaven; those are present in childhood, who are distinguished by the affection of knowing, and therefore communicate with the ultimate or first heaven; those are present in youth and manhood who are in the affection of truth and good, and thence in intelligence, and therefore communicate with the second or middle heaven; but those are present in old age who are in wisdom and innocence, and therefore communicate with the inmost or third heaven. But this adjunction is effected by the Lord with those who are capable of being reformed and regenerated; it is otherwise, however, with those who are not. Yet good spirits are also adjoined to these latter, in order that, through their influence, they may be withheld from evil as much as possible; but their immediate conjunction is with evil spirits who communicate with hell, and who are of like character with themselves. If they be lovers of themselves, or lovers of gain, or lovers of revenge, or lovers of adultery, similar spirits are present, and as it were dwell in their evil affections; and as far as man cannot be restrained from evil by good spirits, so far evil spirits inflame him; and as far as the affection rules, so far they adhere to him and do not recede. Thus a wicked man is conjoined with hell, and a good man with heaven.

296. Man is governed by spirits from the Lord, because he is not in the order of heaven; for he is born into the evils of hell, thus into a state altogether contrary to divine order. Wherefore he must be brought back into order; and this can only be effected by means of spirits. It would be otherwise if man were born into good, which is according to the order of heaven; then he would not be governed of the Lord by spirits, but by order itself, thus by common influx. Man is governed by this influx as to those things which proceed from his thought and will into act, thus as to his words and actions; for both the latter and the former flow according to natural order; with these, therefore, the spirits who are adjoined to man have nothing in common. Animals likewise are governed by influx from the spiritual world, because they are in the order of their life; nor have they been

24

able to pervert and destroy it, because they have not the rational faculty.[1] What the distinction is between men and beasts, may be seen above, n. 39.

297. As to what further concerns the conjunction of heaven with the human race, it is to be remarked that the Lord Himself flows-in with every man, according to the order of heaven,—both into his inmosts and into his ultimates,—and disposes him to receive heaven, and governs his ultimates from his inmosts, and at the same time his inmosts from his ultimates, and thus holds in connection everything that belongs to him. This influx of the Lord is called immediate influx; but the other influx, which is effected through the medium of spirits, is called mediate influx. The latter subsists by means of the former. Immediate influx, which is of the Lord Himself, is from His Divine Human into the will of man, and through the will into his understanding; thus into the good of man, and through his good into his truth, or, what is the same, into his love, and through his love into his faith; but not the reverse, still less into faith without love, or into truth without good, or into the understanding which is not in agreement with the will. This divine influx is perpetual, and is received in good by the good, but not by the evil; these either reject it, or suffocate it, or pervert it. Hence their life is an evil life, which, in the spiritual sense, is death.[2]

---

[1] That the distinction between men and beasts is, that men are capable of being elevated by the Lord to Himself; of thinking about the Divine Being; of loving Him, and thus of being conjoined to the Lord, whence they have eternal life: but that it is otherwise with beasts, n. 4525, 6323, 9231. That beasts are in the order of their life, and that, therefore, they are born into things suitable to their nature; but that man is not born into the order of his life, and that, therefore, he must be brought into it by things intellectual, n. 637, 5850, 6323. That according to general influx, thought falls into speech with man, and will into gestures, n. 5862, 5990, 6192, 6211. Concerning the general influx of the spiritual world into the lives of beasts, n. 1633, 3646.

[2] That there is immediate influx from the Lord, and also a mediate influx through the spiritual world, n. 6063, 6307, 6472, 9682, 9683. That the immediate influx of the Lord is into the most minute of all things, n. 6058, 6474 to 6478, 8717, 8728. That the Lord flows into first and at the same time into last principles, and in what manner, n. 5147, 5150, 6473.

298. The spirits who are with man, as well those who are conjoined with heaven as those who are conjoined with hell, never flow into man from their own memory and consequent thought,—for in that case, man would know no otherwise than that their thoughts were his own, as may be seen above, n. 256. But still, through them, there flows into man from heaven, ar affection which is of the love of good and truth, and from hell, an affection which is of the love of evil and the false. So far, therefore, as the affection of man agrees with that which flows-in, he receives it in his own thought,—for the interior thought of man is in perfect agreement with his affection or love ; but so far as it does not agree, he does not receive it. Since, therefore, thought is not infused into man by spirits, but only the affection of good and the affection of evil, it is evident that man has the power of choice, because he has freedom ; thus that he can in thought receive good, and reject evil, for he knows what is good and what is evil from the Word. What he receives in thought from affection, is also appropriated to him ; but what he does not receive in thought from affection, is not appropriated to him. From these observations the nature of the influx into man of good from heaven, and of evil from hell, may be clearly seen.

299. It has also been granted me to know the origin of anxiety, grief of mind, and interior sadness, called melancholy, wherewith man is afflicted. There are certain spirits who are not yet in conjunction with hell, because they are as yet in their first state,—concerning whom hereafter, when treating of the world of spirits. These love undigested and malignant substances, such as meats in a state of corruption in the stomach ; wherefore they are present where there are such things with man, because these are

---

7004, 7007, 7270. That the influx of the Lord is into the good in man, and through good into truth, and not *vice versa*, n. 5482, 5649, 6027, 8685, 9701, 10153. That the life which flows-in from the Lord varies according to the state of man and according to the quality of his reception, n. 2888, 5986, 6472, 7343. That the good which flows-in from the Lord is turned into evil with the wicked, and truth into the false; from experience, n. 3607, 4632. That the good, and the truth thence derived, which continually flows-in from the Lord, is received so far as evil and the false thence derived do not oppose, n. 2411, 3142, 3147, 5828.

delightful to them, and there they converse with one another from their own evil affection. The affection of their discourse flows thence into man; and if it be contrary to his affection, it becomes in him sadness and melancholy anxiety; but if it be agreeable to his affection, it becomes in him gladness and cheerfulness. These spirits appear near the stomach, some to the left of it, some to the right, some beneath, some above, also nearer and more remote, thus variously, according to the quality of, the affections whereby they are distinguished. That this is what produces anxiety of mind, has been made known to me and proved by much experience; for I have seen such spirits, heard them, felt the anxieties occasioned by them, and conversed with them. They have been driven away, and the anxiety ceased; they have returned, and the anxiety returned; and I have perceived its increase and decrease according to their approach and removal. Hence was made manifest to me the origin of the persuasion entertained by some, who do not know what conscience is,—because they have none themselves,—that its pangs arise from a disordered stomach.[1]

300. The conjunction of heaven with man is not like that of one man with another, but is a conjunction with the interiors which belong to his mind, thus with his spiritual or internal man. But there is a conjunction with his natural or external man by correspondences, which conjunction will be spoken of in the following chapter, where the conjunction of heaven with man by the Word is treated of.

301. That the conjunction of heaven with the human race, and

---

[1] That they who have no conscience do not know what conscience is, n. 7490, 9121. That there are some who laugh at conscience when they hear what it is, n. 7217. That some believe that conscience is nothing; some that it is something natural, which is sad and mournful, arising either from causes in the body, or from causes in the world; and others that it is something peculiar to the vulgar, and occasioned by religion, n. 950. That there is a true conscience, a spurious conscience, and a false conscience, n. 1033. That pain of conscience is anxiety of mind on account of what is unjust, insincere, and in any respect evil, which man believes to be contrary to God, and to the good of his neighbor, n. 7217. That they have conscience who are in love to God and charity toward the neighbor, but not they who are not so principled, n. 831, 965, 2380, 7490.

of the human race with heaven, is such that one subsists from the other, will also be shown in the next chapter.

302. I have conversed with the angels concerning the conjunction of heaven with the human race; and I remarked that the man of the church says, indeed, that all good is from God, and that angels are present with man; but that still few believe that they are conjoined to him, and still less that they are in his thought and affection. To this the angels replied, that they knew there was such a belief, and even such a mode of speaking in the world, and especially within the church, (at which they wondered), where nevertheless is the Word, which teaches them concerning heaven, and concerning its conjunction with man; when yet there exists such conjunction, that man were incapable of the slightest thought unless spirits were adjoined to him, and that his spiritual life depends on this conjunction. They said that the cause of the ignorance on this subject is, that man supposes he lives from himself, without connection with the First Esse of life, and that he is not aware that he has such connection through the heavens; when yet, if that connection were dissolved, he would instantly fall down dead. If man believed,—what is really true,—that all good is from the Lord, and all evil from hell, he then would not take merit to himself on account of his good, nor would evil be imputed to him; for then, in every good thought and act he would look to the Lord, and every evil which flows-in would be rejected to hell whence it came. But because man does not believe in any influx from heaven and from hell, and consequently supposes that all things which he thinks and wills are in himself, and thence from himself, he appropriates evil to himself, and the good which flows-in he defiles with merit.

THE CONJUNCTION OF HEAVEN WITH MAN BY THE WORD.

303. THEY who think from interior reason can see that there is a connection of all things by intermediates with the First, and that whatever is not in connection therewith, drops out of existence; for they know, when they reflect, that nothing can subsist from itself, but everything from what is prior to itself, thus from the First; and that the connection of anything with what is prior to itself, is like that of an effect with its efficient cause; for when the efficient cause is taken away from its effect, the effect is dissolved and destroyed. Since the learned have so thought, therefore they have seen and affirmed that subsistence is perpetual existence; thus that all things perpetually exist, that is, subsist from the First, because from Him they originally existed. But what is the connection of everything with what is prior to itself, thus with the First, from Whom are all things, cannot be explained in a few words, because it is various and diverse; only in general, that there is a connection of the natural world with the spiritual world, and that hence there is a correspondence of all things in the natural world with all things in the spiritual world,—concerning which correspondence, see n. 103 to 115; also that there is a connection, and consequent correspondence, of all things of man with all things of heaven; concerning which also above, n. 87 to 102.

304. Man was so created, that he has connection and conjunction with the Lord, but with the angels of heaven he has only consociation. He has not conjunction with the angels, but only consociation, because from creation he is like an angel as to his interiors which belong to the mind; for the will and understanding of man are like the will and understanding of an angel. Hence it is that after his decease, if he had lived according to divine order, he becomes an angel, and receives wisdom similar to that of the angels. When, therefore, the conjunction of man with heaven is spoken of, his conjunction with the Lord and his consociation with the angels are meant; for heaven is not heaven

from anything proper to the angels, but from the Divine of the Lord. (That the Divine of the Lord makes heaven, may be seen above, n. 7 to 22). Man, however, has something more than the angels, in that he is not only in the spiritual world as to his interiors, but also at the same time in the natural world as to his exteriors. His exteriors, which are in the natural world, are all things which belong to his natural or external memory, and thence are subjects of thought and imagination. These in general are knowledges and sciences, with their delights and pleasures, so far as they savor of the world; also various pleasures which belong to the sensual principles of the body, together with the senses themselves, the speech, and actions. All these things are the ultimates also in which the divine influx of the Lord closes ; for it does not stop in the middle, but proceeds to its ultimates. From these facts it is evident that the ultimate of divine order is in man ; and that, because he is the ultimate, he is also its basis and foundation. Because the divine influx of the Lord does not stop in the middle, but proceeds to its ultimates, as was said, and because the medium [or middle] through which it passes, is the angelic heaven, and the ultimate is in man, and because nothing unconnected can exist, it follows that the connection and conjunction of heaven with the human race are such, that the one subsists from the other ; and that the human race without heaven, would be like a chain without any hook ; and that heaven without the human race, would be like a house without a foundation.[1]

---

[1] That nothing exists from itself, but that everything exists from what is prior to itself, and thus all things from the First; that they also subsist from Him who gave them existence; and that to subsist is to exist perpetually, n. 2886, 2888, 3627, 3628, 3648, 4523, 4524, 6040, 6056. That divine order does not stop in the middle, but proceeds to ultimates, and there terminates; that the ultimate is man, and that divine order therefore terminates in man, n. 634, (2853), 3632, 5897. (6239), 6451, 6465, 9216, (9217), 9824, 9828, 9836, 9905, 10044, 10329, 10335, 10548. That interior things flow by successive order into external things, even to the extreme or ultimate, and that there, also, they exist and subsist, n. 634, 6239, 6465, 9216, 9217. That interior things exist and subsist in what is ultimate in simultaneous order, concerning which, n. 5897, 6451, 8603, 10099. That hence all interior things are held together in connection from the First by the last, n. 9828. That hence the first and the last signify all things in

305. But because man, through the love of self and the world, has broken this connection with heaven, by averting his interiors therefrom and turning them to the world and himself, and has thus withdrawn himself so as no longer to serve as a basis and foundation for heaven, therefore a medium has been provided by the Lord to supply the place of such basis and foundation, and also to serve for the conjunction of heaven with man. This medium is the Word. But how the Word serves for such a medium, has been shown in many passages in the ARCANA CŒLESTIA, all of which may be seen collected together in the little work, concerning THE WHITE HORSE mentioned in the Apocalypse; and also in the APPENDIX to the HEAVENLY DOCTRINE, some passages from which are here adduced in the notes below.[1]

306. I have been informed from heaven, that the most ancient

---

general, and every particular thing, thus the whole, n. 10044, 10329, 10335, and that hence there is strength and power in ultimates, n. 9836.

[1] That the Word in its literal sense is natural, n. 8783, because the natural is the ultimate principle, in which spiritual and celestial things, which are things interior, close, and on which they subsist, as a house upon its foundation, n. 9430, 9433, 9824, 10044, 10436. That the Word, in order to be of such a quality, is written by pure correspondences, n. 1403, 1408, 1409, 1540, (1615), 1659, 1709, 1783, 8615, 10687. That because the Word consists of pure correspondences in the literal sense, it is the continent of the spiritual and celestial sense, n. 9407. That it is accommodated both to men and angels at the same time, n. 1767 to 1772, 1887, 2143, 2157, 2275, 2333, 2395, 2540, 2541, 2547, 2553, 7381, 8862, 10322. That it is the medium for uniting heaven and earth, n. 2310, 2495, 9212, 9216, 9357, 9396, 10375. That the conjunction of the Lord with man is effected by the Word, through the medium of the internal sense, n. 10375. That by the whole Word and by every part of it there is conjunction, and that hence the Word is wonderful above all other writings, n. 10632, 10633, 10634. That since the Word was written, the Lord speaks by it to men, n. 10290. That the church, where the Word is, and where the Lord is known by the Word, when compared with those who are out of the church, and have not the Word, and know not the Lord, is like the heart and lungs in man with respect to the other parts of the body, which live from them as from the fountains of their life, n. 637, 931, 2054, 2853. That the universal church on earth is as one man before the Lord, n. 7396, 9276. Hence it is that unless there was a church on the earth where the Word is, and where the Lord is known by the Word, the human race here would perish, n. 468, 637, 931, 4545, 10452.

people had immediate revelation, since their interiors were turned toward heaven; and that thence there was conjunction of the Lord with the human race at that time. But after their times, that there was not such immediate revelation, but mediate by correspondences; for all the divine worship of the people who succeeded the most ancient, consisted of correspondences; from which circumstance the churches of that period were called representative churches. For the nature of correspondence and representation was at that time well known. They knew that all things which exist on earth corresponded to the spiritual things in heaven and in the church; or, what is the same, represented them; wherefore the natural things which constituted the externals of their worship, served them as mediums for thinking spiritually, thus in unison with the angels. After the science of correspondences and representations was obliterated, then the Word was written, in which all the words and sentences are correspondences; thus they contain a spiritual or internal sense, which the angels understand. Wherefore when man reads the Word, and understands it according to the literal or external sense, the angels understand it according to the internal or spiritual sense; for all the thought of angels is spiritual, but the thought of man is natural. Spiritual and natural thought indeed appear different, but still they are one, because they correspond. Hence it is, that after man removed himself from heaven, and severed the bond of connection therewith, a medium of conjunction by means of the Word was provided by the Lord.

307. How heaven is conjoined with man by means of the Word, I will illustrate by citing a few passages. The New Jerusalem is described in the Apocalypse in these words: *"I saw a new heaven and a new earth; and the former heaven and the former earth had passed away. And I saw the holy city Jerusalem coming down from God out of heaven.—The city was four square, its length as great as its breadth; and the angel measured the city with a reed, twelve thousand furlongs. The length and the breadth and the hight of it were equal; and he measured the wall thereof, a hundred and forty-four cubits, the measure of a man, that is, of the angel. The building of the wall was of jasper; but the city itself was*

25   I

pure gold, and like unto pure glass; and the foundations of the wall were adorned with every precious stone.—The twelve gates were twelve pearls;—and the street of the city was pure gold as it were transparent glass." chap. xxi. 1, 2, 16, [19, 21]. When a man reads these words, he understands them merely according to the sense of the letter, which is, that the visible heaven and earth are to perish, and a new heaven to be created; and that the holy city Jerusalem is to descend upon the new earth, and that it is to be, in all its dimensions, according to this description. But the angels attendant on man understand these things in a manner altogether different,—for they understand spiritually what man understands naturally. By the new heaven and new earth they understand a new church. By the city Jerusalem coming down from God out of heaven, they understand its heavenly doctrine revealed by the Lord. By its length, breadth, and hight, which are equal,—each being twelve thousand furlongs,—they understand all the goods and truths of that doctrine in the complex. By its wall, they understand the truths which protect it. By the measure of the wall, a hundred and forty-four cubits, which is the measure of a man, that is, of the angel, they understand all those protecting truths in the complex, and their quality. By its twelve gates, which were of pearls, they understand the truths which introduce. Pearls also signify such truths. By the foundations of the wall, which were of precious stones, they understand the knowledges on which that doctrine is founded. By the gold like unto clear glass, of which the city and its street consisted, they understand the good of love, from which the doctrine with its truths is transparent. Thus do the angels understand all those things,—in a manner quite different from man. The natural ideas of man thus pass into spiritual ideas with the angels, without their knowing anything of the literal sense of the Word,—as of a new heaven and a new earth, of a new city Jerusalem, of its wall, of the foundations of the wall, and of its dimensions. Nevertheless the thoughts of the angels make one with the thoughts of man, because they correspond. They make one almost like the words of a speaker, and the understanding of them by a hearer who pays no attention to the words, but only to their meaning. From this it may be seen how heaven is conjoined with man by means of the Word.

To take another example from the Word: "*In that day there shall be a path from Egypt to Assyria; and the Assyrian shall come into Egypt, and the Egyptian into Assyria; and the Egyptians shall serve the Assyrians. In that day Israel shall be a third to Egypt and Assyria, a blessing in the midst of the land, which Jehovah of hosts shall bless, saying, Blessed be my people, the Egyptians, and the Assyrian, the work of my hands, and Israel mine inheritance.*" (Isa. xix. 23, 24, 25). How man thinks and how the angels think when these words are read, may be evident from the literal sense of the Word, and from its internal sense. Man thinks, from the sense of the letter, that the Egyptians and Assyrians are to be converted to God, and accepted, and that they are to make one with the Israelitish nation; but the angels think, according to the internal sense, of the man of the spiritual church, who is there described in that sense, whose spiritual mind is Israel, whose natural mind is the Egyptian, and whose rational mind, which is the intermediate, is the Assyrian.[1] Still the literal sense and spiritual sense are one, because they correspond; wherefore when the angels think thus spiritually, and man thus naturally, they are conjoined almost like soul and body. The internal sense of the Word is also its soul, and the literal sense is its body. Such is the Word throughout. Hence it is evident that it is a medium of the conjunction of heaven with man, and that its literal sense serves as a basis and foundation.

308. Those who are out of the church and have not the Word, are likewise conjoined to heaven by means of the Word; for the church of the Lord is universal, and with all who acknowledge a Divine and live in charity. These also are instructed by the

---

[1] That Egypt and Egyptian, in the Word, signify the natural principle, and the scientific thence derived, n. 4967, 5079, 5080, 5095, 5160, 5799, 6015, 6147, 6252, 7355, 7648, 9391, 9340. That Assyria signifies the rational principle, n. 119, 1186. That Israel signifies the spiritual principle, n. 5414, 5801, 5803, 5806, 5812, 5817, 5819, 5826, 5833, 5879, 5951, 6426, 6637, 6862, 6868, 7035, 7062, 7198, 7201, 7215, 7223, 7957, 8234, 8805, 9340.

angels after their decease, and receive divine truths.[1]—On this
subject see below in the chapter that treats of the Gentiles.
The universal church on earth is as one man in the sight of the
Lord, just as heaven is, (concerning which above, n. 59 to 72.)
But the church where the Word is, and where the Lord through
it is known, is as the heart and lungs in that man.   That all the
viscera and members of the whole body derive life from the
heart and lungs by various derivations, is well known ; so likewise that part of the human race, which is without the church
where the Word is, and which constitutes the members of that
man, derives its life [from the church which is in possession of
the Word].   The conjunction of heaven by the Word with those
who are remote from the church, may also be compared to light,
which is propagated from a centre in every direction.   There is
divine light in the Word, and there the Lord with heaven is present ; and in consequence of His presence, even those who are
far off are in the enjoyment of light.   It would be otherwise if
there were no Word.   These truths may receive further elucida-
tion from what was shown above concerning the form of heaven,
according to which are the consociations and communications
there.   But this arcanum is comprehensible to those who are in
spiritual light, yet not to those who are only in natural light ; for
the former see innumerable things which are invisible to the latter, or seen by them as one obscure thing.

309. If such a Word had not been given on this earth, its inhabitants would have been separated from heaven ; and if separated from heaven, they would have been no longer rational, for
the human rational exists from the influx of the light of heaven.
The men of this earth are also incapable of receiving immediate

---

[1] That the church specifically exists where the Word is, and where the
Lord is known by the Word, and thus where divine truths from heaven
are revealed, n. 3857, 10761.   That the church of the Lord is with all in
the universal terrestrial globe, who live in good according to the principles of their religion, n. 3263, 6637, 10765.   That all in every country, who
live in good according to the principles of their religion, and acknowledge
a Divine Being, are accepted of the Lord, n. 2589 to 2604, 2861, 2863, 3263,
4190, 4197, 6700, 9256; and also all infants wherever they are born, n. 2289
to 2309, 4792.

revelation, and of being instructed thereby concerning divine truths, like the inhabitants of other earths, concerning whom I have treated in a separate work; for the former are more immersed in worldly things, thus in things external, than the latter, and internal things are what receive revelation; if external things received it, [*i. e.* if the truth were revealed to those who are in externals] it would not be understood. That such is the character of the men of this earth, appears manifestly from those within the church, who, although they know from the Word about heaven, and hell, and the life after death, still deny them in their hearts; among whom also are some who have acquired the reputation of learning in an eminent degree, and who might therefore be expected to be wiser than others.

310. I have sometimes conversed with the angels concerning the Word, and told them that some despise it on account of its simple style; that nothing whatever is known concerning its internal sense; and that hence it is not believed that such exalted wisdom lies concealed in it. The angels replied, that the style of the Word, although it appears simple in the sense of the letter, is still such, that nothing can by any means be compared to it in point of excellence; since divine wisdom lies concealed not only in all the meaning there, but even in every single word; and that in heaven, that wisdom is manifest as the light. They meant to say that it is the light of heaven, because it is divine truth; for divine truth in heaven emits light (see above, n. 132). They said also, that without such a Word there would be no heavenly light with the men of our earth, and therefore no conjunction of heaven with them; for that conjunction exists in proportion as the light of heaven is present with man; and in the same proportion also divine truth is revealed to him through the Word. Man does not know that that conjunction is effected by the spiritual sense of the Word corresponding with its natural sense, because the man of this earth knows nothing concerning the spiritual thought and speech of the angels, and that it differs from the natural thought and speech of men; and unless this be known, it is impossible to know what the internal sense is, and that through it, therefore, such conjunction can be effected. They said likewise, that if man were aware of the existence of such a

sense, and, when reading the Word, would think from some knowledge of it, he would come into interior wisdom, and into a still closer conjunction with heaven, since by means of it he would enter into ideas similar to those of the angels.

HEAVEN AND HELL ARE FROM THE HUMAN RACE.

311. It is altogether unknown in the Christian world that heaven and hell are from the human race; for it is believed that angels were created from the beginning, and that this was the origin of heaven; and that the devil or satan was an angel of light, but because he became rebellious, he was cast down with his crew; and that this was the origin of hell. The angels wonder very much that such a belief should prevail in the Christian world, and still more that nothing whatever is known about heaven, when yet it is a primary point of doctrine in the church; and because such ignorance prevails, they rejoiced in heart that it has pleased the Lord at this time to reveal to mankind many things respecting heaven, and also respecting hell; and thereby as far as possible to dispel the darkness which is every day increasing, because the church has come to its end. Wherefore they desire me to declare positively from their mouths, that there is not a single angel in the universal heaven who was originally created such, nor any devil in hell who was created an angel of light and cast down; but that all, both in heaven and in hell, are from the human race; in heaven, those who lived in the world in heavenly love and faith; in hell, those who lived in infernal love and faith; and that hell in the whole complex is what is called the devil and satan,—*devil* being the term used to denote the hell at the back which is inhabited by those called evil genii, and *satan* the term used to denote the hell in front, which is inhabited by those called evil spirits.[1] The character of each of these hells will be

---

[1] That the hells taken together, or the infernals taken together, are

made known hereafter. The angels further said that the Christian world had conceived such an idea respecting the inhabitants of heaven and hell from certain passages of the Word, understood merely according to the sense of the letter, and not illustrated by genuine doctrine from the Word; when yet the literal sense of the Word, not illustrated by genuine doctrine, perplexes the mind in regard to many things,—whence come ignorance, heresies, and errors.[1]

312. Another reason why the man of the church so believes is, that he supposes no one can go to heaven or hell before the time of the last judgment, when,—agreeably to the conception he has formed of that event,—all visible things are to perish and new ones to be created, and the soul then to return into its body, and man again to live as a man by virtue of that re-union. This belief involves the other, that angels were created such from the beginning; for it cannot be believed that heaven and hell are from the human race, while it is imagined that no man can enter either until the end of the world. But that man may be convinced that it is not so, I have been permitted to hold intercourse with the angels, and also to converse with the inhabitants of hell; and this now for many years,—sometimes continually from morning to evening,—and thus to be informed concerning heaven and hell. And this experience has been granted me in order that the man of the church may no longer continue in his erroneous belief concerning a resurrection at the day of judgment, and concerning the state of the soul in the meantime, and

called the devil and satan, n. 694. That they who have been devils in the world become devils after death, n. 968.

[1] That the doctrine of the church must be derived from the Word, n. 3464, 5402. 5432. 10763, 10764. That the Word without doctrine is not understood, n. 9025, 9409, 9424, 9430, 10324. 10431, 10582. That true doctrine is a lamp to those who read the Word, n. 10400. That genuine doctrine must be had from those who are in illustration from the Lord, n. 2510, 2516, 2519, 9424, 10105. That they who are in the sense of the letter without doctrine, never attain any understanding respecting divine truths, n. 9409, 9410, 10582. And that they are led away into many errors, n. 10431. What is the difference between those who teach and learn from the doctrine of the church derived from the Word, and those who teach and learn from the literal sense alone, n. 9025.

also concerning angels and the devil; which belief, because it is a belief of what is false, involves the mind in darkness; and, with those who think on these subjects from self-intelligence, it induces doubt, and at length denial. For they say in their hearts, how can so vast a heaven, with so many myriads of stars, and with the sun and moon, be destroyed and dissipated? And how can the stars fall from heaven to the earth, when yet they are larger than the earth? And how can bodies eaten up by worms, wasted by corruption, and scattered to all the winds, be gathered together again and re-united with their souls? Where is the soul in the mean time, and what sort of thing can it be when deprived of the sensibility which it had in the body? Besides many similar things, which, because they are incomprehensible, cannot become objects of faith, and with many destroy all belief in the life of the soul after death, and in heaven and hell, and along with these, everything else which the church believes. That they have destroyed it, is evident from those who say, Who has ever come to us from heaven, and declared what heaven is? What is hell,—or is there any? What can this mean, that man is to be tormented in everlasting fire? What is the day of judgment? Has it not been expected in vain for ages? Besides other things, which imply a denial of all. Lest, therefore, those who think in this manner,—as many do, who, on account of their worldly wisdom are esteemed erudite and learned,—should any longer trouble and seduce the simple in faith and heart, and induce infernal darkness respecting God, heaven, eternal life, and other things which depend on these, the interiors which are of my spirit have been opened by the Lord, and thus I have been permitted to converse with all whom I have ever known in the life of the body,—after their decease; with some for days, with some for months, and with some for a year; and with others also,—so many that I should not exaggerate were I to say a hundred thousand,—of whom many were in the heavens, and many in the hells. I have also conversed with some two days after their decease, and have told them that preparations were now being made for their interment. They replied, that their friends did well to reject that which had served them for a body and its uses in the world; and they wished me to say, that they were not dead but alive, being men now just the same as before, and that they had only migrated from one world to another; and that they were not conscious of having lost any thing, since they were in a body and in the possession of bodily senses as before, and in the enjoyment of understanding and will as before; and that they had thoughts, affections, sensations, and desires, similar to those which they had in the world. Most of those recently deceased, when they saw that they were still alive and men as before, and in a similar state, (for after death every one's state of life is at first such as it had been in the world, but that is successively changed either into heaven or into hell), were affected with new joy at being alive, and declared that they had not believed this. But they wondered very much that they should have lived in such ignorance and blindness concerning the state of their life after death; and especially that the man of the church should be in such ignorance and blindness,—who yet, above all others in the whole world, might be in the enjoyment of light on these subjects.[1] They then first discovered the cause of that blindness and ignorance, which is, that external things, which are those that relate to the world and the body, have occupied and filled their minds to such a degree as to render them incapable of being elevated into the light of heaven, and of having any regard for the things of the church beyond its doctrinals; for when corporeal and worldly things are loved as they are at the

---

[1] That in Christendom, at this day, few believe that man rises again immediately after death, preface to chap. xvi. Gen. and n. 4622, 10758; but believe that he will rise again at the time of the last judgment, when the visible world will perish, n. 10595. The reason that it is so believed, n. 10595, 10758. That nevertheless man rises again immediately after death, and that then he is a man as to all and single things, n. 4527, 5006, 5078, 8939, 8991, 10594, 10758. That the soul which lives after death is the spirit of man, which in man is the man himself, and likewise in the other life is in a perfect human form, n. 322, 1880, 1881, 3633, 4622, 4735, 5883, 6054, 6605, 6626, 7021, 10594; from experience, n. 4527, 5006, 8939: from the Word, n. 10597. What is meant by the dead seen in the holy city, Matt. xxvii. 53, explained, n. 9229. In what manner man is raised from the dead, from experience, n. 168 to 189. Concerning his state after resuscitation, n. 317, 318, 319, 2119, 5079, 10596. False opinions concerning the soul and its resurrection, n. 444, 445, 4527, 4622, 4658.

present day, there flows from them into the mind mere darkness, as soon as men go a step beyond.

313. A great many of the learned from the Christian world are astonished, when they see themselves after their decease, possessed of a body, clad in garments, and dwelling in houses, as in tl e world : and when they call to mind what they had thought concerning the life after death, concerning the soul, concerning spirits, and concerning heaven and hell, they are filled with shame, and confess that they had thought foolishly, and that the simple in faith thought much more wisely than they. The learned, who had confirmed themselves in such things, and who had ascribed all things to nature, were explored, and it was discovered that their interiors were entirely closed, and their exteriors open, so that they had not looked to heaven, but to the world, consequently also to hell ; for in the degree that the interiors are open, man looks to heaven ; but in the degree that the interiors are closed and the exteriors open, he looks to hell : for the interiors of man are formed for the reception of all things of heaven, and the exteriors for the reception of all things of the world ; and they who receive the world, and not heaven at the same time, receive hell.[1]

314. That heaven is from the human race may be further evident from this, that angelic minds and human minds are similar. Both enjoy the faculty of understanding, perceiving, and willing. Both are formed to receive heaven ; for the human mind is capable of wisdom as well as the angelic mind, but it does not become so wise in the world, because it is in an earthly body, and in that the spiritual mind thinks naturally. But it is otherwise when released from its connection with that body ; then it no longer thinks naturally, but spiritually ; and when it thinks spiritually, then it thinks things incomprehensible and ineffable to the natural man ; thus it becomes wise as an angel. From these observations it may be seen that the internal of man, which is called his spirit, is, in its essence, an angel (see above, n. 57),[2]

[1] That in man the spiritual and the natural world are conjoined, n. 6057. That the internal of man is formed to the image of heaven, but the external to the image of the world, n. 3628, 4523, 4524, 6057, 6314, 9706, 10156, 10472.

[2] That there are as many degrees of life in man, as there are heavens,

which, when released from the earthly body is in the human form the same as an angel. (That an angel is in a perfect human form, may be seen above, n. 73 to 77). But when the internal of man is not open above, but only beneath, then after its release from the body it is still in the human form, but hideous and diabolical; for it cannot look upward to heaven, but only downward to hell.

315. Whoever is instructed concerning divine order, may also understand that man was created to become an angel; because in him is the ultimate of order, (n. 304), in which may be formed a subject of heavenly and angelic wisdom capable of being renewed and multiplied. Divine order never stops mid-way, and there forms something without an ultimate,—for it is not then in its fullness and perfection,—but proceeds to its ultimate, and when it reaches that, commences the work of formation; and also through the means there collected, renews itself and goes on to further productions, which it accomplishes by means of procreations. Wherefore there [in the ultimate] is the seminary of heaven.

316. The Lord rose again not only as to the spirit but also as to the body, because when He was in the world He glorified his whole Human, that is, made it Divine. For the soul which He had from the Father, was the very Divine Itself; and the body was made a likeness of the soul, that is, of the Father,— therefore also Divine. Hence it was that He, differently from any man, rose again as to both.[1] This also He manifested to His disciples, who imagined when they beheld Him, that they saw a spirit,—saying: *"Behold my hands and my feet, that it is I Myself: handle Me and see, for a spirit hath not flesh and bones as ye see Me have,"* (Luke xxiv. 36–38); by which He indicated

---

and that they are opened after death according to his life, n. 3747, 9594. That heaven is in man, n. 3884. That men who live a life of love and charity have in them angelic wisdom, but at the time hidden, and that they come into it after death, n. 2494. That man, in the Word, is called an angel, who receives the good of love and of faith from the Lord, n. 10528.

[1] That man rises again only as to spirit, n. 10593, 10594. That the Lord alone rose again as to the body also, n. 1729, 2083, 5078, 10825.

that He was a man not only as to His spirit, but likewise as to His body.

317. In order that it may be known that man lives after death, and goes either to heaven or to hell according to his life in the world, many things have been revealed to me concerning the state of man after death, which will hereafter be treated of in order when speaking of the world of spirits.

THE GENTILES, OR PEOPLES NOT INCLUDED IN THE CHURCH, IN HEAVEN.

318. It is a common opinion that those who are born out of the church, who are called Heathen or Gentiles, cannot be saved, because they have not the Word, and thus are ignorant of the Lord, without whom there can be no salvation. Nevertheless it may be known that they also are saved, from these considerations alone; That the mercy of the Lord is universal, that is, extended toward every individual; that they are born men as well as those within the church, who are respectively few; and that it is no fault of theirs that they are ignorant of the Lord. Every person who thinks from any enlightened reason, may see that no man is born for hell; for the Lord is love itself, and it is agreeable to His love that all be saved. Wherefore also He has provided that all shall have some kind of religion, and thereby be in the acknowledgment of a Divine, and in the enjoyment of interior life: for to live according to religion is to live interiorly; for then man looks up to a Divine; and as far as he looks up to a Divine, so far he does not esteem the world, but removes himself from it, consequently from the life of the world, which is exterior life.[1]

---

[1] That Gentiles are saved alike with Christians, n. 932, 1032, 1059, 2284, 2589, 2590, 3778, 4190, 4197. Concerning the lot of Gentiles and peoples, out of the church in the other life, n. 2589 to 2604. That the church is

319. That Gentiles are saved as well as Christians, may be known to those who understand what it is that makes heaven with man; for heaven is in man, and those who have heaven in themselves enter heaven after death. It is heaven in man to acknowledge a Divine, and to be led by Him. The first and primary thing of every religion is, to acknowledge a Divine. A religion which does not include this acknowledgment, is no religion at all. And the precepts of every religion have respect to worship; thus they teach how the Divine is to be worshiped in a manner acceptable to Him; and when this is settled in one's mind, yea, in the degree that he wills or loves it, in that degree he is led by the Lord. It is known that Gentiles live a moral life as well as Christians, and that many of them live better than Christians. Men live a moral life either for the sake of the Divine, or from a regard to the opinion of the world. The moral life which is lived for the sake of the Divine is spiritual life. Both appear alike in the external form, but in the internal they are altogether different. One saves man; the other does not. For he who lives a moral life from a regard to the Divine, is led by the Divine; but he who lives a moral life from a regard to the opinions of the world, is led by himself. But let this be illustrated by an example. He who shuns the doing of evil to his neighbor, because to do evil is contrary to religion, thus contrary to the Divine, shuns evil from a spiritual ground; but he who shuns the doing of evil to another merely through fear of the law, of the loss of reputation, honor, or gain, thus for the sake of himself and the world, shuns it from a natural ground, and is led by himself. The life of the latter is natural, but that of the former is spiritual. The man whose moral life is spiritual, has heaven in himself; but he whose moral life is merely natural, has

---

specifically where the Word is, and by it the Lord is known, n. 3857, 10761. Nevertheless, that they who are born where the Word is, and where the Lord is known, are not, on that account, of the church, but they who live a life of charity and of faith, n. 6637, 10143, 10153, 10578, 10645, 10829. That the church of the Lord is with all in the universe who live in good according to their religion and acknowledge a Divine, and that they are accepted of the Lord, and come into heaven, n. 2589 to 2604, 2861, 2863, 3263, 4190, 4197, 6700, 9256.

not heaven in himself. The reason is, because heaven flows in from above, and opens man's interiors, and through his interiors flows-in into his exteriors; but the world flows-in from beneath, and opens his exteriors, but not his interiors; for there is no influx from the natural world into the spiritual, but from the spiritual world into the natural; wherefore if heaven be not received at the same time with the world, the interiors are closed. From these observations it may be seen who receive heaven in themselves, and who do not. But heaven is not the same in one as it is in another; it differs in each according to his affection of good and thence of truth. They who are in the affection of good for the sake of the Divine, love divine truth; for good and truth mutually love each other, and desire to be conjoined.[1] Wherefore the Gentiles, although they are not in genuine truths in the world, still receive them in the other life according to the love with which they are imbued.

320. There was a certain spirit from among the Gentiles, who had lived in the world in the good of charity according to his religion; when he heard Christian spirits arguing about articles of belief, (for spirits argue with each other much more ably and acutely than men, especially about goods and truths), he wondered at their disputing in this manner, remarking that he did not like to hear them, for they argued from appearances and fallacies; instructing them in this wise:—If I am good, I can know from good itself what things are true; and what I do not know, I am able to receive.

321. I have often been instructed that Gentiles, who have led a moral life, have lived in obedience and subordination, and in mutual charity according to their religion, and have thence received something of conscience, are accepted in the other life, and are there instructed with anxious care by angels in the goods and truths of faith; and that, while under instruction, they be-

---

[1] That between good and truth there is the resemblance of a marriage, n. 1904, 2173, 2508. That good and truth are in a perpetual tendency to conjunction, and that good desires truth and its conjunction, n. 9206, 9207, 9495. In what manner is the conjunction of good and of truth, and with whom, n. 3834, 3843, 4096, 4097, 4301, 4345, 4353, 4364, 4368, 5365, 7623 to 7627, 9258.

have themselves modestly, intelligently, and wisely, and willingly
receive truths, and are imbued with them; besides, they have
formed to themselves no principles of the false contrary to the
truths of faith, which are to be shaken off, much less scandals
against the Lord,—like many Christians who cherish no other idea
of Him than that of a common man. Not so the Gentiles. When
they hear that God became Man, and thus manifested Himself in
the world, they immediately acknowledge it, and adore the Lord,
saying, that God has, indeed, manifested Himself, because He is
the God of heaven and earth, and because the human race are
His.[1] It is a divine truth, that without the Lord there is no salvation; but this is to be understood to mean that there is no salvation but from the Lord. There are many earths in the universe, and all of them full of inhabitants. Scarcely any there
know that the Lord assumed the Human on our earth. Nevertheless, because they adore the Divine under a human form, they
are accepted and led of the Lord. On this subject, see the little
treatise on THE EARTHS IN THE UNIVERSE.

322. There are among Gentiles, as among Christians, both
wise and simple. That I might be instructed respecting their
character, I have been allowed to converse with both, sometimes
for hours and days. But there are no such wise men now as in
ancient times, especially in the ancient church, which extended
over a great part of Asia, from which religion spread to many
nations. That I might know their quality, I have been allowed
to converse familiarly with some of them. One with whom I

---

[1] The difference between the good in which the gentiles are, and that in
which Christians are, n. 4189, 4197. Concerning truths with the gentiles,
n. 3263. 3778, 4190. That the interiors cannot be so closed with gentiles as
with Christians, n. 9256. That neither can so thick a cloud exist with the
gentiles who live according to their religious principles in mutual charity,
as with Christians who live in no charity, the reasons, n. 1059, 9256.
That gentiles cannot profane the holy things of the church like Christians, because they are not acquainted with them, n. 1327, 1328, 1051.
That they are afraid of Christians, on account of their lives, n. 2596,
2597. That they who have lived well according to their religious principles, are instructed by angels, and easily receive the truths of faith, and
acknowledge the Lord, n. 2049, 2595, 2598, 2600, 2601, 2603, 2661, 2863,
3263.

spoke was formerly classed among those of superior wisdom, and
hence was known also in the learned world. I conversed with
him on various subjects, and had reason to believe that it was
Cicero. And because I knew that he was a wise man, I discoursed with him concerning wisdom, intelligence, order, the
Word, and lastly concerning the Lord. Concerning wisdom he
said, that there is no other wisdom than that which pertains to
life, and that wisdom cannot be predicated of anything else.
Concerning intelligence, that it is derived from wisdom. Concerning order, that it is from the Supreme God; and that to live
according to that order is to be wise and intelligent. As to the
Word, when I read to him a passage from the prophets, he was
exceedingly delighted, especially on learning that every name
and every word signified interior things,—wondering very much
that the learned at this day are not delighted with such study.
I clearly perceived that the interiors of his thought or mind were
open. He said that he could not listen any longer, because he
perceived something more holy than he could bear,—so interiorly
was he affected. At length I spoke with him concerning the
Lord, saying, that He was born a Man, but conceived of God;
and that He put off the maternal human, and put on the Divine
Human; and that it is He who governs the universe. To this he
replied, that he knew many things respecting the Lord, and comprehended according to his fashion, that if mankind were to be
saved, it could have been accomplished in no other way. In the
meantime some wicked Christians threw in various stumbling-
blocks; but he paid no attention to them, saying that it was not
to be wondered at, because in the life of the body they had imbibed unbecoming ideas on the subject; and that until these were
removed out of the way, they could not admit things confirma-
tory of the truth, as those do who are in ignorance.

323. It has also been granted me to converse with others who
had lived in ancient times, and who in their day were classed
among the eminently wise. They appeared at first in front at
some distance, and there they could discern the interiors of my
thoughts, thus many things fully; from one idea of thought they
could know the entire series, and fill it with delightful conceptions of wisdom, combined with charming representations. I

perceived from this that they were among the eminently wise,
and I was told that they were some of the ancients. They then
approached nearer; and when I then read to them a passage
from the Word, they were very much delighted. I perceived
the nature of their delight and gratification, which arose chiefly
from the circumstance, that all and each of the things which they
heard from the Word, represented and signified celestial and
spiritual things. They said that in their time, when they lived
in the world, their mode of thinking and speaking, and also of
writing, was such, and that this was the study of their wisdom.

324. But as to the Gentiles of the present day, they are not so
wise; but many of them are simple in heart. Such of them,
however, as have lived in mutual charity receive wisdom in the
other life. Of these, I am at liberty to adduce an example or two.
Once when I read the xvii. and xviii. chapters of Judges concerning Micah, whose graven image, Teraphim, and Levite, were taken
from him by the sons of Dan, a spirit from among the Gentiles
was present, who in the life of the body had worshiped a graven
image. He listened attentively to the relation of what was done
to Micah, and of the grief which he suffered on account of his
graven image which the Danites took away, and was so affected
by it that interior grief nearly deprived him of the power of
thought. I perceived his grief, and at the same time the innocence which was in all his affections. Some Christian spirits
also were present, who had a similar perception; and they wondered that the worshiper of a graven image should be moved
with such a profound feeling of pity and of innocence. Afterward good spirits conversed with him, and remarked that a
graven image ought not to be worshiped, and that, as a rational
being, he was capable of understanding this; but that, indepen-
dently of a graven image, he ought to think of God the Creator and
Governor of the whole heaven and earth, and that the Lord is
that God. When these remarks were made, the interior affection
of his worship was communicated to me, and I perceived
that it was much more holy than with Christians. From this
circumstance it is evident that Gentiles at the present day enter
heaven more easily than Christians, according to the words of
the Lord in Luke: "*Then shall they come from the east and*

the west, and from the north and the south, and shall sit down
in the kingdom of God: and behold, there are last who shall
be first, and there are first who shall be last," xiii. 29, 30. For
in the state in which that Gentile spirit was, he was capable of
becoming imbued with all the doctrines of faith, and of receiving
them with interior affection. He had compassion, which is
an attribute of love, and in his ignorance there was innocence ;
and when these are present, all the doctrines of faith are received
as it were spontaneousiy, and with joy. He was afterward received among the angels.

325. One morning I heard a number of singers at a distance,
and from the accompanying representations it was given me to
know that they were Chinese ; for they presented the figure of a
he-goat clothed with wool, likewise a cake of millet, and an
ebony spoon, together with the idea of a floating city. They
desired to come nearer to me ; and when they approached, they
wished to be alone with me, that they might reveal their thoughts.
But they were told that they were not alone, and that there were
others present who were displeased at their wishing to be alone,
when yet they were strangers. On perceiving their displeasure,
they began to consider whether they had transgressed against
their neighbor, and whether they had claimed anything as their
own which belonged to others ; and (since all thoughts in the
other life are communicated) it was given me to perceive the
agitation of their minds, which consisted of the acknowledgment
that, possibly, they had done them an injury, also of shame on
account of it, and at the same time of other worthy affections.
Hence I knew that they were indued with charity. Soon after I
entered into conversation with them, and at last spoke to them
concerning the Lord. When I called Him Christ, I perceived
in them a degree of repugnance ; but it was found to originate in
the impression they had received in the world, from knowing
that Christians led worse lives than they did, and that they were
without charity. But when I called Him simply the Lord, they
were then interiorly affected. They were afterward instructed by
angels that the Christian doctrine, above every other in the world,
prescribes love and charity ; but that there are few who live
according to it. There are some Gentiles who, during their life

in the world, knew both from conversation and report, that
Christians lived wicked lives, being addicted to adultery, hatred,
quarrelling, drunkenness, and the like, which they abhorred, be-
ca::se such things are contrary to their religious principles.
These in the other life are more afraid than others of receiving
the truths of faith. But they are instructed by angels that the
Christian doctrine, and indeed the Faith itself, teaches altogether
otherwise ; but that Christians live less according to their doctrine
than Gentiles do. When they learn these things, they receive
the truths of faith, and worship the Lord,—but they advance to
this state slowly.

326. It is common for Gentiles, who have worshiped a god
under the form of an image or statue or some graven thing, to be
introduced, when they enter the other life, to certain ones appointed to take the place of their gods or idols, in order to rid
them of their fantasies. When they have been with them for
some days, they [*i. e.* their fantasies] are then removed. Those
also who have worshiped men are occasionally introduced to
them, or to others who personate them. This is often the case
with the Jews, who are thus introduced to Abraham, Jacob,
Moses, and David ; but when they find that they are human like
others, and that they can give them no help, they are ashamed,
and are carried to their own places according to their lives.
Among the Gentiles in heaven, the Africans are most beloved ;
for these receive the goods and truths of heaven more readily
than others. It is their particular desire to be called obedient,
but not faithful. They say that Christians may be called faithful,
because they have the doctrine of faith ; but not themselves,
unless they receive that doctrine, or, as they say, are able to receive it.

327. I have conversed with some who belonged to the ancient
church. (That is called the ancient church, which existed after
the flood, extending at that time throughout many kingdoms ; as
throughout Assyria, Mesopotamia, Syria, Ethiopia, Arabia,
Lybia, Egypt, Philistea, even to Tyre and Zidon, and the land of
Canaan on both sides of Jordan).[1] They knew when they were in

---

[1] That the first and most ancient church on earth was that which is described in the first chapters of Genesis ; and that that church, above all

the world that the Lord was to come, and were imbued with the
goods of faith; but still they fell away, and became idolaters.
They were in front toward the left, in a dark place, and in a
miserable state. Their speech was like the sound of a pipe, mo-
notonous, almost void of rational thought. They said that they
had been in that place for many ages, and that they are occasionally taken out of it to perform mean uses for others. From their
character and condition I was led to think of many Christians, who
are not idolaters outwardly, but are so inwardly,—being worshipers of themselves and the world, and denying the Lord in heart,
—and to consider what kind of lot awaits them in the other
life.

328. That the church of the Lord is spread over the whole
terrestrial globe, and is thus universal; that it embraces all who
have lived in the good of charity according to their religious belief; and that the church where the Word is, and where by
means of it the Lord is known, is, to those who are out of the
church, as the heart and lungs in man, from which all the viscera
and members of the body live variously according to their forms,
situations, and connections, may be seen above, n. 308.

---

others, was celestial, n. 607, 895, 920, 1121, 1122, 1123, 1124, 2896, 4493,
8891, 9942, 10545. What is the quality of the members of that church in
heaven, n. 1114 to 1125. That there were various churches after the flood,
which are called ancient churches, concerning which, n. 1125, 1126, 1127,
1327, 10355. What was the quality of the men of the ancient church, n.
607, 895. That the ancient churches were representative churches, n. 519,
521, 2896. That the ancient church had a Word, but that it is lost, n.
2897. What was the quality of the ancient church when it began to de-
cline, n. 1128. The difference between the ancient church and the most
ancient, n. 597, 607, 640, 641, 765, 784, 895, 4493. That the statutes, the
judgments, and the laws, which were commanded in the Jewish church, were
in part like those which were in the ancient church, n. 4288, 4449, 10149.
That the Lord was the God of the most ancient church, and also of the
ancient, and that He was called Jehovah, n. 1343, 6846.

INFANTS IN HEAVEN.

329. SOME believe that only the infants who are born within the church go to heaven, but not those born out of the church; and the reason they assign is, that infants within the church are baptized, and are thus initiated into the faith of the church. But they are not aware that no one receives heaven or faith by baptism, for baptism is only for a sign and memorial that man is to be regenerated; and that he can be regenerated who is born within the church, since there is the Word which contains the divine truths by means of which regeneration is effected; there also the Lord is known, by whom it is accomplished.[1] Be it known, therefore, that every infant, wheresoever born,—whether within the church or out of it, whether of pious or of impious parents,—when he dies, is received by the Lord, and is educated in heaven. He is there instructed according to divine order, and is imbued with affections of good, and by them with the knowledges of truth; and afterward, as he is perfected in intelligence and wisdom, he is introduced into heaven and becomes an angel. Every one who thinks from reason may know that no one is born for hell, but all for heaven; and that man himself is in fault if he goes to hell; but that infants can as yet be in no fault.

330. When infants die, they are still infants in the other life. They have the same infantile mind, the same innocence in ignorance, and the same tenderness in all things. They are only in rudimental states introductory to the angelic,—for infants are not angels, but they become angels. Every one after his decease, is in a similar state of life to that in which he was in the world; an

---

[1] That baptism signifies regeneration from the Lord by the truths of faith derived from the Word, n. 4255, 5120, 9088, 10239, 10386, 10387, 10388, 10392. That baptism is a sign that man is of the church where the Lord, from Whom regeneration is derived, is acknowledged; and where the Word exists which contains the truths of faith, by which regeneration is effected, n. 10386, 10387, 10388. That baptism confers neither faith nor salvation, but that it testifies that they who are regenerating will receive them, n. 10391.

infant in a state of infancy, a boy in a state of boyhood, a youth, a man, an old man, in the state of a youth, of a man, and of an old man ; but the state of every one is afterward changed. The state of infants, however, excels that of all others in this respect, that they are in innocence, and evil from actual life has not yet taken root in them. And such is the nature of innocence, that all things of heaven may be implanted in it ; for it is the receptacle of the truth of faith and of the good of love.

331. The state of infants in the other life is far preferable to that of infants in the world ; for they are not clothed with an earthly body, but with a body like that of the angels. The earthly body in itself is of a dull nature. It does not receive its first sensations and motions from the interior or spiritual world, but from the exterior or natural world. Wherefore infants in the world must learn to walk, to use their limbs, and to talk ; yea, their senses, as those of sight and hearing, must be opened in them by use. Not so with infants in the other life. There, being spirits, they act immediately according to their interiors. They walk without practice ; they talk also with the same readiness, but at first from general affections not yet clearly distinguished into ideas of thought. But in a short time they are initiated into these also ; and the reason that this is so easily effected, is because their exteriors are homogeneous with their interiors. That the speech of angels flows from affections variegated by ideas of thought, so that their discourse is altogether conformable to their thoughts from affection, may be seen above, n. 234 to 245.

332. As soon as infants are raised from the dead, which takes place immediately after their decease, they are taken into heaven, and committed to the care of angels of the female sex, who in the life of the body loved little children tenderly, and at the same time loved God. Because these angels when in the world loved all infants from a sort of maternal tenderness, they receive them as their own ; and the little ones also, from an inclination implanted in them, love them as their own mothers. Each one has as many infants under her care, as she desires from a spiritual maternal affection. This heaven appears in front over against the forehead, directly in the line or radius in which the angels look at the Lord. The reason of its being thus situated is, be-

cause all infants are under the immediate auspices of the Lord. They also receive influx from the heaven of innocence, which is the third heaven.

333. Infants differ in their genius,—some partaking of the genius of the spiritual, others, of the celestial angels. They who are of a celestial genius, appear at the right in the heaven above mentioned; they who are of a spiritual genius, at the left. All infants in the GRAND MAN, which is heaven, are in the province of the eyes,—those of a spiritual genius, in the province of the left eye, and those of a celestial genius, in the province of the right eye; and the reason is, because the Lord appears to the angels in the spiritual kingdom before the left eye, and to those in the celestial kingdom before the right eye (see above, n. 118). From the fact that infants are in the province of the eyes in the GRAND MAN or heaven, it is also evident that they are under the immediate view and auspices of the Lord.

334. How infants are educated in heaven shall also be briefly told. From their tutoresses they learn to talk. Their first speech is only a sound of affection, which by degrees becomes more distinct as the ideas of thought enter; for ideas of thought derived from affections constitute all angelic speech. (On this subject see in its proper chapter, n. 234 to 245). Into their affections, which all proceed from innocence, are first insinuated such things as appear before their eyes, and are delightful; and as these are from a spiritual origin, the things of heaven flow into them at the same time, by means of which their interiors are opened; and thus they become more perfect every day. When this first period is completed, they are transferred to another heaven where they are instructed by masters: and so on.

335. Infants are instructed chiefly by representatives suited to their capacities, which are so beautiful, and at the same time so full of wisdom from an interior ground, as to exceed all belief. Thus intelligence, which derives its soul from good, is insinuated into them by degrees. I am allowed to mention here two representatives which I was permitted to see, from which a conclusion may be formed with regard to the rest. First, they represented the Lord rising from the sepulchre, and at the same time the union of His Human with the Divine,—which

was done in a manner so wise as to exceed all human wisdom, and at the same time in an innocent, infantile manner. They also presented the idea of a sepulchre, but not simultaneously an idea of the Lord, except so remotely as scarcely to be perceived that it was the Lord, otherwise than as it were afar off; because in the idea of a sepulchre there is something funereal, which was thus removed. Afterward, they cautiously admitted into the sepulchre something atmospherical which appeared like a thin watery substance, whereby they represented spiritual life in baptism,—and this again with a judicious removal of every thing unbecoming. After that, I saw represented by them the Lord's descent to those that were bound, and His ascent with them into heaven, which was done with incomparable prudence and piety. And there was this peculiarly infantile feature in the representation: They let down little threads, scarcely discernible, very soft and delicate, whereby they raised up the Lord; while a holy fear possessed them, lest any part of the representative should border upon anything wherein was not the spiritual celestial. Not to mention other representatives in use among them, and by means of which they are led into the knowledges of truth and the affections of good,—such as plays suitable to the minds of little children.

336. How tender their understanding is, was also shown me. When I prayed the Lord's prayer, and they then flowed into the ideas of my thought from their intellectual faculty, I perceived that their influx was so tender and soft, as to be almost that of affection alone ; and at the same time I observed that their intellectual faculty was open even from the Lord, for what proceeded from them seemed to be transfluent, [*i. e.* as if it only flowed through them]. The Lord also flows into the ideas of infants chiefly from inmosts, for nothing closes their ideas as with adults. No false principles obstruct their understanding of truth, nor does the life of evil obstruct their reception of good, and thus their reception of wisdom. From these things it is evident, that infants do not arrive to the angelic state immediately after death, but that they are gradually led into it by the knowledges of good and truth, and this according to all heavenly order: for the minutest particulars of their natural disposition are known to the Lord, and

therefore they are led to receive the truths of good and the goods of truth according to every movement of their inclination.

337. How all things are insinuated into them by delights and pleasantnesses suited to their genius, has also been shown me. I was permitted to see little children most elegantly clothed, having around their breasts, and also around their delicate arms, garlands of flowers resplendent with the most pleasing and heavenly colors. On one occasion also, I saw some children with their instructresses accompanied by virgins in a paradisiacal garden most splendidly embellished, not so much with trees, as with laurel espaliers, and so with porticos, together with paths conducting toward the interior recesses. The children themselves were clothed in the manner above mentioned; and when they entered the garden, the clustering flowers above the entrance shot forth a most joyful radiance. From this it may be seen what delights attend them; and also that by means of things pleasant and delightful they are led to the goods of innocence and charity, which goods are continually insinuated into them from the Lord through such agreeable mediums.

338. It was shown me by a mode of communication familiar in the other life, what are the ideas of infants when they see any objects. Every single thing appears to them to be alive; and therefore in every idea of their thought there is life. I also perceived that the ideas of infants on earth, when engaged in their little pastimes, are nearly the same; for they have not yet reflection, like adults, so as to distinguish the animate from the inanimate.

339. It was said above, that infants are of a genius either celestial or spiritual. The distinction between them is obvious. The celestial think, speak, and act, with more gentleness than the spiritual, so that scarcely anything appears [in their conduct and speech] but what flows from the good of love to the Lord and toward other infants. But the spiritual do not exhibit so much gentleness, but something as it were of a fluttering vibratory character manifests itself in all they say or do. This is evident also from their indignation, and from other signs.

340. Many persons may imagine that infants remain such in heaven, and exist as infants among the angels. They who do

not know what constitutes an angel, may have confirmed themselves in this opinion from the images sometimes seen in churches,
where angels are exhibited as infants. But the case is altogether
otherwise. Intelligence and wisdom constitute an angel; and so
long as infants have not intelligence and wisdom, they are not
angels, although they are with angels. But when they become
intelligent and wise, then for the first time they become angels.
Yea,—a thing that I have wondered at,—they then no longer appear as infants, but as adults; for they are then no longer of an
infantile genius, but of a more mature angelic genius. Intelligence and wisdom produce this effect. As infants are perfected
in intelligence and wisdom, they appear more mature, thus as
youths and young men, because intelligence and wisdom are real
spiritual nourishment.[1] For this reason the things which nourish
their minds nourish their bodies also,—and this from correspondence; for the form of the body is but the external form of the interiors. It is to be observed that infants in heaven do not advance
in age beyond the period of early manhood; and there they stop
forever [*i. e.* so far as apparent progress in *age* is concerned].
That I might be assured of this, it was granted me to converse
with some who were educated as infants in heaven, and who had
grown up there; with some also when they were infants, and afterward with the same when they had become young men; and
I heard from them the progress of their life from one age to another.

341. That innocence is the receptacle of all things of heaven,
and thus that the innocence of infants is the plane of all the
affections of good and truth, may be evident from what was said
above, n. 276 to 283, concerning the innocence of the angels in
heaven; it was there shown that innocence consists in a willing-

---

[1] That spiritual food is science, intelligence, and wisdom, and thus the
good and truth from which they are derived, n. 3114, 4459, 4792, 5147,
5293. 5340, 5342, 5410, 5426, 5576, 5582, 5588, 5655, 8562, 9003. Hence that
food, in a spiritual sense, is everything which proceeds from the mouth of
the Lord, n. 681. That bread signifies all food in general, and therefore
every good, celestial and spiritual, n. 276, 680, 2165, 2177, 3478, 6118, 8410.
The reason is, because celestial and spiritual good nourish the mind,
which is of the internal man, n. 4459, 5293, 5576, 6277, 8410.

ness to be led by the Lord, and not by self; consequently that man is so far in innocence as he is removed from his own proprium; and that so far as any one is removed from his own proprium, he is in the proprium of the Lord. The proprium of the Lord is what is called the Lord's justice and merit. But the innocence of infants is not genuine innocence, because it is as yet without wisdom. Genuine innocence is wisdom, for in proportion as any one is wise, he loves to be led by the Lord; or, what is the same, in proportion as any one is led by the Lord, he is wise. Infants therefore are led from external innocence, in which they are at first,—and which is called the innocence of infancy,—to internal innocence, which is the innocence of wisdom. This innocence is the end of all their instruction and progress; wherefore when they come to the innocence of wisdom, the innocence of infancy, which had served them in the meantime as a plane, is then conjoined to them. The nature of infantile innocence was represented to me by a kind of wooden thing almost void of life, which is vivified just as children are perfected by the knowledges of truth and the affections of good. And afterward the nature of genuine innocence was represented by a most beautiful infant, full of life and naked. For those eminently innocent ones, who dwell in the inmost heaven, and thus nearest to the Lord, appear to other angels just like infants, and some of them naked; for innocence is represented by nakedness unaccompanied by shame, —as we read of the first man and his wife in paradise, (Gen. chap. ii. 25). Wherefore also when their state of innocence was lost, they were ashamed of their nakedness, and hid themselves, (chap. iii. 7, 10, 11). In a word, the wiser the angels are, the more innocent they are; and the more innocent they are, the more do they appear to themselves like infants. Hence it is that infancy, in the Word, signifies innocence, (see above, n. 278).

342. I have conversed with angels concerning infants, and inquired whether they are free from evils, because they have no actual evil, like adults. But I was told that they are equally in evil,—yea, that they, too, are nothing but evil;[1] but that they,

---

[1] That all men are born in evils of every kind, insomuch that their proprium is nothing but evil, n. 210, 215, 731, 874, 875, 876, 987, 1047, *307,

like all the angels, are withheld from evil and held in good by the Lord, yet in such a way that it appears to them as if they were in good of themselves. Lest, therefore, infants who have grown up in heaven should entertain a false opinion of themselves, and imagine that the good which they possess is from themselves and not from the Lord, they are sometimes let into the evils which they have received hereditarily, and are left in them until they know, acknowledge, and believe, that their good is all from the Lord. A certain prince who died in his infancy and grew up in heaven, entertained the false opinion just alluded to. Wherefore he was let into the life of the evils wherein he was born; and I then perceived from the sphere of his life, that he had a disposition to domineer over others, and to make light of adulteries. These evils he derived hereditarily from his parents. But after he acknowledged that such was his nature, he was received again among the angels with whom he was before. No one in the other life ever suffers punishment on account of hereditary evil, because it is not his own, thus no fault of his that he is such. But he is punished on account of the actual evil which is his own, and thus in proportion as he has made hereditary evil his own by actual life. Infants, therefore, are let into the state of their hereditary evil when they become adult, not that they may suffer punishment on account of it, but in order that they may be convinced that of themselves they are nothing but evil; that through the mercy of the Lord they are delivered from the

2308, 3518, 3701, 3812, 8480, 8550, 10283, 10284, 10286, 10732. That man therefore must be re-born, that is, regenerated, n. 3701. That the hereditary evil of man consists in loving himself more than God, and the world more than heaven, and in making no account of his neighbor in comparison with himself, except only for the sake of hinself,—which is to love himself,—so that it consists in the love of self and of the world, n. 694, 731, 4317, 5660. That from the love of self and the love of the world, when they predominate, come all evils, n. 1307, 1308, 1321, 1594, 1691, 3413, 7255, 7376, (7480), 7488, 8318, 9335, 9348, 10038, 10742: which evils are contempt of others, enmity, hatred, revenge, cruelty, deceit, n. 6667, 7372, 7373, 7374, 9348, 10038, 10742; and that from these evils comes all that is false, n. 1047, 10283, 10284, 10286. That those loves rush headlong if the reins are given them, and that the love of self aspires even to the throne of God, n. 7375, 8678.

hell which cleaves to them, and introduced into heaven; and that they are in heaven, not from any merit of their own, but from the Lord; and therefore that they may not boast of their goodness before others,—for this is as contrary to the good of mutual love, as it is to the truth of faith.

343. Several times when a number of infants have been present with me in choirs,—while they were as yet altogether infantile,—their voices were heard as something tender, but confused, proving that they did not yet act in unison, as they do afterward when they become more mature; and what I wondered at, the spirits who were with me could not refrain from leading them to speak. Such desire is innate in spirits. But I observed that on all such occasions the infants resisted, and were unwilling to speak as they were led. Their refusal and resistance were attended with a species of indignation, as I often perceived; and when they were permitted to speak freely, they only said *that it is not so.* I have been informed that such is the temptation of infants, permitted in order that they may learn and become accustomed, not only to resist what is false and evil, but also that they may not think, speak, and act from others; and therefore that they may not suffer themselves to be led by any other than the Lord alone.

344. From these instances it may be evident what the education of infants in heaven is; namely, that through the intelligence of truth and the wisdom of good they are introduced into angelic life, which is love to the Lord and mutual love; and in those loves there is innocence. But how contrary is the education of children on earth in many cases, may appear from this instance: I was in the street of a great city, and saw little boys fighting with each other. A crowd gathered around and gazed upon the spectacle with much pleasure; and I was informed that the parents themselves incite their little sons to such combats. The good spirits and angels who saw through my eyes what was passing, were so shocked by it that I perceived their horror, and that it was caused especially by the conduct of the parents who incite their children to such deeds. They said that thus, in their earliest years, parents extinguish in them all mutual love and all innocence which infants receive from the Lord, and initiate them

into hatred and revenge; consequently that they, by their own efforts, exclude their children from heaven, where there is nothing but mutual love. Let parents therefore, who wish well to their children, beware of such practices.

345. The difference between those who die infants, and those who die adults, shall also be stated. They who die adults have a plane acquired from the terrestrial and material world, and carry it with them. This plane is their memory and its corporeal natural affection. After death this plane remains fixed, and is quiescent; but still it serves their thought for an ultimate plane, for the thought flows into it. Hence it is, that such as that plane is, and such as is the correspondence of the rational with the things thereto belonging, such is the quality of the man after death. But those who die in infancy, and are educated in heaven, have not such a plane, but a spiritual-natural one, since they derive nothing from the material world and the terrestrial body; wherefore they cannot be in such gross affections and thence thoughts, for they derive all things from heaven. Besides, infants do not know that they were born in the world, and therefore believe that they were born in heaven; consequently they know nothing of any birth but the spiritual birth, which is effected by the knowledges of good and truth, and by intelligence and wisdom, by virtue of which man is man; and because these are from the Lord, they believe, and love to believe, that they are the children of the Lord Himself. Nevertheless the state of men who grow up on earth, may become just as perfect as the state of infants who grow up in heaven, provided they remove corporeal and terrestrial loves,—which are the loves of self and the world,—and in their place receive spiritual loves.

THE WISE AND THE SIMPLE IN HEAVEN.

346. It is believed that the wise will enjoy glory and eminence in heaven above the simple, because it is said in Daniel: "*The*

intelligent shall shine as with the brightness of the firmament; and they that turn many to righteousness, as the stars forever." xii. 3. But few know who are meant by the intelligent, and by those who turn many to righteousness. It is generally believed that they are those who are called the educated and learned, especially those who have been teachers in the church, and have excelled others in learning and preaching, and still more those among them who have converted many to the faith. All such in the world are believed to be the intelligent; but still they are not the intelligent in heaven, of whom the above words are spoken, unless their intelligence be heavenly intelligence, the nature of which will be told in what now follows.

347. Heavenly intelligence is interior intelligence, arising from the love of truth, not for the sake of glory in the world, nor for the sake of glory in heaven, but for the sake of truth itself, whereby they are inmostly affected and delighted. They who are affected and delighted with the truth itself, are affected and delighted with the light of heaven; and they who are affected and delighted with the light of heaven, are also affected and delighted with divine truth, yea, with the Lord Himself; for the light of heaven is divine truth, and divine truth is the Lord in heaven, (see above, n. 126 to 140). This light enters into the interiors of the mind alone,—for the interiors of the mind are formed to receive it,—and as it enters, it also affects and delights; for whatever flows-in from heaven and is received, contains in itself something delightful and pleasant. Hence comes the genuine affection of truth, which is the affection of truth for its own sake. They who are in this affection, or, what is the same, in this love, are in heavenly intelligence, and shine in heaven as with the brightness of the firmament. They shine, because the divine truth, wheresoever it is in heaven, gives light, (see above, n. 132); and the firmament of heaven from correspondence signifies that intellectual, both with angels and men, which is in the light of heaven. But they who are in the love of truth either for the sake of glory in the world or of glory in heaven, cannot shine in heaven, since they are not delighted and affected with the light of heaven, but with the light of the world; and this light without

the other, is in heaven nothing but thick darkness.[1] With all such, self-glory predominates, because it is the end they have in view; and when self-glory is the end, man regards himself in the first place, and the truths which are subservient to his own glory he regards only as means to that end, and as his servants. For he who loves divine truths for the sake of his own glory, regards himself in divine truths, and not the Lord; consequently he turns his sight,—which is that of the understanding and faith,— away from heaven to the world, and away from the Lord to himself. Hence such persons are in the light of the world, and not in the light of heaven. In the external form, and therefore in the sight of men, they appear as intelligent and well-instructed as those who are in the light of heaven, because they converse like them, and sometimes to all appearance more wisely, because excited by self-love, and well-versed in the art of counterfeiting heavenly affections; but still in the internal form in which they appear before the angels, they are of a totally different character. From these considerations it may be evident in some measure who they are that are meant by the intelligent, who will shine in heaven as with the brightness of the firmament. But who they are that are meant by those who turn many to righteousness, and who will shine as the stars, shall now be told.

348. By those who turn many to righteousness, are meant those who are wise; and in heaven they are called wise who are in good, and they are in good there, who commit divine truths immediately to life; for when divine truth is reduced to life, it becomes good, for it becomes a possession of the will and love; and whatever belongs to the will and love is called good. These therefore are called wise, for wisdom is of the life. But they

---

[1] That the light of the world is for the external man, and the light of heaven for the internal man, n. 3222, 3223, 3337. That the light of heaven flows into natural light, and that the natural man is wise so far as he receives the light of heaven, n. 4302, 4408. That from the light of the world, which is called natural light, the things which are in the light of heaven cannot be seen, but *vice versa*, n. 9754. Wherefore they who are in the light of the world alone do not perceive those things which are in th. light of heaven, n. 3108. That the light of the world is thick darkness to the angels, n. 1521, 1783, 1880.

are called intelligent, who do not admit divine truths immediately into the life, but first into the memory, whence they are afterward brought forth and applied to life. In what manner and to what extent the intelligent differ from the wise in heaven, may be seen in the chapter which treats of the two kingdoms of heaven, the celestial and the spiritual, (n. 20 to 28), and in that which treats of the three heavens, (n. 29 to 40). They who are in the Lord's celestial kingdom, and therefore in the third or inmost heaven, are called just, from the fact that they attribute nothing of justice to themselves, but all to the Lord. The justice of the Lord in heaven is the good which is from the Lord.[1] These, then, are the persons who are here meant by those who justify; these also are they, concerning whom the Lord says: " *The just shall shine as the sun in the kingdom of My Father.*" Matt. xiii. 43. It is said that they shall shine as the sun, because they are in love to the Lord from the Lord, and because that love is meant by the sun, (see above, n. 116 to 125). The light also with them is flamy, and the ideas of their thought partake of a flamy nature, because they receive the good of love immediately from the Lord as the sun in heaven.

349. All who have procured for themselves intelligence and wisdom in the world, are accepted in heaven, and become angels, every one according to the quality and amount of his intelligence and wisdom. For whatever a man acquires in the world, this remains, and is carried with him after death, when also it is increased and filled, but within the degree of his affection and desire of truth and good, not beyond it. They who have had but little affection and desire, receive but little, yet still as much as they are able to receive within that degree; but they who have had much affection and desire, receive much. The degree itself

---

[1] That the merit and righteousness of the Lord are the good which rules in heaven, n. 9486, 9986. That a righteous and justified person is one to whom the merit and righteousness of the Lord are ascribed; and that he is unrighteous who has his own righteousness and self-merit, n. 5069, 9263. What is the quality of those in the other life who claim righteousness to themselves, n. 942, 2027. That justice or righteousness, in the Word, is predicated of good, and judgment of truth; and that hence to do justice and judgment is to do what is good and true, n. 2235, 9857.

of affection and desire is as a measure, which is filled to the brim. To him, therefore, whose measure is large, much is added; and little, to him whose measure is little. The reason of all this is, because the love, to which belong affection and desire, receives everything which is agreeable to itself; hence the greater is one's love, the more he receives. This is meant by the Lord's words; "*To every one that hath, shall be given, that he may have more abundantly.*" Matt. xiii. 12; chap. xxv. 29. "*Into the bosom shall be given good measure, pressed down, shaken together, and running over.*" Luke vi. 38.

350. All are received into heaven, who have loved truth and good for their own sake. They, therefore, who have loved much, are called wise; and they who have loved little, are called simple. The wise in heaven are in great light, but the simple are in less light,—every one according to the degree of his love of good and truth. To love truth and good for their own sake, is to will them and do them; for they who will and do them, are those that love them, but not they who do not will and do them. The former also are they who love the Lord, and are loved by Him, since good and truth are from the Lord; and because they are from Him, He is also in them; therefore He is also with those who receive good and truth in their life, by willing and doing them. Man, too, regarded in himself, is nothing else but his own good and truth. because good is of his will, and truth is of his understanding, and the man is such as his will and understanding are. Hence it is evident that man is loved by the Lord, in proportion as his will is formed by good, and his understanding by truth. To be loved by the Lord is also to love the Lord, since love is reciprocal; for to him who is loved, the Lord gives the ability to love in return.

351. It is believed in the world, that they who possess much knowledge,—whether relating to the doctrines of the church and the Word, or to the sciences,—see truths more interiorly and quickly than others, and thus are more intelligent and wise. Such men also entertain a similar opinion of themselves. But the nature of true intelligence and wisdom, and also of that which is spurious and false, shall be told in what now follows.

True intelligence and wisdom is to see and perceive what is

true and good, and thence what is false and evil, and accurately to distinguish the one from the other, and this by an interior intuition and perception. There are interiors and exteriors with every man. The interiors are those things which belong to the internal or spiritual man, but the exteriors are those which belong to the external or natural man. The quality of a man's understanding and perception depends upon the form of his interiors, and the degree in which they make one with his exteriors. The interiors of man can be formed only in heaven, but his exteriors are formed in the world. When the interiors are formed in heaven, there is an influx from them into the exteriors which are from the world, and thus they are brought into correspondence, that is, into unity of action. When this takes place, the man sees and perceives from the interior. In order that the interiors may be formed, the only way is for a man to look to the Divine and to heaven; for, as was just said, the interiors are formed in heaven. And a man looks to the Divine when he believes in the Divine, and believes that all truth and good, and hence all intelligence and wisdom, are from Him; and he believes in the Divine when he is willing to be led by Him. In this way, and in no other, are a man's interiors opened. The man who is in this faith, and in a life according to it, has the power and faculty of becoming intelligent and wise. But in order to become so, he must learn many things, not only such as relate to heaven, but such as relate to the world also. Those which relate to heaven are to be learned from the Word and from the church; and those which relate to the world, from the sciences. In proportion as man learns these things, and applies them to life, he becomes intelligent and wise; for in the same proportion the interior sight which is that of his understanding, and the interior affection which is that of his will, are perfected. The simple of this sort are they whose interiors are open, but not so much cultivated by spiritual, moral, civil, and natural truths; these perceive truths when they hear them, but they do not see them in themselves. But the wise of this class are they whose interiors are not only open, but cultivated; these also see truths in themselves, and perceive them. From these considera tions it is evident what true intelligence and wisdom are.

352. Spurious intelligence and wisdom consist, not in seeing and perceiving from an interior ground what is true and good, and thence what is false and evil, but only in believing that to be true and good, and that to be false and evil, which is declared to be so by others, and in confirming it afterward. They who do not see what is true from truth itself, but from the persuasion of another, may embrace and believe what is false just as readily as what is true, and may also confirm it until it appears to be true; for whatever is confirmed puts on the appearance of truth; and there is nothing which cannot be confirmed. The interiors of such persons are open only from beneath, but their exteriors are open in proportion as they have confirmed themselves; wherefore the light by which they see is not the light of heaven, but the light of the world, which is called natural light [*lumen*]. In this light falses may shine like truths, yea, when confirmed, may appear resplendent, but not in the light of heaven. Of this class the less intelligent and wise are they who have confirmed themselves much, and the more intelligent and wise are they who have confirmed themselves but little. From these considerations it may be seen, what spurious intelligence and wisdom are. But those are not of this class, who, in childhood, have supposed those things to be true which they heard from their teachers, provided that, in their riper years, when they think from their own understanding, they do not obstinately cling to them, but desire truth, and earnestly seek after it, and are interiorly affected by it when they find it. Such persons are affected with truth for its own sake, and therefore see it to be truth before they confirm it.[1] This may be illustrated by an example. A conversation arose among certain spirits upon the question, why animals are

---

[1] That wisdom consists in seeing and perceiving whether a thing be true before it is confirmed, but not in confirming what is said by others, n. 1017, 4741, 7012, 7680, 7950. That to see and to perceive whether a thing be true before it is confirmed, is given only to those who are affected with truth for its own sake, and for the sake of life, n. 8521. That the light of confirmation is natural light and not spiritual, and that it is sensual light, which has place even with the wicked, n. 8780. That all things, even falses, may be confirmed, so as to appear like truths, n. 2482, 2490, 5033, 6865, 8521.

born into all the science suitable to their nature, but not man; and the reason assigned was, that animals are in the order of their life, but that man is not; wherefore he must be brought into order by knowledges and sciences. But if man were born into the order of his life, which is to love God above all things and his neighbor as himself, he would be born into intelligence and wisdom, and thence also into the belief of all truth, so far as he was made acquainted therewith through the acquisition of knowledges. The good spirits immediately saw this, and perceived that it was so, purely from the light of truth; but the spirits who had confirmed themselves in faith alone, and had thence cast aside love and charity, could not understand it, because the light of the false which they had confirmed obscured the light of truth.

353. False intelligence and wisdom is all that which is without the acknowledgment of a Divine; for all those who do not acknowledge a Divine, but nature instead, think from the corporeal-sensual, and are merely sensual, how much soever they may be esteemed in the world for their erudition and learning.[1] Their erudition, however, does not ascend beyond such things as appear in the world before their eyes. These they retain in their memory, and look at almost materially, although the same sciences are what serve the truly intelligent for the formation of their understanding. By the sciences are meant the various kinds of experimental

---

[1] That the sensual principle is the ultimate of the life of man, adhering to, and inhering in, his corporeal principle, n. 5077, 5767, 9212, 9216, 9331, 9730. That he is called a sensual man, who judges and concludes all things from the senses of the body, and who believes nothing but what he sees with his eyes and touches with his hands, n. 5094, 7693. That such a man thinks in his outermost principles, and not interiorly in himself, n. 5089, 5094, 6564, 7693. That his interiors are closed, so that he sees nothing of divine truth, n. 6564, 6844, 6845. In a word, that he is in gross natural light, and thus perceives nothing which is derived from the light of heaven, n. 6201, 6310, 6564, 6844, 6845, 6598, 6612, 6614, 6622, 6624. That therefore he is inwardly opposed to all things which are of heaven and the church, n. 6201, 6316, 6844, 6845, 6948, 6949. That the learned, who have confirmed themselves against the truths of the church, are sensual men, n. 6316. The quality of the sensual man is described, n. 10236.

knowledge, as physics, astronomy, chemistry, mechanics, geometry, anatomy, psychology, philosophy, the history of kingdoms, and also the criticisms and languages of the learned world. The dignitaries of the church who deny a Divine, do not elevate their thoughts above the sensual things appertaining to the external man; they regard the contents of the Word as others regard the sciences, nor do they make them matters of thought or of any intuition by an enlightened rational mind, because their interiors are closed, and also the exteriors which are nearest to their interiors. These are closed, because they have turned themselves away from heaven, and have retroverted those faculties which were capable of looking in that direction, which are the interiors of the human mind, as observed above. Hence it is that they cannot see what is true and good, since to them these are in thick darkness, but what is false and evil is in the light. Nevertheless sensual men can reason,—some of them more ingeniously and acutely than other men,—but from the fallacies of the senses confirmed by their scientifics. And because they possess such skill in reasoning, they also think themselves wiser than others.[1] The fire which warms their reasonings with its affection, is the fire of the love of self and the world. These are they who are in false intelligence and wisdom, and who are meant by the Lord in Matthew: "*Seeing they see not, and hearing they hear not, neither do they understand,*" xiii. 13, 14, 15. And in another place: "*These things are hid from the intelligent and wise, and revealed unto babes,*" xi. 25, 26.

354. I have been allowed to converse with many of the learned after their departure from the world; with some who enjoyed the most distinguished reputation, and were celebrated in the literary world on account of their writings; and with others who were not so celebrated, but who, nevertheless, possessed hidden wisdom. Those who in heart denied a Divine,—how much soever they

---

That sensual men reason acutely and cunningly, because they make intelligence to consist in speaking from the corporeal memory, n. 195, 196, 5700, 10236; but that they reason from the fallacies of the senses, n. 5084, 6948, 6949, 7693. That sensual men are more cunning and malicious than others, n. 7693, 10236. That such were called by the ancients serpents of the tree of science, n. 195, 196, 197, 6398, 6949, 10313.

confessed Him with their lips,—had become so stupid, that they could scarcely comprehend any civil truth, much less any spiritual truth. I perceived and also saw that the interiors of their mind· were so closed as to appear black, (such things appear visibly in the spiritual world), and thus that they could not endure any heavenly light, neither could they admit any influx from heaven. That blackness in which their interiors appeared, was greater and more extended with those who had confirmed themselves against the Divine by their learned scientifics. Such persons in the other life receive with delight all that is false, and imbibe it as a sponge does water; and repel all truth, as a bony elastic surface repels what falls upon it. It is said also that the interiors of those who have confirmed themselves against the Divine and in favor of nature, are ossified. Their heads likewise appear hard as if made of ebony, and this appearance reaches even to the nose,—a sign that they no longer have any perception. Spirits of this character are immersed in quagmires, which appear like bogs, where they are harassed by the fantasies into which their false notions are turned. Their infernal fire is the lust of glory and a name, which prompts them to assail each other, and from infernal ardor to torment those who do not worship them as deities. In this way they torture each other by turns. Into such things is all worldly learning changed, which has not received into itself light from heaven by the acknowledgment of the Divine.

355. That the learned of this class are such in the spiritual world, when they arrive there after death, may be concluded from this single circumstance: That all things which are in the natural memory, and immediately conjoined to the sensuals of the body,—like the scientifics mentioned just above,—are then quiescent, and the rational conclusions thence derived form the sole basis of the thought and speech. For man carries with him all his natural memory, but the things which are in that memory are not under his view, and do not enter into his thought, as they did when he lived in the world. He can take nothing from that memory, and exhibit it in spiritual light, because the things therein have no relation to that light. But the rational or intellectual principles, which a man has acquired from the sciences

while he lived in the body, are in agreement with the light of the spiritual world; wherefore in proportion as the spirit of man is made rational by knowledges and sciences in the world, he is rational after the dissolution of the body; for then man is a spirit, and it is the spirit which thinks in the body.[1]

356. But those who have procured to themselves intelligence and wisdom by means of knowledges and sciences,—as is the case with those who have applied all things to the use of life, and at the same time have acknowledged a Divine, loved the Word, and lived a spiritual moral life, (concerning which above, n. 319),—the sciences have served as a means of becoming wise, and also of corroborating the things which appertain to faith. I have perceived and also seen the interiors of their minds, and they appeared as if transparent from light of a white, flamy, or azure color, like that of diamonds, rubies, and sapphires, which are pellucid; and this according to the confirmations in favor of a Divine and of divine truths, which they had derived from the sciences. Such is the appearance of true intelligence and wisdom, when presented in the spiritual world in a visible form. This appearance they derive from the light of heaven, which is the divine truth proceeding from the Lord, which is the source of all intelligence and wisdom, (see above, n. 126 to 133). The planes of that light, in which variegations like those of colors exist, are the interiors of the mind; and the confirmations of divine truths by such things as are in nature, and therefore in the sciences, produce those variegations.[2] For the interior mind of man looks into the stores of the natural memory, and seizing upon those things therein which are confirma-

---

[1] That scientifics belong to the natural memory, which man has in the body, n. 5212, 9922. That man carries all the natural memory with him after death, n. 2475; from experience, n. 2581 to 2486: but that he cannot bring anything forth from that memory as in the world, for several reasons, n. 2476, 2477, 2749.

[2] That most beautiful colors appear in heaven, n. 1053, 1624. That colors in heaven are derived from the light there, and that they are its modifications or variegations, n. 1042, 1643, 1053, 1624, 3993, 4530, 4922, 4742. Thus that they are the appearances of truth derived from good, and signify such things as belong to intelligence and wisdom, n. 4530, 4922, 4677, 9466.

tive, it sublimates them as it were by the fire of heavenly love, withdraws them, and purifies them even into spiritual ideas. That such a process takes place is unknown to man while he lives in the body, since he therein thinks both spiritually and naturally; but the things which he then thinks spiritually, he does not perceive, but only those which he thinks naturally; but when he comes into the spiritual world he then has no perception of what he thought naturally in the world, but of what he thought spiritually; thus his state is changed. From these considerations it is evident that man is made spiritual by knowledges and sciences, and that these are a means of becoming wise, but only to those who have acknowledged a Divine in faith and life. These also are accepted in heaven before others, and are among those there who are in the midst, (n. 43), because they are in light more than others. These are the intelligent and wise in heaven, who shine as with the brightness of the firmament, and who shine as the stars. But the simple there, are those who have acknowledged a Divine, loved the Word, and lived a spiritual-moral life, but the interiors of whose minds were not so much cultivated by knowledges and sciences. The human mind is like ground, which is such as it is made by cultivation.

THE RICH AND POOR IN HEAVEN.

357. THERE are various opinions concerning reception into heaven. Some suppose that the poor are received, and not the rich; others, that the rich and the poor are received alike; and others, that the rich cannot be received, unless they give up their

------

Extracts from the ARCANA CŒLESTIA concerning the sciences.

That man ought to be imbued with sciences and knowledges, since by them he learns to think, afterwards to understand what is true and good, and at length to grow wise, n. 129, 1450, 1451, 1453, 1548, 1802. That scientifics are the first principles, on which the life of man, civil, moral, and

wealth. and become as the poor; and each confirms his opinion from the Word. But they who make a distinction between the

---

spiritual, is built and founded; and that they are acquired for the sake of use as an end, n. 1489. 3310. That knowledges open the way to the internal man, and afterwards conjoin that man with the external according to uses, n. 1563, 1616. That the rational principle is born by sciences and knowledges, n. 1895, 1900, 3086; not by knowledges themselves, but by the affection of the uses derived from them, n. 1895.

That there are scientifics which admit divine truths, and others which do not admit them, n. 5213. That empty scientifics ought to be destroyed, n. 1489, 1492, 1499, 1580. That empty scientifics are those which have for their end, and which confirm, the loves of self and of the world, and which withdraw from love to God and love toward the neighbor; because such scientifics close the internal man so that man cannot afterward receive anything from heaven, n. 1563, 1600. That scientifics are the means of growing wise, and the means of becoming insane; that by them the internal man is either opened or closed, and that thus the rational principle is either cultivated or destroyed, n. 4156. 8628, 9922.

That the internal man is opened and successively perfected by scientifics, if man has good use for an end, especially the use which respects eternal life, n. 3086. That in this case scientifics, which are in the natural man, are met by spiritual and celestial things from the spiritual man, which adopt such of them as are suitable, n. 1495. That in this case the uses of heavenly life are extracted, purified, and elevated, from the scientifics which are in the natural man, by the internal man from the Lord, n. 1895, 1896, 1900, 1901, 1902, 5871, 5874, 5901; and that incongruous and opposing scientifics are cast aside and exterminated, n. 5871, 5886, 5889.

That the sight of the internal man calls forth from the scientifics of the external man nothing but what accords with its love, n. 9394. That beneath the sight of the internal man, those things which are of the love are in the midst and in brightness, but those which are not of the love are at the sides and in obscurity, n. 6068, 6085. That suitable scientifics are successively implanted in man's loves, and as it were dwell in them, n. 6325. That man would be born into intelligence, if he were born into love toward his neighbor; but since he is born into the love of self and of the world, he is therefore born in total ignorance, n. 6323. 6325. That science, intelligence, and wisdom, are the offspring of love to God and of love toward the neighbor, n. 1226, 2049, 2116.

That it is one thing to be wise, another thing to understand, another to know, and another to do; but that still, with those who are in spiritual life, they follow in order, and exist together in act, n. 10331. That it is also one thing to know, another to acknowledge, and another to have faith, n. 896.

rich and the poor as to facility of admission into heaven, do not understand the Word. The Word in its bosom is spiritual, but

---

That scientifics, which belong to the external or natural man, are in the light of the world; but that truths, which have been made truths of faith and of love, and have thus gained life, are in the light of heaven, n. 5212. That the truths which have gained spiritual life, are comprehended by natural ideas, n. 5510. That spiritual influx proceeds from the internal or spiritual man into the scientifics which are in the external or natural man, n. 1940, 8005. That scientifics are the receptacles, and as it were the vessels, of the truth and good which belong to the internal man, n. 1469, 1496, 3068, 5489, 6004, 6023, 6052, 6071, 6077, 7770, 9922. That scientifics are as it were mirrors, in which the truths and goods of the internal man appear as in an image, n. 5201. That they are there together as in their ultimate, n. 5373, 5874, 5886, 5901, 6004, 6023, 6052, 6071.

That influx is spiritual and not physical; that is, that there is influx from the internal man into the external, and thus into the scientifics of the external man, but that there is no influx from the external man into the internal, and therefore none from the scientifics of the external man into the truths of faith, n. 3219, 5119, 5259, 5427, 5428, 5478, 6322, 9110, 9111. That from the truths of the doctrine of the church, which are derived from the Word, a principle is to be drawn; that those truths are first to be acknowledged, and that afterward it is allowable to consult scientifics, n. 6047. Thus that it is allowable for those who are in an affirmative principle concerning the truths of faith, to confirm them intellectually by scientifics, but not for those who are in a negative principle, n. 2568, 2588, 4760, 6047. That he who does not believe divine truths unless he be persuaded by scientifics, never believes, n. 2094, 2832. That to enter into the truths of faith from scientifics is contrary to order, n, 10236. That they who do so become infatuated as to those things which pertain to heaven and the church, n. 128, 129, 140. That they fall into falses of evil, n. 232, 233, 6047; and that in the other life, when they think on spiritual subjects, they become as it were drunken, n. 1072. What their further quality is, n. 196. Examples illustrating that things spiritual cannot be comprehended if entered into by scientifics, n. 233, 2094, 2196, 2203, 2209. That many of the learned are more insane in spiritual things than the simple, because they are in a negative principle, and confirm it by scientifics which they have continually and in abundance before their view, n. 4760, 8629.

That they who reason from scientifics against the truths of faith, reason acutely, because from the fallacies of the senses, which are engaging and persuasive, since it is with difficulty that they can be dispersed, n. 5700. What and of what quality the fallacies of the senses are, n. 5084, 5094, 6400, 6948. That they who understand nothing of truth, and also they

in the letter it is natural; wherefore they who take the Word
only according to the literal sense, and not according to any spiritual sense, err upon many points, especially in regard to the rich

---

who are in evil, can reason about the truths and goods of faith, and yet
not understand them, n. 4214. That it is not the part of an intelligent
person merely to confirm a dogma, but to see whether it be true or not,
before it is confirmed, n. 4741, 6047.

That sciences are of no avail after death, but what man has imbibed in
his understanding and life by means of sciences, n. 2480. That still all scientifics remain after death, but that they are quiescent, n. 2476 to 2479,
2481 to 2486.

That the same scientifics with the evil are falses, because they are applied to evils, and with the good are truths, because they are applied to
good, n. 6917. That scientific truths with the evil are not truths, however
they may appear as truths when they are spoken, because there is evil
within them, n. 10331.

What is the quality of the desire of knowing, which spirits have; an
example, n. 1973. That with the angels there is an immense desire of
knowing and of growing wise, since science, intelligence, and wisdom are
spiritual food, n. 3114, 4459, 4792, 4976, 5147, 5293, 5340, 5342, 5410, 5426,
5576, 5582, 5588, 5655, 6277, 8562, 9003. That the science of the ancients
was the science of correspondences and representations, by which they introduced themselves into the knowledge of spiritual things; but that that
science is now altogether obliterated, n. 4844, 4749, 4964, 4965.

Spiritual truths cannot be comprehended, unless the following universals be known : I. That all things in the universe have reference to good
and truth, and to the conjunction of both, that they may be something;
thus to love and faith, and their conjunction. II. That man possesses understanding and will; that the understanding is the receptacle of truth,
and the will the receptacle of good; and that all things have reference to
these two principles in man, and to their conjunction, as all things have
reference to truth and good and their conjunction. III. That there is an
internal man and an external man, and that they are as distinct from each
other as heaven and the world; and yet that they ought to make one, that
man may be truly man. IV. That the internal man is in the light of heaven, and the external man in the light of the world; and that the light
of heaven is the divine truth itself, which is the source of all intelligence.
V. That there is a correspondence between the things which are in the
internal man and those which are in the external man, and that hence
they appear in all cases under another aspect, insomuch that they are
not discerned except by the science of correspondences. Unless these
and many other things be known, no ideas can be conceived and formed
of spiritual and celestial truths except such as are incongruous; and thus

and poor; as, in supposing that it is as difficult for the rich to enter heaven, as for a camel to go through the eye of a needle; and that it is easy for the poor because they are poor, since it is said: "*Blessed are the poor, for theirs is the kingdom of the heavens.*" [Matt. v. 3]; Luke vi. 20, 21. But they who know anything of the spiritual sense of the Word, are of a different opinion. They know that heaven is for all who live the life of faith and love, whether they be rich or poor. But who are meant in the Word by the rich, and who by the poor, will be shown in what follows. From much conversation and intercourse with the angels, it has been granted me to know for a certainty that the rich enter heaven as easily as the poor; that no man is excluded on account of his great possessions, and that no one is received because he is poor. Both rich and poor are there, and many of the rich in greater glory and happiness than the poor.

358. It is proper to observe in the outset, that a man may acquire riches and accumulate wealth as far as opportunity is given, provided it be not done with craft and dishonesty; that he may eat and drink daintily, provided he does not make life consist in that; may dwell magnificently according to his condition, may converse with others as others do; may frequent places of amusement, and talk about worldly affairs; and that he has no need to assume a devout aspect, to be of a sad and sorrowful countenance, and to bow down his head, but may be glad and cheerful; nor to give his goods to the poor, except so far as inclination leads him; in a word, he may live outwardly altogether like a man of the world; and these things will not prevent his going to heaven, provided that inwardly in himself he thinks properly about God, and acts sincerely and justly with his neighbor. For man is such as his affection and thought are, or such as his love and faith are; thence all his outward acts derive their life, for to act is to will, and to speak is to think, since every one acts from will and speaks from thought. Wherefore, when it is

---

scientifics and knowledges, which are of the natural man, without these universals can be of little use to the rational man for understanding and improvement. Hence it is evident how necessary scientifics are.

said in the Word that man shall be judged according to his deeds, and that he shall be rewarded according to his works, the meaning is, that he shall be judged and rewarded according to his thought and affection from which his deeds proceed, or which are in his deeds; for deeds are of no account without these, and are altogether such as these are.[1] Hence it is evident that the external of man is of no account, but that his internal,—from which his external is derived,—is what is judged. For illustration: If any one acts sincerely, and does not defraud another merely because he fears the law, the loss of reputation and consequently of honor or gain, he would defraud him to the utmost of his power if he were not restrained by that fear. His thought and will are fraudulent, though his actions are outwardly sincere. Such a man has hell within him, because he is interiorly insincere and fraudulent. But he who acts sincerely, and does not defraud another because it is against God and his neighbor, would not defraud him even if he had the opportunity, for his thought and will are conscience; he has heaven in himself. The deeds of both appear similar in the external form, but in the internal they are altogether dissimilar.

359. Since a man may live in the external form just as others do, may grow rich, keep a bountiful table, dwell in a splendid house, and wear costly apparel according to his condition and

---

[1] That it is very frequently said in the Word, that man shall be judged, and that he shall be recompensed according to his deeds and his works, n. 3934. That by deeds and works in such passages are not meant deeds and works in the external form, but in the internal; because good works in the external form are done also by the wicked, but in the external and at the same time in the internal form, only by the good, n. 3934, 6073. That works, like all acts, derive their esse and existere, and their quality, from the interiors of man, which are of his thought and will, inasmuch as they proceed thence; wherefore such as the interiors are, such are the works, n. 3934, 8911, 10331. Thus they are such as the interiors are in regard to love and faith, n. 3934, 6073, 10331, 10333. That works, therefore, contain those principles, and are love and faith in effect, n. 10331. Wherefore to be judged and recompensed according to deeds and works, denotes according to love and faith, n. 3147, 3934, 6073, 8911, 10331, 10333. That works are not good so far as they respect self and the world, but only so far as they respect the Lord and the neighbor, n. 3147.

employment, enjoy delights and gratifications, and engage in worldly affairs for the sake of occupation and business, and for sustenance of mind and body, provided he interiorly acknowledges a Divine and wishes well to his neighbor, it is evident that it is not so difficult to walk in the way of heaven as many suppose. The only difficulty is, to be able to resist the love of self and the love of the world, and to prevent their predominance · for these are the source of all evils.[1] That it is not so difficult to tread the heavenward path as many imagine, is evident from these words of the Lord: "*Learn of Me, for I am meek and lowly of heart; and ye shall find rest unto your souls: for My yoke is easy, and My burden is light.*" Matt. xi. 29, 30. The Lord's yoke is easy and His burden light, because in the degree that man resists the evils which flow from the loves of self and the world, he is led by the Lord and not by himself; and because the Lord afterward resists those evils in man, and removes them.

360. I have conversed with some after death, who, while on earth, renounced the world, and gave themselves up to an almost solitary life, that by the withdrawal of their thoughts from worldly concerns they might have leisure for pious meditations, imagining that they should thus be treading the path of heaven. But such persons in the other life are of a melancholy temper, and despise others who are not like themselves. They are indignant that they do not attain happiness above others, which they think they have merited. They care nothing about others, and turn away from offices of charity, by means of which there is conjunction with heaven. They desire heaven more than others, but when they are elevated among the angels, they induce anxieties which disturb their happiness; wherefore they are separated from them, and then they betake themselves to desert places, where they lead a life similar to that which they led in

---

That all evils are derived from the love of self and the world, n. 1307, 1308, 1321, 1594, 1691, 3413, 7255, 7376, 7480, 7488, 8318, 9335, 9348, 10038, 10742; which are contempt of others, enmities, hatred, revenge, cruelty, deceit, n. 6667, 7372, 7373, 7374, 9348, 10038, 10742. That man is born into those loves, and thus that his hereditary evils are in them, n. 694, 4317, 5660.

the world.   Man cannot be formed for heaven except by means of the world.   The ultimate effects, wherein every one's affection must be terminated, are there ; for unless one's affection exert itself, or flow forth into acts,—which is done in the society of many persons,—it is suffocated, and at length to such a degree that the man no longer regards his neighbor, but himself alone. Hence it is evident that a life of charity toward the neighbor,— which consists in doing what is just and right in every work and in every office,—leads to heaven, but not a life of piety without a life of charity ;[1] consequently that the exercises of charity, and thence the increments of the life thereof, can be given in the degree that man is busy with some occupation ; and cannot be given in the degree that he removes himself therefrom.   On this subject I will now speak from experience.   Many who were engaged in trade and merchandise in the world, and who also became rich by those pursuits, are in heaven ; but fewer of those who were in stations of honor, and who became rich by their offices.   The reason is, because these latter, by the gains and honors bestowed on them for dispensing what is just and right, as also posts of honor and emolument, were induced to love themselves and the world, and thereby to remove their thoughts and affections from heaven and turn them to themselves : for as far as man loves himself and the world, and regards himself and the world in everything, so far he alienates himself from the Divine, and removes himself from heaven.

361. The lot of the rich in heaven is such, that they excel all others in opulence.   Some of them dwell in palaces, in which everything is refulgent as with gold and silver.   They have an abundance of all things which contribute to the uses of life. They do not, however, in the least degree, set their hearts on such things, but on the uses themselves.   These they see in clearness, and as it were in the light ; but the gold and silver, in

---

[1] That charity toward the neighbor consists in doing what is good, just, and right, in every act and every employment, n. 8120, 8121, 8122. Hence that charity toward the neighbor extends itself to all and every-thing which man thinks, wills, and does, n. 8124.   That a life of piety without a life of charity is of no avail, but with it, is profitable for all things, n. 8252, 8253.

obscurity, and as it were in the shade respectively. The reason is, because they loved uses in the world, and gold and silver only as means and instruments thereof. Uses themselves glitter thus in heaven; the good of use as gold, and the truth of use as silver.[1] The opulence and the delight and the happiness of the rich in heaven, are therefore according to the uses which they performed in the world. Good uses consist in a man's providing the necessaries of life for himself and family; in desiring an abundance for the sake of his country, and also for the sake of his neighbor, whom a rich man can benefit more than a poor one in many ways; and because he can thus withdraw his mind from a life of idleness, which is a pernicious life,—for in idleness a man thinks evil from the innate evil in himself. These uses are good, so far as they have the Divine in them; that is, so far as a man looks to the Divine and heaven, places his good in them, and regards wealth only as a subservient good.

362. But very different is the lot of the rich who have not believed in a Divine, and have rejected from their minds the things which belong to heaven and the church. These are in hell, where filth, misery, and want abound. Riches, when loved as an end, are changed into such things; and not the riches only, but also the uses themselves, which are either that they may live as they like, and indulge in pleasures, and may be able to give up the mind more fully and freely to the commission of wickedness, or that they may rise above others whom they despise. Such riches and such uses become filthy, because they have nothing spiritual in them, but only what is terrestrial;—for a spiritual principle in riches and their uses is like a soul in the body,

[1] That every good has its delight from use, and according to use, n. 3049, 4984, 7038, and also its quality; consequently such as the use is, such is the good, n. 3049. That all the happiness and delight of life is from uses, n. 997. In general, that life is the life of uses, n. 1964. That angelic life consists in the goods of love and charity, and thus in performing uses, n. 452. That the Lord, and the angels from Him, look only at the ends which man regards, which ends are uses, n. 1317, 1645, 5844. That the kingdom of the Lord is a kingdom of uses, n. 454, 696, 1103, 3645, 4054, 7038. That to serve the Lord is to perform uses, n. 7038. That the quality of all is according to the quality of the uses which they perform, n. 4054, 6815; illustrated, n. 7038.

and like the light of heaven in moist ground ;—they also become
putrid like a body without a soul, and like moist ground without
the light of heaven.   These are they whom riches have seduced,
and withdrawn from heaven.

363. Every man's ruling affection or love remains with him
after death, nor is it extirpated to eternity; since the spirit of
man is altogether such as his love is, and,—what is an arcanum,
— the body of every spirit and angel is the external form of his
love, perfectly corresponding to the internal form which is that of
his natural and rational mind [*animi et mentis*].   Hence it is
that the character of spirits is known from their faces, their
gestures, and their speech ; and man might also be known as to
the quality of his spirit while he lives in the world, if he had
not learned, by his face, gestures, and speech, to counterfeit virtues
which do not belong to him.   It is therefore manifest that man
remains to eternity of the same quality as his ruling affection or
love.   It has been granted me to converse with some who lived
seventeen centuries ago, and whose lives are well known from
the writings of that period ; and it was found that every one was
still influenced by the love which ruled him when he lived in the
world.   Hence also it may be manifest that the love of riches,
and of the uses to be performed by riches, remains with every
one to eternity, and that it is altogether such as was procured in
the world ; yet with this difference, that with those who had
employed them in the promotion of good uses, riches are turned
into delights according to the uses ; but with those who had employed them in the promotion of evil uses, they are turned into
filth.   Then also the evil are delighted with such filth, in like
manner as in the world they were delighted with riches for the
sake of evil uses.   They are then delighted with filth, because
the filthy pleasures and infamies which were the uses to which
they applied their riches, and also avarice, which is the love of
riches without regard to use, correspond to filth.   Spiritual filth
is nothing else.

364. The poor do not go to heaven on account of their poverty, but on account of their life.   Every one's life follows him,
whether he be rich or poor.   There is no peculiar mercy for one

more than for another.[1] He who has lived well is received, and he who has lived ill is rejected. Besides, poverty seduces and withdraws man from heaven as much as wealth. Great numbers among the poor are not contented with their lot, but are eager after many things, and believe riches to be blessings.[2] They are angry, therefore, when they do not receive them, and think evil concerning the Divine Providence. They also envy others the good things which they possess. Besides, they are as ready as the wicked among the rich to defraud others, and to live in sordid pleasures when they have the opportunity. But it is otherwise with the poor who are content with their lot, who are faithful and diligent in their calling, who love labor better than idleness, who act sincerely and honestly, and then at the same time live a Christian life. I have several times conversed with those who were of the rustic class and of the lower order in society, who, while they lived in the world, believed in God, and did what was just and right in their vocations. They inquired what charity and faith are, because they were in the affection of knowing truth, and because in the world they had heard much about faith, but in the other life, much about charity. Wherefore they were told, that charity is everything which relates to life, and faith everything which relates to doctrine; consequently, that charity is to will and do what is just and right in every transaction, but faith, to think justly and rightly; and that faith and charity conjoin themselves like doctrine and a life according to it, or like thought and will; and that faith becomes charity, when that which a man thinks justly and rightly he also wills and does, and that then charity and faith are not two but one. This they understood perfectly; and rejoiced, saying, that

---

[1] That there is no such thing as immediate mercy, but that mercy is mediate, and is exercised toward those who live according to the Lord's precepts; because, from a principle of mercy, He leads them continually in the world, and afterward to eternity, n. 8700, 10659.

[2] That dignities and riches are not real blessings, and therefore that they are given to the wicked as well as to the good, n. 8939, 10775, 10776. That real blessing is the reception of love and faith from the Lord, and thereby conjunction; for thence comes eternal happiness, n. 1420, 1422, 2846, 3017, 3408, 3504, 3514, 3530, 3565, 3584, 4216, 4981, 8939, 10495.

when they were in the world they never conceived that believing was anything else than living.

365. From these considerations it may be manifest, that the rich go to heaven as well as the poor, and the one just as easily as the other. It is believed that the poor enter easily, and the rich with difficulty, because the Word has not been understood where the rich and poor are mentioned. By the rich there are meant, in the spiritual sense, those who abound in the knowledges of good and truth, thus those who are within the church where the Word is ; and by the poor, those who are deficient in these knowledges, and yet desire them,—thus those who are out of the church in countries where the Word is not. By the rich man who was clothed in purple and fine linen, and was cast into hell, is meant the Jewish nation, which is called rich because it had the Word, and thence abounded in the knowledges of good and truth ; by garments of purple are also signified the knowledges of good, and by garments of fine linen, the knowledges of truth :[1] but by the poor man who lay at his gate, and desired to be filled with the crumbs which fell from the rich man's table, and was carried by the angels into heaven, are meant the Gentiles, who had not the knowledges of good and truth, and yet desired them. (Luke xvi. 19, 31). By the rich who were invited to a great supper, and excused themselves, is also meant the Jewish nation, and by the poor introduced in their place, are meant the gentiles who were out of the church. (Luke xiv. 16 to 24). Who are meant by the rich man, of whom the Lord said, "*It is easier for a camel to go through the eye of a needle than for a rich man to enter into the kingdom of God*," (Matt. xix. 24), shall also be told. In this passage, the rich man denotes those who are rich in both senses, the natural as well as the spiritual. In the natural sense, the rich are those who abound in riches, and set their hearts upon them ; but in the spiritual sense, they are those who abound in knowledges and sciences,—for these are

---

[1] That garments signify truths, thus knowledges, n. 1073, 2576, 5319, 5954, 9212, 9216, 9952, 10536. That purple signifies celestial good, n. 9467. That fine linen signifies truth from a celestial origin, n. 5319, 9469, 9744.

spiritual riches,—and by means of them desire to introduce themselves into the things which belong to heaven and the church according to their own intelligence ; and because this is contrary to divine order, it is said that it is easier for a camel to go through the eye of a needle ; for by a camel in this sense is signified the principle of knowledge and science in general, and by the eye of a needle, spiritual truth.[1] That a camel and the eye of a needle have this signification, is not known at this day, because hitherto the science which teaches what is signified in the spiritual sense by those things which are said in the letter of the Word, has not been disclosed. For in every particular of the Word there is a spiritual sense, and also a natural sense ; for the Word,—in order that there might be conjunction of heaven with the world, or of angels with men,—after immediate conjunction ceased, was written by pure correspondences of natural things with spiritual. Hence it is evident who are specifically meant by the rich man in the above passage. That by the rich in the Word, in the spiritual sense, are meant those who are in the knowledges of truth and good, and by riches the knowledges themselves, which also are spiritual riches, may be evident from various passages ; as from Isaiah chap. x. 12, 13, 14 ; chap. xxx. 6, 7 ; chap. xlv. 3 ; Jer. chap. xvii. 3 ; chap. xlviii. 7 ; chap. l. 36, 37 ; chap. li. 13 ; Dan. chap. v. 2, 3, 4 ; Ezek. chap. xxvi. 7, 12 ; chap. xxvii. 1 to

---

[1] That a camel, in the Word, signifies the principle of knowledge and of science in general, n. 3048, 3071, 3143, 3145. What is meant by needle-work by working with a needle and hence by a needle, n. 9688. That to enter into the truths of faith from scientifics is contrary to divine order, n. 10236. That they who do so, become infatuated as to those things which are of heaven and the church, n. 128, 129, 130, 232, 233, 6047 ; and that in the other life, when they think about spiritual things, they become as it were drunken, n. 1072. Their quality further explained, n. 196. Examples to illustrate that spiritual things cannot be comprehended, if entrance to them be made by scientifics, n. 233, 2094, 2196, 2203, 2209. That from spiritual truth it is allowable to enter into the scientifics which are of the natural man, but not *vice versa ;* because spiritual influx into the natural principle is given, but not natural influx into the spiritual principle, n. 3219, 5119, 5259, 5427, 5428, 5478, 6322, 9110, 9111. That the truths of the Word and the church ought to be acknowledged first, and then it is allowable to consult scientifics, but not *vice versa,* n. 6047.

the end ; Zech. chap. ix. 3, 4 ; Psalm xl. 13 ; Hosea chap. xii. 9 ; Rev. chap. iii. 17, 18 ; Luke chap. xiv. 33 ; and elsewhere : and that by the poor in the spiritual sense, are signified those who have not the knowledges of good and truth, and yet desire them, Matt. chap. xi. 5 ; Luke chap. vi. 20, 21 ; chap. xiv. 21 ; Isaiah chap. xiv. 30 ; chap. xxix. 19 ; chap. xli. 17, 18 ; Zeph. chap. iii. 12, 18. All these passages may be seen explained according to the spiritual sense in the Arcana Cœlestia, n. 10227.

MARRIAGES IN HEAVEN.

366. Because heaven is from the human race, and the angels of heaven are therefore of both sexes ; and because it was ordained from creation that the woman should be for the man and the man for the woman, and thus that each should be the other's ; and because this love is innate in both ; it follows that there are marriages in the heavens as well as on earth. But marriages in the heavens are very different from those on earth. What therefore marriages in the heavens are, and in what they differ from marriages on earth, shall be told in what now follows.

367. Marriage in the heavens is the conjoining of two into one mind. What this conjunction is shall be first explained. The mind consists of two parts, one of which is called the understanding, the other the will. When these two parts act in unity, they are then called one mind. In heaven the husband acts that part which is called the understanding, and the wife that which is called the will. When this conjunction, which is of the interiors, descends into the inferiors, which are of the body, it is perceived and felt as love ; that love is conjugial love.* Hence

---

* [This word *conjugial* is not in common use in our language, but *conjugal* instead. Both are from the Latin, in which language they are written *conjugialis* and *conjugalis*. Though both these Latin words are alike classical, our author, when speaking of what he calls "conjugial love," has

it is evident, that conjugial love derives its origin from the conjunction of two into one mind. This is called in heaven cohabitation; and it is said that they are not two but one. Wherefore two married partners in heaven are not called two but one angel.[1]

368. That there is also such a conjunction of husband and wife in the inmosts, which are of their minds, results from creation itself; for the man is born to be intellectual, thus to think from the understanding, but the woman is born to be voluntary, thus to think from the will. This is evident from the inclination or connate disposition of each, as also from their form. *From the disposition*, in that the man acts from reason, but the woman from affection. *From the form*, in that the man has a rougher and less beautiful face, a harsher voice, and a more robust body; but the woman has a milder and more beautiful face, a softer voice, and a more delicate body. There is a similar distinction between the understanding and the will, or between thought and affection; similar also between truth and good, and between faith and love; for truth and faith belong to the understanding, and good and love to the will. Hence it is that in the Word, by

confined himself to the use of the former. The reason of this is doubtless to be found in the etymology of the two words. *Conjugialis* is derived, through *conjugium* (*marriage*, and *conjux,—a married partner*), from *conjungo*, which means *to conjoin*. Whereas *conjugalis* is from *conjugo*, which means *to yoke together*. Now while the idea of *conjunction* is quite in harmony with the author's doctrine concerning marriage, that of a *yoking together* is not—for in this latter is involved something of domination and servitude, which do not belong to true marriage. It is easy to see, therefore, why he selected the term *conjugialis*, instead of *conjugalis*. And as the original ideas remain in the words, when anglicized by lopping off their termination, the translators of Swedenborg have generally adopted the appropriate though unusual word, *conjugial*, instead of the common but less appropriate word, *conjugal.*—TR.]

[1] That it is unknown at this day what and whence conjugial love is, n. 2727. That conjugial love consists in mutually and reciprocally willing what the other wills, n. 2731. That they who are in conjugial love cohabit in the inmost principles of life, n. 2732. That in them there is a union of two minds, which from love becomes one, n. 10168, 10169; for the love of minds, which is spiritual love, is union, n. 1594, 2057, 3939, 4018, 5807, 6195, 7081 to 7086, 7501, 10130.

a young man and a man, in the spiritual sense, is meant the understanding of truth, and by a virgin and a woman, the affection of good ; and also that the church, from the affection of good and truth, is called a woman, and likewise a virgin ; also that all those who are in the affection of good are called virgins, as Apoc. xiv. 4.[1]

369. Every one,—man as well as woman,—possesses understanding and will ; but still with man the understanding predominates, and with woman the will, and the character of a person is determined by that which predominates. But in marriages in the heavens there is no predominance ; for the will of the wife is also that of the husband, and the understanding of the husband is also that of the wife ; since each loves to will and to think as the other, thus mutually and reciprocally. Hence their conjunction into one. This conjunction is actual conjunction ; for the will of the wife enters into the understanding of the husband, and the understanding of the husband into the will of the wife, more especially when they look each other in the face ; for, as has been often stated above, there is a communication of thoughts and affections in the heavens, and especially between conjugial partners, because they mutually love each other. From these considerations it may be manifest that the conjunction of minds, which makes marriage and produces conjugial love in the heavens, consists in this : that each one wishes all he has to be the other's, and thus reciprocally.

370. I have been told by the angels, that as far as two married partners are in such conjunction, so far they are in conjugial love, and at the same time in the like degree in intelligence, wis-

---

[1] That young men, in the Word, signify the understanding of truth, or one that is intelligent, n. 7668. That men have a like signification, n. 158, 265, 749, 915, 1007, 2517, 3134, 3236, 4823, 9007. That a woman signifies the affection of good and truth, n. 568, 3160, 6014, 7337, 8994: also the church, n. 252, 253, 749, 770: and that a wife signifies the same, n. 252, 253, 409, 749, 770: with what difference, n. 915, 2517, 3236, 4510, 4822. That husband and wife, in the supreme sense, are predicated of the Lord and of his conjunction with heaven and the church, n. 7022. That a virgin signifies the affection of good, n. 3067, 3110, 3179, 3189, 6731, 6742; and also the church, n. 2362, 3081, 3963, 4638, 6729, 6775, 6778.

dom, and happiness, because divine good and divine truth, from which all intelligence, wisdom, and happiness are derived, flow principally into conjugial love; consequently that conjugial love is the very plane of the divine influx, because it is at the same time the marriage of truth and good; for the conjunction of truth and good is as the conjunction of understanding and will; since the understanding receives divine truth, and is also formed of truths, and the will receives divine good, and is also formed of goods; for what a man wills, is to him good; and what he understands, is to him truth. Hence, whether we say the conjunction of the understanding and will, or the conjunction of truth and good, it is the same thing. The conjunction of truth and good makes an angel, and also his intelligence, wisdom, and happiness; for the quality of an angel is according to the degree in which good with him is conjoined to truth, and truth to good; or, what is the same, according to the degree in which love is conjoined to faith, and faith to love.

371. The Divine proceeding from the Lord flows principally into conjugial love, because conjugial love descends from the conjunction of good and truth; for, as just observed, whether we say the conjunction of understanding and will, or the conjunction of good and truth, it is the same thing. The conjunction of good and truth derives its origin from the Lord's divine love toward all who are in heaven and on earth. From the divine love proceeds divine good, and divine good is received by angels and men in divine truths. Truth is the only receptacle of good; wherefore nothing from the Lord and from heaven can be received by any one who is not in truths. As far, therefore, as truths with man are conjoined to good, so far he is conjoined to the Lord and heaven. This is the very origin of conjugial love; and therefore that love is the very plane of the divine influx. Hence it is that the conjunction of good and truth is called in the heavens the heavenly marriage; and that heaven is compared to a marriage in the Word, and is also called a marriage; and that the Lord is called the bridegroom and husband, and heaven with the church, the bride and wife.[1]

---

[1] That love truly conjugial derives its origin, cause, and essence from

L*

372. Good and truth conjoined in an angel or a man, are not
two but one, since good then belongs to truth and truth to good.
This conjunction is as when a man thinks what he wills, and
wills what he thinks; then thought and will make one, thus one
mind, for the thought forms, or exhibits in form, that which the
will wills, and the will imparts delight to the thought. Hence
also it is, that two conjugial partners in heaven are not called
two but one angel. This, too, is what is meant by the words
of the Lord: "*Have ye not read, that He who made* [*them*]
*from the beginning, made them male and female, and said:
For this cause shall a man leave father and mother, and
cleave to his wife, and they two shall be one flesh? Wherefore they are no more two, but one flesh. What, therefore,
God hath joined together, let not man put asunder.—All do not
comprehend this saying, but they to whom it is given.*" Matt.
xix. 4, 5, 6, 11; Mark x. 6, 7, 8, 9; Gen. ii. 24. Here is described the heavenly marriage in which the angels are, and at the
same time the marriage of good and truth; and by man's not
separating what God hath joined together, is meant that good
ought not to be separated from truth.

373. From these truths the origin of love truly conjugial may
now be seen; namely, that it is first formed in the minds of those
who are in marriage, and that descending thence, it is derived
into the body, and is there perceived and felt as love; for whatever is felt and perceived in the body derives its origin from
man's spiritual part, because from his understanding and will;

the marriage of good and truth, and thus that it is from heaven, n. 2728,
2729. Concerning angelic spirits, who have a perception whether there be
a conjugial principle, from the idea of the conjunction of good and truth,
n. 10756. That conjugial love is circumstanced altogether like the conjunction of good and truth, n. 1094, 2173, 2429, 2503, 3101, 3102, 3155, 3179,
3180, 4358, 5407, 5835, 9206, 9495, 9637. In what manner the conjunction
of good and truth is effected, and with whom, n. 3834, 4096, 4097, 4301,
4315, 4353, 4364, 4368, 5365, 7623 to 7627, 9258. That it is not known what
love truly conjugial is, except by those who are in good and truth from the
Lord, n. 10171. That marriage in the Word signifies the marriage of
good and truth, n. 3132, 4434, 4835. That the kingdom of the Lord and
heaven is in love truly conjugial, n. 2737.

and these make the spiritual man. Whatever descends from the spiritual man into the body, presents itself there under another form ; but still it is similar and accordant, like soul and body, and like cause and effect ; as may be manifest from what was said and shown in the two chapters concerning correspondences.

374. I heard an angel describing love truly conjugial and its heavenly delights, in this manner : that it is the Divine of the Lord in the heavens,—which is the divine good and the divine truth,—united in two beings, yet in such a manner that they are not two but' as one. He said that two conjugial partners in heaven are that love,—because every one is his own good and his own truth,—as to mind as well as to body ; for the body is the effigy of the mind, because formed in its likeness. Hence he concluded that the Divine is effigied in two, who are in love truly conjugial ; and because the Divine is effigied in them, so also is heaven,—for the universal heaven is the divine good and the divine truth proceeding from the Lord,—and that hènce all things of heaven are inscribed on that love, with beatitudes and delights more than can be numbered. He expressed the number by a term which involves myriads of myriads. He wondered that the man of the church knows nothing of this, when yet the church is the Lord's heaven on earth, and heaven is the marriage of good and truth. He said that he was astonished to think that adulteries are committed and also justified within the church more than out of it, when yet the delight of adultery is really nothing else, in the spiritual sense,—and consequently in the spiritual world,—than the delight of the love of the false conjoined with evil. This delight is infernal, because it is diametrically opposite to the delight of heaven, which is the delight of the love of truth conjoined with good.

375. Every one knows that two conjugial partners, who love each other, are interiorly united, and that the essential of marriage is the union of minds. Hence also it may be known, that the quality of their love and the nature of their union depend upon the essential character of their minds. The rational mind is formed solely of truths and goods ; for all things in the universe nave relation to good and truth, and also to their conjunction. Wherefore the union of minds is altogether such as are

the truths and goods from which they are formed ; consequently the union is most perfect between minds that are formed of genuine truths and goods. It is to be observed that no two things mutually love each other more than truth and good ; wherefore love truly conjugial descends from that love.[1] The false and the evil also love each other, but this love is afterward changed into hell.

376. From what has now been said concerning the origin of conjugial love, it may be inferred who are in that love, and who are not ; that they are in conjugial love who are in divine good from divine truths ; and that conjugial love is so far genuine as the truths which are conjoined to good are genuine ; and because all good, which is conjoined to truths, is from the Lord, it follows that no one can be in love truly conjugial, unless he acknowledge the Lord and His Divine ; for without that acknowledgment the Lord cannot flow-in, and be conjoined with the truths which are with man.

377. From these remarks it is evident that they are not in conjugial love who are in falses, and still less they who are in falses derived from evil. With those who are in evil and thence in falses, the interiors, which are of the rational mind, are also closed ; wherefore conjugial love can therein have no origin ; but beneath those interiors, in the external or natural man separate from the internal, there is the conjunction of the false and evil, which is called the infernal marriage. I have been permitted to see what the marriage is between those who are in the falses of evil, which is called the infernal marriage. They converse with each other, and are also conjoined from a lascivious principle ; but interiorly they burn with deadly hatred toward each other,— a hatred so intense as to surpass all description.

---

[1] That all things in the universe, both in heaven and in the world, have relation to good and truth, n. 2451, 3166, 4390, 4409, 5232, 7256, 10122 ; and to their conjunction, n. 10555. That between good and truth there is a marriage, n. 1094, 2173, 2503. That good loves, and from love desires, truth, and its conjunction with itself, and that hence they are in a perpetual tendency to conjunction, n. 9206, 9207, 9495. That the life of truth is from good. n. 1589, 1997, 2579, 4070, 4096, 4097, 4736, 4757, 4884, 5147, 9667. That truth is the form of good, n. 3049, 3180, 4574, 9154. That truth is to good as water to bread, n. 4976.

378. Neither can conjugial love exist between two who are
of a different religion, since the truth of the one does not agree
with the good of the other, and two dissimilar and discordant
principles cannot make one mind out of two; wherefore the
origin of their love partakes not at all of the spiritual. If they
cohabit and agree together, it is only from natural causes.[1] For
this reason marriages in the heavens are contracted between
those who are of the same society, because they are in similar
good and truth; but not between members of different societies.
(That all who are in the same society, are in similar good and
truth, and differ from those in other societies, may be seen above,
n. 41, and following paragraphs). This was also represented
with the Israelitish nation by marriages being contracted within
tribes, and specifically within families, and not out of them.

379. Neither can love truly conjugial be given between one
husband and more wives than one; for this destroys its spiritual
origin, which is the formation of one mind out of two; consequently it destroys interior conjunction, which is that of good
and truth, from which is the very essence of conjugial love.
Marriage with more than one wife is like an understanding divided
among more wills than one; and like a man who is attached
to more churches than one, whereby his faith is so distracted that
it becomes no faith. The angels say, that to have a plurality of
wives is altogether contrary to divine order; and that they know
this from many causes, and from this likewise, that as soon as
they think of marriage with more than one, they are estranged
from internal blessedness and heavenly felicity, and that they then
become like drunken persons, because good with them is disjoined from its truth; and because the interiors which are of their
minds come into such a state, from the mere thought of poly-
gamy with any intention, they clearly perceive that marriage
with more than one closes the internal man, and causes conjugial
love to be supplanted by the love of lasciviousness, which love
draws away from heaven.[2] They say further, that it is hard

[1] That marriages between those who are of a different religion are un-
lawful, on account of the non-conjunction of similar good and truth in
the interiors, n. 8998.
[2] Since husband and wife ought to be one, and to cohabit in the inmost

for man to comprehend this, because there are few who are in genuine conjugial love ; and they who are not in it, know nothing whatever of the interior delight inherent in that love, but only of the delight of lasciviousness, which is turned into what is undelightful after they have lived together for a short time. But the delight of love truly conjugial not only endures to old age in the world, but also becomes the delight of heaven after death, and is then filled with interior delight, which is perfected to eternity. They also said that the blessednesses of love truly conjugial might be reckoned at many thousands, of which not even one is known to man, or can be conceived of by the understanding of any one who is not in the marriage of good and truth from the Lord.

380. The love of exercising dominion one over the other, completely takes away conjugial love and its heavenly delight ; for, as was said above, conjugial love and its delight consist in this, that the will of one be that of the other, and this mutually and reciprocally. The love of dominion in marriage destroys this ; for he who domineers wishes that his will alone should be in the other, and none of the others reciprocally in himself; hence there is nothing mutual, consequently no reciprocal communication of one's love and its delight with the other ; yet this communication, and thence conjunction, is the interior delight itself in marriage, which is called blessedness. The love of dominion completely extinguishes this blessedness, and with it all celestial and spiritual love, so that it is not known that it exists ; and if its existence should be admitted, it would be accounted so worthless, that at the bare mention of blessedness from such a source they would

principle of their lives ; and since they together constitute one angel of heaven ; therefore love truly conjugial cannot exist between one husband and several wives, n. 1907, 2740. That to marry more wives than one at the same time, is contrary to divine order, n. 10837. That marriage cannot exist except between one husband and one wife, is clearly perceived by those who are in the Lord's celestial kingdom, n. 865, 3246, 9961, 10172. The reason is, because the angels there are in the marriage of good and truth, n. 3246. That the Israelitish nation were permitted to marry several wives, and to adjoin concubines to wives, but that Christians are not so permitted ; because the Israelites were in externals without internals, but Christians may be in internals, and thus in the marriage of good and truth, n. 3246, 4837, 8809.

either laugh or be angry. When one wills or loves what the other does, both enjoy freedom, for all freedom is the offspring of love; but where there is dominion, neither is free; one is a slave, and so is the other that exercises dominion, because he is led as a slave by the lust of domineering. But this is utterly incomprehensible to him who is ignorant of the freedom of heavenly love. Still, from what has been said above concerning the origin and essence of this love, it may be known that as far as dominion enters, so far minds are not conjoined but divided; for dominion subjugates, and a subjugated mind has either no will, or an opposite will. If it has no will, it also has no love; and if it has an opposite will, there is hatred instead of love. The interiors of those who live in such a marriage, are in mutual collision and combat with each other, as is the case between two opposites, however the exteriors may be restrained and kept quiet for the sake of peace. The collision and combat of their interiors reveal themselves after death; when they generally meet together and fight like enemies, and mutually lacerate each other; for they then act according to the state of their interiors. I have several times been permitted to witness their combats and tearings, some of which were full of revenge and cruelty; for the interiors of every one are set at liberty in the other life, and are no longer restrained by externals on account of worldly considerations, for then every one appears openly such as he is interiorly.

381. There exists with some a certain resemblance of conjugial love, but still it is not conjugial love if they are not in the love of good and truth. It is a love appearing like conjugial from many causes; as, that they may be served at home; that they may live in security, or in tranquility, or at ease; or that they may be taken care of in sickness and old age; or for the sake of their children whom they love. In some instances it is constrained through fear of the other partner, or of loss of reputation, or of evil consequences; and in others the appearance is induced by lasciviousness. Conjugial love differs also with the two partners, with one there may be more or less of it, with the other little or nothing; and because it differs, heaven may be the portion of one, and hell of the other.

382. There is genuine conjugial love in the inmost heaven, be-

cause the angels of that heaven are in the marriage of good and
truth, and also in innocence.   The angels of the inferior heavens
are also in conjugial love, but only so far as they are in innocence, for conjugial love, regarded in itself, is a state of innocence ; wherefore married partners who are in conjugial love
enjoy heavenly delights, which appear before their minds almost
like the sports of innocence, as among infants ; for everything
delights their minds, because heaven with its joy flows into each
of the things of their life.   Wherefore conjugial love is represented in heaven by the most beautiful objects.   I have seen it
represented by a virgin of inexpressible beauty, encompassed
with a bright cloud ; and I have been told that the angels in heaven derive all their beauty from conjugial love.   The affections
and thoughts which flow from it are represented by adamantine
auras sparkling as with carbuncles and rubies ; and such representations are attended with delights which affect the interiors of
their minds.   In a word, heaven represents itself in conjugial
love, because heaven with the angels is the conjunction of good
and truth, and this conjunction makes conjugial love.

Marriages in the heavens differ from marriages on earth in
this respect, that, besides other uses, marriages on earth are
for the procreation of offspring, but not in the heavens ; there,
instead of such procreation, there is the procreation of good
and truth.   This procreation is instead of the former, because
marriage in the heavens is the marriage of good and truth,—as
was shown above,—and in that marriage, good and truth and their
conjunction are loved above all else ; these, therefore, are what
are propagated from marriages in the heavens.   Hence it is, that
by nativities and generations in the Word are signified spiritual
nativities and generations, which are those of good and truth.
Mother and father signify truth conjoined to good which procre-
ates ; sons and daughters, the truths and goods which are pro-
created ; and sons-in-law and daughters-in-law, the conjunctions
of these ; and so on.[1]   From these things it is evident that mar-

---

[1] 'That conceptions, births, nativities, and generations signify spiritual
conceptions, births, and nativities, which are those of good and t.uth, or
of love and faith, n. 613, 1145, 1155, 2020, 2584, 3860, 3868, 4070, 4668

riages in the heavens are not like marriages on earth. In the heavens the nuptials are spiritual, and should not be called nuptials, but conjunctions of minds from the marriage of good and truth; but on earth they are nuptials, because they are not only of the spirit, but also of the flesh. And because there are no nuptials in the heavens, therefore two married partners there are not called husband and wife, but each is called,—from the angelic idea of the conjunction of two minds into one,—by a term which signifies what is each one's mutual reciprocally. From these things it may be known, how the Lord's words concerning nuptials are to be understood. Luke xx. 35, 36.

383. How marriages are contracted in the heavens, I have also been allowed to see. Everywhere in heaven those who are alike are consociated, and those who are unlike are dissociated. Hence every society of heaven consists of like ones; they who are alike are brought together, not of themselves but of the Lord, (see above, n. 41, 43, 44 *et seq.*). In like manner conjugial partners, whose minds are capable of being conjoined into one, are drawn together; wherefore at first sight they deeply love each other, and see that they are conjugial partners, and enter into marriage. Hence it is that all the marriages in heaven are of the Lord alone. They also hold a festival on the occasion, which is attended by a numerous company. The festivities differ in different societies.

384. The angels regard marriages on earth as most holy, because they are the seminaries of the human race, and also of the angels of heaven,—for, as was shown above in its proper chapter, heaven is from the human race; also because they are from a spiritual origin, namely, from the marriage of good and truth; and because the Divine of the Lord flows primarily into conju-

6239, 8042, 9325, (10197). That hence generation and nativity signify regeneration and re-birth by faith and love, n. 5160, 5598, 9042, 9845. That a mother signifies the church as to truth, and thus also the truth of the church; and a father the church as to good, and thus also the good of the church, n. 2691, 2717, 3703, 5580, 8897. That sons signify the affections of truth, and thus truths, n. 489, 491, 533, 2623, 3373, 4257, 8649, 9807. That daughters signify the affections of good, and thus goods, n. 489, 490, 491, 2362, 3963, 6729, 6775, 6778, 9055. That a son-in-law signifies truth associated to the affection of good, n. 2389. That a daughter-in-law signifies good associated to its truth, n. 4843.

gial love   And on the other hand, they regard adulteries as profane, because they are contrary to conjugial love ; for as in marriages the angels behold the marriage of good and truth, which is
heaven, so in adulteries they behold the marriage of the false and
evil, which is hell.   Wherefore when they only hear adultery
mentioned, they turn themselves away.   This also is the reason
why heaven is closed against a man when he commits adultery
from delight ; and when heaven is closed, he no longer acknowledges the Divine, nor anything pertaining to the faith of the
church.[1]   That all who are in hell are in opposition to conjugial
love, it has been given me to perceive from the sphere thence
exhaling, which was like a perpetual endeavor to dissolve and
violate marriages.   From this it was evident that the ruling
delight in hell is the delight of adultery ; and that the delight of
adultery is also the delight of destroying the conjunction of
good and truth, which conjunction makes heaven.   Hence it
follows that the delight of adultery is an infernal delight, altogether opposed to the delight of marriage, which is a heavenly
delight.

385. There were certain spirits who, from habit acquired in
the life of the body, infested me with peculiar cunning, and this
by an influx gentle and as it were undulatory, like that of well-
disposed spirits ; but I perceived that there was craftiness and
similar evils in them, which prompted them to ensnare and deceive.   At length I spoke with one of them, who, I was told,
had been the leader of an army when he lived in the world ; and
perceiving that something lascivious lurked in the ideas of his
thought, I spoke with him concerning marriage, in spiritual language with representatives, whereby the sense intended is fully

---

[1] That adulteries are profane, n. 9961, 10174.   That heaven is closed
against adulterers, n. 2750.   That they who have taken delight in adulteries, cannot enter into heaven, n. 539, 2733, 2747, 2748, 2749, 2751, 10175.
That adulterers are unmerciful, and without a religious principle, n. 824,
2747, 2748.   That the ideas of adulterers are filthy, n. 2747, 2748.   That in
the other life they love filth, and are in filthy hells, n. 2755, 5394, 5722.
That by adulteries, in the Word, are signified the adulterations of good;
and by whoredoms the perversions of truth, n. 2466, 2729, 3399, 4865,
8904, 10648.

expressed, and many ideas in a moment. He said that in the life of the body he made light of adulteries. But it was given me to tell him that adulteries are heinous, although from the delight with which they captivate such as himself, and from the persuasion thence induced, they appear not to be so, yea, to be allowable; that he might also be convinced of this, from the fact that marriages are the seminaries of the human race, and thence also of the kingdom of heaven; and that therefore they ought on no account to be violated, but to be accounted holy; as also from the fact, which he ought to be aware of,—being then in the other life, and in a state of perception,—that conjugial love descends from the Lord through heaven, and that from that love as from a parent is derived mutual love, which is the support of heaven; also from this, that adulterers, when they only approach the heavenly societies, are made sensible of their own stench, and cast themselves headlong thence toward hell; that at least he might know, that to violate marriages is contrary to the divine laws, and contrary to the civil laws of all kingdoms, as well as to the genuine light of reason, because contrary to order both divine and human; not to mention many other considerations. But he replied, that he had never thought of such things in the life of the body. He wished to reason whether it were so, but was told, that truth does not admit of reasonings, for they favor delights, thus evils and falses; and that he ought first to think of the things which had been said, because they are truths; or even from that principle so well known in the world, that no one ought to do to another what he is not willing that another should do to him; and that if any one had so deceived his wife whom he had loved, as is always the case in the first period of marriage, then if he spoke from the state of wrath excited by the outrage, whether he himself would not also have detested adulteries; and then, as a man of good capacity, whether he would not have confirmed himself more than others against them, and have condemned them even to hell.

386. It has been shown me how the delights of conjugial love progress toward heaven, and the delights of adultery toward hell. The progression of the delights of conjugial love toward heaven was into blessednesses and happinesses continually increasing in

number, until they became innumerable and ineffable; and the more interiorly they progressed, the more innumerable and ineffable they became, until they reached the very blessednesses and happinesses of the inmost heaven, which is the heaven of innocence, and this with the most perfect freedom; for all freedom is from love, and therefore the most perfect freedom is from conjugial love, which is heavenly love itself. But the progression of adultery was toward hell, and by degrees to the lowest, where there is nothing but what is direful and horrible. Such is the lot which awaits adulterers after their life in the world. By adulterers are meant those who perceive delight in adulteries, and no delight in marriages.

THE EMPLOYMENTS OF THE ANGELS IN HEAVEN.

387. It is impossible to enumerate or describe specifically the employments of heaven, for they are innumerable and various according to the offices of the societies; but only something may be said of them in a general way. Every society performs a peculiar office; for as the societies are distinct according to goods, (see above, n. 41), they are also distinct according to uses, since goods with all in the heavens are goods in act, which are uses. Every one there performs a use, for the kingdom of the Lord is a kingdom of uses.[1]

388. There are in the heavens, as on earth, various administrations; for there are ecclesiastical affairs, civil affairs, and domestic affairs. That there are ecclesiastical affairs, is manifest

---

[1] That the kingdom of the Lord is a kingdom of uses, n. 454, 696, 1103, 3645, 4054, 7038. That to serve the Lord is to perform uses, n. 7038. That all in the other life must perform uses, n. 1103, even the wicked and infernal; but in what manner, n. 696. That all derive their quality from the uses which they perform, n. 4054, 6815; illustrated, n. 7038. That angelic blessedness consists in the goods of charity, and thus in performing uses, n. 454.

from what was said and shown above concerning divine worship,
(n. 221 to 227) ; that there are civil affairs, is manifest from what
was said concerning governments in heaven, (n. 213 to 220) ; and
that there are domestic affairs, is manifest from what was said
concerning the habitations and mansions of the angels, (n. 183
to 190), and concerning marriages in heaven, (n. 366 to 386).
Hence it is evident, that there are many employments and administrations in every heavenly society.

389. All things in the heavens are instituted according to divine
order, which is everywhere guarded by administrations executed
by the angels; the wiser angels taking charge of those things
belonging to the general good or use, and the less wise, of such
as relate to particular goods or uses ; and so on. They are subordinated, just as in divine order, uses are subordinated. Hence also
dignity is attached to every employment according to the dignity
of the use. No angel, however, arrogates the dignity to himself,
but ascribes it all to the use ; and because use is the good which he
performs, and all good is from the Lord, therefore he ascribes it
all to the Lord. Wherefore he who thinks of honor for himself
and thence for use, and not for use and thence for himself, cannot
perform any office in heaven ; because he looks backward from
the Lord, regarding himself in the first place and use in the
second. When use is spoken of, the Lord also is meant, because,
as remarked just above, use is good, and good is from the Lord.

390. From these considerations it may be inferred what subordinations in the heavens are, namely, that as every one loves,
esteems, and honors use, so also he loves, esteems, and honors
the person to whom that use is adjoined ; and also that the person is loved, esteemed, and honored, in the degree that he does
not ascribe the use to himself, but to the Lord ; for in that degree
he is wise, and the uses which he performs are performed from
a principle of good. Spiritual love, esteem, and honor, are
nothing else than the love, esteem and honor of use in the person
who performs it; and the honor of the person is from the use,
and not that of the use from the person. He also who regards
men from spiritual truth, regards them in no other way ; for he
sees that one man is like another, whether he be in great dignity
or in little; that they differ only in wisdom, and that wisdom

consists in loving use, and thus in loving the good of a fellow citizen, of society, of the country, and of the church. In this also consists love to the Lord, because all good, which is the good of use, is from the Lord; and love toward the neighbor also, because the neighbor is the good which is to be loved in a fellow-citizen, in society, in the country, and in the church, and which is to be done to them.[1]

391. All the societies in the heavens are distinct according to uses, since they are distinct according to goods, as was said above, (n. 41, *et seq.*); and the goods are goods in act, or the goods of charity, which are uses. There are societies whose employments consist in taking care of infants; there are other societies whose employments are to instruct and educate them as they grow up; there are others who in like manner instruct and educate boys and girls, who are of a good disposition from education in the world, and who thence come into heaven; others who teach the simple good from the Christian world, and lead them in the way to heaven; others who perform the same office for the various Gentile nations; others who defend novitiate spirits, —those who have recently come from the world,—from infestations by evil spirits; some also who are attendant on those in the lower earth; and some who are present with those in hell, and restrain them from tormenting each other beyond the prescribed limits; there are some also who attend upon those who are being raised from the dead. In general, angels of every society are

---

[1] That to love the neighbor is not to love his person, but to love that which appertains to him, and which constitutes him, n. 5025, 10336. That they who love the person, and not that which appertains to the man, and constitutes the man, love the evil and the good alike, n. 3820: and that they do good alike to the evil and to the good, when yet to do good to the evil is to do evil to the good, which is not to love the neighbor, n. 3820, 6703, 8120. The judge who punishes the evil that they may be amended, and to prevent the good being contaminated and injured by them, loves his neighbor, n. 3820, 8120, 8121. That every man and every society, our country and the church, and in a universal sense the kingdom of the Lord, are the neighbor; and that to do good to them from the love of good according to the quality of their state, is to love the neighbor. Their good therefore, which is to be consulted, is the neighbor, n. 6818 to 6824, 8123.

sent to men, that they may guard them, and withdraw them from evil affections and consequent evil thoughts, and inspire them with good affections, so far as they receive them freely. By means of these affections also they rule the deeds or works of men, removing from them evil intentions as far as possible. When angels are with men, they have their abode as it were in their affections ; and they are near a man, in proportion as he is in good derived from truths ; but more remote, in proportion as his life is distant from good.[1] But all these employments of the angels are functions performed by the Lord through them ; for the angels perform them, not from themselves, but from the Lord. Hence it is that by angels in the Word, according to its internal sense, are not meant angels, but something of the Lord ; and for the same reason angels in the Word are called gods.[2]

392. These employments of the angels are their general employments ; but to each one is assigned his particular use ; for every general use is composed of innumerable others, which are called mediate, ministering, and subservient uses. All and each of these are co-ordinated and sub-ordinated according to divine order, and, taken together, they constitute and perfect the general use, which is the common good.

393. Ecclesiastical affairs in heaven are under the charge of those who, when in the world, loved the Word, and earnestly sought for the truths which it contains, not for the sake of honor or gain, but for the sake of the use of life, both their own and others. These are in illustration and in the light of wisdom in

---

[1] Concerning angels who attend on infants, and afterward on boys successively, n. 2303. That man is raised from the dead by angels, from experience, n. 168 to 189. That angels are sent to those who are in the hells, to prevent their tormenting each other beyond measure, n. 967. Concerning the offices of angels toward men who come into the other life, n. 2131. That spirits and angels are attendant on all men, and that man is led by spirits and angels from the Lord, n. 50. 697, 2796. 2887. 2888, 5847 to 5866, 5976 to 5993, 6209. That angels have dominion over evil spirits, n. 1755.

[2] That by angels, in the Word, is signified something divine from the Lord. n. 1925, 2821, 3039, 4085. 6280. 8192. That angels, in the Word, are called gods, from their reception of divine truth and good from the Lord, n. 4295, 4402, 8192, 8301.

heaven according to their love and desire of use; for they come into that light in the heavens from the Word, which is not natural there as in the world, but spiritual, (see above, n. 259). These perform the office of preachers; and according to divine order there, those are in a superior place, who excel others in wisdom from illustration. Civil affairs are administered by those who, while in the world, loved their country and its general good in preference to their own, and did what is just and right from the love of justice and rectitude. Such men possess capacity for administering offices in heaven, in proportion as their love of rectitude has prompted them to inquire into the laws of justice, and thence to become intelligent. The offices which they administer correspond exactly to the degree of their intelligence, and their intelligence is then in like degree also with their love of use for the general good. Moreover, there are so many offices and administrations in heaven, and so many employments also, that it is impossible to enumerate them on account of their multitude. Those in the world are comparatively few. All, how many soever there be, are in the delight of their occupation and labor from the love of use, and no one from the love of self or gain; nor is any one influenced by the love of gain for the sake of maintenance, because all the necessaries of life are given them gratis,—their habitations, their garments, and their food. From these things it is evident, that they who have loved themselves and the world more than use, have no lot in heaven; for every one's own love or affection remains with him after his life in the world, nor is it extirpated to eternity, (see above, n. 363).

394. Every one in heaven is in his work according to correspondence; and the correspondence is not with the work, but with the use of every work, (see above, n. 112); and there is a correspondence of all things, (see n. 106). He in heaven, who is in an employment or work corresponding to his use, is in a state of life exactly like that in which he was in the world,—for what is spiritual and what is natural act as one by correspondences—but with this difference: that he is in more interior delight, because in spiritual life, which is interior life, and hence more receptive of heavenly blessedness.

HEAVENLY JOY AND HAPPINESS.

395. SCARCELY any one at the present day knows what heaven and heavenly joy are. They who have thought about both, have conceived an idea concerning them so gross and general, that it scarcely amounts to an idea. From the spirits who pass out of the world into the other life, I have been able to learn most accurately what notion they entertained about heaven and heavenly joy; for, when left to themselves, they think in the same manner as they did in the world. It is not known what heavenly joy is, because they who have thought about it have formed their judgment from the external joys which belong to the natural man; and have known nothing of the internal or spiritual man, and therefore nothing of his delight and blessedness. Wherefore if it had been declared by those who have been in spiritual or internal delight, what the nature of heavenly joy is, it would not have been comprehended, for it would have fallen into an unknown idea, thus not into perception; wherefore it would have been among those things which the natural man would have rejected. Yet every one may know that man, when he leaves the external or natural man, comes into the internal or spiritual; hence it may be known that heavenly delight is internal and spiritual, not external and natural; and because it is internal and spiritual, that it is purer and more exquisite than natural delight, and that it affects the interiors of man which belong to his soul or spirit. From these considerations alone, every one may conclude that his delight in the other world will be of the same nature as the delight of his spirit in this world; and that the delight of the body, which is called the delight of the flesh, is respectively not heavenly. Moreover, that which is in the spirit of man when he leaves the body remains with him after death; for then he lives a man-spirit.

396. All delights flow from love; for what a man loves, he feels to be delightful, nor is there delight from any other source. Hence it follows, that such as the love is, such is the delight. The delights of the body or the flesh all flow from the love of

self and the love of the world, whence also are concupiscences
and their attendant pleasures; but the delights of the soul or
spirit all flow from love to the Lord and love toward the neighbor, whence also are the affections of good and truth, and interior
satisfactions. These loves with their delights flow-in from the
Lord and from heaven by an internal way, which is from above,
and affect the interiors; but the former loves with their delights
flow-in from the flesh and from the world by an external way,
which is from beneath, and affect the exteriors. In the degree,
therefore, that those two loves of heaven are received and affect
man, the interiors which belong to the soul or spirit are opened,
and look from the world to heaven; but in the degree that those
two loves of the world are received and affect him, the exteriors
which are of the body or the flesh are opened, and look from
heaven to the world. As loves flow in and are received, so do
their delights also flow in with them,—the delights of heaven
into the interiors, and the delights of the world into the exteriors; since, as has been said, all delight is of love.

397. Heaven in itself is so full of delights, that, viewed in
itself, it is nothing but delight and blessedness; for the divine
good proceeding from the Lord's divine love makes heaven both
in general and in particular with every one there; and the divine
love wills the salvation and happiness of all from inmosts and
completely. Hence it is, that whether we speak of heaven or of
heavenly joy, it is the same thing.

398. The delights of heaven are ineffable and likewise innumerable; but innumerable as they are, not one can be known or
believed by him who is in the mere delight of the body or the
flesh, since, as observed above, his interiors look from heaven to
the world, thus backward; for he who is altogether in the delight
of the body or the flesh, or what is the same, in the love of self
and the world, feels no delight but in honor, gain, and the pleasures of the body and the senses; and these so extinguish and
suffocate interior delights, which are of heaven, as to destroy all
belief in their existence. Such a man therefore would greatly
wonder, if he were only told that when the delights of honor and
of gain are removed, other delights remain; and still more, if he
were told that the delights of heaven which succeed in the place

of them are innumerable, and of such a nature that the delights of the body and the flesh, which are principally those of honor and gain, cannot be compared with them. Hence the reason is plain why the nature of heavenly joy is not known.

399. How great the delight of heaven is, may appear from this circumstance alone, that it is delightful to all there to communicate their delights and blessings to each other; and because all in the heavens are of this character, it is obvious how immense is the delight of heaven; for, (as was shown above, n. 268), there is in the heavens communication of all with each, and of each with all. Such communication flows from the two loves of heaven, which, as was said, are love to the Lord and love toward the neighbor; and it is the nature of these loves to communicate their delights. Love to the Lord is of this nature, because the Lord's love is the love of communicating all that He has to all His creatures, for He wills the happiness of all; and a similar love is in each of those who love Him, because the Lord is in them. Hence there is with the angels a mutual communication of their delights to each other. That love toward the neighbor is also of a similar quality, will be seen in what follows. From these considerations it may be evident that it is the nature of those loves to communicate their delights. It is otherwise with the loves of self and of the world. The love of self withdraws and takes away all delight from others, and directs it to itself, for it wishes well to itself alone; and the love of the world wishes that what is the neighbor's were its own. Wherefore these loves are destructive of delights with others. If they are communicative, it is for the sake of themselves, and not for the sake of others; wherefore in respect to others they are not communicative, but destructive, except so far as the delights of others respect themselves, or are in themselves. That the loves of self and of the world, when they rule, are of this character, has often been granted me to perceive by living experience. Whenever spirits, who were in those loves while they lived as men in the world, approached me, my delight receded and vanished; and I have been told that if such spirits only approach toward any heavenly society, the delight of those in the society is diminished precisely according to the degree of their presence; and,

what is wonderful, those wicked spirits are then in their delight. Hence it became evident what is the state of the spirit of such a man when in the body, for it is similar to what it is after separation from the body ; namely, that he desires or covets the delights or goods of another, and that as far as he obtains them, so far he is delighted.   From these considerations it may be seen, that the loves of self and of the world are destructive of the joys of heaven, thus altogether opposite to heavenly loves, which are communicative.

400. It is, however, to be observed, that the delight experienced by those who are in the loves of self and of the world, when they approach any heavenly society, is the delight of their concupiscence, and is therefore utterly opposed to the delight of heaven.   They come into the delight of their concupiscence, when they deprive or remove heavenly delight from those who are in it.   The case is otherwise when such deprivation and removal are not effected ; for then they cannot approach, because in the degree that they advance, they come into anguish and distress.   On this account they seldom venture to come near.   This, too, it has been given me to know by repeated experience, some of which I will also relate.   Spirits who come from the world into the other life, desire nothing more than to be admitted into heaven.   Almost all seek to gain admittance, imagining that heaven consists only in being introduced and received.   Wherefore also because they desire it, they are conveyed to some society of the lowest heaven ; but when they who are in the love of self and the world approach the first threshold of that heaven, they begin to be so distressed and tormented interiorly, that they feel hell in themselves rather than heaven ; wherefore they cast themselves down headlong thence, nor do they find rest until they come into hell among their like.   It has often happened also that such spirits desired to know what heavenly joy is ; and when they heard that it is in the interiors of the angels, they have wished to have it communicated to themselves.   Wherefore this also was granted, —for whatever a spirit desires, who is not yet in heaven or in hell, is granted him if it be beneficial.   But when the communication was made, they began to be tortured to such a degree that they knew not into what posture to screw their bodies on account

of the pain. I saw them force their heads down even to their feet, cast themselves upon the ground, and there writhe themselves into folds in the manner of a serpent, and this by reason of the inward agony. Such was the effect which heavenly delight produced upon those who were in delights from the love of self and the world. The reason is, because those loves are altogether opposite to the loves of heaven; and when one opposite acts upon another, such pain is produced. Heavenly delight enters by an internal way; when, therefore, it is communicated to the wicked, it flows into a contrary delight, and bends backward the interiors which are in that delight, thus turns them into what is contrary to their nature. Hence arise such tortures. The opposition of heavenly and infernal loves results from their very nature; for, as was said above, love to the Lord and love toward the neighbor wish to communicate all their own to others, for this is their delight; and the love of self and of the world wish to take from others what belongs to them, and to appropriate it to themselves, and are in their delight so far as they succeed. From these considerations it may also be known why hell is separated from heaven; for all who are in hell, when they lived in the world, were in the mere delights of the body and the flesh from the love of self and the world; but all who are in heaven, when they lived in the world, were in the delights of the soul and the spirit from love to the Lord and love toward the neighbor. Because these loves are opposite, therefore the heavens and the hells are so entirely separated, that a spirit who is in hell dares not raise the crown of his head, or even put forth a finger thence; for the moment he attempts it, he is racked and tortured. This, too, I have often seen.

401. The man who is in the loves of self and the world, so long as he lives in the body, feels delight from those loves, and also in each of the pleasures to which they give birth: but the man who is in love to God and in love toward the neighbor, does not, so long as he lives in the body, feel a manifest delight from those loves and from the good affections thence derived, but only a blessedness almost imperceptible, because it is stored up in his interiors, and veiled by the exteriors which are of the body, and blunted by worldly cares. But the states are entirely changed

after death.　The delights of the love of self and the world are then turned into painful and horrible sensations, which are called hell-fire, and occasionally into things defiled and filthy, corresponding to their unclean pleasures, which,—strange to say,—are then delightful to them; but the obscure delight and almost imperceptible blessedness, which had been enjoyed by those in the world who were in love to God and in love toward the neighbor, are then turned into the delight of heaven, which becomes perceptible and sensible in all manner of ways; for that blessedness, which lay stored up and hidden in their interiors when they lived in the world, is then revealed and brought forth into manifest sensation, because they are then in the spirit, and that was the delight of their spirit.

402. All the delights of heaven are conjoined with uses, and are inherent in them, because uses are the goods of love and charity in which the angels are; wherefore every one has delights corresponding in quality with his uses, and in degree with his affection for use.　That all the delights of heaven are the delights of use, may be manifest from comparison with the five senses of the body.　To every sense is given a delight according to its use; to the sight is given its delight; to the hearing, smell, taste, and touch,—to each its own delight.　The sight derives its delight from the beauties of color and form; the hearing, from harmonious sounds; the smell, from pleasant odors; and the taste, from things savory.　The uses which each sense respectively performs, are known to those who inquire into such subjects, and more fully to those who are acquainted with their corresponlences.　The sight has such delight, on account of the use which it performs to the understanding, which is the internal sight; the hearing, on account of its use to the understanding and the will by hearkening; the smell, on account of the use which it performs to the brain and also to the lungs; and the taste, on account of its use to the stomach, and thence to the whole body, in the matter of nourishment.　Conjugial delight, which is a purer and more exquisite delight of touch, surpasses all the rest on account of its use, which is the procreation of the human race, and thence of the angels of heaven.　These delights are in those sen

sories on account of the influx from heaven, where every delight is from use and according to use.

403. Certain spirits, from an opinion conceived in the world, believed heavenly happiness to consist in an idle life, and in being served by others ; but they were told that happiness by no means consists in mere rest from employment, because every one would then desire that others' happiness should be his own ; and if every one had this desire, none would be happy. Such a life would not be active but indolent, and through indolence the faculties would become torpid; when yet they might know, that without an active life there can be no happiness, and that cessation from employment is only for the sake of recreation, that one may return with greater alacrity to the active business of his life. It was afterward shown by numerous evidences, that angelic life consists in performing the goods of charity, which are uses, and that the angels find all their happiness in use, from use, and according to use. They who entertained the idea that heavenly joy consisted in living an idle life, and in breathing eternal delight without employment, were allowed to perceive the quality of such a life, in order to make them ashamed ; and it was found to be extremely sad, and that after a short time—all joy having thus departed—they felt only disgust and loathing for it.

404. Some spirits who believed themselves better instructed than others, said that it was their belief in the world that heavenly joy consisted solely in praising and glorifying God, and that this was an active life. But they were told, that to praise and glorify God is not such an active life, and that God has no need of praises and glorification, but that His will is that they perform uses, and thus the good works which are called goods of charity. But they could have no idea of heavenly joy in doing the goods of charity, but an idea of servitude. The angels however testified, that in the performance of such good works there is the highest freedom, because it proceeds from interior affection, and is conjoined with ineffable delight.

405. Almost all who enter the other life, suppose that every one is in the same hell, or in the same heaven ; when yet there are infinite varieties and diversities in both. The hell of one is never precisely like that of another, nor is the heaven of one ex

actly the same as the heaven of another; just as no man, spirit,
or angel is ever exactly like another, even as to the face. When
I only thought that two might be exactly alike or equal, the angels were astonished, saying that every whole [*unum*] is formed
by the harmonious agreement of many parts, and that the character of the whole is according to that agreement: and that thus every
society of heaven makes a one, and all the societies of heaven collectively; and this from the Lord alone by love.[1] In like manner
uses in the heavens are according to all variety and diversity.
The use of one angel is never exactly similar to, or the same as,
that of another; nor is the delight of one altogether like the
delight of another. And further still,—the delights of every
one's use are innumerable; and those innumerable delights are
in like manner various, but yet conjoined in such order that they
mutually regard each other, like the uses of every member, organ, and viscus in the body, and still more like the uses of every
vessel and fibre in each member, organ, and viscus; each and all
of which are so connected together, that every one regards its
own good in another, and thus each in all and all in each.
From this universal and particular regard they act as one.

406. I have several times conversed with spirits who had recently come from the world, concerning the state of eternal life,
remarking that it is important to know who is the Lord of
the kingdom, what the nature of the government, and what
its form; for, as nothing is of greater moment to those in the
world who remove to another kingdom, than to know who the
king is, and what his character, what the nature of his government, and many other particulars relating to that kingdom, so it
is of still greater importance that such knowledge be had respect-

---

[1] That one thing consists of various things, and hence receives form
and quality and perfection according to the quality of their harmony and
agreement, n. 457, 3241, 8003. That variety is infinite, and that in no
case is any one thing the same as another, n. 7236, 9002. That a like variety exists in heaven, n. 5744, 4005, 7236, 7833, 7836, 9002. That hence
all the societies in the heavens, and every angel in every society, are distinct from each other, because in various good and use, n. 690, 3241, 3519,
3804, 3986, 4067, 4149, 4263, 7236, 7833, 7986. That the divine love of the
Lord arranges all into a heavenly form, and conjoins them so that they
are as one man, n. 457, 3986, 5598.

ing this kingdom, in which they are to live to eternity. Let them know, therefore, that the Lord is the King who governs heaven, and also the universe,—for He who governs one governs the other; thus that the kingdom wherein they now are is the Lord's, and the laws of this kingdom are eternal truths which are all based upon this law, that they love the Lord above all things and their neighbor as themselves; and still further,—if now they wished to be like the angels,—they ought to love their neighbor better than themselves. On hearing these things, they were unable to make any reply, because in the life of the body they had heard something of the kind, but had not believed it. They marveled that there should be such love in heaven, and that it were possible for any one to love his neighbor more than himself. But they were informed that all goods increase immensely in the other life, and that man's life while in the body is such that he cannot go beyond loving his neighbor as himself, because he is in corporeal principles; but when these are removed the love becomes more pure, and at length angelic, which is to love the neighbor more than themselves; for in the heavens it is delightful to do good to another, and not delightful to do good to themselves unless that the good may become another's, thus for the sake of another; and that this is to love the neighbor more than themselves. The possible existence of such love was urged from the conjugial love of some persons in the world, in that they have preferred death rather than suffer a consort to be injured; from the love of parents toward their children, in that a mother would suffer hunger rather than see her little child in want of food: as also from sincere friendship, in that one friend will expose himself to perils for the sake of another; and from civil and pretended friendship, which seeks to emulate the genuine, in that it will offer its choicest things to those for whom it professes good-will,—carrying such good-will also in the mouth, though not in the heart; finally, from the nature of love, which finds its joy in serving others, not for its own sake but for theirs. B t these things they could not comprehend who loved themselves more than others, and who, in the life of the body had been greedy of gain; and least of all could the covetous.

407. A certain one who, in the life of the body, had been

35   M*

man of superior power, retained also in the other life his desire
to command ; but he was told that he was in another kingdom,
which is eternal ; that the authority which he had on earth had
expired ; and that, in the world where he now is, no one is esteemed except according to good and truth, and that measure
of the Lord's mercy whereof he is in the enjoyment on account of
his life in the world ; also that this kingdom is circumstanced like
kingdoms on earth, where men are esteemed on account of their
wealth, and on account of their favor with the sovereign ; wealth
here being good and truth, and favor with the sovereign being
the Lord's mercy, which is dispensed to every one according to
his life in the world ; and that if he desired to rule in any other
way, he is a rebel, for he is in the kingdom of another sovereign.   On hearing these things he was ashamed.

408. I have conversed with spirits who supposed heaven and
heavenly joy to consist in being great ; but they were told, that in
heaven he is greatest who is least, for he is called least who has
no power and wisdom and desires to have none from himself, but
from the Lord : He who is least in this sense, has the greatest
happiness ; and because he has the greatest happiness, it thence
follows that he is the greatest ; for thus he has all power from the
Lord, and excels all others in wisdom.   And what is it to be the
greatest, unless to be most happy ?—for to be most happy is what
the powerful seek by power, and the rich by riches.   They were
further told, that heaven does not consist in desiring to be the
least with a view to being the greatest,—for then one sighs and
longs to be the greatest,—but in cordially desiring the good of
others more than one's own, and in serving them for the sake of
their happiness, not with any selfish regard to recompense, but
from love.

409. Heavenly joy itself, such as it is in its essence, cannot be
described, because it is in the inmosts of the life of the angels, and
thence in every particular of their thought and affection, and
from these in every particular of their speech and action.   It is
as if their interiors were wide open and free to receive delight
and blessedness, which is distributed to every single fibre, and
thus throughout the whole frame.   The perception and sensation
of delight and blessedness thence resulting, surpass all descrip-

tion; for that which commences from the inmosts, flows into every particular thence derived, and propagates itself with continual augmentation toward the exteriors. When good spirits, who are not yet in that delight, because not yet taken up into heaven, perceive it from an angel by the sphere of his love, they are filled with such delight that they come as it were into a delicious trance. This has often occurred with those who desired to know the nature of heavenly joy.

410. Certain spirits also were desirous to know what heavenly joy is; therefore they were allowed to perceive it to such a degree that they could bear it no longer; but still it was not angelic joy,—scarcely in the least degree angelic. This was proved by its actual communication to me, when I perceived that it was so slight as almost to partake of something rather frigid; and yet they called it most celestial, because it was their inmost joy. Hence it was manifest, not only that there are degrees of the joys of heaven, but also that the inmost joy of one scarcely approaches the ultimate or middle joy of another; also, that when any one receives that which is the inmost to him, he is in his own heavenly joy, and cannot bear a more interior degree thereof, but would find it painful.

411. Certain spirits, not evil, fell into a state of repose like sleep, and were thus as to the interiors of their minds translated to heaven,—for spirits, before their interiors are opened, may be translated to heaven, and instructed concerning the happiness of those there. I saw them in this state of repose for about half an hour; after which they relapsed into their exteriors in which they were before, but still retaining the recollection of what they had seen. They said that they had been among the angels in heaver, and had there seen and perceived things stupendous, all shining as with gold, silver, and precious stones, admirable in form and astonishing in variety; and that the angels were not delighted with the external things themselves, but with those which they represented, which were divine, ineffable, and of infinite wisdom, and that these were to them a source of joy; besides innumerable other things, not the ten thousandth part of which could be expressed in human language, or fall into ideas which partake in any degree of materiality.

412. Almost all who enter the other life, are ignorant of the nature of heavenly blessedness and felicity, because they do not know what and of what quality internal joy is, forming their idea of it from corporeal and worldly joy and gladness. What they are ignorant of they therefore regard as nothing, when yet corporeal and worldly joys are comparatively of no account. In order therefore that the well-disposed, who are unacquainted with the nature of heavenly joy, may understand and know what it is, they are first conveyed to paradisiacal scenes which surpass every conception of the imagination. They now suppose that they have come into the heavenly paradise; but they are taught that this is not, in reality, heavenly happiness. It is therefore granted them to experience the interior states of joy perceptible to their inmosts. They are then brought into a state of peace even to their inmost, when they confess that nothing of its nature can ever be expressed or conceived. Finally they are brought into a state of innocence, even to their inmost sense thereof. Hence it is granted them to know what spiritual and celestial good really is.

413. But in order that I might know what, and of what nature, heaven and heavenly joy are, it has been often, and for a long time, granted me by the Lord to perceive the delights of heavenly joys. Since, therefore, I have had living experience of them, I know what they are, but can never describe them. But in order that some idea of them may be formed, a few things shall be told concerning them.

Heavenly joy is an affection of innumerable delights and joys, which, taken together, constitute a certain general state or affection, wherein are the harmonies of innumerable affections which do not come distinctly but obscurely to the perception, because the perception is of the most general kind. Still it was granted me to perceive that innumerable things were included in it, so arranged that they could not possibly be described. Those innumerable things are such as flow from the order of heaven. Such is the order in each of the particulars of the affection, even the most minute, which are presented to the mind and perceived only as one most general whole, according to the capacity of the person who is their subject. In a word, infinite things arranged in the most orderly form are contained in every general thing; and there is not one of them that does not live, and exert an influence, and all indeed from the inmosts, for thence all heavenly joys proceed. I also perceived that the joy and delight came as from the heart, diffusing themselves very gently through all the inmost fibres, and thence into the collections of fibres, with such an inmost sense of enjoyment, that every fibre seemed as it were nothing but joy and delight, and thence all the perceptive and sensitive faculties in like manner seemed alive with happiness. The joy of bodily pleasures, compared with those joys, is like coarse and offensive grime, compared with the pure and sweetest aura.* I observed that when I wished to transfer all my delight to another, there flowed-in continually a delight more interior and full, in place of the former; and the more intensely I desired to do this, the more abundant was the influx of this delight; and this I perceived to be from the Lord.

414. They who are in heaven are continually advancing toward the spring-time of life; and the more thousands of years they live, the more delightful and happy is the spring to which they attain. And this goes on forever, with augmentations according to the progress and degrees of their love, charity, and faith. Those of the female sex, who have died old and worn out with age, and who have lived in faith in the Lord, in charity toward their neighbor, and in happy conjugial love with a husband, after a succession of years, come more and more into the bloom of youth, and into a beauty surpassing every conception of beauty formed from that which the eye has ever seen. Goodness and charity are what mould their form, presenting it in their own likeness, and causing the delight and beauty of charity to shine forth from every feature of the face, so that they are themselves the forms of charity. Some who have seen them, have been amazed at the sight. The form of charity, which is seen to the

---

* [*Aura* is a term often employed by the author, to describe an atmosphere of the third or highest degree of purity. For he makes the atmospheres, both in the spiritual and the natural world, to consist of three degrees; to the lowest of these,—being the one perceptible to the senses,— he gives the name of air (*aer*); to the middle, that of ether (*æther*); and to the third or highest, that of *aura*.—Tr.]

life in heaven, is such that charity itself is what effigies and is effigied; and this so perfectly, that the whole angel, and especially the face, is as it were charity, which is both plainly seen and perceived. When this form is attentively surveyed, it is seen to be beauty ineffable, affecting with charity the very inmost life of the mind. In a word, to grow old in heaven is to grow young. They who have lived in love to the Lord and in charity toward the neighbor, become such forms or such beauties in the other life. All the angels are such forms, with innumerable variety; and of these heaven consists.

THE IMMENSITY OF HEAVEN.

415. THAT the Lord's heaven is immense, may appear from many things which have been said and shown in the foregoing chapters; and especially from this, that heaven is from the human race, (see above, n. 311 to 317), not from those only who are born within the church, but also from those who are born without it, (n. 317 to 328), thus from all who have lived in good since the first creation of this earth. How vast is the multitude of men in all this terrestrial globe, any one may conclude who has any knowledge of the quarters, regions, and kingdoms of this earth. Whoever goes into the calculation, will find that many thousands of men die every day, and some myriads or millions every year; and this has been going on from the earliest times, since which, some thousands of years have elapsed; and of these, all after their decease have entered the other world, which is called the spiritual world, and are still entering it continually. But how many of them have become, and are now becoming, angels of heaven, it is impossible to say. I have been told that in ancient times their number was very great, because at that period men thought more interiorly and spiritually, and thence were in heavenly affection; but that in the following ages they became

less numerous, because in process of time man became more external, and began to think more naturally, and thence to be in earthly affection. From these facts it may be evident in the outset, that the heaven formed solely from the inhabitants of this earth, must be of vast magnitude.

416. That the heaven of the Lord is immense, may be manifest from this one fact: that all little children, whether born within the church or out of it, are adopted by the Lord and become angels. The number of these amounts to a fourth or fifth part of the entire human race on earth. That every little child wheresoever born,—whether within the church or without it, whether of pious or impious parents,—is received by the Lord when he dies, educated in heaven, taught according to divine order, imbued with affections of good and by them with the knowledges of truth, and that afterwards,—as he is perfected in intelligence and wisdom,—he is introduced into heaven, and becomes an angel, may be seen above, (n. 329 to 345). It may therefore be concluded how vast a multitude of angels of heaven, have sprung from this source alone since the first creation to the present time.

417. The immensity of the Lord's heaven may also be manifest from this consideration, that all the planets which are visible to the eye in our solar system, are earths; and that, besides these, there are innumerable others in the universe, all full of inhabitants. These have been particularly treated of in a small work concerning those earths, from which I will adduce the following passage:

"That there are many earths inhabited by men, from whom come spirits and angels, is well known in the other life; for every one there, who desires it from the love of truth and thence of use, is allowed to converse with spirits from other earths, and thence to be assured of the existence of a plurality of worlds, and to be informed that the human race belongs not to one earth only, but to innumerable ones. I have several times conversed on this subject with spirits from our earth, and observed, that any intelligent person may know from many things with which he is acquainted, that there are numerous earths inhabited by men; for it may be reasonably inferred that immense bodies like the

planets, some of which exceed this earth in magnitude, are not
empty masses, created merely to circulate round the sun, and
shed their scanty light upon a single earth. but that their use
must be more important than that. He who believes, as every
one ought to believe, that the Divine created the universe for no
other end than the existence of the human race, and thence of
heaven,—for the human race is the seminary of heaven,—cannot
help believing that wheresoever there is an earth, there must also
be men. That the planets,—which are visible to us, because
within the limits of our solar system,—are earths, may be readily
inferred from the fact, that they are bodies of earthy matter, as
is evident from their reflecting the light of the sun ; and when
viewed through telescopes, they do not appear like stars glowing
with flame, but like earths variegated with shadows ; also from
the fact, that they in like manner as our earth, are carried round
the sun, and travel through the zodiac, thereby causing years, and
the seasons of the year, spring, summer, autumn, and winter ;
likewise that they revolve on their own axis like our earth,
whence they have days, and the times of the day, morning,
mid-day, evening, and night ; and besides, that some of them
have moons, called satellites, which revolve around their prima-
ries in fixed periods, as the moon around our earth ; and that the
planet Saturn, on account of its great distance from the sun, has
also a large luminous belt, which gives much light, though re-
flected, to that earth. Who that is acquainted with these facts,
and thinks from reason, can ever say that these are empty
bodies? Moreover, I have remarked, when conversing with
spirits, that man may believe that there are more earths in the
universe than one, from the fact that the starry heaven is so immense, and the stars therein of various magnitudes so innumerable, every one of which, in its place or system, is a sun, and
similar to the sun of our world. Whoever duly considers the
subject, must conclude that all this immense apparatus cannot
but be a means to an end, which is the ultimate end of creation ;
that end is, the existence of a heavenly kingdom, in which the
Divine may dwell with angels and men. For the visible universe or heaven, bright with so many stars which are so many
suns, is only a means provided for the existence of earths. with

men upon them, from whom may be formed a heavenly king dom. From these things a rational man cannot but conclude, that so vast a means provided for so great an end, was not made for the human race of one earth only. What would this be for the Divine, who is infinite, and to whom thousands, yea, myriads of earths, and all full of inhabitants, would be but little, and scarcely anything? There are spirits whose only study it is to acquire knowledges, because in these alone they find delight. Therefore they are permitted to pass out of this solar system into others, and to procure for themselves knowledges. These have told me that there are earths inhabited by men not only in this solar system, but also beyond it in the starry heaven, and that their number is immense. These spirits are from the planet Mercury. It has been calculated that if there were a million of earths in the universe, and three hundred millions of men on every earth, and two hundred generations in six thousand years, and a space of three cubic ells were allowed to every man or spirit, the total number would not fill the space of this earth, and scarcely more than the space occupied by a satellite of one of the planets. This would be a portion of the universe so small as to be almost invisible, for a satellite is scarcely visible to the naked eye. What is this for the Creator of the universe, to whom it would not be enough if the whole universe were filled, for He is infinite? I have conversed with the angels on this subject, and they said that they entertain a similar idea concerning the fewness of the human race in respect to the infinity of the Creator; but that still they do not think from spaces, but from states; and that, according to their idea, earths to the number of as many myriads as can possibly be conceived, would still be absolutely nothing to the Lord."

Concerning the earths in the universe, with their inhabitants, and the spirits and angels who come from them, see in the above-mentioned little work. Its contents were revealed and shown to me, in order that it may be known that the Lord's heaven is immense, and that it is all from the human race; also that our Lord is everywhere acknowledged as the God of heaven and earth.

418. That the heaven of the Lord is immense, may also be

36

manifest from this consideration : That heaven in the whole complex resembles one man, and also corresponds to all and each of the parts of man ; and that this correspondence can never be filled up, since it is not only a correspondence with every member, organ, and viscus of the body in general, but also in particular and singular with all and each of the little viscera and little organs within them, yea, with every single vessel and fibre ; and not with these only, but also with the organic substances which interiorly receive the influx of heaven, and are the immediate sources of interior activities subservient to the operations of the mind ; for whatever exists interiorly in man, exists in forms which are substances ; and what does not exist in substances as its subjects is nothing.   There is a correspondence of all these things with heaven, as may be seen in the chapter on the correspondence of all things of heaven with all things of man, (n. 87 to 102).   This correspondence can never be filled up, because heaven becomes more perfect in proportion to the number of angelic associations which correspond to any one member.   The reason that perfection in the heavens increases with the increase of numbers, is because all there have one end, and all unanimously look to that end.   This end is the common good ; and when this rules, every individual derives good from the common good, and the common good results from the good of each individual.   This results from the fact that the Lord turns all in heaven toward Himself, (see above, n. 123), thereby causing them to be one in Him.   That the unanimity and concord of many, especially when derived from such an origin and united in such a bond. produces perfection, every one whose reason is in any degree enlightened, may clearly see.

419. I have likewise been permitted to behold the extent of the heaven which is inhabited, and of that also which is not inhabited ; and I saw that the extent of the heaven which is not inhabited, is so vast that it conld not be filled to eternity, even if there were myriads of earths, and in every earth as great a multitude of people as in ours.   On this subject also see the small work concerning the Earths in the Universe, n. 168.

420. That heaven is not immense, but of limited extent, is a conclusion drawn by some from certain passages of the Word

understood according to the sense of the letter; as from those wherein it is said, that none but the poor are received into heaven; also none but the elect; and only those who are within the church, and not those who are out of it; that it is only the former for whom the Lord intercedes; that heaven will be shut when it is full, and that the time for this is predetermined. But such persons are not aware that heaven will never be shut, and that there is no such time predetermined, nor any definite number to be admitted; that those are called the elect, who are in the life of good and truth;[1] and that the poor are those who are not in the knowledges of good and truth, and still desire them; these also, on account of that desire, are called the hungry.[2] They who have conceived the opinion that heaven is small in extent, in consequence of not understanding the Word, suppose that it is in one place, where there is a general assembly of all; when yet heaven consists of innumerable societies. (see above, n. 41 to 50). And they also imagine that heaven is granted to every one from immediate mercy, and thus that admission and reception depend solely upon the good pleasure [of the Lord]. They do not understand that the Lord from mercy leads every one who receives Him; and that he receives Him who lives according to the laws of divine order, which are the precepts of love and faith; and that to be thus led by the Lord from infancy to the end of life in the world, and afterward to eternity, is what is meant by mercy. Let all such know, therefore, that every man is born for heaven; and that he is received who receives heaven in himself while in the world, and that he is excluded who does not receive it.

---

[1] That they are the elect who are in the life of good and truth, n. 3755, 3900. That there is no election and reception into heaven from mere mercy, as is generally understood, but according to life, n. 5057, 5058. That the Lord's mercy is not immediate, but mediate; that it is shown to those who live according to His precepts, and that from a principle of mercy He leads them continually in the world, and afterward to eternity, n. 8700, 10659.

[2] That by the poor, in the Word, are meant those who are spiritually poor, that is, who are in ignorance of truth, but still desire to be instructed, n. 9209, 9253, 10227. They are said to hunger and thirst, to denote their desire of the knowledges of good and truth, by which introduction into the church and heaven is obtained, n. 4958, 10227.

WORLD OF SPIRITS,

THE STATE OF MAN AFTER DEATH.

WHAT THE WORLD OF SPIRITS IS.

421. THE world of spirits is neither heaven nor hell, but an intermediate place or state between both. For thither man goes first after death; and then, after a certain period, the duration of which depends upon what kind of a life he has lived in the world, he is either elevated into heaven or cast into hell.

422. The world of spirits is an intermediate place between heaven and hell, and also the intermediate state of man after death. That it is an intermediate place, was made evident to me from the fact, that the hells are beneath and the heavens above; and that it is an intermediate state, from the fact, that so long as man is there, he is neither in heaven nor in hell. The state of heaven with man is the conjunction of good and truth with him; and the state of hell is the conjunction of evil and the false. When good with a man-spirit [*i. e.* a man now become a spirit] is conjoined with truth, he then enters heaven, because, as just remarked, that conjunction is heaven with him; but when with a man-spirit evil is conjoined with the false, he then enters hell, because that conjunction is hell with him. This conjunction takes place in the world of spirits, since man is then in the intermediate state. Whether we say the conjunction of the understanding and the will, or the conjunction of truth and good, it is the same thing.

423. First, something is to be said here concerning the con-

junction of the understanding and the will, and its likeness to
the conjunction of truth and good, since that conjunction takes
place in the world of spirits. Man possesses understanding and
will. The understanding receives truths, and is formed from
them ; and the will receives goods, and is formed from them.
Wherefore whatever a man understands and thence thinks, he
calls true, and whatever he wills and thence thinks, he calls good.
Man can think from the understanding, and thence perceive what
is true, and likewise what is good ; but still he does not think it
from the will, unless he wills and does what the understanding
approves. When he thus wills and acts, then truth is in both
the understanding and the will, consequently in the man ; for the
understanding alone does not make the man, nor the will alone,
but the understanding and the will together ; what therefore is
in both, is in the man, and is appropriated to him. What is in
the understanding only, is indeed with the man, but not in him ;
it is merely a thing of his memory, and of science in the memory, whereof he can think when he is not in himself, but out of
himself with others ; thus it is something about which he can
converse and reason, and conformable to which he can also feign
affections and manner.

424. Man has the capacity of thinking from the understanding
and not at the same time from the will, in order that he might be
capable of reformation ; for man is reformed by means of truths ;
and truths, as just remarked, belong to the understanding. Man
is born into all evil as to the will, and thence of himself he
wills good to no one but himself alone ; and he who wills good
to himself alone, delights in the misfortunes that befall others,
especially if they tend to his own advantage : for he wishes to
appropriate to himself the goods of all others, whether they be
honors or riches, and inwardly rejoices so far as he is successful.
In order that this state of the will may be amended and reformed,
man is gifted with the capacity of understanding truths, and of
subduing thereby the evil affections which spring from the will.
Hence it is that man is able to think truths from the understanding, and also to speak them and do them ; but still he cannot
think them from the will, until he is such that he wills and does
them from himself, that is, from the heart. When such is the

quality of a man, then the truths which he thinks from the understanding are of his faith, and those which he thinks from the will are of his love; wherefore faith and love are then conjoined with him, like understanding and will.

425. So far, therefore, as the truths of the understanding are conjoined to the goods of the will, that is, so far as man wills truths and thence does them, he has heaven in himself, because, as was said above, the conjunction of good and truth is heaven; but so far as the falses of the understanding are conjoined to the evils of the will, man has hell in himself, because the conjunction of the false and the evil is hell; but so far as the truths of the understanding are not conjoined to the goods of the will, man is in an intermediate state. Almost every man at this day is in such a state, that he is acquainted with truths, and thence also thinks from knowledge and understanding, and either does many of them, or few, or none, or acts against them from the love of evil and thence the belief of what is false. In order therefore that he may be a subject either of heaven or hell, he is brought after death first into the world of spirits, and there the conjunction of good and truth takes place with those who are to be elevated into heaven, and the conjunction of evil and the false with those who are to be cast into hell. For no one either in heaven or in hell is allowed to have a divided mind, understanding one thing and willing another; but what one wills he must understand, and what he understands he must will. Wherefore he who wills good in heaven must understand truth, and he who wills evil in hell must understand falsity. Therefore with the good, falses are removed in the world of spirits, and truths are given them suitable and conformable to their good; and with the evil, truths are removed, and falses given them suitable and conformable to their evil. From these disclosures it may be evident what the world of spirits is.

426. In the world of spirits there is a vast number, because the first meeting of all [after their decease] is there, and all are there examined and prepared for their final abode. The period of their sojourn in that world is not in all cases the same. Some only enter it, and shortly after are either conveyed to heaven or cast down to hell; some remain there only a few weeks; others, sev

eral years, but not more than thirty. The varieties in the term
of sojourn there, arise from the correspondence or non-corre-pon-
dence of the interiors and exteriors with man. But in what manner a person in that world is led from one state to another, and
prepared for his final abode, will be told in what follows.

427. As soon as men enter the world of spirits after their decease, they are accurately discriminated by the Lord. The evil
are immediately bound to the infernal society in which they were
as to their ruling love when in the world, and the good are immediately bound to the heavenly society in which they were
when in the world as to love, charity and faith. But although
they are thus distinguished, still those who have been friends and
acquaintances in the life of the body, all meet and converse
together in the world of spirits, when they desire it; especially
wives and husbands, and also brothers and sisters. I have seen
a father conversing with six sons whom he recognized; and
many others conversing with their relations and friends; but as
their characters were dissimilar in consequence of their life in
the world, after a short time they separated. But they who pass
from the world of spirits into heaven or hell, afterward see each
other no more, nor do they know anything about each other, unless
they are of similar disposition from similar loves. They see each
other in the world of spirits, and not in heaven nor in hell, because they who are in the world of spirits are brought into states
similar to those which they had experienced in the life of the
body, being led from one into another; but afterward, all are
brought into a permanent state similar to that of their ruling
love; and in that state one knows another only from similitude
of love; for (as shown above, n. 41 to 50) similitude conjoins,
and dissimilitude separates.

428. As the world of spirits is an intermediate state with man
between heaven and hell, so likewise it is an intermediate place.
Beneath are the hells, and above are the heavens. All the hells
are shut toward that world, being open only through holes and
clefts as of rocks, and through wide chasms, which are guarded
to prevent any one going out except by permission, which also is
granted in cases of urgent necessity, of which I shall speak hereafter. Heaven likewise is enclosed on all sides, nor is there ac-

ress to any heavenly society except by a narrow way, the entrance
of which is also guarded. Those outlets and these entrances are
what are called, in the Word, the gates and doors of hell and of
heaven.

429. The world of spirits appears like an undulating valley
between mountains and rocks. The gates and doors leading to the
heavenly societies do not appear, except to those who are prepared
for heaven ; nor are they found by any others. To every society
there is one entrance from the world of spirits, beyond which there
is one path, which in its ascent branches into several. Nor do the
gates and doors leading to the hells appear, except to those who are
about to enter, to whom they are then opened ; and when opened,
there appear dusky and as it were sooty caverns, tending obliquely downward to the deep, where again there are more doors.
Through these caverns exhale noisome and fetid stenches, which
good spirits flee from, because they have an aversion to them, but
which evil spirits draw near to, because they are delightful to
them ; for as every one in the world is delighted with his own
evil, so after death he is delighted with the stench to which his
evil corresponds. Such persons may be compared, in this respect, to rapacious birds and beasts, as ravens, wolves, and swine,
which fly and run to carrion and dunghills when they scent their
stench. I once heard a certain spirit utter a loud cry, as if from
inward torture, on being struck by the breath exhaled from heaven ; and I saw the same spirit serene and joyful when struck by
the breath exhaled from hell.

430. There are two gates also with every man, one of which
opens toward hell, and is open to the evils and falses thence proceeding ; the other opens toward heaven, and is open to the
goods and truths thence proceeding. The gate of hell is open to
those who are in evil and thence in falsity, and only through
clefts from above a few rays of light flow-in from heaven,
whereby the man is able to think, reason, and talk ; but the gate
of heaven is open to those who are in good and thence in truth.
For there are two ways which lead to man's rational mind ; a
superior or internal way, through which good and truth from
the Lord enter, and an inferior or external way, through which
evil and falsity steal in from hell. The rational mind itself is in

the middle toward which the ways lead; therefore in the degree that light from heaven is admitted, man is rational, but in the degree that it is not admitted, he is not rational, however the case may appear to himself. These observations are made, in order that it may also be known what is the correspondence of man with heaven and with hell. His rational mind, during the time of its formation, corresponds to the world of spirits; whatever is above it corresponds to heaven, and whatever is beneath it, to hell. The parts above it are opened, and those beneath it are shut, against the influx of evil and falsity with those who are being prepared for heaven; but the parts beneath it are opened, and those above it are shut, against the influx of goodness and truth with those who are being prepared for hell. Hence the latter cannot look otherwise than beneath them, that is, toward hell; and the former cannot look otherwise than above them, that is, toward heaven. To look above themselves, is to look to the Lord, because He is the common centre toward which all things of heaven look; but to look beneath themselves is to look back from the Lord to the opposite centre, toward which all things of hell look and tend, (see above, n. 123 and 124).

431. Wherever spirits are mentioned in the preceding pages, those who are in the world of spirits are meant; and by angels, those who are in heaven.

EVERY MAN IS A SPIRIT AS TO HIS INTERIORS.

432. WHOEVER duly considers the subject, may know that the body does not think, because it is material; but that the soul does think, because it is spiritual. The soul of man, about the immortality of which so many have written, is his spirit; for this is immortal as to all that pertains to it. It is this also which thinks in the body, for it is spiritual; and what is spiritual receives what is spiritual, and lives spiritually, which is to think and to will. All the rational life, therefore, which appears in

the body, belongs to the spirit, and nothing of it to the body ; for the body, as was said above, is material ; and materiality, which is proper to the body, is added, and almost as it were adjoined, to the spirit, in order that the spirit of man may live and perform uses in the natural world, whereof all things are material, and in themselves void of life. And since what is material does not live, but only what is spiritual, it may be evident that whatever lives in man is his spirit, and that the body only serves it, as an instrument is subservient to a living moving force. It is said, indeed, of an instrument, that it acts, moves, or strikes ; but to believe that these acts are those of the instrument, and not of him who acts, moves, or strikes by means of it, is a fallacy.

433. Since everything that lives in the body, and from life acts and feels, belongs exclusively to the spirit, and nothing of it to the body, it follows that the spirit is the real man ; or, what is similar, that man considered in himself is a spirit, and that the spirit is also in a form similar to that of the body ; for whatever lives and feels in man belongs to his spirit,—and everything in him, from his head to the sole of his foot, lives and feels. Hence it is, that when the body is separated from its spirit, which is called dying, the man still continues a man, and lives. I have heard from heaven that some who die, when they are lying upon the bier, before they are resuscitated, think even in their cold body ; nor do they know otherwise than that they still live, except that they are unable to move a single material particle belonging to the body.

434. Man cannot think and will, unless there be a subject which is a substance, from which and in which he may think and will. Whatever is supposed to exist without a substantial subject, is nothing. This may be known from the fact that man cannot see without an organ which is the subject of his sight, nor hear without an organ which is the subject of his hearing. Sight and hearing are nothing without these, nor can they exist. It is the same also with thought, which is internal sight ; and with perception, which is internal hearing : unless these existed in and from substances, which are organic forms that are the subjects of those faculties, they could not exist at all. From these considerations it may be manifest that the spirit of man is

in a form as well as his body, and that its form is the human; and that it enjoys sensories and senses when separated from the body, just the same as when it was in it; and that all of the life of the eye, and all of the life of the ear, in a word, all of the sensitive life that man enjoys, belongs not to his body, but to his spirit; for his spirit dwells in them, and in every minutest part thereof. Hence it is that spirits see, hear, and feel. the same as men; but after separation from the body, not in the natural world, but in the spiritual. The natural sensation which the spirit had when it was in the body, was by means of the material which was adjoined to it; but even then it enjoyed spiritual sensation at the same time, by thinking and willing.

435. These observations are made in order that the rational man may be convinced, that man, in himself considered, is a spirit, and that the corporeal frame adjoined to him for the sake of performing functions in the natural and material world, is not the man, but only an instrument for the use of his spirit. But confirmations from experience are preferable, because the deductions of reason are not comprehended by many, and because they who have confirmed themselves in the contrary opinion, turn them into matters of doubt by reasonings drawn from the fallacies of the senses. It is usual for those who have confirmed themselves in the contrary opinion, to think that beasts live and feel the same as man, and thus that they, too, have a spiritual nature like that of man; and yet that dies with the body. But the spiritual of beasts is not the same as the spiritual of man. For man has (and beasts have not) an inmost, into which the Divine flows, and thereby elevates man to, and conjoins him with, Himself. Hence man, above the beasts, is able to think of God, and of the divine things which belong to heaven and the church, and to love God from and in those things, and thus be conjoined to Him; and whatever is capable of being conjoined to the Divine, cannot be dissipated, but whatever is incapable of such conjunction, is dissipated. The inmost, which man has above beasts, was treated of above, n. 39; and it is here repeated, because it is important that the fallacies thence conceived [*i. e.* through ignorance of the difference between man and beast] be dissipated; and these fallacies prevail with many,

who, from a deficiency of knowledges, and a contracted understanding, are incapable of forming rational conclusions on such subjects. The words in the passage referred to, are these: " I will relate a certain arcanum concerning the angels of the three heavens, which has never before entered the mind of any one, because no one has hitherto understood the subject of degrees. The arcanum is this: that with every angel, and also with every man, there is an inmost or supreme degree, or an inmost or supreme something, into which the Divine of the Lord first or proximately flows, and from which it arranges the other interior things which succeed according to the degrees of order with the angel or man. This inmost or supreme [region] may be called the Lord's entrance to angels and men, and His veriest dwelling-place with them. By virtue of this supreme or inmost, man is man, and is distinguished from brute animals; for these do not possess it. Hence it is that man, different from animals, can, as to all the interiors of his rational and natural minds (*mentis et animi ejus*) be elevated by the Lord to Himself, can believe in Him, be affected with love toward Him, and thus see Him; and that he can receive intelligence and wisdom, and converse in a rational manner. It is for this reason also that he lives forever. But what is disposed and provided by the Lord in this inmost [region], does not come manifestly to the perception of any angel, because it is above his thought, and transcends his wisdom."

436. That man is a spirit as to his interiors, has been taught me by much experience, which, were I to adduce the whole of it, would fill volumes,—to use a common saying. I have conversed with spirits as a spirit, and I have conversed with them as a man in the body. And when I conversed with them as a spirit, they knew no otherwise than that I myself was a spirit, and in the human form as they were. Thus my interiors appeared to them; for when I conversed with them as a spirit, my material body did not appear.

437. That man is a spirit as to his interiors, may appear from the fact, that after his separation from the body, which takes place at death, he still lives a man as before. That I might be confirmed in this, I have been permitted to converse with almost

all whom I ever knew when they lived in the body; with some for hours, with others for weeks and months, and with others for years, and this chiefly in order that I might be sure of it, and bear testimony to its truth.

438. I may add to what has already been said, that every man, as to his spirit, is in society with spirits even while he lives n the body, although he does not know it. By them as mediums a good man is in some angelic society, and an evil man in some infernal society; and after death he comes into the same society. This has been often told and shown to those, who after death have come among spirits. The man does not, indeed, appear as a spirit in that society while he lives in the world, because he then thinks naturally; but those who think abstractedly from the body sometimes appear in their own society, because they are then in the spirit. And when they appear, they are easily distinguished from the spirits who are there, for they walk about in a state of meditation, say nothing, and pay no attention to others, acting as if they did not see them; and as soon as any spirit addresses them, they vanish.

439. To elucidate the truth that man is a spirit as to his interiors, I will relate from experience what it is to be withdrawn from the body, and what it is to be carried of the spirit to another place.

440. In regard to the first, that is, being withdrawn from the body, it occurs thus: The man is brought into a certain state, midway between sleeping and waking; and when in this state, he cannot know but that he is perfectly awake. All his senses are as thoroughly awake as in the highest state of bodily wakefulness, the sight as well as the hearing, and what is wonderful, the touch, which is then more exquisite than it ever can be when the body is awake. In this state also, spirits and angels are seen in all the 'reality of life; they are likewise heard, and what is wonderful, they are touched, scarcely anything of the body then intervening. This is the state which is called being *absent from the body*, and not knowing *whether one is in the body or out of the body*.* I have been let into this state only three or four

* [As in the case of the Apostle Paul, 2 Cor. xii. 2, 3.—Tr.]

times, merely that I might know what it is, and at the same time be convinced that spirits and angels enjoy every sense, and man also, as to his spirit, when he is withdrawn from the body.

441. As to the other,—being carried of the spirit to another place,—I have been shown by living experience what that is, and the manner in which it occurs; but this only two or three times. I will adduce a single instance. Walking along the streets of a city, and through fields, conversing also with spirits at the same time, I knew no otherwise than that I was awake, and seeing as at other times. Thus I walked on without mistaking the way, being in vision meanwhile, seeing groves, rivers, palaces, houses, men, and various other objects. But after walking thus for some hours, I suddenly returned into my bodily sight, and discovered that I was in another place. I was greatly astonished at this, and perceived that I had been in a state like that experienced by those, of whom it is said, that they were *carried by the spirit to another place;*[*] for while it continues, the distance is not thought of, even though it were many miles; neither is time attended to, though it were many hours or days; nor is there any consciousness of fatigue; the person is also led unerringly, through ways whereof he is ignorant, even to the place of his destination.

442. But these two states of man, which are states appertaining to him when he is in his interiors, or what is the same, when he is in the spirit, are extraordinary, and were shown to me only that I might understand their nature, their existence being known within the church. But to converse with spirits, and to be with them as one of their number, has been granted me even in full wakefulness of the body, and this now for many years.

443. That man as to his interiors is a spirit, may be further confirmed from what was said above, (n. 311 to 317), where it was shown that heaven and hell are from the human race.

444. By man's being a spirit as to his interiors, is meant as to those things which belong to his thought and will, since these are the interiors themselves which cause him to be man, and such a man as he is in respect to these.

---

[*] [As happened to Philip, (Acts viii. 39); and often to the prophets, (1 Kings xviii. 12; 2 Kings ii. 16.)—Tr.]

THE RESUSCITATION OF MAN FROM THE DEAD, AND HIS ENTRANCE INTO ETERNAL LIFE.

445. WHEN the body is no longer capable of performing its functions in the natural world, corresponding to the thoughts and affections of its spirit which are from the spiritual world, then a man is said to die. This occurs when the respiratory motions of the lungs and the systolic motions of the heart cease. But still the man does not die, but is only separated from the corporeal part, which was of use to him in the world; for the man himself lives. It is said that the man himself lives, because man is not man by virtue of the body, but by virtue of the spirit; since it is the spirit in man which thinks, and thought together with affection makes the man. Hence it is evident that when man dies, he only passes from one world into another. Hence it is that death, in the internal sense of the Word, signifies resurrection and continuation of life.[1]

446. The inmost communication of the spirit is with the respiration, and with the motion of the heart; its thought with the respiration, and affection which is of love, with the heart.[2] When therefore these two motions cease, the separation of the spirit from the body takes place immediately. These two motions,— the respiratory motion of the lungs and the systolic motion of the heart,—are the very bonds, on the sundering of which the spirit is left to itself; and the body, being then without the life of its spirit, grows cold and putrefies. The inmost communication of the spirit of man is with the respiration and the heart, because

---

[1] That death, in the Word, signifies resurrection, because, when man dies, his life is still continued, n. 3498, 3505, 4618, 4621, 6036, 6222.

[2] That the heart corresponds to the will, thus likewise to the affection which is of love; and that the respiration of the lungs corresponds to the understanding, thus to thought, 3888. That hence the heart, in the Word, signifies the will and love, n. 7542, 9050, 10336; and that the soul signifies understanding, faith, and truth. Hence from the soul and from the heart signifies from the understanding, faith, and truth; and from the will, denotes from the love, and good, n. 2930, 9050. Concerning the correspondence of the heart and lungs with the GRAND MAN or heaven, n. 3883 to 3896.

all the vital motions depend upon those two, not only in the body
generally, but also in every part of it.[1]

447. The spirit of man, after the separation, remains a little
while in the body, but not after the motion of the heart has entirely ceased. This takes place sooner or later, according to the
nature of the disease of which the man dies; for in some cases
the motion of the heart continues a long time, while in others it
quickly ceases. As soon as this motion ceases, the man is resuscitated; but this is done by the Lord alone. By resuscitation is
meant the drawing forth of the spirit from the body, and its introduction into the spiritual world, which is commonly called
resurrection. The spirit of man is not separated from the body
until the motion of the heart has ceased, because the heart corresponds to the affection which is of love, and love is the very life
of man; for every one has vital heat from love.[2] Wherefore so
long as this union continues [*i. e.* the union between the body
and the spirit], correspondence is maintained, and thence the
life of the spirit in the body.

448. How resuscitation is effected, has not only been told me,
but also shown by living experience. I was myself the subject of
that experience, in order that I might fully comprehend the process.

449. I was brought into a state of insensibility as to the bodily
senses, thus nearly into the state of dying persons, while yet the
interior life and the faculty of thought remained entire, so that I
could perceive and retain in memory the things which transpired,
and which happen to those who are being raised up from the
dead. I perceived that the respiration of the body was almost
taken away, while the interior respiration, which is that of the
spirit, remained conjoined with a gentle and tacit respiration of
the body. There was then opened, in the first place, a communication as to the pulse of the heart with the celestial kingdom,

---

[1] That the pulse of the heart and the respiration of the lungs prevail in
the body throughout, and flow mutually into every part, n. 3887, 3889,
3890.

[2] That love is the esse of the life of man, n. 5002. That love is spiritual heat, and thence the essential vital principle of man, n. 1589, 2146,
3338, 4906, 7081 to 7086, 9954, 10740. That affection is the continuous
principle of love, n. 3938.

since that kingdom corresponds to the heart with man.[1] Angels from that kingdom were also visible ; some were at a distance, and two were seated near my head. Thereby all affection proper to myself was taken away, but thought and perception still remained. I was in this state for some hours. The spirits who were around me then withdrew, supposing that I was dead. There was also perceived an aromatic odor, like that of an embalmed corpse ; for when celestial angels are present, the effluvium from the corpse is perceived as a fragrant perfume. When spirits perceive this, they are unable to approach. By this means, also, evil spirits are prevented from coming near the spirit of man, when he is first introduced into eternal life. The angels who were seated near my head were silent, only communicating their thoughts with mine ; and when these are received, they know that the spirit of man is in a state capable of being drawn forth from the body. The communication of their thoughts was effected by looking into my face, for in this way are such communications made in heaven. Because thought and perception remained with me, in order that I might learn and remember how resuscitation takes place, I perceived that these angels first inquired what my thought was, whether it was similar to that of dying persons, which is usually about eternal life ; and that they wished to keep my mind in that thought. It was told me afterward, that the spirit of man is held in the last thought which he has when expiring, until he returns to the thoughts which proceed from the general or ruling affection that belonged to him in the world. It was given me particularly to perceive, and also to feel, that there was a drawing, and as it were a pulling out, of the interiors of my mind, thus of my spirit, from the body ; and I was told that this is from the Lord, and that the resurrection is effected in this way.

450. The celestial angels who attend upon a resuscitated person, do not leave him, because they love every one ; but if the spirit be of such a character that he can no longer continue in the company of celestial angels, he desires to depart from them. When this occurs, angels from the Lord's spiritual kingdom

---

[1] That the heart corresponds to the Lord's celestial kingdom, nd the lungs to His spiritual kingdom, n. 3635, 3886, 3887.

come to him, and give him the use of light; for before, he saw nothing, but only thought. I was also shown how this is done. Those angels seemed, as it were, to roll off the coat of the left eye toward the septum of the nose, that the eye might be opened, and sight be given. This is merely an appearance, but the spirit perceives it as a reality. When the coat of the eye seems to have been rolled off, something lucid but indistinct appears, like what is seen through the eyelids on first awaking from sleep This obscure light seemed to me of a sky-blue color; but I was afterward told that the color varies with different persons. After this, there is a sensation as if something were gently rolled off from the face, and this is succeeded by a state of spiritual thought. This rolling off from the face is also an appearance, whereby is represented the change from a state of natural to one of spiritual thought. The angels are extremely careful to suppress any idea in the resuscitated person, which does not savor of love. They then tell him that he is a spirit. After the spiritual angels have given the use of light to the new spirit, they perform for him all the kind offices which he can ever desire in that state, and instruct him concerning the things of another life, so far as he is able to comprehend them. But if he is not willing to receive instruction, then he wishes to be separated from their company. But still the angels do not leave him, but he dissociates himself from them; for the angels love every one, and desire nothing more than to perform kind offices, to instruct, and lead to heaven. In this consists their chief delight. When the spirit thus dissociates himself, he is received by good spirits, who also render him all kind offices while he continues with them. But if his life in the world had been such that he could not endure the society of the good, he then wishes to leave them also; and these changes continue, until at length he associates himself with spirits who are in perfect agreement with his life in the world. With them he finds his life; and, strange to say, he then leads a similar life to what he had led in the world.

451. But this commencing state of man's life after death continues only a few days. How he is afterward led from one state to another, and at last either into heaven or hell, will be told in what follows. This, too, I have learned from much experience.

452. I have conversed with some on the third day after their decease, when the process described above, (n. 449, 450), was completed. Three of these had been known to me in the world, and I told them that preparations were now being made for the burial of their bodies. I said " for their burial ;" on hearing which, they were struck with a sort of amazement, saying that they were alive, but that they buried only that which had served them in the world. They afterward wondered exceedingly that, during their life in the body, they did not believe in such a life after death, and especially that the same unbelief prevailed almost universally within the church. They who, while in the world, did not believe in any life of the soul after the death of the body, are very much ashamed when they find themselves alive. But they who had confirmed themselves in such unbelief, are consociated with their like, and separated from those who had believed in man's immortality. Such sceptics are, for the most part, bound to some infernal society, because they have also denied a Divine, and despised the truths of the church : for so far as any one confirms himself against the everlasting life of his soul, he confirms himself also against the things which belong to heaven and the church.

MAN AFTER DEATH IS IN A PERFECT HUMAN FORM.

453. THAT the form of man's spirit is the human form, or that the spirit is a man even as to its form, is evident from what has been shown in several of the foregoing chapters, especially in those where it was shown that every angel is in a perfect human form, (n. 73 to 77) ; that every man is a spirit as to his interiors, (n. 432 to 444) ; and that the angels in heaven are from the human race, (n. 311 to 317). This may be seen still more clearly from the consideration, that man is man by virtue of his spirit, and not by virtue of his body ; and that the corporeal form is added to the spirit according to the form thereof, and not the reverse ; for the spirit is clothed with a body according to its own form

Wherefore the spirit of man acts upon every part of the body, even the most minute, insomuch that the part which is not acted upon by the spirit, or in which the spirit is not active, does not live.   This every one may know from this single consideration, that thought and will actuate all parts of the body, both in general and in particular, so absolutely that every part responds to their be..iests ; and whatever does not respond, is no part of the body, and is also cast out as a thing void of any living principle. Thought and will belong to the spirit of man, and not to the body.   Although the spirit is in the human form, it does not appear to man after its separation from the body, nor is it seen in another man while living in the world, because the eye,—the organ of bodily sight, so far as concerns its seeing in the world,— is material ; and what is material sees nothing but what is material, but what is spiritual sees what is spiritual ; wherefore, when the material of the eye is veiled, and deprived of its co-operation with the spiritual, spirits appear in their own form, which is the human,— not only spirits who are in the spiritual world, but also the spirit that is in another while he is yet in his body.

454. The form of the spirit is human, because man as to his spirit was created according to the form of heaven ; for all things belonging to heaven and to its order, are collated into those which appertain to the mind of man ;[1] and hence he has the faculty of receiving intelligence and wisdom.   Whether we say the faculty of receiving intelligence and wisdom, or the faculty of receiving heaven, it is the same, as may appear from what was shown concerning the light and heat of heaven, n. 126 to 140 ; concerning the form of heaven, n. 200 to 212 ; concerning the wisdom of the angels, n. 265 to 275 ; and in the chapter, that heaven as to its form, both in the whole and in part, resembles one man, n. 59 to 77 ; and this from the Divine Human of the Lord, from which heaven and its form are derived.

455. A rational man can understand the statements here ad-

---

[1] That man is the being into whom are collated all things of divine order, and that from creation he is divine order in form, n. 4219, 4220, 4223, 4523, 4524, 5114, 5368, 6013, 6057, 6605, 6626, 9706, 10156, 10472. That man appears perfect and beautiful in the other life in proportion *as he* lives according to divine order, n. 4839, 6605, 6626.

vanced, for he can view things from a chain of causes, and from
truths in their order; but a man who is not rational, will not un
derstand them. There are several reasons for this, the chief of
which is, that he does not wish to understand them, because they
are contrary to his falses which he has made his truths; and he
who, on this account, does not wish to understand, has closed his
rational faculty against the influx from heaven; which, nevertheless, may still be opened, provided the will does not resist; (see
above, n. 424). That man can understand truths, and be rational, if he is only willing, has been proved to me by much experience. I have often seen evil spirits, who had become irra-
tional in the world by denying the Divine and the truths of the
church, and who had confirmed themselves in such denial, turned
by a divine power toward spirits who were in the light of truth;
and then they comprehended like the angels all the truths which
they had before denied, confessing that they were truths, and also
that they comprehended them all; but the moment they relapsed
into themselves, and were turned to the love appertaining to their
will, they comprehended nothing, and affirmed what was directly
the opposite. I have also heard infernal spirits say, that they know
and perceive that what they do is evil, and that what they think
is false; but that they cannot resist the delight of their love, thus
their will, which leads their thoughts to see evil as good, and the
false as truth. Thus it was made plain, that they who are in
falses derived from evil might understand, and therefore be rational, but that they were not willing; and that the reason why
they were not willing, was because they loved falses rather than
truths, since falses agreed with the evils in which they were.
To love and to will are the same thing; for what a man wills he
loves, and what he loves he wills. Since the state of men
is such that they can understand truths if they only desire
to understand them, I am permitted to confirm the spiritual
truths of heaven and the church even by rational considerations;
and this in order that the falses, which have closed the rational
with many, may be dispersed by the conclusions of reason, and
that thus, perchance, their mental eye may in some measure be
opened. For such confirmations of spiritual truth are allowed to
all who are principled in truths. Who could ever understand

the Word from its literal sense, unless he saw the truths which it contains from an enlightened rational faculty? Whence, otherwise, so many heresies from the same Word?[1]

456. That the spirit of man, after its separation from the body, is itself a man, and similar in form, has been proved to me by the daily experience of many years; for I have seen, heard, and conversed with spirits thousands of times, and have even talked with them on the prevailing disbelief that spirits are men, and have told them that the learned regard those as simple who think so. The spirits were grieved at heart that such ignorance still continues in the world, and especially within the church. But they remarked that this infidelity had emanated chiefly from the learned, who have thought of the soul from their corporeal-sensual apprehensions, and thence have concluded that it is mere thought, which, when viewed without any subject in and from which it exists, is like a volatile breath of pure ether, which cannot but be dissipated when the body dies. But because the church, on the authority of the Word, believes in the immortality of the soul, they could not but ascribe to it some vital principle, like thought, although they deny it a sensitive principle such as man has, until it is again conjoined to the body. This is the foundation of the prevailing doctrine of the resurrection, and of the belief that the soul and the body will be again united at the time of the last judgment. Hence it is, that when any one thinks about the soul according to the prevailing doctrine and at the same time hypothesis, he does not at all comprehend that it is a spirit and in human form. In addition to this, scarcely any one at this day is aware what the spiritual nature is, and still less that spiritual beings,—as all spirits and angels are,—have any hu-

---

[1] That we ought to begin with the truths of doctrine of the church which are derived from the Word, and acknowledge those truths first, and that afterward it is allowable to consult scientifics, n. 6047. Thus that those who are in an affirmative principle concerning the truths of faith, may confirm them rationally by scientifics, but that it is not allowable for those who are in a negative principle, n. 2568, 2588, 4760, 6047. That it is according to divine order to enter rationally from spiritual truths into scientifics, which are natural truths, but not *vice versa*, because spiritual influx into natural things is given, but not natural or physical influx into things spiritual, n. 3219, 5119, 5259, 5427, 5428, 5478, 6322, 9110, 9111.

:naii rorm. Hence it is that almost all who pass out of this world into the other, are greatly astonished to find themselves alive, and that they are men equally as before; that they see, hear, and speak; that their bodies enjoy the sense of touch as before; and that there is no discernible difference whatever (see above, n. 74); but when they cease to wonder at themselves, they then wonder that the church knows nothing about such a state of man after death, thus nothing about heaven and hell; when yet all who have ever lived in the world, have passed into the other life, and are living as men. And because they also wondered why this was not revealed to man by visions, seeing it is an essential of the faith of the church, they were told from heaven that this might have been done,—since nothing is easier when it pleases the Lord,—but that still they who have confirmed themselves in falses in opposition to these truths, would not believe even the evidence of their senses; moreover that it is dangerous to confirm anything by visions, because they would first believe, and afterward deny, and thus with those who are in falses, would profane the truth itself,—for to believe and afterward to deny, is to commit profanation; and they who profane truths are thrust down into the lowest and most grievous of all the hells.[1] This danger is what is meant by the Lord's words:

---

[1] That profanation is the commixture of good and evil, or of the true and the false in man, n. 6348. That none can profane truth and good, or the holy things of the Word and the church, but those who first acknowledge them; and that the profanation is more grievous if they live according to them, and afterward deny them, recede from the faith, and live to themselves and the world, n. 593, 1008, 1010, 1059, 3398, 3399, 3898, 4289, 4601, 10284, 10287. That if man after repentance of heart relapses into his former evils, he is guilty of profanation, and his last state is worse than his first, n. 8394. That they cannot profane holy things, who have not acknowledged them, and still less they who do not know them, n. 1008, 1010, 1059, 9188, 10284. That the Gentiles, who are out of the church, and have not the Word, cannot profane it, n. 1327, 1328, 2051, 2081. That on this account interior truths were not discovered to the Jews, because if they had been discovered and acknowledged, that people would have profaned them, n. 3398, 3399, 6963. That the lot of profaners in the other life is the worst of all, because the good and truth, which they have acknowledged, remain, and also the evil and the false; and because they

"*He hath blinded their eyes, and hardened their hearts, lest they should see with their eyes, and understand with the heart, and convert themselves, and I should heal them,*" (John xii. 40.) And that they who are in falses would still not believe, is meant by these words : "*Abraham said to the rich man in hell, They have Moses and the prophets, let them hear them; but he said, Nay, father Abraham, but if one went unto them from the dead, they would be converted. But Abraham said to him, If they hear not Moses and the prophets, neither will they believe though one rose from the dead,*" (Luke xvi. 29, 30, 31.)

457. When the spirit of man first enters the world of spirits, which takes place shortly after his resuscitation, (concerning which above) he has a similar face and similar tone of voice to what he had in the world, because he is then in the state of his exteriors, and his interiors are not yet disclosed. This is the first state of man after death. But afterward, his face is changed and becomes entirely different, assuming the likeness of his ruling affection or love in which the interiors of his mind were in the world, and in which his spirit was in the body,—for the face of a man's spirit differs exceedingly from that of his body. The face of his body is derived from his parents, but the face of his spirit is derived from his affection, of which it is the image. Into this his spirit comes after his life in the body, when the exteriors are removed and the interiors are revealed. This is the third state of man. I have seen some spirits shortly after their arrival from the world, and knew them by their face and speech ; but when I saw them afterward, I did not know them. They who were principled in good affections appeared with beautiful faces, but they who were principled in evil affections, with faces deformed ; for the spirit of man, viewed in itself, is nothing but his affection, whereof the face is the external form. The reason also why the face is changed, is because in the other life no one is allowed to counterfeit affections which are not properly his own, nor, consequently, to put on looks which are contrary to his real

cohere, their life is rent asunder, n. 571, 582, 6348. That therefore the utmost provision is made by the Lord to prevent profanation, n. 2426, 10384.

love. All in the spiritual world, therefore, whoever they may be, are brought into such a state as to speak as they think, and to express by their faces and gestures the inclinations of their will. Hence the faces of all become the forms and images of their affections. And hence it is that all who have known each other in the world, know each other also in the world of spirits, but not in heaven nor in hell, as stated above, n. 427.[1]

458. The faces of hypocrites are changed more slowly than those of others, because from practice they have formed the habit of disposing their interiors so as to imitate good affections. Wherefore they appear for a long time not unbeautiful. But because their assumed appearance is successively put off, and the interiors which belong to their minds are disposed according to the form of their affections, they afterward become more deformed than others. Hypocrites are those who have talked like angels, but who interiorly have acknowledged nothing but nature, and thus have denied the Divine, and consequently the truths which belong to heaven and the church.

459. It is worthy of remark, that the human form of every man after death is the more beautiful, the more interiorly he had loved divine truths and had lived according to them; for the interiors of every one are opened and formed according to their love and life; wherefore the more interior is the affection, the more conformable it is to heaven, and hence the more beautiful is the face. Therefore the angels of the inmost heaven are the most beautiful, because they are forms of celestial love. But they who have loved divine truths externally, and have therefore lived externally according to them, are less beautiful; for the

---

[1] That the face is formed in correspondence with the interiors, n. 4791 to 4805, 5695. Concerning the correspondence of the face and its expressions with the affections of the mind, n. 1568, 2988, 2989, 3631, 4796, 4797, 4800, 5165, 5168, 5695, 9306. That, with the angels of heaven, the face makes one with the interiors which are of the mind, n. 4796 to 4799, 5695, 8250. That on this account, the face, in the Word, signifies the interiors which are of the mind, that is, which are of the affection and thought, n. 1999, 2434, 3527, 4066, 4796, 5102, 9306, 9546. How the influx from the brain into the face has been changed in process of time, and with it the face itself, as regards its correspondence with the interiors, n. 4326, 8250

exteriors only shine forth from their faces, and no interior heavenly love shines through their exteriors, consequently not the form of heaven as it really is. There appears something respectively obscure in their faces, which is not vivified by the translucence of interior life. In a word, all perfection increases toward the interiors, and decreases toward the exteriors; and as perfection increases and decreases, so likewise does beauty. I have seen the faces of angels of the third heaven, which were so beautiful that no painter, with all his art, could ever impart to colors any such animation as to equal a thousandth part of the brightness and life which appeared in their faces. But the faces of the angels of the ultimate heaven may, in some degree, be equalled by a painter.

460. I will mention, in conclusion, an arcanum hitherto unknown. It is this: that every good and truth which proceeds from the Lord and makes heaven, is in the human form, and this not only in the whole and the greatest, but also in every part even in the least; and that this form affects every one who receives good and truth from the Lord, and causes every one in heaven to be in the human form, according to the measure of his reception. Hence it is that heaven is similar to itself in general and in particular, and that the human form belongs to the whole, to every society, and to every angel, as was shown in the four chapters, from n. 59 to 86;—to which may here be added, that the human form exists in every single thought with the angels which proceeds from heavenly love. This arcanum, however, is hard to be understood by any man, but it is clearly comprehended by the angels, because they are in the light of heaven.

MAN AFTER DEATH HAS EVERY SENSE, AND ALL THE
MEMORY, THOUGHT, AND AFFECTION, WHICH HE HAD IN
THE WORLD; AND HE LEAVES BEHIND HIM NOTHING
BUT HIS TERRESTRIAL BODY.

461. THAT when a man passes from the natural into the spiritual world, he takes with him all things belonging to him as a
man except his terrestrial body, has been proved to me by manifold
experience. For when he enters the spiritual world, or the life
after death, he is in a body as he was in the natural world ; and
to all appearance in the same body, since neither touch nor sight
can detect any difference. But his body is spiritual, and thus is
separated or purified from things terrestrial ; and when what is
spiritual touches and sees what is spiritual, it is just the same to
sense as when what is natural touches and sees what is natural.
Hence when a man first becomes a spirit, he is not aware that he
has deceased, and believes that he is still in the body which he
had when he was in the world. A human spirit also enjoys
every external and internal sense which he possessed in the
world. He sees as before ; he hears and speaks as before ; he
smells and tastes as before ; and when he is touched he feels as
before. He also longs, desires, wishes, thinks, reflects, is affected, loves, and wills, as before. And he who is delighted
with studies, reads and writes as before. In a word, when man
passes from one life into the other, or from one world into the
other, it is just as if he passed from one place to another; and he
carries with him all things which he possessed in himself as a
man, so that it cannot be said that man after death,—which is only
the death of the terrestrial body,—has lost anything that belonged
to himself. He carries with him his natural memory also, for he
retains all things whatsoever which he has heard, seen, read,
learned, and thought, in the world, from earliest infancy even to
the end of life. But because the natural objects which are in the
memory, cannot be re-produced in the spiritual world, they are
quiescent, just as they are with a man in this world when he
does not think of them : but still they are re-produced when the

Lord pleases. But concerning this memory and its state after death, more will be said shortly. The sensual man cannot possibly believe that such is the state of man after death, because he does not comprehend it; for the sensual man cannot think otherwise than naturally, even about spiritual things; whatever therefore is not palpable to the bodily sense, that is, whatever he does not see with his eyes and touch with his hands, he affirms has no existence; as we read of Thomas, in John xx. 25, 27, 29. What the sensual man is, may be seen above, n. 267, and in the notes there.

462. Still, however, the difference between the life of man in the spiritual world, and his life in the natural world, is great, as well with respect to the external senses and their affections, as with respect to the internal senses and their affections. The senses of those in heaven are far more exquisite than they were in the world; that is, they see and hear more perfectly and also think more wisely; for they see by the light of heaven, which exceeds by many degrees the light of the world (see above, n. 126); and they hear by a spiritual atmosphere, which also surpasses by many degrees the atmosphere of the earth (n. 235). The difference between these external senses is like the difference between a clear sky and a dark mist, or between the light of noon-day and the shade of evening. For since the light of heaven is divine truth, it enables the sight of the angels to perceive and discriminate the minutest objects. Their external sight also corresponds to their internal sight, or their understanding; for with the angels one sight flows into the other, and they act as one. Hence their wonderful acuteness of vision. In like manner also their hearing corresponds to their perception, which is both of the understanding and the will; hence in the tone and the words of the speaker, they perceive the minutest particulars of his affection and thought,—in his tone, the things which belong to his affection, and in his words, the things which belong to his thought (see above, n. 234 to 245). But the other senses with the angels are not so exquisite as the senses of sight and hearing, because these are conducive to their intelligence and wisdom, but not the rest. Were the other senses as exquisite as these, they would take away the light and delight of their wisdom, and

introduce the delight of pleasures belonging to the various appetites and to the body, which obscure and debilitate the understanding in proportion as they predominate. This also is the
case with men in the world, who become dull and stupid as to
spiritual truths, in proportion as they indulge the sense of bodily
taste, and yield to the blandishments of the touch. That the interior senses of the angels of heaven, which are those of their
thought and affection, are also more exquisite and perfect than
they were in the world, is evident from the chapter concerning
the wisdom of the angels of heaven, (n. 265 to 275). The state
of those who are in hell is also widely different from their state
in the world; for in the degree that the external and internal
senses with the angels in heaven are excellent and perfect, in
like degree are they imperfect with those in hell; but the state of
these will be treated of hereafter.

That man takes all his memory with him when he leaves the
world, has been confirmed by many things worthy of mention
which have been seen and heard, some of which I will relate
in order. There were those who denied their crimes and enormities which they had perpetrated in the world; wherefore, lest
they should be believed innocent, all their deeds were discovered,
and recounted in order from their own memory, from their earliest age to the latest. They consisted chiefly of adulteries and
whoredoms. There were some who had deceived others by
wicked arts, and who had stolen; their tricks and thefts were
also enumerated in order, although many of them were known
to scarcely any one in the world, except themselves alone.
They also acknowledged them, because they were made manifest in the light, together with every thought, intention,
delight, and fear, which passed through their minds at the
time. There were others who had accepted bribes, and made
gain of judgment; these were in like manner explored from
their memory, and from it were recounted all their official
misdeeds from first to last. Every particular was recalled,—
the amount and nature of each bribe, the time when it was
offered, their state of mind and intention in accepting it, were all
at the same time brought to their recollection, and visibly exhibited; and the number of their offenses amounted to many hun-

dreds. This was done in several cases; and, what is wonderful, even their memorandum-books themselves, wherein they had made a record of such transactions, were opened and read before them page by page. There were others who had enticed virgins to acts of fornication, and who had violated chastity; these were called to a similar judgment, and every particular of their crimes was drawn forth and recited from their memory; the very faces of the virgins and women were also exhibited as if present, together with the places, conversation, and purposes, and this as suddenly as when anything is presented to view. The manifestations sometimes continued for several hours. There was one who had made light of the evil of backbiting. I heard his backbitings and defamations recounted in order, and in the very words he had used; the persons whom he had defamed, and those to whom he had defamed them, were also made known. All these things were produced, and at the same time exhibited to the life; and yet every particular had been studiously concealed by him when he lived in the world. Another spirit who had deprived a relation of his inheritance by a fraudulent pretext, was convicted and judged in the same way; and, what was wonderful, the letters and papers which had passed between them, were read in my hearing, and I was told that not a word was wanting. The same person also, shortly before his death, clandestinely destroyed a neighbor by poison, which crime was disclosed in this manner: he was seen to dig a hole in the ground, out of which when dug, a man came forth as out of a grave, and cried out to him, What hast thou done to me? And then every particular was revealed; the friendly conversation of the poisoner with his victim; how he held out the cup to him; what he thought before, and what transpired afterward. When these disclosures were made, he was sentenced to hell. In a word, all evils, villanies, robberies, artifices, deceits, are made manifest to every evil spirit, and are drawn forth from his own memory, and his guilt is established beyond a doubt; nor is there any room for denial, because all the circumstances appear together. The memory of a certain spirit was seen and examined by angels, and I heard what his thoughts had been for a month together day after day; and all without the least mistake, the particulars being recalled

just as they were in his mind on those days. From these examples, it is evident that man carries all his memory with him
into the other world; and that there is nothing, however concealed here, which is not made manifest hereafter in the presence
of many; according to the Lord's words: "*There is nothing
hidden which shall not be uncovered, and nothing secret which
shall not be known. Therefore whatsoever ye have spoken in
darkness shall be heard in the light; and what ye have spoken
into the ear shall be proclaimed upon the housetops,*" Luke xii.
2, 3.

463. When a man's actions are disclosed to him after death,
the angels to whom is assigned the duty of making inquisition,
look into his face and extend their examination through the
whole body, beginning with the fingers of each hand, and so
proceeding through the whole. I was surprised at this, and the
reason of it was therefore explained to me, which was this:
that, as all the particulars of thought and will are inscribed on
the brain,—for their beginnings are there,—so likewise are they
inscribed on the whole body; since all the things of thought and
will proceed thither from their beginnings, and there terminate
as in their ultimates. Hence it is, that whatever is inscribed on
the memory from the will and its consequent thought, is not
only inscribed on the brain, but also on the whole man, and there
exists in order according to the order of the parts of the body.
By this it was made plain that the whole man is such as his will
is, and his thought thence derived; so that a bad man is his own
evil, and a good man, his own good.[1] From these things it may
also be evident what is meant by the book of man's life, spoken
of in the Word, namely this: that all things, as well those
which he has done as those he has thought, are inscribed on the
whole man, and appear as if read in a book when they are
called forth from the memory, and as if seen in effigy when the

---

[1] That a good man, spirit, or angel, is his own good and his own truth;
that is, he is wholly such as his good and truth are, n. 10298, 10367; because good makes the will, and truth the understanding, and the will and
understanding make the all of life appertaining to man, to spirit, and to
angel, n. 3332, 3623, 6065. In like manner it may be said that every man,
spirit, and angel is his own love, n. 6872, 10177, 10284.

spirit is viewed in the light of heaven. To these things I will add a certain memorable circumstance concerning the permanence of memory after death, whereby I was confirmed in the truth, that not only things in general, but also the most minute particulars which enter the memory, remain, and are never obliterated. I saw some books with writing in them just like those in the world; and I was informed that they were taken from the memory of their authors, and that not one word contained in the book written by the same person when in the world, was wanting there; and that thus the most minute circumstances may be called forth from the memory of another, even those which the man himself had forgotten in the world. The reason was also disclosed to me, which was: That man has an external memory and an internal memory,—an external memory which belongs to his natural man, and an internal memory which belongs to his spiritual man; and that everything which a man has thought, willed, spoken, done, also which he has heard and seen, is inscribed on his internal or spiritual memory;[1] and that whatever is recorded in that memory, is never erased, since it is inscribed at the same time on the spirit itself, and on the members of its body, as was said above; and thus that the spirit is formed according to the thoughts and acts of the will. I am aware that

---

[1] That man has two memories, one exterior and the other interior, or one natural and the other spiritual, n. 2469 to 2494. That man does not know that he has an interior memory, n. 2470, 2471. How much the interior memory excels the exterior, n. 2473. That the things contained in the exterior memory are in the light of the world, but the things contained in the interior memory are in the light of heaven, n. 5212. That it is from the interior memory that man is able to think and speak intellectually and rationally, n. 9394. That everything which man speaks or does, and everything which he sees and hears, is inscribed on the interior memory, n. 2474, 7398. That the interior memory is the book of man's life, n. 2474, 9386, 9841, 10505. That the truths which have been made truths of faith, and the goods which have been made goods of love, are in the interior memory, n. 5212, 8067. That those things which have become habitual, and have been made matters of life, are obliterated in the exterior memory, but remain in the interior memory, n. 9394, 9723, 9841. That spirits and angels speak from the interior memory, and that hence they have a universal language, n. 2472, 2476, 2490, 2493. That languages in the world belong to the exterior memory, n. 2472, 2476.

these things will appear like paradoxes, and will scarcely be believed, but still they are true. Let no man, therefore, imagine that anything which he has thought within himself, and which he has done in secret, remains hidden after death; but let him be assured that every thought and deed is then laid open as in the clear light of day.

464. Although the external or natural memory is in man after death, still the merely natural things in that memory are not reproduced in the other life, but the spiritual things which are adjoined to them by correspondences; which things, nevertheless, when they are exhibited to the sight, appear in a form altogether similar to things in the natural world; for all things which appear in the heavens, appear in like manner as in the world, although in their essence they are not natural, but spiritual, as was shown in the chapter concerning representatives and appearances in heaven, (n. 170 to 176). But the external or natural memory, so far as regards the ideas which are derived from materiality, time, space, and all other things proper to nature, does not serve the spirit for the same use which it had served it in the world; for when man in the world thought from the external sensual, and not at the same time from the internal sensual, or the intellectual, he thought naturally and not spiritually; but in the other life, being a spirit in the spiritual world, he does not think naturally but spiritually. To think spiritually is to think intellectually or rationally. Hence it is that the external or natural memory, as to all material ideas, is quiescent after death, and only those things come into use which man has imbibed in the world by means of the natural memory, and has made a part of his rational life. The external memory is quiescent as to things material, because material ideas cannot be reproduced in the spiritual world; for spirits and angels speak from the affections and the thoughts thence proceeding, which belong to their minds; and therefore they cannot utter anything which does not agree with their affections and thoughts, as may appear from what was said concerning the speech of the angels in heaven, and concerning their speech with man, (n. 234 to 257). Hence it is, that in proportion as man becomes rational in the world by means of languages and sciences, he is rational after death, and not at all

in proportion to his skill in languages and sciences. I have conversed with many who were reputed learned when in the world, because they were acquainted with the ancient languages, as the Hebrew, Greek, and Latin, and who had not cultivated their rational faculty by means of the things written in those languages. Some of them seemed as simple as those who had known no language but their own, and some appeared stupid; but still they retained a conceited persuasion of their superior wisdom. I have conversed with some who imagined, when in the world, that a man is wise in proportion to the extent of his memory, and who also had stored their memories with a great many things; and they conversed almost exclusively from those things, thus from others and not from themselves; nor had they employed the stores of their memory to perfect their rational faculty. Some of them were stupid, others foolish, not at all comprehending any truth, so as to see whether it be truth or not, and seizing with avidity upon all falses which were put forth for truths by those who called themselves learned; for of themselves they are unable to discern the truth or falsehood of any proposition, and consequently can understand nothing rationally which they hear from others. I have also conversed with some who had written much in the world, and indeed on scientific subjects of every kind, and who had thus acquired an extensive reputation for learning. Some of them, indeed, were able to reason about truths, and to argue whether they were truths or not; others, when they turned to those who were in the light of truth, could understand that they were truths, but still they did not wish to understand them; wherefore they denied them when they sunk into their own falses, thus into themselves. Some were as destitute of wisdom as the unlearned vulgar. Thus they differed, one from another, according to the degree in which they had cultivated their rational faculty by the scientific works which they had written or copied. But they who were opposed to the truths of the church, and had thought from scientifics, and thereby had confirmed themselves in falses, did not cultivate their rational faculty, but only the faculty of arguing. This, indeed, the world calls rationality, but it is quite distinct from it, for it is merely the faculty of confirming whatever a man pleases. Such men, therefore, from pre-conceived principles and from fallacies, see falses as truths, and are not able to discern truth itself; nor can they ever be induced to acknowledge truths, since truths cannot be seen from falses, but falses may be seen from truths. The rational faculty of man is like a garden and flower-bed, and also like ground newly ploughed. The memory is the ground, scientific truths and knowledges are the seeds, and the light and warmth of heaven cause them to spring forth; and as there is no natural germination without the light and heat of the sun, so also there is no spiritual germination without the light and heat of hea ven. The light of heaven is divine truth, and the heat of heaven is divine love. From these alone is the rational faculty. The angels are very much grieved that so many of the learned ascribe all things to nature, and have thereby closed the interiors of their minds, so that they can see nothing of truth from the light of truth, which is the light of heaven. In the other life, therefore, they are deprived of the faculty of arguing, lest by their reasonings, they should disseminate falses among the simple good, and seduce them; and they are sent into desert places.

465. A certain spirit was indignant because he could not remember many things with which he was acquainted in the life of the body, grieving at the loss of a delight which had afforded him so much enjoyment. But he was told that he had lost nothing at all; that he still knew everything which he ever knew, but that in the world which he now inhabits, no one is allowed to recall such things; that it was sufficient that he could think and speak much better and more perfectly than before, without immersing his rational faculty as he used to do, in gross, obscure, material, and corporeal things, which are of no use in the kingdom which he had just entered; that he now possessed everything conducive to the uses of eternal life, and that thus he might become blessed and happy, but not otherwise; that therefore it was the part of ignorance to believe, that, in the kingdom in which he now is, intelligence perishes with the removal and quiescence of material things in the memory; when yet the truth is, that in proportion as the mind is withdrawn from the sensuals which belong to the external man or to the body, it is elevated to things spiritual and celestial.

466. What the memories are, is sometimes visibly represented
in the other life by forms peculiar to that state of being, (for
many things there appear vividly before the sight, which m an
can contemplate only in thought). The exterior memory is there
exhibited to appearance like a callus, and the interior memory
like a medullary substance, similar to that in the human brain.
The character of spirits may be known from these appearances.
With those who, during the life of the body, have labored only
to store the memory, and thus have neglected to cultivate the
rational faculty, the callosity appears hard, and streaked within
as with tendons. With those who have filled the memory with
falses, it appears hairy and rough, and this from the confused
mass of things which are therein. With those who have labored
in storing the memory for the sake of self-love and the love of
the world, its fibres appear glued together and ossified. With
those who have wished to penetrate into divine mysteries by
means of scientifics, and especially by what is called philosophy,
and who would not believe spiritual truths unless they were
demonstrated by science, the memory appears dark, and the
darkness is such as to absorb the rays of light and turn them into
darkness. With those who have practiced deceit and hypocrisy,
it appears hard and bony like ebony, which reflects the rays of
light. But with those who have been in the good of love and
the truths of faith, there appears no such callus, because their
interior memory transmits the rays of light into the exterior; in
the objects or ideas of which, as in their basis or ground, the rays
terminate, and there find delightful receptacles; for the exterior
memory is the ultimate of order, wherein spiritual and celestial
things gently terminate and dwell, when goods and truths are
there.

467. Men who are in love to the Lord and in charity toward
the neighbor, have angelic intelligence and wisdom within them
while they live in the world, but stored up in the inmosts of their
interior memory, and not at all apparent to them until they put
off corporeal things. The natural memory is then laid asleep,
and they awake into the interior memory, and gradually there-
after into angelic memory itself.

468. How the rational faculty may be cultivated shall also be

told in a few words. The genuine rational consists of truths, and not of falses. What is formed from falses is not the rational. Truths are of three kinds, civil, moral, and spiritual. Civil truths relate to matters of civil law, and to whatever belongs to government in states; in general, to justice and equity there. Moral truths relate to such things as belong to every man's life in relation to society and his intercourse with others; in general, to sincerity and uprightness, and specifically to the virtues of every kind. But spiritual truths relate to those things which belong to heaven and the church; in general, to the good which is of love, and to the truth which is of faith. There are three degrees of life with every man, (see above, n. 267). The rational faculty is opened to the first degree by civil truths; to the second degree by moral truths; and to the third degree by spiritual truths. But it is to be observed that the rational faculty is not formed and opened by the mere knowledge of those truths, but by living according to them; and by living according to them, is meant to love them from spiritual affection; and to love them from spiritual affection, is to love what is just and equitable because it is just and equitable, what is sincere and right because it is sincere and right, and what is good and true because it is good and true. But to live according to civil, moral, and spiritual truths, and to love them from corporeal affection, is to love them for the sake of one's self, his reputation, honor, or gain. Wherefore in proportion as man loves them from corporeal affection, he is not rational, because he does not really love them, but himself, whom the truths serve as servants a master. And when truths become servants, they do not enter into man, and open any degree of his life, not even the first, but they reside only in the memory as scientifics under a material form, and there conjoin themselves with the love of self which is corporeal love. From these considerations it may appear how man becomes rational; namely, that he becomes rational to the third degree by the spiritual love of good and truth, which are the constituents of heaven and the church; to the second degree by the love of what is sincere and right; and to the first degree by the love of what is just and equitable. The two latter loves also become spiritual from the spiritual love of good and truth, because this flows into them, conjoins itself with them, and forms in them as it were its own likeness.

469. Spirits and angels have memory just the same as men; for whatever they hear, see, think, will, and do, remains with them, and is the means whereby their rational faculty is continually cultivated, and this forever. Hence it is that spirits and angels are perfected in intelligence and wisdom, the same as men, by means of the knowledges of truth and good. That spirits and angels have memory, I have also learned from much experience; for I have seen that all things which they had thought and done, both in public and in private, were called forth from their memory when they were with other spirits; and also that they who were in any truth from simple good, were imbued with knowledges, and thereby with intelligence, and were afterward taken up into heaven. But it is to be observed, that none are imbued with knowledges, and thereby with intelligence, beyond the degree of affection for good and truth in which they were when in the world; for the affection of every spirit and angel remains, both in quality and intensity, such as it had been in the world, although it is afterward perfected by impletion, which also is continued throughout eternity; for there is nothing but what is capable of being filled up to eternity, since everything may be infinitely varied, thus enriched by various things, consequently multiplied and fructified. No end can be assigned to any good thing, because it springs from the Infinite. That spirits and angels are continually perfecting in intelligence and wisdom by the knowledges of truth and good, may be seen in the chapters on the wisdom of the angels of heaven, (n. 265 to 275); on the Gentiles and peoples without the church in heaven, (n. 318 to 328); and on infants in heaven, (n. 329 to 345); and that this perfecting is accomplished to the degree of the affection for good and truth in which they were when in the world, and not beyond it, (n. 349).

THE CHARACTER OF MAN AFTER DEATH, IS DETERMINED BY HIS LIFE IN THE WORLD.

470. THAT every one's life remains with him after death, is known to every Christian from the Word; for it is there declared in many passages, that man will be judged and rewarded according to his deeds and works. Every one also, who thinks from good and from real truth, cannot help seeing that he who lives well will go to heaven, and that he who lives wickedly will go to hell. But they who are immersed in evil, are not willing to believe that their state after death will be according to their life in the world; but they think, especially when they are sick, that heaven is granted to every one out of pure mercy, however he may have lived, and that it is given according to one's faith, which they separate from life.

471. That man will be judged and recompensed according to his deeds and works, is declared in many passages in the Word, some of which I will here adduce; "*The Son of Man shall come in the glory of His Father with His angels, and then He shall render to every one according to his works,*" (Matt. xvi. 27). "*Blessed are the dead who die in the Lord:—Yea, saith the spirit, that they may rest from their labors; and their works do follow them,*" Rev. xiv. 13. "*I will give unto every one according to his works,*" Rev. ii. 23. "*I saw the dead, small and great, standing before God; and the books were opened;—and the dead were judged by those things which were written in the books, according to their works. And the sea gave up the dead that were in it; and death and hell delivered up those that were in them; and they were judged every one according to his works,*" Rev. xx. 12, 13. "*Behold I come;—and my reward is with me to give to every one according to his works,*" Rev. xxii. 12. "*Every one that heareth my words and doeth them, I will liken to a prudent man; —but every one who heareth my words and doeth them not, is likened unto a foolish man,*" Matt. vii. 24, 26. "*Not every one that saith unto me, Lord, Lord, shall enter into the king-*

*dom of the heavens; but he that doeth the will of my Father
who is in the heavens. Many will say unto me in that day,
Lord, Lord, have we not prophesied by thy name, and in thy
name cast out devils, and in thy name done many wonderful
works? But then will I confess to them, I never knew you;
depart from me, ye workers of iniquity,"* Matt. vii. 22, 23.
*"Then shall ye begin to say, We have eaten and drunk in thy
presence, and thou hast taught in our streets; but He shall
say, I tell you, I know you not, ye workers of iniquity,"* Luke
xiii. 25, 26, 27. *"I will recompense them according to their
work, and according to the deed of their hands,"* Jer. xxv. 14.
*"Jehovah, whose eyes are open on all the ways of man, to give
to every one according to his ways, and according to the fruit
of his works,"* Jer. xxxii. 19. *"I will visit upon his ways, and
recompense to him his works,"* Hosea iv. 9. *"Jehovah dealeth
with us according to our ways, and according to our works,"*
Zec. i. 6. Where the Lord prophesies concerning the last judgment, He mentions nothing but works, and declares that they
who have done good works shall enter into eternal life, and that
they who have done evil works shall enter into damnation, (see
Matt. xxv. 32 to 46, and many other passages which treat of
the salvation and condemnation of man). It is evident that
works and deeds are the external life of man, and that the quality of his internal life is manifested through them.

472. But by the deeds and works according to which man is
judged, are not meant such deeds and works as are merely exhibited in the external form, but such also as they are internally; for
every one knows that every deed and work proceeds from man's
will and thought; for if it were otherwise, his deed would be
mere motion, like that of an automaton or image. Wherefore a
deed or work in itself considered, is nothing but an effect which
derives its soul and life from the will and thought, so that it is
will and thought in effect, therefore will and thought in an external form. Hence it follows, that such as are the will and
thought which produce a deed or work, such also is the deed or
work. If the thought and will be good, the deeds and works are
good; but if the thought and will be evil, the deeds and works
are evil, although outwardly they may appear alike. A thou-

sand men may act alike; that is, they may exhibit a similar deed, —so similar, that as to the outward form their deeds can scarcely be distinguished; and yet the deeds may all be essentially unlike, because they proceed from dissimilar wills. Take for example, the case of acting sincerely and justly with the neighbor; one man may act sincerely and justly with him, in order that he may appear to be sincere and just for the sake of himself and his own honor; another, for the sake of the world and of gain; a third, for the sake of reward and merit; a fourth, for the sake of friend-ship; a fifth, through fear of the law, or the loss of reputation and employment; a sixth, that he may draw some one to his own side,—wrong though it be; a seventh, that he may deceive; and others from other motives. But the deeds of all these, al-though they appear good,—for it is good to act sincerely and justly with one's neighbor,—still are evil, since they are not done for the sake of sincerity and justice, because they love them, but for the sake of self and the world. These are the objects which they really love; and outward sincerity and justice are sub-servient to this love, as servants to a master, who despises and dismisses them when they are not serviceable to him. The sin cere and just conduct of those who act from the love of sincerity and justice, appears similar in the external form to that of the others. Some of these act from the truth of faith, or from obe-dience, because it is so commanded in the Word; some from the good of faith or from conscience, because from religious princi-ple; some from the good of charity toward the neighbor, because his good ought to be consulted; and some from the good of love to the Lord, because good ought to be done for its own sake, and therefore also sincerity and justice. They love sincerity and jus-tice because these are from the Lord, and because the Divine which proceeds from the Lord is in them, and thence, viewed in their very essence, they are divine. The deeds or works of these are interiorly good, and therefore also they are exteriorly good; for, as was said above, deeds or works are altogether such as the thought and will from which they proceed; and without these, they are not deeds and works, but only inanimate motions. From these considerations, it is manifest what is meant by deeds and works in the Word.

o*

473. Because deeds and works are of the will and thought therefore also they are of the love and faith, and consequently they are of the same quality as the love and faith; for whether we say the love or the will of a man, it is the same thing; and whether we say the faith or the determinate thought of a man, it is also the same; for what a man loves, he also wills; and what he believes, he also thinks. If a man loves what he believes, he also wills it, and as far as possible does it. Every one may know that love and faith reside in man's will and thought, and not out of them, since the will is what is enkindled by love, and the thought is what is enlightened in matters of faith; wherefore only those who can think wisely are enlightened, and they, according to the degree of their illumination, think truths and will them; or, what is the same, they believe truths and love them.[1]

474. But it is to be observed, that the will makes the man, and the thought only so far as it proceeds from the will, and that deeds or works proceed from both; or, what is the same, that love makes the man, and faith only so far as it proceeds from love, and that deeds or works proceed from both. Hence it follows, that the will or love is the man himself; for whatever proceeds belongs to that from which it proceeds. To proceed is to be brought forth and exhibited in a suitable form, in order that it may be comprehended and seen.[2] From these considerations it

---

[1] That as all things in the universe, which exist according to order, have reference to good and truth, so, with man, they have reference to will and understanding, n. 803, 10122; because the will is the recipient of good, and the understanding is the recipient of truth, n. 3332, 3623, 5232, 6065, 6125, 7503, 9300, 9995. It amounts to the same thing, whether we speak of truth or of faith, because faith is of truth and truth is of faith; and it amounts to the same thing whether we speak of good or of love, because love is of good and good is of love, n. 4353, 4997, 7178, 10122, 10367. Hence it follows that the understanding is the recipient of faith, and the will of love, n. 7179, 10122, 10367; and since the understanding of man is capable of receiving faith in God, and the will is capable of receiving love to God, it follows that man is capable of being conjoined with God in faith and love; but a being who is capable of conjunction with God by faith and love can never die, n. 4525, 6323, 9231.

[2] That the will of man is the very *esse* of his life, because it is the re-

is manifest that faith separate from love is not faith, but mere science, which in itself is void of spiritual life ; in like manner that a deed or work without love, is not a deed or work of life, but a deed or work of death, wherein there is an appearance of life derived from the love of evil and from faith of what is false. This appearance of life is what is called spiritual death.

475. It is further to be observed, that the whole man is exhibited in his deeds or works ; and that his will and thought, or his love and faith, which are his interiors, are not complete until they exist in deeds or works, which are his exteriors ; for these latter are the ultimates wherein the former terminate, and without which terminations they are as things vague and unlimited which have as yet no existence, and therefore are not yet in the man. To think and to will without doing, when there is opportunity, is like a flame shut up in a close vessel, whereby it is extinguished ; it is also like seed cast upon sand, which does not germinate, but perishes with its prolific principle : but to think and to will, and thence to do, is like a flame in the open air, which diffuses heat and light all around ; and it is like seed in the ground, which grows up into a tree or flower, and so attains a living and visible existence. Every one may know that to will and not to do, when there is opportunity, is in reality not to will ; and that to love good and not to do it, when it is possible, is in reality not

---

ceptacle of love or good ; and that the understanding is the *existere* of life thence derived, because it is the receptacle of faith or truth. n. 3619, 5002, 9282. Thus that the life of the will is the principal life of man, and that the life of the understanding proceeds from it, n. 585, 590, 3619, 7342, 8885, 9282, 10076, 10109, 10110,—as light proceeds from fire or flame. n. 6032, 6314. Hence it follows that man is man by virtue of his will and of his understanding as derived from his will, n. 8911, 9069, 9071, 10076, 10109, 10110. Every man is loved and esteemed by others according to the good of his will, and of his understanding thence derived ; for he is loved and esteemed who wills well and has a good understanding, but he is rejected and despised who understands well and does not will well, n. 8911, 10076 That man after death remains such as his will is and his understanding thence derived, n. 9069, 9071, 9386, 10153 ; and consequently such as his love is and his faith thence derived ; and that the things which are of faith, and not at the same time of love, vanish after death, because they are not in man, and form no part of him, n. 553, 2364, 10153.

to love it. Will, which stops short of action, and love which does not do the good that is loved, is a mere thought separate from will and love, which vanishes and comes to nothing. Love and will is the very soul of a deed or work, forming its body in the sincere and just actions which a man performs. The spiritual body, or the body of a man's spirit, is from no other origin; that is, it is formed from nothing else but the things which the man does from his love or will, (see above, n. 463). In a word, all things which belong to the man and to his spirit, are in his deeds or works.[1]

476. From these considerations it may now be evident what is meant by the life which remains with man after death; namely, that it is his love and the faith thence derived—not love and faith merely in potency, but also in act; thus that it is his deeds or works, because these contain within themselves all things which belong to the man's love and faith.

477. It is his ruling love that remains with a man after death; nor is this ever changed to eternity. Every one has many loves, but still they all have reference to his ruling love, and make one with it, or together compose it. All things of the will which agree with the ruling love are called loves, because they are loved. These loves are interior and exterior; some of them are immediately conjoined to the ruling love, and some mediately; some are nearer to it, and some more remote; but all are in some manner its servants. Taken together, they constitute as it were a kingdom; for although man is entirely ignorant of it, their arrangement within him resembles the subordinations of a kingdom. But something of this is manifested to him in the other life, for according to their arrangement he has extension of

---

[1] That interior things flow successively into things exterior, until they reach the extreme or ultimate, and that there they exist and subsist, n. 634, 6451, 6465, 9216. That they not only flow-in, but also form in the ultimate what is simultaneous, and in what order, n. 5897, 6451, 8603, 10099. That hence all interior things are held together in connection, and subsist, n. 9828. That deeds or works are ultimates, which contain interior things, n. 10331. Wherefore to be recompensed and judged according to deeds and works, is to be recompensed and judged according to all things of love and faith, or of will and thought, because these are the interior things contained in them, n. 3147, 3934, 6073, 8911, 10331, 10338.

thought and affection there,—extension into heavenly societies if his ruling love consist of the loves of heaven, but into infernal societies if his ruling love consist of the loves of hell. That all the thought and affection of spirits and angels have extension into societies, may be seen above in the chapter concerning the wisdom of the angels of heaven; also in that concerning the form of heaven, according to which the consociations and communications there are regulated.

478. But the truths which have been hitherto advanced affect only the thought of the rational man; that they may also be presented in a form that the senses can take cognizance of, I will adduce some facts from experience whereby the same things may be illustrated and confirmed. FIRST, it shall be shown that man after death is his own love or his own will. SECONDLY, that man remains to eternity such as he is in respect to his will or ruling love. THIRDLY, that the man whose love is celestial and spiritual goes to heaven, and that he whose love is corporeal and worldly, destitute of that which is celestial and spiritual, goes to hell. FOURTHLY, that faith does not remain with man, if it be not from heavenly love. FIFTHLY, that it is love in act which remains with man, therefore that it is his life.

479. *That man after death is his own love or his own will*, has been testified to me by manifold experience. The universal heaven is distinguished into societies according to the differences of the love of good, and every spirit who is elevated into heaven and becomes an angel, is conveyed to that society which is distinguished by his ruling love. On his arrival there, he is as though he were at home, and living in the house where he was born. The angel perceives this, and is there consociated with those like himself. When he departs thence, and goes to some other place, he is always sensible of a certain inward resistance, attended with a desire to return to his like, and thus to his ruling love. It is in this way that consociations in heaven are effected. The like occurs in hell, where also they are consociated according to loves which are the opposite of the loves of heaven. That heaven and hell consist of societies, and that they are all distinct according to the differences of love, may be seen above, (n. 41 to 50, and n. 200 to 212). That man after death is his

own love, has also been made evident from this, that those things are then removed, and as it were taken away from him, which do not make one with his ruling love. If he is good, all things discordant or disagreeing with his good are removed, and as it were taken away, and he is thus let into his own love. The like occurs if he is evil,—but with this difference, that truths are taken away from the evil, and falses from the good; and this process goes on, until at last everyone becomes his own love. This takes place when the man-spirit is brought into the third state, which will be treated of in what follows. When this is accomplished, he turns his face steadfastly to his own love, which he has continually before his eyes in whatever direction he turns himself. (see above, n. 123, 124). All spirits may be led at pleasure, provided that they be kept in their ruling love; nor can they resist, even though they are perfectly aware of being so led, and think that they will resist. The experiment has often been tried, whether they could do anything contrary to it, but to attempt it was in vain. Their love is like a cord or rope fastened around them as it were, whereby they can be drawn along, and from which they cannot extricate themselves. The case is similar with men in the world; for their own love leads them also, and by means of it they are led by others. Still more is this the case when they become spirits, because then it is not allowable to assume the appearance of any other love, and to counterfeit what is not their own. That the spirit of man is his ruling love, is manifest in all social intercourse in the other life; for so far as any one acts and speaks according to another's love, the latter appears conspicuously, with a full, cheerful, and lively countenance; but so far as any one acts and speaks in opposition to the love of another, his countenance begins to change, to become obscure, and to fade from the sight, until at last he disappears entirely, as if he had not been there. I have often wondered at this, because nothing of the kind can take place in the world; but I was told that the case is similar with the spirit in man, which, when it turns itself away from another, is no longer visible to him. That a spirit is his ruling love, was also made evident by this circumstance, that every spirit seizes and appropriates to himself whatever agrees with his love, and rejects and

removes from himself everything that does not agree with it.
Every one's love is like spongy and porous wood, which imbibes
such fluids as promote its growth, and repels others. It is also
like animals of every kind, which know their proper food, and
seek that which agrees with their nature, and turn away from
whatever disagrees; for every love desires to be nourished by its
proper aliments,—evil love by falses, and good love by truths.
I have several times observed that certain simple good. spirits
wished to instruct the evil in truths and goods, but that the latter
fled far away from the proffered instruction; and when they came
to their associates, they caught with much pleasure at the falses
which were in agreement with their love. I have also seen
good spirits conversing with each other about truths, which were
listened to with eager affection by the good spirits present; but
some evil spirits who were also present paid no attention to what
was said, and behaved as if they did not hear. In the world of
spirits there appear ways, some of which lead to heaven and some
to hell, and every one to some society. The good spirits go only
in those ways which lead to heaven, and to the society distinguished by the good of their peculiar love; nor do they see the
ways that tend in other directions; but the evil spirits go only in
the ways which lead to hell, and to that society there distinguished by the evil of their peculiar love; nor do they see the
ways that tend in other directions; and if they do see them, still
they are unwilling to walk in them. Such ways in the spiritual
world are real appearances, which correspond to truths or falses;
wherefore ways in the Word signify truths or falses.[1] By these
proofs from experience, the truths before advanced from reason
are confirmed, namely, that every man after death is his own
love and his own will. It is said his own will, because the will
of every one is his love.

480. *That man after death remains to eternity such as he is
as to his will or ruling love*, has also been confirmed by abun-

---

[1] That a way, a path, a road, a street, and a broad street, signify truths,
which lead to good, and also falses which lead to evil, n. 627, 2333, 10422.
That to sweep a way denotes to prepare for the reception of truths, n.
3142. That to make a way known, when spoken concerning the Lord,
denotes to instruct in truths which lead to good, n. 10565.

dant experience. I have been permitted to converse with some
who lived two thousand years ago, whose lives are known because described in history; and I found that they still retained
their distinctive characters, and were exactly such as they had
been described, for the quality of their love, from and according
to which their lives were formed, remained the same. I have
also been permitted to converse with others who lived seventeen
centuries ago, and whose lives are known from history; with
others who lived four centuries ago; with others who lived three;
and so on; and it was found that an affection similar to that
which distinguished them in the world, ruled in them still. The
only difference was, that the delights of their love were turned
into such things as correspond to them. I have been told by the
angels that the life of the ruling love is never changed with any
one to eternity, since every one is his own love; wherefore to
change that love in a spirit, would be to deprive him of his life,
or to annihilate him. They also stated the reason, which is, that
man after death is no longer capable of being reformed by instruction, as in the world, because the ultimate plane, which consists of natural knowledges and affections, is then quiescent, and
cannot be opened because it is not spiritual, (see above, n. 464);
that the interiors which belong to the rational and natural minds
rest upon that plane, like a house on its foundation; and that it
is on this account that man remains to eternity such as the life
of his love had been in the world. The angels wonder exceedingly that man does not know that every one is such as his ruling love is; that many should believe they can be saved by immediate mercy, and by faith alone, whatever be the quality of
their lives; also that they do not know that the divine mercy operates through means, and consists in being led by the Lord both
in the world and afterward to eternity; and that those are led by
mercy who do not live in evil. They are also surprised that men
do not know that faith is the affection of truth proceeding from
heavenly love, which is from the Lord.

481. *That the man whose love is celestial and spiritual goes
to heaven, and he whose love is corporeal and worldly without
celestial and spiritual, goes to hell*, has been made plain to me
from all whom I have seen taken up into heaven and cast into

hell. The life of those who were taken up into heaven had been from celestial and spiritual love; but the life of those who were cast into hell had been from corporeal and worldly love. Heavenly love is to love what is good, sincere and just, for their own sake, and from the love of such things, to do them. Thence is derived the life of goodness, sincerity and justice, which is heavenly life. They who love goodness, sincerity, and justice, for their own sake, and practice or live them, love the Lord above all things, because these are from Him; and they also love the neighbor, because these are the neighbor that is to be loved.[1] But corporeal love is to love what is good, sincere, and just, not for their own sake, but for the sake of self, because they are loved only as the means of securing reputation, honor, and gain. They who are in such love do not regard the Lord and the neighbor in what is good, sincere, and just, but themselves and the world, and experience delight in fraud; and goodness, sincerity, and justice, practiced with fraudulent intent, are evil, insincerity, and injustice; and these latter are the things which they love in the former. Because the loves thus determine the quality of every one's life, therefore all are examined on their first entrance after

---

[1] That the Lord is our neighbor in the supreme sense, because He ought to be loved above all things; but that to love the Lord is to love that which is from Him, because He Himself is in everything which is from Himself; thus it is to love the good and the true, n. 2425, 3419, 6706, 6711, 6819, 6823, 8123. That to love the good and the true, which is from Him, is to live according to them, and that this is to love the Lord, n. 10143, 10153, 10310, 10336, 10578, 10645. That every man and every society, also a man's country and the church, and in the universal sense, the kingdom of the Lord, are our neighbor, and that to do them good from the love of good according to the quality of their state, is to love the neighbor; thus their good, which is to be consulted, is the neighbor, n. 6818 to 6824, 8123. That moral good also, which is sincerity, and civil good, which is justice, are our neighbor; and that to act sincerely and justly from the love of sincerity and justice is to love the neighbor, n. 2915, 4730, 8120, 8121 to 8123. That hence charity toward the neighbor extends itself to all things of the life of man, and that to do what is good and just, and to act sincerely from the heart in every occupation and in every work, is to love the neighbor, n. 2417, 8121, 8124. That doctrine in the ancient church was the doctrine of charity, and that hence that church had wisdom, n. 2417, 2385, 3419, 3420, 4844, 6628.

42

death into the world of spirits; and when their quality is ascertained, they are joined to those who are in similar love. They who are in heavenly love are joined to their like in heaven, and they who are in corporeal love, to their like in hell. And when they have passed through their first and second states, the two classes are so completely separated, that they no longer see or know each other; for every one becomes his own love, not only as to his interiors which belong to the mind, but also as to his exteriors which belong to the face, body, and speech; for every one becomes the image of his own love, even in external appearance. They who are corporeal loves, appear gross, obscure, black, and deformed; but they who are heavenly loves appear fresh, bright, fair, and beautiful. In their minds and thoughts also, they are altogether unlike. They who are heavenly loves are also intelligent and wise; but they who are corporeal loves are stupid and as it were foolish. When permission is given to inspect the interiors and exteriors of the thought and affection of those who are in heavenly love, their interiors appear like light,—those of some like flaming light,—and their exteriors appear of various beautiful colors like those of the rainbow; but the interiors of those who are in corporeal love appear like something black, because they are closed; and in some cases they have a dusky, fiery appearance; these latter are they who have been interiorly in malignant deceit; but their exteriors appear of a shocking color, and melancholy to look upon. (The interiors and exteriors which belong to the rational and natural minds, are exhibited visibly in the spiritual world, whenever the Lord pleases). They who are in corporeal love can see nothing in the light of heaven, that light being thick darkness to them; but the light of hell, which is like that from ignited coals, is to them as clear light. Their interior sight is also darkened, in the light of heaven, to such a degree that they become insane; wherefore they shun that light, and hide themselves in dens and caverns, at a depth proportioned to their falses derived from evils. But on the other hand, those who are in heavenly love see all things more clearly in proportion as they enter more interiorly or superiorly into the light of heaven; and all things appear to them more beautiful also, and truths are perceived more intelligently and wisely in the same proportion. They who are in corporeal love cannot possibly live in the heat of heaven, for the heat of heaven is heavenly love; but the heat of hell is agreeable to them, which heat is the love of exercising cruelty toward those who do not favor them. Contempt of others, enmity, hatred, and revenge, are the delights of that love. When they are in these delights, they are in their life, being utterly ignorant of what it is to do good to others from good itself, and for the sake of good itself, but only skilled in doing good from evil, and for the sake of evil. Nor can those who are in corporeal love breathe in heaven. When any evil spirit is conveyed thither, he draws his breath like one who struggles in a contest. But they who are in heavenly love breathe more freely and live more perfectly in proportion as they enter more interiorly into heaven. From these considerations it may be evident that celestial and spiritual love is heaven with man, because all things of heaven are inscribed on that love; and that corporeal and worldly love, without that which is celestial and spiritual, is hell with man, because all things of hell are inscribed on those loves. Hence it is plain that he who is in celestial and spiritual love goes to heaven, and he who is in corporeal and worldly love, without that which is celestial and spiritual, goes to hell.

482. *That faith does not remain with man, unless it spring from heavenly love,* has been made manifest to me by so much experience, that were I to recite all that I have seen and heard upon this subject, it would fill a volume. This I can testify, that there is no faith at all, neither can there be any, with those who are in corporeal and worldly love without that which is celestial and spiritual; and that what some may regard as faith, is mere science, or a persuasion that such a thing is true, because it serves their love. Many also from among those who supposed that they had faith, have been brought to those who really had it; and when communication with them was opened, they perceived that their faith was no faith at all. They also confessed afterward that mere belief in the truth and in the Word is not faith, but that to love truth from heavenly love, and to will and do it from interior affection, is faith. It was also shown that their persuasion, which they called faith, was only as the light of

winter, in which there is no heat. In that season, therefore, all things on the earth being bound in frost, become torpid and lie buried beneath the snow. Wherefore as soon as the rays of the light of heaven fall upon the light of this persuasive faith, with them it is not only extinguished, but also becomes as thick darkness, wherein no one sees himself. And their interiors become so darkened at the same time, that they understand nothing whatever, and at length become insane from falses. Wherefore all the truths which such persons had learned from the Word and from the doctrine of the church, and had called the truths of their faith, are taken away from .them, and they are imbued, instead, with every false persuasion which is in agreement with the evil of their life; for all are let into their own loves, and into the falses which agree with them; and then they hate and turn from and thus reject truths, because they are repugnant to the falses of evil in which they are. This I can testify from all my experience concerning the things of heaven and hell, that all who have acknowledged the doctrine of salvation by faith alone, and have led evil lives, are in hell. I have seen many thousands of them cast down thither, concerning whom see in the treatise on the Last Judgment and the destruction of Babylon.

483. *That it is love in act, thus that it is the life of man, which remains,* follows as a conclusion from the experimental evidence that has now been adduced, and from what has been said above concerning deeds and works. Love in act is work and deed.

484. It is to be observed that all works and deeds belong to moral and civil life, and hence regard sincerity and uprightness, justice and equity. Sincerity and uprightness belong to moral life; justice and equity, to civil life. The love from which they are practiced, is either heavenly or infernal. The works and deeds of moral and civil life are heavenly, if they are done from heavenly love; for whatever is done from heavenly love is done from the Lord, and whatever is done from the Lord is good. But the deeds and works of moral and civil life are infernal, if they are done from infernal love; for whatever is done from this love, —which is the love of self and the world,—is done from man himself, and whatever is done from man himself is in

itself evil; because man, viewed in himself, or as to his proprium, is nothing but evil.[1]

THE DELIGHTS OF EVERY ONE'S LIFE ARE, AFTER DEATH, TURNED INTO CORRESPONDING DELIGHTS.

485. THAT the ruling affection or dominant love remains with every one to eternity, was shown in the preceding chapter; but that the delights of that affection or love are turned into corresponding delights, is now to be shown. By being turned into corresponding delights, is meant into spiritual ones which correspond to natural. That these are turned into spiritual delights in the other world, may be evident from the fact that so long as man is in the natural world he is in a terrestrial body; but when he leaves that body he enters the spiritual world and puts on a spiritual body. (That the angels are in a perfect human form, and men likewise after death, and that the bodies with which they are then clothed are spiritual, may be seen above, n. 73 to 77; and n. 453 to 460. And for what is meant by the correspondence of spiritual things with natural, see n. 87 to 115).

486. All the delights which man enjoys are those of his ruling love; for he feels nothing to be delightful except what he loves;

---

[1] That the *proprium* of man consists in loving himself more than God, and the world more than heaven, and in making light of his neighbor in comparison with himself; thus that it consists in the love of self and of the world, n. 694, 731, 4317. That man is born into this *proprium*, and that it is dense evil, n. 210, 215, 731, 874, 875, 876, 987, 1047, 2307, 2308, 3518, 3701, 3812, 8480, 8550, 10283, 10284, 10286, 10732. That not only all evil, but also every false, comes from the *proprium* of man, n. 1047, 10283, 10284, 10286. That the evils, which are from the *proprium* of man, are contempt of others, enmity, hatred, revenge, cruelty, deceit, n. 6667, 7370, 7373, 7374, 9348, 10038, 10742. That as the *proprium* of man has rule, the good of love and the truth of faith are either rejected, or suffocated, or perverted, n. 2041, 7491, 7492, 7643, 8487, 10455, 10742. That the *proprium* of man is hell with him, n. 694, 8480. That the good, which man does from the *proprium*, is not good, but is in itself evil, n. 8480.

consequently that which he loves supremely, is in the highest degree delightful. It amounts to the same, whether we say the
ruling love, or that which is loved above all things. Those delights are various. There are in general as many as there are ruling loves, and therefore as many as there are men, spirits, and
angels,—for the ruling love of one is never in all respects like
that of another. Hence it is that the face of one is never exactly like that of another; for the face of every one is an image
of his mind, and in the spiritual world is an image of his ruling
love. The delights of every individual in particular are also of
infinite variety; nor is a single delight of any one altogether similar to, or the same as, that of another, whether we regard those
which succeed one after another, or those which exist simultaneously one with another. One delight is never given exactly like
another. But still these specific delights with every individual
refer themselves to the one love belonging to him, which is his
ruling love; for they compose it, and thus make one with it. In
like manner all delights in general have reference to one universally ruling love; which, in heaven, is to love the Lord, and in
hell, the love of self.

487. What and of what nature are the spiritual delights into
which the natural delights of every one are turned after death, can
only be known from the science of correspondences. This teaches
in general, that no natural thing exists to which something spiritual does not correspond; and it also teaches in particular, what
and of what nature the corresponding thing is. Wherefore a
person skilled in that science may learn and know his own state
after death, provided he knows his own love, and its relation to
that universally ruling love just spoken of, to which all loves have
reference. But it is impossible for those who are in the love of
self to know their ruling love, because they love whatever is
their own, and call their evils goods, and the falses which favor
and thereby confirm their evils, they at the same time call truths.
Nevertheless, if they wish, they may learn it from others who
are wise, since these see what they themselves do not; but this is
not possible with those who are so filled with the love of self, as
to spurn all the instruction of the wise. But those who are in
heavenly love receive instruction; and on being brought into the

evils into which they were born, see them from truths,—for it is these which make evils manifest. Every one can see evil and its falsity by means of truth derived from good; but no one can see the good and the true from evil, because the falses of evil are darkness, and likewise correspond to darkness. They who are in falses derived from evil are therefore like blind persons, who do not see the objects which are in light. They also shun truths, as creatures of the night[1] shun the light of day. But truths derived from good are light, and likewise correspond to light, (as may be seen above, n. 126 to 134); wherefore they who are in truths derived from good, are seers, having their eyes open, and discerning the things which are of light and of shade. In these truths I have also been confirmed by experience. The angels in the heavens both see and perceive the evils and falses which sometimes rise up in themselves, and likewise the evils and falses wherein are the spirits who, in the world of spirits, are connected with the hells; but the spirits themselves cannot see their own evils and falses. What the good of heavenly love is, what conscience, what sincerity and justice,—except as practiced for some selfish end,—and what it is to be led by the Lord, they do not comprehend. They declare that there are no such things, and therefore that they are nothing. These things are said to induce man to examine himself, and from his delights learn the quality of his love, and thence what will be the state of his life after death, so far as he understands the science of correspondences.

488. How the delights of every one's life are turned into corresponding delights after death, may indeed be known from the science of correspondences; but because that science is not yet generally known, I will illustrate the subject by some examples from experience. All those who are in evil, and have confirmed

---

[1] That from correspondence darkness, when mentioned in the Word, signifies falses, and thick darkness the falses of evil, n. 1839, 1860, 7688, 7711. That the light of heaven is thick darkness to the evil, n. 1861, 6832, 8197. That the inhabitants of hell are said to be in darkness, because they are in the falses of evil, n. 3340, 4418, 4531. That the blind, in the Word, signify those who are in falses, and are not willing to be instructed, n. 2383, 6990.

dant experience. I have been permitted to converse with some
who lived two thousand years ago, whose lives are known because described in history; and I found that they still retained
their distinctive characters, and were exactly such as they had
been described, for the quality of their love, from and according
to which their lives were formed, remained the same. I have
also been permitted to converse with others who lived seventeen
centuries ago, and whose lives are known from history; with
others who lived four centuries ago; with others who lived three;
and so on; and it was found that an affection similar to that
which distinguished them in the world, ruled in them still. The
only difference was, that the delights of their love were turned
into such things as correspond to them. I have been told by the
angels that the life of the ruling love is never changed with any
one to eternity, since every one is his own love; wherefore to
change that love in a spirit, would be to deprive him of his life,
or to annihilate him. They also stated the reason, which is, that
man after death is no longer capable of being reformed by instruction, as in the world, because the ultimate plane, which consists of natural knowledges and affections, is then quiescent, and
cannot be opened because it is not spiritual, (see above, n. 464);
that the interiors which belong to the rational and natural minds
rest upon that plane, like a house on its foundation; and that it
is on this account that man remains to eternity such as the life
of his love had been in the world. The angels wonder exceedingly that man does not know that every one is such as his ruling love is; that many should believe they can be saved by immediate mercy, and by faith alone, whatever be the quality of
their lives; also that they do not know that the divine mercy operates through means, and consists in being led by the Lord both
in the world and afterward to eternity; and that those are led by
mercy who do not live in evil. They are also surprised that men
do not know that faith is the affection of truth proceeding from
heavenly love, which is from the Lord.

481. *That the man whose love is celestial and spiritual goes
to heaven, and he whose love is corporeal and worldly without
celestial and spiritual, goes to hell*, has been made plain to me
from all whom I have seen taken up into heaven and cast into

hell. The life of those who were taken up into heaven had been from celestial and spiritual love; but the life of those who were cast into hell had been from corporeal and worldly love. Heavenly love is to love what is good, sincere and just, for their own sake, and from the love of such things, to do them. Thence is derived the life of goodness, sincerity and justice, which is heavenly life. They who love goodness, sincerity, and justice, for their own sake, and practice or live them, love the Lord above all things, because these are from Him; and they also love the neighbor, because these are the neighbor that is to be loved.[1] But corporeal love is to love what is good, sincere, and just, not for their own sake, but for the sake of self, because they are loved only as the means of securing reputation, honor, and gain. They who are in such love do not regard the Lord and the neighbor in what is good, sincere, and just, but themselves and the world, and experience delight in fraud; and goodness, sincerity, and justice, practiced with fraudulent intent, are evil, insincerity, and injustice; and these latter are the things which they love in the former. Because the loves thus determine the quality of every one's life, therefore all are examined on their first entrance after

[1] That the Lord is our neighbor in the supreme sense, because He ought to be loved above all things; but that to love the Lord is to love that which is from Him, because He Himself is in everything which is from Himself; thus it is to love the good and the true, n. 2425, 3419, 6706, 6711, 6819, 6823, 8123. That to love the good and the true, which is from Him, is to live according to them, and that this is to love the Lord, n. 10143, 10153, 10310, 10336, 10578, 10645. That every man and every society, also a man's country and the church, and in the universal sense, the kingdom of the Lord, are our neighbor, and that to do them good from the love of good according to the quality of their state, is to love the neighbor; thus their good, which is to be consulted, is the neighbor, n. 6818 to 6824, 8123. That moral good also, which is sincerity, and civil good, which is justice, are our neighbor; and that to act sincerely and justly from the love of sincerity and justice is to love the neighbor, n. 2915, 4730, 8120, 8121 to 8123. That hence charity toward the neighbor extends itself to all things of the life of man, and that to do what is good and just, and to act sincerely from the heart in every occupation and in every work, is to love the neighbor, n. 2417, 8121, 8124. That doctrine in the ancient church was the doctrine of charity, and that hence that church had wisdom, n. 2417, 2385, 3419, 3420, 4844, 6628.

42

truths and the Word from interior affection, or from the affection
of truth itself, in the other life dwell in light, in elevated places
which appear like mountains, and there they are continually in
the light of heaven. They have no idea of darkness like that
of night in the world. And they also live in a vernal temperature.   There are exhibited before them as it were fields and
harvests, and likewise vineyards. Everything in their houses
glistens as if made of precious stones. To look through the
windows, is like looking through pure crystals. These are the
delightful objects of their sight; but the same things are interiorly delightful on account of their correspondence with divine-
celestial things; for the truths derived from the Word which they
have loved, correspond to harvests, vineyards, precious stones,
windows, and crystals.[1] They who have applied the doctrinals of
the church derived from the Word immediately to life, are in the
inmost heaven, and in the enjoyments of the delight of wisdom
above the rest.   In every single object they behold things divine.
They see the objects, indeed, but the divine things corresponding
to them flow immediately into their minds, and fill them with a
blessedness wherewith all their sensations are affected.   Hence
all objects, to their eyes, seem as it were to laugh, sport, and live.
(On this subject see above, n. 270).   They who have loved the
sciences, and have cultivated their rational faculty by means of
them, and thence have procured to themselves intelligence, and
have at the same time acknowledged the Divine, find the pleasure
which they derived from the sciences, and their rational delight,
turned in the other life into spiritual delight, which is that of the
knowledges of good and truth.   They dwell in gardens, where
appear beds of flowers and grass-plats beautifully arranged, and
rows of trees round about, together with porticoes and walks.

That a harvest, when mentioned in the Word, signifies a state of
reception and the increase of truth derived from good, n. 9294. That
a standing crop signifies truth in conception, n. 9146. That vineyards
signify the spiritual church, and the truths of that church, n. 1069, 9139.
That precious stones signify the truths of heaven and the church transparent from good, n. 114, 9863, 9865. 9868, 9873. 9905. That a window signifies the intellectual principle which is of the internal sight, n. 655, 658,
3391.

The trees and flowers are varied every day. The view of the whole in general presents delights to their minds, and the varieties in particular continually renew them ; and because these objects correspond to things divine, and those who behold them are in the science of correspondences, they are perpetually replenished with new knowledges, whereby their spiritual rational faculty is perfected. *They are sensible of these delights, because gardens, beds of flowers, grass-plats, and trees, correspond to sciences and knowledges, and to intelligence thence derived.[1] They who have ascribed all things to the Divine, and have regarded nature respectively as dead, only subservient to things spiritual, and have confirmed themselves in this belief, dwell in heavenly light, which renders all things that appear before their eyes transparent ; and in that transparency they behold innumerable variegations of light, which their internal sight imbibes as it were immediately ; thence they perceive interior delights. The objects which appear in their houses are as if made of diamonds, resplendent with similar variegations of light. I have been told that the walls of their houses are like crystal, thus also transparent ; and in them appear as it were moving forms representative of heavenly things, also with perpetual variety. And these phenomena exist, because such transparency corresponds to an understanding enlightened by the Lord, and free from the shades which originate in faith merely natural, and in the love of natural things. Such are the things, with numberless others, concerning which it has been said by those who have been in heaven, that they have beheld things which eye hath not seen, and,—from a perception of divine things thence communicated,—that they have heard things which the ear never heard. They who have not acted clandestinely, but have been willing that all their thoughts should be known abroad, so far as was consistent with the interests and customs of civil life,—because they

---

[1] That a garden, a grove, and a paradise signify intelligence, n. 100, 108, 3220. That therefore the ancients celebrated holy worship in groves, n. 2722, 4552. That flowers and flower-beds signify scientific truths and knowledges, n. 9553. That herbs, grasses, and grass-plats signify scientific truths, n. 7571. That trees signify perceptions and knowledges, n. 103, 2163, 2682, 2722, 2972, 7692.

have thought nothing but what was sincere and just from the Divine,—appear in heaven with radiant faces, wherein every affection and thought are imaged, while their speech and actions are the very forms of their affections. Hence they are loved more than others. When they speak, their faces become a little obscure ; but when they have done speaking, the same things which they have spoken appear simultanéously in their faces, clearly manifest to the sight. All the objects which exist around them also,—because they correspond with the interiors,—assume such an appearance, that what they represent and signify is clearly perceived by others. When the spirits who have taken delight in acting clandestinely, see these ingenuous ones at a distance, they shun them, and appear to themselves to crawl away from them like serpents. They who have regarded adulteries as abominable, and have lived in the chaste love of marriage, are beyond all others in the order and form of heaven, and thence in all beauty, and forever remain in the bloom of youth. The delights of their love are ineffable, and increase throughout eternity ; for all the delights and joys of heaven flow into that love, because it descends from the conjunction of the Lord with heaven and the church, and in general from the conjunction of good and truth, which conjunction is heaven itself in general, and with every individual angel in particular, (see above, n. 366 to 386). Their external delights are such as no human language can describe. But these are only a few of the things which have been revealed to me concerning the correspondences of the delights with those who are in heavenly love.

490. From the things here related it may be known, that the delights of all after death are turned into corresponding ones, the love itself still remaining to eternity ; as conjugial love, the love of what is just, sincere, good, and true, the love of the sciences and of knowledges, the love of intelligence and wisdom, and all other loves. The things which flow from love like streams from their fountain, are delights, which also are permanent, but exalted to a superior degree, when from natural delights they are raised to spiritual.

THE FIRST STATE OF MAN AFTER DEATH.

491. THERE are three states through which man passes after death, before he enters either heaven or hell. The first state is that of his exteriors; the second, that of his interiors; and the third, that of his preparation. These states are passed through in the world of spirits. But there are some who do not pass through them, but, immediately after death are either taken up into heaven or cast into hell. They who are immediately taken up into heaven, are those who have been regenerated, and thus prepared for heaven, in the world. They who have become so regenerated and prepared that they need only to cast off natural defilements with the body, are immediately conveyed by the angels to heaven. I have seen them taken up soon after the hour of death. But they who have been interiorly wicked, though to outward appearance good, and thus have filled their wickedness with deceit, and have used goodness as a means of deceiving, are immediately cast into hell. I have seen some such cast into hell directly after death,—one of the most deceitful, with his head downward and feet upward; and others in other ways. There are also some, who immediately after death are cast into caverns, and are thus separated from those who are in the world of spirits, and are taken out thence and let in thither by turns; these are they, who, under civil pretences, have dealt wickedly with the neighbor. But the latter and the former are few in comparison with those who are kept in the world of spirits, and there according to divine order are prepared for heaven or for hell.

492. As to what concerns the first state, which is the state of the exteriors, man comes into that immediately after death. Every man as to his spirit has exteriors and interiors. The exteriors of the spirit are those whereby he accommodates his body in the world, especially his face, speech, and gestures, to consociation with others; but the interiors of the spirit are those which belong to his own proper will and consequent thought, which are rarely manifested in the face, the speech, and the man-

ner. For man is accustomed from infancy to assume the appearance of friendship, of benevolence, and of sincerity, and to conceal the thoughts of his own proper will; hence from habit he assumes a moral and civil life in externals, whatever he may be in internals. In consequence of this habit, a man scarcely knows what his interiors are, nor does he pay any attention to them.

493. The first state of man after death is similar to his state in the world, because then in like manner he is in externals. He has also a similar face, similar speech, and a similar mind [*animus*], thus a similar moral and civil life. In consequence of this, he is not aware but that he is still in the world, unless he adverts to those things which present themselves, and to those which were said to him by the angels when he was raised up, that he is now a spirit, (n. 450). Thus one life is continued into the other, and death is only the passage [from the natural to the spiritual world].

494. Because the spirit of man recently departed from the world is such, therefore he is then recognized by his friends, and by those whom he had known in the world; for spirits recognize another, not only from his face and speech, but also from the sphere of his life when they come near him. When any one in the other life thinks of another, he also brings the other's face before him in thought, and at the same time many of the circumstances of his life; and when he does this, the other becomes present, as if he were sent for and called. This occurs in the spiritual world, from the fact that thoughts are there communicated, and that there are no spaces there, such as exist in the natural world, (see above, n. 191–199). Hence it is that all, when they first come into the other life, are recognized by their friends, relations, and those with whom they were in any way acquainted; and that they also converse together, and afterward associate according to their friendship in the world. I have frequently heard that those who came from the world, rejoiced at seeing their friends again, and that their friends in turn rejoiced that they had come to them. This is a common occurrence: that one married partner meets the other, and they mutually congratulate each other; they also remain together for a time, longer or shorter according to the delight that had attended their dwelling

together in the world. Nevertheless, if love truly conjugial,—which is the conjunction of minds from heavenly love,—had not conjoined them, after remaining together for some time, they are separated. But if their minds had been discordant, and they interiorly had an aversion to each other, they break out into open enmity, and sometimes actually fight; notwithstanding which, they are not separated until they enter the second state, which will be treated of in what presently follows.

495. Because the life of spirits recently deceased is not unlike their life in the natural world, and because they know nothing about the state of their life after death, nor about heaven and hell, except what they have learned from the sense of the letter of the Word, and preaching thence,—therefore after wondering at finding themselves in a body, and in the enjoyment of every sense which they had in the world, and at beholding similar objects, they are seized with a desire to know what heaven and hell are, and where they are situated. Wherefore they are instructed by their friends concerning the state of eternal life, and are likewise led about to various places, and into various companies; some are taken into cities, and also into gardens and paradises, generally to magnificent things, since such things delight the externals in which they are. They are then brought by turns into their own thoughts, which they had entertained in the life of the body about the state of the soul after death, and about heaven and hell, until they feel indignant that they should have been entirely ignorant of such things, and likewise at the ignorance of the church. Almost all are anxious to know whether they shall go to heaven; most of them believe they shall, because in the world they have led a moral and civil life; not considering that the evil and the good lead a similar life in externals, alike doing good to others, frequenting churches, listening to sermons, and engaging in prayer; not being at all aware that external acts and the externals of worship are of no avail, but the internals from which externals proceed. Out of some thousands, scarcely one knows what internals are, and that man has heaven and the church in these; and still less do they know that external acts are such as the intentions and thoughts are, and the love and faith therein, from which the acts proceed; and when they are instructed, they

do not comprehend how thinking and willing can be of any avail, but only speaking and acting. Such are most of those who, at the present day, enter the other life from the Christian world.

496. Nevertheless they are examined by good spirits as to their quality, and this by various methods, since in this first state the evil as well as the good speak truths, and do good deeds; because,—as stated above,—they also have led an outwardly moral life, since they have lived under governments and in subjection to laws, and since they have thereby acquired the reputation of being just and sincere, have secured favor, been exalted to honors, and obtained wealth. But evil spirits are distinguished from the good especially by this circumstance, that they attend eagerly to what is said about external things, and give but little heed to what is said about internal things, which are the truths and goods of heaven and the church. They hear these things indeed, but not with attention and gladness. They are also distinguished by this, that they frequently turn themselves toward certain quarters, and, when left to themselves, walk in the ways which tend in those directions. From the quarters toward which they turn, and the ways in which they go, the quality of the love that leads them is known.

497. All the spirits who arrive from the world, are indeed connected with some society in heaven or in hell, but only as to their interiors. But the interiors are not manifested so long as they remain in their exteriors, for external things cover and conceal things internal, especially with those who are in interior evil; but afterward they appear plainly when they come into the second state, because their interiors are then opened and their exteriors laid asleep.

498. This first state of man after death continues with some for days, with some for months, and with some for a year, but seldom with any for more than a year: in each instance the duration is shorter or longer according to the agreement or disagreement of the interiors with the exteriors. For with every one the exteriors and interiors must act in unity, and must correspond. It is not allowable for any one in the spiritual world to think and will in one way, and to speak and act in another. Every one

there must be the image of his own affection, or of his own love; so that what he is in his interiors, he must be in his exteriors. The exteriors of a spirit are therefore first uncovered and reduced to órder, that they may serve as a plane corresponding to the interiors.

THE SECOND STATE OF MAN AFTER DEATH.

499. THE second state of man after death is called the state of his interiors, because he is then let into the interiors which belong to his mind, or to his will and thought: and his exteriors, in which he had been in his first state, are laid asleep. Every one who observes the life of man, and his speech and actions, may know that with every one there are things exterior and interior, or exterior and interior thoughts and intentions. This may be known from the following considerations: Every one in civil life thinks of others according to what he has heard and understood concerning them, either from report or from conversation; nevertheless he does not speak with them according to his tnought; and although they are evil, still he treats them with civility. That this is the case is especially evident from pretenders and flatterers, who speak and act altogether different from what they think and will: and from hypocrites, who talk about God, and heaven, and the salvation of souls, and the truths of the church, and their country's good, and their neighbor, as if from faith and love; when yet in heart they believe quite differently from what they talk, and love themselves alone. From these considerations it may be evident, that there are two classes of thoughts, one exterior and the other interior; and that people speak from their exterior thought, and in their interior they entertain different sentiments; and that these two classes of thoughts are separated, care being taken lest the interior flow into the exterior, and in any way appear. Man is so formed by creation that his interior thought should act as one with his exte-

rior by correspondence; and it likewise does so act with those who are in good, for they think and speak only what is good. But with those who are in evil, interior thought does not act in unity with exterior, for they think what is evil and speak what is good. With these, order is inverted; for good with them is without, and evil within. Hence it is that evil with them has dominion over good, and subjects it to itself as a servant, that it may serve it as a means to obtain its ends, which are the things belonging to their love. And because such an end lies concealed in the good which they speak and do, it is evident that the good appertaining to them is not good, but infected with evil, however it may appear as good, in the external form, to those who are not acquainted with their interiors. It is otherwise with those who are in good; with them order is not inverted, but good from interior thought flows into the exterior, and thus into the speech and actions. This is the order into which man was created; for when men are in this order their interiors are in heaven and in the light of heaven; and because the light of heaven is divine truth proceeding from the Lord, consequently is the Lord in heaven, (n. 126–140), therefore they are led by the Lord. These things are said that it may be known that every man has interior thought and exterior thought, and that these are distinct from each other. When thought is mentioned, the will is also meant, since thought is from the will, for without the will no one can think. From these things it is evident what is the state of man's exteriors, and the state of his interiors.

500. When mention is made of the will and the thought, then by the will is also meant affection and love, together with all the delight and pleasure which belong to affection and love, because these have reference to the will as to their subject; for what a man wills, this he loves, and feels as pleasurable and delightful; and conversely, what a man loves and feels as pleasurable and delightful, this he wills. But by the thought is then meant all that also whereby a man confirms his affection or love; for thought is nothing else but the form of the will, or the medium whereby that which a man wills may appear in the light. This form is presented by various rational analyses, which derive their

origin from the spiritual world, and belong properly to man's spirit.

501. It is to be observed that man is altogether such as he is in respect to his interiors, and not such as he is in respect to his exteriors separate from his interiors. The reason is, because the interiors belong to his spirit, and the life of man is the life of his spirit, for the body lives from the spirit; wherefore also such as a man is as to his interiors, such he remains to eternity. But since his exteriors belong also to the body, they are separated after death, and those of them which adhere to the spirit are laid asleep, and only serve as a plane for the interiors, as was shown above in treating of the memory of man which remains after death. Hence it is evident what really belongs to man, and what is not properly his own; namely, with the wicked all those things which belong to the exterior thought from which they speak, and to the exterior will from which they act, are not properly theirs, but those things which belong to their interior thought and will.

502. When the first state is passed through, which is the state of the exteriors treated of in the preceding chapter, the man-spirit is let into the state of his interiors, or into the state of his interior will and the thought thence proceeding, in which he had been in the world, when being left to himself he thought freely and without restraint. He falls into this state without being aware of it, just as in the world when he withdraws the thought which is next to speech, or from which speech proceeds, toward his interior thought, and abides in the latter. Wherefore when the man-spirit is in this state, he is in himself, and in his very life; for to think freely from the affection properly his own, is the very life of man, and is himself.

503. The spirit in this state thinks from his own will, thus from his own affection, or from his own love; and then his thought makes one with his will, and so completely one, that he scarcely appears to think, but merely to will. It is nearly the same when he speaks; yet there is this difference, that he feels some degree of fear lest the thoughts of his will should go forth naked, since by social intercourse in the world this reserve has also become the habit of his will.

504. All men without exception are let into this state after death, because it is the proper state of their spirits. The former state is such as that of the man was, as to his spirit, when he was in company, which state is not properly his own. That this state, or the state of his exteriors, in which a man is at first after death,—as treated of in the preceding chapter,—is not properly his own, may be evident from many considerations; as from this, that spirits not only think but also speak from their own affection; for their speech proceeds from their affection, as may appear from what was said and shown in the chapters concerning the speech of angels, (n. 234-245). The man also thought in a similar manner in the world when he thought within himself; for then he did not think from the speech of his body, but only saw the things thought of; and at the same time saw more within a minute, than he could afterward utter in half an hour. That the state of man when he is in his exteriors is not properly his own, or that of his spirit, is also evident from this consideration, that when he is in company in the world, he speaks according to the laws of moral and civil life, and his interior thought governs his exterior, as one person governs another, to prevent its passing beyond the limits of decorum and good manners. The same is evident also from this, that when a man thinks within himself, he also thinks how he must speak and act in order to please, and to obtain friendship, good-will, and favor; and this by methods foreign to his inclination, thus otherwise than he would do if he acted from his own proper will. From these facts it is evident that the state of his interiors into which the spirit is let, is the state that properly belongs to him, and was therefore the man's real state when he lived in the world.

505. When a spirit is in the state of his interiors, it manifestly appears of what quality the man was in himself when in the world, for he then acts from his proprium. He who was interiorly in good in the world, then acts rationally and wisely,—more wisely indeed than in the world, because he is released from his connection with the body, and thence with terrestrial things which caused obscurity, and as it were interposed a cloud. But he who was in evil in the world, then acts foolishly and insanely,—more insanely indeed than he did in the world, because he is in free-

dom and under no restraint. For when he lived in the world, he was sane in externals, since he thereby assumed the appearance of a rational man; wherefore when his externals are removed from him, his insanities are revealed. A bad man, who in externals puts on the semblance of a good one, may be compared to a vessel exteriorly bright and polished, and covered with a lid, within which is concealed every kind of filth; according to the Lord's declaration: "*Ye are like unto whited sepulchres, which outwardly appear beautiful, but within are full of the bones of the dead, and of all uncleaftness,*" Matt. xxiii. 27.

506. All who have lived in good in the world, and have acted from conscience,—who are those that have acknowledged the Divine and have loved divine truths, especially those who have applied them to life,—appear to themselves, when let into the state of their interiors, like persons who are awakened out of sleep, and like those who come from darkness into light. They also think from the light of heaven, thus from interior wisdom, and they act from good, thus from interior affection. Heaven flows-in likewise into their thoughts and affections with an interior blessedness and delight, whereof before they had no knowledge; for they have communication with the angels of heaven. Then also they acknowledge the Lord, and worship Him from their very life; for they are in their own proper life when in the state of their interiors, as stated just above, (n. 505). And they likewise acknowledge and worship Him from freedom, for freedom belongs to interior affection. Thus also they recede from external sanctity, and come into internal sanctity, wherein essential worship really consists. Such is the state of those who have led a Christian life according to the precepts in the Word. But the state of those who in the world have lived in evil, and have had no conscience, and have thence denied the Divine, is diametrically the opposite; for all who live in evil, interiorly in themselves deny the Divine, however they may imagine, when in their externals, that they do not deny but acknowledge Him; for to acknowledge the Divine and to live wickedly are opposites. Such persons in the other life, when they come into the state of their interiors, and are heard to speak and seen to act, appear as

if infatuated; for from their evil lusts they break out into all
manner of abominations,—into contempt of others, ridicule,
blasphemy, hatred, and revenge; they contrive plans of mischief,
some of them with such cunning and malice, that it can scarcely
be believed that anything of the kind could exist in any man.
For in the state in which they then are, they are free to act according to the thoughts of their will, because they are separated
from their exteriors, which in the world restrained and checked
them. In a word, they are deprived of rationality, because in
the world the rational had not resided in their interiors but in
their exteriors; nevertheless they then appear to themselves to
be wise beyond all others. Such being their character, therefore
when they are in this second state, they are occasionally remit-
ted for a short time into the state of their exteriors, and then into
the remembrance of their actions when they were in the state of
their interiors. Some are then ashamed, and acknowledge that
they have been insane; some are not ashamed; and some are
indignant at not being allowed to remain continually in the state
of their exteriors. But it is shown to these latter what sort of
persons they would be if they were continually in this state;
namely, that they would endeavor to commit the same evils clandestinely, and by appearances of goodness, of sincerity and justice, would seduce the simple in heart and faith, and would utterly destroy themselves; for their exteriors would at length burn
with a fire similar to that which rages in their interiors, and this
would consume all their life.

507. When spirits are in this second state, they appear altogether such as they were in themselves when in the world, and
the things which they did and spoke in concealment are also
published; for then, being no longer restrained by external considerations, they say similar things openly, and likewise endeavor
to do similar things, having no fear for their reputation as in the
world. They are then also brought into many states of their
own evils, that their true quality may appear to angels and good
spirits. Thus hidden things are laid open, and secret things are
uncovered, according to the Lord's words: "*There is nothing
covered which shall not be uncovered, neither hidden which
shall not be known: what ye have said in darkness, shall be*

reard in the light, and what ye have spoken into the ear in closets, shall be preached upon the house-tops," Luke xii. 2, 3. And in another place : *"I say unto you, whatsoever useless word men have spoken, they shall give an account thereof in the day of judgment,"* Matt. xii. 36.

508. What sort of beings the wicked are in this state, cannot be described in a few words, for every one is then insane according to his lusts, and these are various. I shall therefore only adduce some particular instances, from which a conclusion may be formed respecting the rest. They who have loved themselves above all things, and in their offices and employments have regarded their own honor, and have performed uses not for the sake of the uses and because they took delight in them, but for the sake of reputation that they might be esteemed more worthy than others on account of them, and have thus been delighted with the fame of their own honor,—these, when in the second state, are more stupid than others ; for in proportion as any one loves himself, he is removed from heaven ; and in proportion as he is removed from heaven, he is removed from wisdom. But they who have been in self-love, and at the same time have been crafty, and have raised themselves to honors by artful practices, consociate themselves with the worst of spirits, and learn magic arts, which are abuses of divine order, whereby they trouble and infest all who do not honor them. They lay snares, they cherish hatred, they burn with revenge, and seek to vent their rage against all who do not submit themselves. And they rush into all these enormities in proportion as the wicked crew favors them ; and at last they deliberate with themselves how they may climb up into heaven so as to destroy that, or be worshiped there as gods. To such lengths does their madness go. Those of this class who have been of the Roman Catholic religion, are more insane than the rest ; for they are possessed with the notion that heaven and hell are subject to their power, and that they can remit sins at pleasure. They arrogate to themselves every divine attribute, and call themselves Christ. Their persuasion that all this is true, is so strong, that wherever it flows in it disturbs the mind, and induces a darkness that is even painful. These spirits are nearly the same in both states, but in the second they are without ration-

ality. But concerning their insanities, and concerning their lot
after they have passed through this state, some particulars will
be related in the little work concerning the Last Judgment and
the Destruction of Babylon. They who have ascribed creation
to nature, and hence in heart, though not with the lips, have
denied the Divine, consequently all things of the church and of
heaven, consociate themselves with their like in this state, and
call every one a god who excels in craftiness, even worshiping
him with divine honor. I have seen such spirits assembled together, adoring a magician, debating about nature, and behaving
like fools, as if they were beasts under a human form ; among
them also were some, who in the world had been exalted to posts
of dignity, and some who had been reputed learned and wise.
And so in other instances. From these few examples it may be
concluded what sort of persons those are, whose interiors which
belong to the mind are closed toward heaven, as is the case with
all those who have not received any influx from heaven through
an acknowledgment of the Divine, and a life of faith. Every
one may judge from himself what sort of a person he would be
if he were of this character, and were at liberty to act without
fear of the law, or of the loss of life, and without external restraints,
which are fears lest he should suffer in his reputation, and be
deprived of honor, of gain, and of the pleasures thence resulting. Nevertheless their insanity is restrained by the Lord, so as
to prevent it from rushing beyond the limits of use,—for some
use is performed by every one even of this character. Good
spirits see in them what evil is, and what is its nature, and what
man would be if he were not led of the Lord. It is also one of
their uses to collect together wicked spirits like themselves, and
to separate them from the good. It is also a use that the truths
and goods, whereof the wicked have assumed an appearance in
externals, are taken away from them, and they are brought into
the evils of their own life, and into the falses of evil, and are
thus prepared for hell. For no one goes to hell until he is in his
own evil and in the falses of evil, since it is not allowed any one
there to have a divided mind, that is, to think and speak one
thing, and to will another. Every evil spirit must there think
what is false derived from evil, and must speak from such falsity ;

in both cases from the will, thus from his own proper love and its delight and pleasure, as he did in the world when he thought in his spirit, that is, as he thought in himself when he thought from interior affection. The reason is, because the will is the man himself, and not the thought, except so far as it partakes of the will; and the will is the man's very nature or disposition; wherefore to be let into his will is to be let into his nature or disposition, and also into his life, for man puts on a nature according to his life; and after death, he remains of such a nature as he had procured to himself by his life in the world, which, with the wicked, can no longer be amended and changed by means of thought, or the understanding of truth.

509. In this second state evil spirits rush headlong into evils of every kind, and are therefore frequently and grievously punished. Punishments in the world of spirits are manifold; nor is any respect had to person, whether the culprit when in the world had been a servant or a king. All evil carries its punishment with it; evil and punishment are indissolubly conjoined; wherefore whoever is in evil, is also in the punishment of evil. But still no one there suffers punishment on account of the evil deeds which he had committed in the world, but on account of the evils which he does there. Yet it amounts to the same, and is the same thing, whether it be said that men suffer punishment on account of the evils which they did in the world, or on account of the evils which they do in the other life; since every one after death returns into his own life, and thus into similar evils; for the man is of such a character as he had been in the life of his body, (n. 470-484). That they are punished, is because the fear of punishment is the only means of subduing evils in this state. Exhortation is no longer of any avail, nor instruction, nor fear of the law, or of the loss of reputation, since the spirit now acts according to his nature, which cannot be restrained nor broken except by punishments. But good spirits are never punished, although they have done evils in the world, for their evils do not return. And it has also been revealed to me, that their evils were of a different kind or nature; for they were not done from purpose contrary to the truth, nor from any evil heart other than that which they had received hereditarily from their parents;

45

but they were led into the evil which they did, from a blind delight, when they were in externals separate from internals.

510. Every one goes to his own society in which his spirit was while he lived in the world; for every man as to his spirit is conjoined to some society, either infernal or heavenly,—a wicked man to an infernal society, a good man to a heavenly society. (That every one returns to his own society after death, may be seen, n. 438). The spirit is led to that society by successive steps, and at last enters it. An evil spirit, when he is in the state of his interiors, is turned by degrees toward his own society, and at length directly to it before this state is completed; and when completed, the evil spirit of his own accord casts himself into the hell where are those like himself. When casting himself down, he appears like one falling headlong, with the head downward and the feet upward. The reason of this appearance is, because he is in inverted order; for he had loved the things of hell, and rejected those of heaven. Some evil spirits in this second state, go into and out of their hells alternately; but these do not then appear to fall headlong, as they do when fully vastated. The society itself, in which they were as to their spirit when in the world, is likewise shown them when they are in the state of their exteriors, that they may thence know that they were in hell even while in the life of the body; but still not in a similar state with those who are in hell itself, but in one similar to that of those who are in the world of spirits; concerning whose state, as compared with that of those who are in hell, more will be said in what follows.

511. The separation of evil spirits from good ones is effected in this second state, for in the first state they are together; since while a spirit is in his exteriors, he is as he was in the world, thus as an evil person with a good one there, and as a good person with an evil one. But it is otherwise when he is brought into his interiors, and left to his own nature or will. The separation of the good from the evil is effected in various ways; generally by their being led around to those societies with which they had had communication by good thoughts and affections in their first state, and so to those whom they had induced, by external appearances, to believe that they were not evil. They

are usually led around through an extensive circle, and everywhere their real character is shown to the good spirits. At the sight of them, the good spirits turn themselves away; and as they turn away, so likewise the evil spirits who are led around, turn their faces away from them to the quarter where their infernal society is, which they are about to enter. Not to mention other methods of separation, which are many.

THE THIRD STATE OF MAN AFTER DEATH, WHICH IS THE STATE OF INSTRUCTION OF THOSE WHO GO TO HEAVEN.

512. THE third state of man after death, or of his spirit, is a state of instruction. This state is experienced by those who go to heaven and become angels; but not by those who go to hell, since these cannot be instructed. Wherefore the second state of these latter is likewise their third, which ends in their being altogether turned to their own love, thus to the infernal society which is in similar love. When this takes place, they think and will from that love; and because that love is infernal, they will nothing but what is evil and think nothing but what is false, these things being delightful to them because they are objects of their love; and hence they reject everything good and true, which they had before adopted because it served as a means of gratifying their love. But the good are brought from the second state into the third, which is the state of their preparation for heaven, by means of instruction. For no one can be prepared for heaven except by the knowledges of good and truth, that is, except by instruction; for no one can know what spiritual good and truth are, nor what evil and falsity, which are their opposites, unless he be instructed. What civil and moral good and truth are, which are called justice and sincerity, may be known in the world; because in the world there are civil laws which teach what is just, and there is the intercourse of society, in which man learns to live according to moral laws, all of which have

reference to what is sincere and right. But spiritual good and truth are not learned from the world, but from heaven. They may, indeed, be known from the Word, and from the doctrine of the church which is drawn from the Word; but still they cannot flow into the life, unless man, as to his interiors which belong to his mind, be in heaven : and man is in heaven when he acknowledges the Divine, and at the same time acts justly and sincerely from the conviction that he ought to do so because it is commanded in the Word; for he then lives justly and sincerely for the sake of the Divine, and not for the sake of himself and the world as ends. But no one can so act, unless he be first instructed in such truths as these : That there is a God; that there is a heaven and a hell; that there is a life after death; that God ought to be loved above all things, and the neighbor as one's self; and that the things which are in the Word ought to be believed, because the Word is divine. Without the knowledge and acknowledgement of these truths, man cannot think spiritually; and without thought concerning them, he does not will them; for a man cannot think of the things about which he knows nothing; and the things which he does not think of, he cannot will. When therefore a man wills these truths, then heaven, that is, the Lord through heaven, flows into his life; for He flows into the will, and through the will into the thought, and through both into the life; for all the life of man is from his will and thought. From these considerations it is evident, that spiritual good and truth are not learned from the world but from heaven, and that no one can be prepared for heaven but by means of instruction. In proportion also as the Lord flows into any one's life, He instructs him; for in that proportion He enkindles in his will the love of knowing truths, and enlightens his thought to discern them. And so far as these effects take place, the man's interiors are opened, and heaven is implanted in them; and still further,—what is divine and heavenly flows into the sincere acts of his moral life, and into the just acts of his civil life, and makes them spiritual; since the man then does them from the Divine, because for the sake of the Divine. For the sincere and just actions belonging to his moral and civil life, which the man performs from the above origin, are the very effects of spiritual life; and the effect derives all that belongs to it from its efficient cause; for such as the cause is, such is the effect.

513. The instructions are given by the angels of many societies, especially by those which are in the northern and southern quarters, for those angelic societies are in intelligence and wisdom derived from the knowledges of good and truth. The places of instruction are toward the north, and are various, arranged and distinguished according to the genera and species of heavenly goods, so that every one there may be instructed according to his peculiar genius and faculty of reception. These places extend in all directions there to a considerable distance. The good spirits who are to be instructed, are conveyed thither by the Lord after they have completed their second state in the world of spirits. All, however, are not taken to them; for they who have been instructed in the world, were there also prepared by the Lord for heaven, and are conveyed to heaven by another way; some, immediately after death; some, after a short stay with good spirits, where the grosser things of their thoughts and affections, which they contracted from honors and riches in the world, are removed, and thus they are purified. Some are first vastated, which is effected in places under the soles of the feet, called the lower earth, where some suffer severely. These are they who have confirmed themselves in falses, and yet have led good lives,—for falses confirmed inhere with great tenacity; and until they are dispersed, truths cannot be seen, thus cannot be received. But the subject of vastations, and the ways in which they are effected, has been treated of in the ARCANA CŒLESTIA, extracts from which may be here seen in the notes.[1]

---

[1] That vastations are effected in the other life, that is, that they who come thither from the world are vastated, n. 698, 7122, 7474, 9763. That the well-disposed are vastated as to falses, and the ill-disposed as to truths, n. 7474, 7541, 7542. That with the well-disposed vastations are effected also in order to put off earthly and worldly principles, which they contracted while they lived in the world, n. 7186, 9763; and that evils and falses may be removed, and thus place be given for the influx of goods and truths out of heaven from the Lord, together with the faculty of receiving them, n. 7122, 9331. That they cannot be elevated into heaven until such things are removed, because they oppose and do not agree with heavenly things, n. 6928, 7122, 7186, 7541, 7542, 7543, 9763. That thus likewise they

514. All who are in places of instruction dwell in distinct classes; for every one of them is interiorly connected with the society of heaven which he is soon to enter. Wherefore since the societies of heaven are arranged according to the heavenly form, (see above, n. 200–212), so likewise are the places where the instructions are given. Therefore when viewed from heaven, these places appear like heaven in a lesser form. They extend lengthwise from east to west, and breadthwise from south to north; but the breadth, to appearance, is less than the length. The arrangements in general are as follows: In front are those who died when they were infants, and have been educated in heaven to the period of early youth; these, after passing the state of infancy with their instructresses there, are brought thither by the Lord and instructed. Behind them, are the places where those are instructed who died adults, and who in the world were in the affection of truth from the good of life. Behind these, are such as have professed the Mahomedan religion.

---

are prepared, who are to be elevated into heaven, n. 4728, 7090. That it is dangerous to come into heaven before they are prepared, n. 537, 538. Concerning the state of illustration, and concerning the joy of those who come out of vastation, and are elevated into heaven, and concerning their reception there, n. 2699, 2701, 2704. That the region where those vastations are effected is called the lower earth, n. 4728, 7090. That that region is under the soles of the feet, surrounded by the hells; its quality described, n. 4940 to 4951, 7090; from experience, n. 699. What the hells are, which infest and vastate more than the rest, n. 7317, 7502, 7545. That they who have infested and vastated the well-disposed, are afterward afraid of them, shun them and hold them in aversion, n. 7768. That those infestations and vastations are effected in different ways, according to the inherence of evils and falses, and that they continue according to their quality and quantity, n. 1106 to 1113. That some are willing to be vastated, n. 1107. That some are vastated by fears, n. 4942. Some by infestations from their own evils which they have done in the world, and from their own falses which they have thought in the world, whence come anxieties and pangs of conscience, n. 1106. Some by spiritual captivity, which is ignorance and interception of truth conjoined with the desire of knowing truths, n. 1109, 2694. Some by sleep; some by a middle state between wakefulness and sleep, n. 1108. That they who have placed merit in works, appear to themselves to cut wood, n. 1110. Others in other ways with much variety, n. 699.

and in the world led a moral life, and acknowledged one D.vine, and the Lord as the Great Prophet. These, when they withdraw from Mahomed, because he is not able to help them, approach the Lord, and worship Him, and acknowledge His Divine, and then are instructed in the Christian religion. Behind these, more to the north, are the places of instruction of various Gentile nations, who in the world have led a good life in conformity with their religion, and have thence acquired a species of conscience, and have done what is just and right, not so much from a regard to the laws of their country, as from a regard to the laws of their religion, which they believed ought to be sacredly observed, and in no way to be violated by their actions. All these, when instructed, are easily led to acknowledge the Lord, because it is impressed on their hearts that God is not invisible, but visible under a human form. These exceed the rest in number. The best of them are from Africa.

515. But all are not instructed in the same manner, nor by similar societies of heaven. They who from infancy have been educated in heaven, are instructed by angels of the interior hea vens, inasmuch as they have not imbibed falses from falses of religion, nor defiled their spiritual life by the gross principles which have regard to honors and riches in the world. They who have died adult, are for the most part instructed by the angels of the ultimate heaven, because these angels are better adapted to them than the angels of the interior heavens; for the latter are in interior wisdom, which they are not yet able to receive. But the Mahomedans are instructed by angels who had once been in the same religion, and were converted to Christianity. Gentiles also are instructed by angels who were once Gentiles.

516. All instruction is there given from doctrine derived from the Word, and not from the Word without doctrine. Christians are instructed from heavenly doctrine, which is in perfect agreement with the internal sense of the Word. All others, as the Mahomedans and Gentiles are instructed from doctrines suited to their comprehension, which differ from heavenly doctrines only in this, that spiritual life is taught through the medium of a

moral life in agreement with the good tenets of their religion, according to which they formed their life in the world.

517. Instructions in the heavens differ from instructions on earth in this, that knowledges are not committed to the memory, but to the life; for the memory of spirits is in their life, inasmuch as they receive and imbibe all things which agree with their life, and do not receive, still less imbibe, those things which disagree with it; for spirits are affections, and thence in a human form similar to their affections. This being the case with them, the affection of truth is continually inspired for the sake of the uses of life; for the Lord provides that every one may love the uses suited to his genius, which love is also exalted by the hope of becoming an angel. And because all the uses of heaven have reference to the common use, which is the good of the Lord's kingdom,—this kingdom being their country,—and whereas all special and particular uses are excellent in proportion as they more nearly and fully have regard to that common use, therefore all special and particular uses, which are innumerable, are good and heavenly. With every one, therefore, the affection of truth is so perfectly conjoined with the affection of use, that they act as one. Truth is thereby implanted in use, so that the truths which they learn are truths of use. Thus angelic spirits are instructed, and prepared for heaven. The affection of truth suitable to the use which they are to perform, is insinuated by various methods, most of which are unknown in the world; chiefly by representatives of uses, which in the spiritual world are exhibited in a thousand ways, and with such delights and pleasantnesses, that they penetrate the spirit from the interiors, which belong to his mind, to the exteriors which belong to his body, and thus affect the whole of him. Hence the spirit becomes, as it were, his own use. Wherefore when he enters his own society, into which he is initiated by instruction, he is in his own life when in his own use.[1] From these considerations

---

[1] That every good has its delight from uses, and according to uses, and likewise its quality, whence such as the use is, such is the good, n. 3049, 4984, 7038. That angelic life consists in the goods of love and charity, thus in performing uses. n. 454. That nothing in man is regarded by the Lord, and thence by the angels, but ends which are uses, n. 1317, 1645,

it may be evident that knowledges, which are external truths, do not introduce any one into heaven, but life itself, which is the life of use, implanted by means of knowledges.

518. There were some spirits, who, from what they had conceived in the world, had persuaded themselves that they should go to heaven, and be received before others, because they were learned, and knew many things from the Word, and from the doctrines of their churches,—imagining that they were therefore wise, and that they were meant by those of whom it is said, *that they should shine as the brightness of the firmament, and as the stars,* Dan. chap. xii. 3. But they were examined, to ascertain whether their knowledges resided in the memory, or in the life. They who were in the genuine affection of truth,—which is the love of it for the sake of uses unconnected with corporeal and worldly ends, which uses in themselves are spiritual,—after they had been instructed, were also received into heaven; and it was then given them to know what it is that shines in heaven, namely, that it is the divine truth, which is there the light of heaven, embodied in use; for use is the plane that receives the rays of that light, and turns them into manifold splendors. But they with whom knowledges resided only in the memory, and who had thence acquired the faculty of reasoning about truths, and of confirming whatever notions they assumed as principles, which, although false, after confirmation appeared to them as truths,—these were in no light of heaven; and yet they believed, from the pride which usually accompanies such intelligence, that they were more learned than others, and should therefore go to heaven and be served by the angels. In order therefore, that they might be withdrawn from their infatuated faith, they were taken up to the first or ultimate heaven, that they might enter some angelic society. But in the very entrance, their eyes began to be darkened by the influx of the light of heaven, then their understandings were confused, and at length they panted for breath like persons at the point of death; and

---

5949. That the kingdom of the Lord is a kingdom of uses, n. 454, 696, 1103, 3645, 4054, 7038. That to serve the Lord is to perform uses, n. 7038. That man's quality is according to the quality of the uses appertaining to him, n 1568, 3570, 4054, 6571, 6935, 6938, 10284.

when they felt the heat of heaven, which is heavenly love, they began to be inwardly tortured. Wherefore they were cast down thence; and afterward they were instructed that knowledges do not make an angel, but the life itself which is acquired by means of them; since knowledges viewed in themselves are out of heaven, but life acquired by knowledges is within heaven.

519. After spirits have, by means of instructions, been prepared for heaven in the places above mentioned,—which is effected in a short time, by reason that they are in spiritual ideas which comprehend many things at once,—they are then clothed with angelic garments, which for the most part are white as if made of fine linen; and then they are brought to the way which leads upward toward heaven, and are delivered to the angel-guards there, and afterward are received by other angels, and introduced into societies and into many gratifications there; and finally every one is led to his own society by the Lord. This also is done by leading them through various ways, some of which wind about intricately. The ways through which they are led are not known to any angel, but to the Lord alone. When they come to their own society, their interiors are opened; and because these are conformable to the interiors of the angels who are in that society, therefore they are immediately acknowledged and received with joy.

520. To what has been said, I will add a remarkable circumstance concerning the ways which lead from those places to heaven, and by which the novitiate angels are introduced. There are eight ways. two from each place of instruction, one of which ascends toward the east, the other toward the west. They who enter the Lord's celestial kingdom, are introduced by the eastern way; but they who enter the spiritual kingdom, are introduced by the western way. The four ways which lead to the Lord's celestial kingdom, appear adorned with olive-trees and fruit-trees of various kinds; but those which lead to the Lord's spiritual kingdom, appear adorned with vines and laurels. This arises from correspondence; because vines and laurels correspond to the affection of truth and to its uses, while olives and fruits correspond to the affection of good and its uses.

NO ONE GOES TO HEAVEN FROM IMMEDIATE MERCY.

521. THEY who are not instructed concerning heaven and the
way thither, and concerning the life of heaven with man, suppose that to be received into heaven is purely of mercy, which is
granted to those who are in faith, and for whom the Lord intercedes, thus that it is admission out of mere favor. They therefore suppose that all men without exception might be saved, if
it were the Lord's good pleasure; yea, some imagine that even
those in hell might be saved. But such persons are totally
unacquainted with the nature of man, not being aware that his
quality is altogether such as his life is, and that his life is such as
his love is, not only as to his interiors which belong to his will
and understanding, but also as to his exteriors which belong to
his body; and that the corporeal frame is only an external form,
wherein the interiors present themselves in effect; and hence that
the whole man is his own love (see above, n. 363). ⁴ Nor are
they aware that the body does not live of itself, but from its
spirit, and that the spirit of man is his affection itself, and that
his spiritual body is nothing else but the man's affection in a
human form, such as he also appears in after death, (see above,
n. 453-460). So long as these truths are unknown, man may be
induced to believe that salvation is nothing but the good pleasure
of the Lord, which is called mercy and grace.

522. But it shall first be declared what the divine mercy is.
Divine mercy is the pure mercy of the Lord, which seeks the salvation of the whole human race; and it is likewise continual with
every man, and in no case recedes from any one, so that every
one is saved who can be saved. But no one can be saved except
by divine means, which are revealed by the Lord in the Word.
Divine means are what are called divine truths. These teach
how man must live, in order that he may be saved. By means
of these truths, the Lord leads man to heaven and implants
within him the life of heaven. This the Lord does with all.
But the life of heaven cannot be implanted in any one, unless he
abstains from evil, for evil opposes. So far therefore as man

abstains from evil, the Lord out of pure mercy leads him by His divine means from infancy to the end of his life in the world, and afterward to eternity. This is the Divine mercy which is meant. Hence it is evident that the mercy of the Lord is pure mercy, but not immediate; that is, not such as to save all out of mere good pleasure, however they may have lived.

523. The Lord never acts contrary to order, because He is order itself. The divine truth proceeding from the Lord is what makes order; and divine truths are the laws of order according to which the Lord leads man. Wherefore, to save man by immediate mercy is contrary to divine order; and what is contrary to divine order is contrary to the Divine. Divine order is heaven with man; this order man has perverted with himself by a life contrary to the laws of order, which are divine truths. Into that order man is brought back by the Lord out of pure mercy, by means of the laws of order; and so far as he is brought back, he receives heaven in himself; and he who receives heaven in himself, goes to heaven after death. Hence, again, it is evident that the divine mercy of the Lord is pure mercy, but not immediate mercy.[1]

---

[1] That divine truth proceeding from the Lord is that from which order is, and that divine good is the essential of order, n. 1728, 2258, 8700, 8988. That hence the Lord is order, n. 1919, 2011, 5110, 5703, 10336, 10619. That divine truths are the laws of order, n. 2447, 7995. That the universal heaven is arranged by the Lord according to his divine order, n. 3038, 7211, 9128, 9338, 10125, 10151, 10157. That hence the form of heaven is a form according to divine order, n. 4040 to 4043, 6607, 9877. That so far as man lives according to order, thus so far as he lives in good according to divine truths, so far he receives heaven in himself, n. 4839. That man is the being into whom are collated all things of divine order, and that from creation he is divine order in form, because he is its recipient, n. 4219, 4220, 4223, 4523, 4524, 5114, 5368, 6013, 6057, 6605, 6626, 9706, 10156, 10472. That man is not born into good and truth, but into evil and the false, thus not into divine order, but into what is contrary to order, and that hence it is that he is born into mere ignorance; and that on this account it is necessary that he be born anew, that is, be regenerated, which is effected by divine truths from the Lord, that he may be brought back into order, n. 1047, 2307, 2308, 3518, 3812, 8480, 8550, 10283, 10284, 10286, 10731. That the Lord, when He forms man anew, that is, regenerates him, arranges all things with him according to order, which is into the form of heaven,

524. If men could be saved by immediate mercy, all would be saved even they who are in hell; yea, there would be no hell, because the Lord is mercy itself, love itself, and good itself. Wherefore it is contrary to his Divine, to say that He is able to save all immediately, and does not save them. It is known from the Word that the Lord wills the salvation of all, and the damnation of no one.

525. Most of those who go from the Christian world into the other life, carry with them the belief that they are to be saved by immediate mercy, for they implore that mercy. But when they are examined, they are found to believe that to come into heaven is merely to be admitted; and that those who are admitted, are in heavenly joy,—being totally unacquainted with the nature of heaven and of heavenly joy. Wherefore they are told that heaven is not denied to any one by the Lord, and that they can be admitted if they wish, and tarry there as long as they please. They who desired this, have also been admitted; but when they reached the first threshold, they were seized with such anguish of heart, from the breathing upon them of heavenly heat, which is the love in which the angels are, and from the influx of heavenly light, which is divine truth, that they experienced infernal torment instead of heavenly joy; and in consequence of the shock, they cast themselves headlong thence. Thus they were instructed by living experience, that heaven cannot be given to any one from immediate mercy.

526. I have occasionally conversed on this subject with the angels, and have told them that most of those in the world who live in evil, when they talk with others about heaven and eternal life, seem to have no other idea than that to enter heaven is merely to be admitted from mercy alone, and that this is especially believed by those who make faith the only medium of salvation; for such persons, from the principles of their religion, have no regard to the life and to the deeds of love which make the life, thus neither to any other means whereby the Lord implants heaven in man, and ren-

---

n. 5700, 6690, 9931, 10303. That evils and falses are contrary to order, and that still they who are in them are ruled by the Lord, not according to order but from order, n. 4839, 7877, 10778. That it is impossible for a man who lives in evil to be saved by mercy alone, because this is contrary to divine order, n. 8700.

ders him receptible of heavenly joy; and because they thus reject every actual means, they settle down in the belief, which follows of necessity from the principles assumed, that man goes to heaven from mercy alone, to which they believe that God the Father is moved by the intercession of the Son. To these things the angels replied, that they are aware that such a tenet follows of necessity from the assumption that man is saved by faith alone; and inasmuch as that dogma is the head of all the rest, and into that, because it is not true, no light from heaven can flow, thence comes the ignorance, wherein the church is at this day, concerning the Lord, and heaven, and the life after death, and heavenly joy, and the essence of love and charity, and in general concerning good, and its conjunction with truth; consequently concerning the life of man, whence it is, and what is its quality; yet no one ever derives this from thought, but from will and the deeds thence, and only so far from thought as this partakes of the will; thus not from faith, except so far as faith partakes of love. The angels grieve that these same persons do not know that faith alone cannot exist with any one, since faith without its origin, which is love, is merely science, and with some a kind of persuasion which has the semblance of faith, (see above, n. 482); which persuasion is not in the man's life, but out of it, for it is separated from the man if it does not cohere with his love. They further said, that they who are in such a principle concerning the essential medium of salvation with man, cannot do otherwise than believe in immediate mercy; because they comprehend from natural lumen, and likewise from the experience of sight, that faith alone does not constitute a man's life, since they who lead an evil life can think and persuade themselves in like manner as others. Hence it comes to be believed, that the wicked can be saved as well as the good, provided that they speak with confidence at the hour of death concerning intercession, and mercy procured thereby. The angels confessed that they had never yet seen any one received into heaven by an act of immediate mercy, who had lived an evil life, however he had spoken in the world from that trust or confidence, which is understood by faith in an eminent sense. On being questioned concerning Abraham, Isaac, Jacob, and David, and concerning the apostles, whether they were not received into heaven from immediate mercy, they replied, Not one of them;—and declared that every one was received according to his life in the world; and that they knew where they were; and that they are not more highly esteemed there than others. The reason, they said, that they are mentioned with honor in the Word, is, because by them in the internal sense is meant the Lord; by Abraham, Isaac, and Jacob, the Lord as to the Divine and the Divine Human; by David, the Lord as to the Divine Royalty; and by the apostles, the Lord as to divine truths; and that they have not the least perception of those individuals, when the Word is read by man, since their names do not enter heaven; but instead of them, they have a perception of the Lord, as just stated; and that therefore in the Word which is in heaven, (see above, n. 259), those individuals are no where mentioned, since that Word is the internal sense of the Word which is in the world.[1]

527. I can testify from much experience, that it is impossible to implant the life of heaven in those who have led an opposite life in the world. There were some who imagined that they should easily receive divine truths after death, when they heard them from the angels, and that they should believe them, and consequently should live a different life, and thus be received into heaven. But the experiment was made with great numbers, yet only with those who were in such a belief, to whom the trial

---

[1] That by Abraham, Isaac, and Jacob, in the internal sense of the Word is meant the Lord as to the Divine Itself, and the Divine Human, n. 1893, 4615, 6098, 6185, 6276, 6804, 6847. That Abraham is unknown in heaven, n. 1834, 1876, 3229. That by David is meant the Lord as to the Divine Regal, n. 1888, 9954. That the twelve apostles represented the Lord as to all things of the church, thus all things which are of faith and love, n. 2129, 3354, 3488, 3858, 6397. That Peter represented the Lord as to faith, James as to charity, and John as to the works of charity, n. 3750, 10087. That by the twelve apostles sitting on twelve thrones, and judging the twelve tribes of Israel, is signified that the Lord will judge according to the truths and goods of faith and love, n. 2129, 6397. That the names of persons and places in the Word do not enter heaven, but are turned into things and states; and that neither in heaven can the names be uttered, n. 1876, 5225, 6516, 10216, 10282, 10432. That the angels also think abstractedly from persons, n. 8343, 8985, 9007.

was permitted in order that they might know that repentance after death is not given. Some of those with whom the trial was made, understood truths, and seemed to receive them; but as soon as they turned to the life of their love, they rejected them, and even spoke against them. Some rejected them immediately, being unwilling to hear them. Some were desirous that the life of the love which they had contracted in the world, might be taken away from them, and that angelic life, or the life of heaven, might be infused in its place. This also by permission was accomplished for them; but when the life of their love was taken away, they lay as if dead, having no longer the use of any of their faculties. From these and other experiments, the simple good were instructed, that no one's life can possibly be changed after death, and that evil life can by no means be changed into good life, nor infernal life into angelic, since every spirit from head to foot is of the same quality as his love, and therefore of the same quality as his life; and that to transmute this life into the opposite, were to destroy the spirit altogether. The angels declare that it were easier to change a bat into a dove, or an owl into a bird of paradise, than an infernal spirit into an angel of heaven. That man after death remains of such a quality as his life had been in the world, may be seen above in its proper chapter, (n. 470–484). From these considerations it may now be manifest, that no one can be received into heaven by an act of immediate mercy.

IT IS NOT SO DIFFICULT TO LIVE THE LIFE WHICH LEADS TO HEAVEN, AS SOME SUPPOSE.

528. SOME people imagine that, to live the life which leads to heaven, which is called spiritual life, is difficult, because they have been told that man must renounce the world, and deprive himself of what are called the lusts of the body and the flesh, and must live in a spiritual manner. By this they understand

that they must reject worldly things, which consist chiefly in riches and honors; must live continually in pious meditation about God, salvation, and eternal life; and spend their life in prayer, and in reading the Word and books of piety. This they conceive to be renouncing the world, and living to the spirit and not to the flesh. But that the case is altogether otherwise, I have learned by much experience, and from conversation with the angels; yea, I have learned that they who renounce the world and live in the spirit in this manner, procure to themselves a sorrowful life, which is not receptible of heavenly joy; for every one's own life remains after death. But in order that man may receive the life of heaven, it is altogether necessary that he live in the world, and engage in its duties and employments, and that then by moral and civil life he receive spiritual life. In no other way can spiritual life be formed with man, or his spirit be prepared for heaven; for to live an internal life and not an external one at the same time, is like dwelling in a house which has no foundation, which successively either sinks into the ground, or becomes full of chinks and breaches, or totters till it falls.

529. If the life of man be viewed and explored by rational intuition, it will be found to be threefold; that is to say, there is a spiritual life, a moral life, and a civil life, all distinct from each other. For there are men who live a civil life, yet not a moral and spiritual one; and there are those who live a moral life, and still not a spiritual one; and there are others who live a civil life, a moral life, and a spiritual life, all at once. The latter live the life of heaven; but the former live the life of the world separate from the life of heaven. From these considerations it is manifest in the first place, that spiritual life is not separate from natural life, or from the life of the world, but that the former is conjoined with the latter as the soul with its body; and if it were separated, that it would be like living in a house without a foundation, as was said above. For moral and civil life is the activity of spiritual life; for it is the part of spiritual life to will well, and of moral and civil life to act well; and if the latter be separated from the former, spiritual life consists merely in thought and speech,

and the will recedes because it has no basis to rest upon ; and yet the will is the very essential spiritual constituent of man.

530. That it is not so difficult to live the life which leads to heaven as some suppose, may be seen from the following considerations. Who cannot live a civil and moral life?—for everyone is initiated into it from infancy, and is acquainted with it from living in the world. Every one also does lead such a life, the evil as well as the good ; for who does not wish to be called sincere and just? Almost all practice sincerity and justice in externals, so that they appear to be sincere and just in heart, or to act from real sincerity and justice. The spiritual man ought to do the same, and he can do it as easily as the natural man ; only there is this difference, that the spiritual man believes in a Divine, and acts sincerely and justly, not merely because civil and moral laws require it, but also because it is agreeable to the divine laws ; for the spiritual man, because he thinks about the divine laws in all that he does, communicates with the angels of heaven ; and so far as he does this, he is conjoined with them, and thus his internal man is opened, which, viewed in itself, is the spiritual man. When a man is of this character, he is adopted and led by the Lord, although he is not himself conscious of it ; and then, in practicing the sincerity and justice which belong to moral and civil life, he acts from a spiritual origin ; and to do what is sincere and just from a spiritual origin, is to do it from sincerity and justice itself, or to do it from the heart. His justice and sincerity in the external form, appear exactly like the justice and sincerity practiced by natural men, and even by wicked men and infernals ; but in their internal form, they are totally different. For the wicked act justly and sincerely only for the sake of themselves and the world ; and therefore if they did not fear the law and its penalties, also the loss of reputation, honor, gain, and life, they would act altogether insincerely and unjustly ; since they have no fear of God nor of any divine law, and therefore are not restrained by any internal bond. Wherefore if external restraints were removed, they would defraud, plunder, and spoil others, as far as they were able to do so, and would take delight in doing it. That they are inwardly of such a character, is abundantly evident from those who are like them in the other life.

where external things are removed, and the internals of all are opened, wherein they live to eternity, (see above, n. 499–511) ; for being then free from external restraints, which are, as was said above, fear of the law, and of the loss of reputation, honor, gain, and life, they act insanely and laugh at sincerity and justice. But they who have acted sincerely and justly from a regard to the divine laws, when external considerations are taken away and they are left to their internal promptings, act wisely, because they are conjoined with the angels of heaven, from whom wisdom is communicated to them. From these considerations it may now first appear evident, that a spiritual man can act precisely like a natural man in the affairs of civil and moral life, provided he be conjoined to the Divine as to his internal man, or as to his will and thought; (see above, n. 358–360).

531. The laws of spiritual life, of civil life, and of moral life, are also delivered in the ten precepts of the decalogue ; in the first three,* the laws of spiritual life, in the four following, the laws of civil life, and in the last three, the laws of moral life. The merely natural man lives in outward conformity to all these precepts, in the same manner as the spiritual man ; for like him he worships the Divine, goes to church, hears sermons, and assumes a devout look ; does not kill, nor commit adultery, nor steal, nor bear false witness, nor defraud his neighbors of their goods. But he does this only for the sake of himself and the world, in order to keep up appearances. The same person, in the internal form, is altogether opposite to what he appears in the external because in heart he denies the Divine, in worship acts the hypocrite, and when left to himself and his own thoughts, laughs at the holy things of the church, believing that they only serve to

---

* [It should be borne in mind, that the division of the commandments followed by the author, is the same as that adopted in the Roman Catholic and Lutheran Churches; according to which, the first commandment includes the first and second of the Church of England division; and the last in the Church of England division is divided into two. Thus the first three, as mentioned above, are what are commonly reckoned, among Protestant Christians, the first four; the next four are what are commonly called the fifth, sixth, seventh, and eighth; and the last three are those commonly reckoned the ninth and tenth.—Tr.]

restrain the simple multitude. Hence he is altogether disjoined from heaven ; and because he is not a spiritual man, therefore he is neither a moral nor a civil man.   For although he commits no murder, still he hates every one who opposes him, and burns with revenge inspired by such hatred ; wherefore, unless restrained by civil laws and external bonds, which are fears, he would commit murder ; and because he desires to do it, it follows that he is continually committing murder.   Although he does not commit adultery, yet because he believes it allowable, he is perpetually an adulterer ; for he does commit it as far as it is possible, and as often as he can with impunity.   Although he does not steal, yet because he covets the goods of others, and does not regard fraud and wicked artifices as contrary to what is lawful, in his mind he is continually acting the thief. The case is similar in regard to the precepts of moral life, which teach that we must not bear false witness, nor covet the goods of others.   Such is the character of every man who denies the Divine, and has no conscience formed from religion.   That all such are of this character, appears manifestly from similar spirits in the other life, when their externals are removed, and they are let into their internals ; then, because they are separated from heaven, they act in unity with hell, and are therefore consociated with those who are in hell.   It is otherwise with those who in heart have acknowledged the Divine, and in their actions have had respect to the divine laws, and have obeyed the first three precepts of the decalogue as well as the rest.   When these, on the removal of their externals, are let into their internals, they are wiser than they were in the world.   Coming into their internals is like passing from shade into light, from ignorance into wisdom, and from a sorrowful life into a blessed one, since they are in the Divine, thus in heaven.   These things are said in order that the real character of both these classes of persons may be known, although they have lived a similar external life.

532. Every one may know that thoughts move and tend according to the intentions, or in the direction which a man intends ; for the thought is a man's internal sight, which is like the external sight in this respect that it is turned and fixed on the object to which it is bent and directed.   If, therefore, the inter-

nal sight or thought be turned to the world, and fixed on that, it
follows that the thought becomes worldly; if it be turned to self
and self-honor, that it becomes corporeal: but if it be turned to
heaven, that it becomes heavenly. It therefore follows, that if
the thought be turned to heaven, it is elevated; if to self, it is
withdrawn from heaven, and immersed in what is corporeal; and
if to the world, it is also turned away from heaven, and spent
upon those objects which are presented to the eyes. It is a
man's love which makes his intention, and which determines
his internal sight or thought to its objects. Thus the love of self
determines the thought to self and its objects; the love of the
world, to worldly things; and the love of heaven, to the things
of heaven. Hence it may be known what is the state of a man's
interiors, which belong to his mind, provided his love be known;
namely, that the interiors of him who loves heaven are elevated
toward heaven, and are open above; and that the interiors of
him who loves the world and himself are closed above, and open
exteriorly. Hence it may be concluded, that if the superior faculties belonging to the mind are closed above, man can no longer
see the things which belong to heaven and the church, these being in thick darkness with him; and the things which are in
thick darkness are either denied or not understood. Hence
it is, that they who love themselves and the world above all
things, because the superior faculties of their minds are closed, in
heart deny divine truths; and if they say anything about them
from memory, still they do not understand them: they regard
them also in the same way that they regard worldly and corporeal things. Such being their character, they cannot attend to
anything but what enters through the bodily senses, and are delighted with nothing else. And among these things are many
which are filthy, obscene, profane, and wicked; nor can they be
removed, because with such persons there is no influx from heaven into their minds, since these are closed above, as was said.
A man's intention, from which his internal sight or thought is
determined, is his will; for what a man wills, he intends, and
what he intends, he thinks. If, therefore, his intention be toward
heaven, his thought is determined thither, and with it his whole
mind, which is thus in heaven; whence he afterward surveys the

things belonging to the world beneath him, like one who looks from the roof of a house.   Hence it is, that the man who has the interiors of his mind open, can discern the evils and falses appertaining to him, for these are beneath the spiritual mind ; and on the other hand, the man whose interiors are not open, cannot see his own evils and falses, because he is in them, and not above them.   From these considerations a conclusion may be formed respecting the origin of wisdom with man, and the origin of insanity ; also what a man will be after death, when he is left to will and to think, also to act and to speak, according to his interiors.   These things are said that it may be known what man is interiorly ;—suggesting also the conclusion, that persons exteriorly alike may be interiorly very different.

· 533. That it is not so difficult to live the life of heaven as is believed, is evident from this : that, whenever anything is suggested to a man which he knows to be insincere and unjust, and to which his mind is inclined, it is only necessary for him to reflect that it ought not to be done, because it is contrary to the divine commandments.   If he accustoms himself to think in this manner, and from practice acquires the habit of so thinking, he then by degrees is conjoined to heaven ; and so far as he is conjoined to heaven, the superior faculties of his mind are opened , and so far as these are opened, he sees what is insincere and unjust ; and so far as these things are discovered they are capable of being removed,—for it is impossible for any evil to be removed until it is seen.   This is a state into which man may enter from freedom,—for who cannot think from a free principle in the manner just described?   But when he has made a beginning, the Lord works in him for the production of all kinds of good, and enables him not only to see his evils, but also not to will them, and finally to abhor them.   This is meant by the Lord's words : "*My yoke is easy, and my burden is light,*" Matt. xi. 30. But it is to be observed, that the difficulty of so thinking, and also of resisting evils, increases in proportion as man from the will commits evils ; for so far as he does this, he becomes accustomed to them, until at length he does not see them, and at last comes to love them, and from the delight of love to excuse them, and by all sorts of fallacies to confirm them, declaring them to be allowable and good. But this occurs with those, who at the age of maturity plunge into evils as if regardless of all restraint, and at the same time reject divine things from the heart.

534. There was once represented to me the way which leads to heaven, and that which leads to hell. There was a broad way tending to the left, or toward the north; and there appeared many spirits walking in it; but at a distance was seen a stone of considerable magnitude, where the broad way terminated. From that stone there then branched off two ways, one to the left, and one in an opposite direction, to the right: the way that turned to the left was narrow or strait, leading through the west to the south, and so into the light of heaven; the way that turned to the right was broad and spacious, leading obliquely down toward hell. All seemed at first to go the same way, until they came to the great stone at the parting of the two ways; but when they arrived there, they were separated. The good turned to the left, and entered the strait way which led to heaven; but the evil did not see the stone at the parting of the ways, and therefore fell upon it and were hurt; and when they got up, they ran along the broad way to the right, which tended to hell. It was afterward explained to me what all those things signified. By the first way, which was broad, in which many both good and bad walked along together, and conversed with each other like friends,—because no difference between them was apparent to the sight,—were represented those who in externals live alike sincerely and justly, and who cannot be distinguished by their appearance. By the stone at the parting or angle of the ways, upon which the evil stumbled, and from which they afterward ran along the way leading to hell, was represented the divine truth, which is denied by those who look toward hell; in the supreme sense, by the same stone was signified the Divine Human of the Lord. But they who acknowledged the divine truth, and at the same time the Divine of the Lord, were conducted along the way which led to heaven. From these representations it was made still more evident, that outwardly the wicked lead the same kind of life as the good, or go in the same way, thus one as easily as the other; and yet that they who acknowledge the Divine from the heart, especially they within the church who acknowledge the Divine of the Lord, are

led to heaven, and they who do not, are conveyed to hell. The thoughts of man, which proceed from his intention or will, are represented in the other life by ways. Ways are also there presented to appearance in perfect agreement with the thoughts from intention; and every one likewise walks in them, according to his thoughts which proceed from intention. Hence it is that the quality of spirits, and of their thoughts, is known from their ways. From these things it was also made evident what is meant by the Lord's words: "*Enter ye in through the strait gate; for wide is the gate and broad is the way which leads to destruction, and many there are who walk in it; narrow is the way and strait the gate which leads to life, and few there be who find it,*" Matt. vii. 13, 14. The way which leads to life is narrow, not because it is difficult, but because there are few who find it, as it is said. From that stone, seen in the corner where the broad and common way terminated, and from which two ways were seen leading in opposite directions, it was made evident what is signified by these words of the Lord: "*Have ye not read what is written, the stone which the builders rejected is become the head of the corner? Whosoever shall fall upon that stone shall be broken,*" Luke xx. 17, 18. A stone signifies the divine truth; and the stone (or rock) of Israel, the Lord as to the Divine Human; the builders are the members of the church; the head of the corner is where the two ways meet; to fall and be broken is to deny and perish.[1]

535. I have been permitted to converse with some in the other life, who had withdrawn themselves from the business of the world, that they might live a pious and holy life; and with others also, who had afflicted themselves in various ways, because they imagined that this was to renounce the world, and to subdue the concupiscences of the flesh. But the greater portion of these,—having by such austerities contracted a sorrowful life, and removed themselves from the life of charity, which can only be lived in the world,—cannot be consociated with angels, be-

---

[1] That stone signifies truth, n. 114, 643, 1298, 3720, 6426, 8609, 10376. That therefore the law was inscribed on tables which were of stone, n. 10376. That the stone of Israel is the Lord as to divine truth and as to the Divine Human, n. 6426.

cause the life of the angels is one of gladness resulting from bliss, and consists in performing acts of goodness, which are works of charity. And besides, they who have led a life withdrawn from worldly affairs, are possessed with the idea of their own merit, and are thence continually desirous of being admitted into heaven, and think of heavenly joy as a reward, being totally ignorant of what heavenly joy is. And when they are admitted among the angels, and to a perception of their joy, which is without the thought of merit, and consists in active duties and services openly performed, and in the blessedness arising from the good which they thereby promote, they are astonished like persons who witness things altogether foreign to their expectation; and because they are not receptible of that joy, they depart and consociate with spirits like themselves, who have lived a similar life in the world. But they who have lived in outward sanctity, continually frequenting temples and there repeating prayers, and who have afflicted their souls, and at the same time have thought continually about themselves that they would thus be esteemed and honored above others, and at length after death be accounted saints, in the other life are not in heaven, because they have done such things for the sake of themselves. And since they have defiled divine truths by the love of self in which they have immersed them, some of them are so insane as to think themselves gods. Wherefore they are in hell among those like themselves. Some are cunning and deceitful, and are in the hells of the deceitful; these are they who have performed such pious acts outwardly with art and cunning, whereby they have induced the common people to believe that a divine sanctity was in them. Of this character are many of the Roman Catholic saints, with some of whom also I have been permitted to converse; and their life was then faithfully described to me, such as it had been in the world, and such as it was afterward. These statements are made in order that it may be known, that the life which leads to heaven is not a life of retirement from the world, but of action in the world; and that a life of piety, without a life of charity,—which can only be acquired in the world,—does not lead to heaven, but a life of charity does; and this consists in acting sincerely and justly in every occupation, in

48

every transaction, and in every work, from an interior, and thus from a heavenly origin; and such origin is inherent in such a life, when a man acts sincerely and justly because it is according to the divine laws.   Such a life is not difficult; but a life of piety, separate from a life of charity, is difficult; yet this life leads away from heaven, as much as it is believed to lead to heaven.[1]

---

[1] That a life of piety without a life of charity is of no avail, but with the latter is of advantage in every respect, n. 8252, 8253.   That charity toward the neighbor consists in doing what is good, just, and right, in every work and in every employment, n. 8120, 8121, 8122.   That charity toward the neighbor extends itself to all and each of the things which a man thinks, wills, and acts, n. 8124.   That a life of charity is a life according to the Lord's precepts, n. 3249.   That to live according to the Lord's precepts is to love the Lord, n. 10143, 10153, 10310, 10578, 10648.   That genuine charity is not meritorious, because it is from interior affection, and from the delight thence resulting, (2340), 2371, (2400), 3887, 6388 to 6393.   That man after death remains of such a quality as was his life of charity in the world, n. 8256.   That heavenly blessedness flows in from the Lord into the life of charity, n. 2363.   That no one is admitted into heaven by merely thinking, but by willing and doing good at the same time, n. 2401, 3459.   That unless the doing good is conjoined with willing good and with thinking good, there is no salvation, nor any conjunction of the internal man with the external, n. 3987.

HELL.

THE LORD GOVERNS THE HELLS.

536. In treating above concerning heaven, it has been everywhere shown that the Lord is the God of heaven, and especially in n. 2 to 6: thus that all the government of the heavens is the Lord's. And because the relation of heaven to hell, and of hell to heaven, is like that between two opposites which mutually act against each other, from whose action and reaction results an equilibrium wherein all things subsist, therefore in order that all things and every single thing may be held in equilibrium, it is necessary that He who governs the one should also govern the other; for unless the same Lord restrained the assaults of the hells, and repressed the insanities there, the equilibrium would be destroyed, and with it the whole universe.

537. But here something shall first be said upon the subject of equilibrium. It is known that when two things mutually act against each other, and when one reacts and resists as much as the other acts and impels, neither of them has any force, there being the same power exerted on either side; in such case, both may be acted upon at pleasure by a third; for when the force of the two is neutralized by their equal opposition, the force of a third does everything, and acts as easily as if there were no opposition. Such is the equilibrium between heaven and hell. Yet it is not an equilibrium as between two bodily combatants, whose strength is equal; but it is a spiritual equilibrium which is that of the false against the true, and of evil against good. From hell there continually exhales falsity derived from evil, and from heaven there continually exhales truth derived from good. It is this spiritual equilibrium which keeps man in the freedom

of thinking and willing; for whatever a man thinks and wills has relation either to evil and the false thence derived, or to good and the truth thence derived; consequently when he is in that equilibrium, he enjoys the liberty of either admitting or receiving evil and the false thence derived from hell, or good and the truth thence derived from heaven. Every man is held in this equilibrium by the Lord, because the Lord governs both heaven and hell. But why man is held in this freedom by means of equilibrium, and why evil and falsity are not removed from him, and good and truth implanted by Divine power, will be explained hereafter in its proper chapter.

538. I have several times been allowed to perceive the sphere of the false from evil exhaling from hell. It was like an incessant effort to destroy all that is good and true, combined with anger and a kind of raving madness at not being able to do so; and especially an effort to annihilate and destroy the Divine of the Lord, because all good and truth are from Him. But there was perceived as emanating from heaven a sphere of truth derived from good, whereby the madness of the effort ascending from hell was restrained. Hence comes equilibrium. This sphere from heaven was perceived to be from the Lord alone, although it appeared to come from the angels in heaven. The reason that it was perceived to be from the Lord alone and not from the angels, was because every angel in heaven acknowledges that nothing of good and truth is from himself, but that all is from the Lord.

539. All power in the spiritual world belongs to truth derived from good, and there is no power at all in the false derived from evil. The reason that all power belongs to truth derived from good, is because the Divine Itself in heaven is divine good and divine truth; and the Divine has all power. The false from evil has no power at all, because all power belongs to truth from good; and in the false from evil there is nothing of truth from good. Hence it is that there is all power in heaven, and none in hell; for every one in heaven is in truths derived from good, and every one in hell is in falses derived from evil. For no one is admitted into heaven until he is in truths derived from good, nor is any one cast down into hell until he is in falses derived from

evil; that this is the case, may be seen in the chapters treating of the first, second, and third state of man after death, (n. 491–520). That all power belongs to truth derived from good, may be seen in the chapter concerning the power of the angels of heaven, (n. 228–233).

540. Such, then, is the equilibrium between heaven and hell. They who are in the world of spirits are in that equilibrium, for the world of spirits is intermediate between heaven and hell. And thence also all men in the world are kept in a like equilibrium, for men in the world are governed by the Lord through the medium of spirits who are in the world of spirits, which subject will be treated of below in its proper chapter. Such an equilibrium could not exist, unless the Lord governed both heaven and hell, and regulated the effort on each side; otherwise falses derived from evils would preponderate, and affect the simple good who are in·the ultimates of heaven, and who can be more easily perverted than the angels themselves; and thus the equilibrium would be destroyed, and with it the freedom of man.

541. Hell is distinguished into societies in the same manner as heaven, and also into as many societies as heaven; for every society in heaven has a society opposite to it in hell, and this for the sake of equilibrium. But the societies in hell are distinct according to evils and the falses thence derived, because the societies in heaven are distinct according to goods and the truths thence derived. That to every good there is an opposite evil, and to every truth an opposite falsity, may be known from the fact that nothing exists without relation to its opposite; and that from the opposite, we may learn what it is in kind and in degree, and that all perception and sensation result from this. Wherefore the Lord continually provides, that every society of heaven shall have its opposite in a society of hell, and that between them there shall be equilibrium.

542. Because hell is distinguished into as many societies as heaven, therefore also there are as many hells as there are societies of heaven; for as every society of heaven is a heaven in a less form, (see above, n. 51–58), so every society of hell is a hell in a less form. Because there are in general three heavens, therefore there are likewise in general three hells; the lowest, which is op-

posite to the inmost or third heaven; the middle, which is opposite to the middle or second heaven; and the upper one, which is opposite to the ultimate or first heaven.

543. But in what manner the hells are governed by the Lord, shall also be briefly explained. The hells are governed in general by a common afflux of divine good and divine truth from the heavens, whereby the general endeavor issuing from the hells is checked and restrained; and likewise by a special afflux from each heaven, and from each society of heaven. The hells are governed in particular by angels, who are appointed to inspect them, and to restrain the insanities and disturbances which prevail there. Sometimes also angels are sent thither, to moderate those insanities and disturbances by their presence. But in general, all the inhabitants of hell are governed by fears; some, by fears implanted in the world, which still retain their influence; but because these fears are not sufficient, and likewise lose their force by degrees, they are governed by fear of punishments, and this fear is the principal means of deterring them from doing evils. The punishments in hell are various, more gentle and more severe according to the nature of the evils to be restrained. For the most part, the more malignant who excel in cunning and artifice, and are able to keep the rest in a state of submission and slavery by punishments and the terror thereby inspired, are set over the others; but these governors dare not go beyond the limits prescribed to them. It is to be observed, that the fear of punishment is the only means of restraining the violence and fury of those in the hells. There is no other.

544. It has hitherto been believed in the world, that there is some one devil who presides over the hells; and that he was created an angel of light, but after he became rebellious, was cast down with his crew into hell. This belief has prevailed, because in the Word mention is made of the Devil and Satan, and also of Lucifer, and the Word in those passages has been understood according to the literal sense; when yet by the Devil and Satan is there meant hell,—by the Devil, that hell which is behind, and where the worst dwell, who are called evil genii; and by Satan, that hell which is in front, the inhabitants of which are not so malignant, and are called evil spirits; and by

Lucifer are meant those who belong to Babel or Babylon, being those who claim dominion even over heaven itself. That there is no single devil to whom the hells are subject, is also evident from the fact, that all who are in the hells, like all who are in the heavens, are from the human race, (see n. 311-317); and that those who have gone thither from the beginning of creation to the present time, amount to myriads of myriads, every one of whom is a devil of such a quality as he had acquired in the world by a life in opposition to the Divine: (see above on this subject, n. 311-312).

THE LORD CASTS NO ONE DOWN INTO HELL, BUT THE SPIRIT CASTS HIMSELF DOWN.

545. THE opinion has prevailed with some, that God turns his face away from man, rejects him, and casts him into hell, and that He is angry with him on account of sin; and it is still further supposed by some that God punishes man, and brings evil upon him. In this opinion they confirm themselves from the literal sense of the Word, where such things are declared, not being aware that the spiritual sense of the Word, which explains that of the letter, is altogether different; and that hence the genuine doctrine of the church, which is according to the spiritual sense of the Word, teaches otherwise; namely, that God never turns His face away from man, never rejects him, never casts any one into hell, and is never angry.[1] Every one,

---

[1] That anger and wrath in the Word are attributed to the Lord, but that they appertain to man, and that it is so expressed because it so appears to man when he is punished and damned, n. 5798, 6997, 8284, 8483, 8875, 9306, 10431. That evil also is attributed to the Lord, when yet from the Lord is nothing but good, n. 2447, 6073, 6992, 6997, 7533, 7632, 7877, 7926, 8227, 8228, 8632, 9306. Why it is so expressed in the Word, n. 6073, 6992, 6997, 7643, 7632, 7679, 7710, 7926, 8282, 9009, 9128. That the Lord is pure mercy and clemency, n. 6997, 8875.

also, whose mind is in a state of illustration when he reads the Word, perceives this from the single consideration that God is good itself, love itself, and mercy itself; and that good itself cannot do evil to any one; nor can love itself and mercy itself cast man away from them, because it is contrary to their very essence, thus contrary to the Divine Itself. Wherefore they who think from an enlightened understanding when they read the Word, clearly perceive that God never turns Himself away from man; and because He never turns Himself away from him, that He deals with him from good, love, and mercy; in other words, that He wills his good, that He loves him, and is merciful to him. Hence also they see, that the literal sense of the Word which teaches such things, conceals within itself a spiritual sense, according to which those expressions are to be explained, which, in the sense of the letter, are spoken in accommodation to the apprehension of man, and according to his first and general ideas.

546. They who are in a state of illustration, see further, that good and evil are two opposites, as contrary to each other as heaven is to hell, and that all good is from heaven, and all evil from hell; and because the Divine of the Lord makes heaven, (n. 7-12), therefore nothing but good flows in from the Lord with man, and nothing but evil from hell; and that thus the Lord is continually withdrawing man from evil, and leading him to good, while hell is continually leading him into evil. Unless man were between both, he would have no thought, nor any will, still less any freedom and choice; for man enjoys all these in consequence of the equilibrium between good and evil; wherefore if the Lord were to turn Himself away, and man were left to evil alone, he would no longer be a man. From these considerations it is evident, that the Lord flows-in with good into every man, the bad as well as the good; but with this difference, that He is continually withdrawing the bad man from evil, and continually leading the good man to good; and that the cause of such difference is with man, because he is the recipient.

547. Hence it may be manifest that man does evil from hell, and good from the Lord; but because he believes that whatever he does he does from himself, therefore the evil which he does

adheres to him as his own. Hence it is that man is the cause ot his own evil, and not the Lord. Evil with man is hell with him ; for whether we speak of evil or of hell, it is the same thing. Now since man is the cause of his own evil, therefore also he leads himself into hell, and not the Lord ; and so far is the Lord from leading man into hell, that He delivers him from hell, as far as man does not will and love to abide in his own evil. All of man's will and love remains with him after death, (n. 470–484) ; he who wills and loves evil in the world, wills and loves the same evil in the other life ; and then he no longer suffers himself to be withdrawn from it. Hence it is, that the man who is in evil is tied to hell, and is actually there as to his spirit ; and after death he desires nothing more than to be where his own evil is. Wherefore man after death casts himself into hell, and not the Lord.

548. How this is done, shall also be told. When man enters the other life, he is first received by angels, who perform for him all good offices, and likewise converse with him concerning the Lord, concerning heaven, concerning angelic life, and instruct him in truths and goods. But if the man, now a spirit, be one of those who knew such things in the world, but in heart denied or despised them, he then, after some conversation, desires and also seeks to be separated from their company. When the angels perceive this, they leave him ; after joining several other companies, he is at last associated with those who are in similar evil with himself, (see above, n. 445–452) ; when this takes place, he turns himself away from the Lord, and turns his face toward the hell with which he had been conjoined while in the world, where those reside who are in a similar love of evil. From these facts it is evident that the Lord draws every spirit toward Himself by means of the angels, and likewise by influx from heaven ; but that the spirits who are in evil strenuously resist, and as it were tear themselves away from the Lord, and are drawn by their own evils, thus by hell, as by a rope ; and because they are drawn, and by reason of their love of evil are willing to follow, it is manifest that they cast themselves into hell of their own free choice. That this is the case, cannot be believed in the world, in consequence of the idea entertained of

hell: nor does it in the other life appear otherwise than in the world, before the eyes of those who are out of hell. But it does not appear so to those who cast themselves thither, for they enter of their own accord; and they who enter from an ardent love of evil, appear as if they were cast headlong, with their heads downward and their feet upward. On account of this appearance, it seems as if they were cast down to hell by Divine Power; (on this subject more may be seen below, n. 574). From what has been said, it may now be seen that the Lord casts no one down to hell, but that every one casts himself down, not only while he lives in the world, but also after death when he comes among spirits.

549. The Lord, from His divine essence,—which is good, love, and mercy,—cannot deal in the same manner with every man, because evils and the falses thence derived not only resist and blunt, but also reject, His divine influx. Evils and the falses thence derived are like black clouds, which interpose themselves between the sun and man's eye, and take away the sunshine and serenity of the day. The sun, however, still continues in the perpetual effort to dissipate the obstructing clouds; for it is behind them and operating toward their dispersion; and in the meantime, also, transmits something of shady light to the eye through various indirect passages. It is the same in the spiritual world. There, the sun is the Lord and the divine love, (n. 116–140); and the light is the divine truth, (n. 126–140); the black clouds there, are falses derived from evil, and the eye is the understanding. In proportion as any one in that world is in falses derived from evil, he is encompassed by such a cloud, which is black and dense according to the degrees of his evil. From this comparison it may be seen that the Lord is constantly present with every one, but that He is received differently.

550. Evil spirits are severely punished in the world of spirits, in order that they may thereby be deterred from doing evil. It also appears as if this were the Lord's doing, when yet nothing of the punishment which they there suffer is from Him, but from evil itself; for evil is so conjoined with its own punishment, that they cannot be separated. For the infernal crew desire and love nothing more than to do injury, especially to inflict punishment

and torture upon others; and they also do injury to, and inflict punishment on, every one who is not protected by the Lord. Wherefore when evil is done from an evil heart, then, because it casts away from itself all protection from the Lord, infernal spirits rush upon him who does such evil, and punish him. This may be illustrated in some measure by crimes and their punishments in the world, where also they are conjoined; for the laws prescribe some punishment for every crime, so that whoever rushes into crime, rushes also into the punishment thereof. The only difference is, that in the world crime may be concealed; but in the other life concealment is impossible. From these considerations it may be seen that the Lord does evil to no one; and that herein the case is similar to what we find in the world, where not the king, nor the judge, nor the law, is the cause of punishment to the guilty, because neither of them is the cause of the crime committed by the evil-doer.

ALL WHO ARE IN THE HELLS ARE IN EVILS, AND IN THE FALSES THENCE DERIVED, ORIGINATING IN SELF-LOVE AND THE LOVE OF THE WORLD.

551. ALL who are in the hells are in evils, and in the falses thence derived, and no one there is in evils and at the same time in truths. Nearly all the wicked in the world are acquainted with spiritual truths, which are the truths of the church; for they have learned them in childhood, and then from preaching and from reading the Word, and afterward from the conversation they have had respecting them. Some have even induced others to believe that they were Christians in heart. because they knew how to discourse from truths with pretended affection, and also to act sincerely as if from spiritual faith. But such of them as have thought within themselves contrary to those truths, and have abstained from the doing of evils agreeable to their thoughts only on account of the

laws of their country, and with a view to reputation, honors, and gain, are all evil in heart, and are in truths and goods only as to the body, and not as to the spirit. When, therefore, external things are removed from them in the other life, and the internal things belonging to their spirits are revealed, they are altogether in evils and falses, and not in any truths and goods; and it is made manifest that truths and goods resided in their memory merely as scientifics, which they brought forth in conversation, putting on the semblance of good as if from spiritual love and faith. When such persons are let into their internals, and consequently into their evils, they can no longer speak truths, but only falses, since they speak from their evils; for to speak truths from evils is impossible, because the spirit is then nothing but his own evil, and what proceeds from evil is falsity. Every evil spirit is reduced to this state before he is cast into hell, (see above, n. 499–512). This is called being vastated as to truths and goods;[1] and vastation is nothing else than being let into one's internals, that is, into the proprium of his spirit, or into his spirit itself. (On this subject see also above, n. 425).

552. When a man after death is brought into this state, he is no longer a man-spirit, such as he is in his first state, (concerning which above, n. 491–498), but he is truly a spirit; for one who is truly a spirit has a face and body corresponding to his internals, which belong to his mind; thus his external form is the type or effigy of his internals. Such is the spirit after passing through the first and second states, spoken of above. Wherefore it is then known, the moment he is seen, what his true character is, not only from his face, but also from his whole personal appearance, and likewise from his speech and gestures. And

---

[1] That the evil, before they are cast down into hell, are devastated as to truths and goods, and that when those are taken away they are carried of themselves into hell, n. 6977, 7039, 7795, 8210, 8232, 9330. That the Lord does not devastate them, but that they devastate themselves, n. 7643, 7926. That every evil has in it what is false, wherefore they who are in evil are also in the false, although some of them do not know it, n. 7577, 8094. That they who are in evil, cannot but think what is false, when they think from themselves, n. 7437. That all who are in the hells speak falses from evil, n. 1695, 7351, 7352, 7357, 7392, 7689.

because he is now in himself, he cannot abide elsewhere than among those who are like him. For in the spiritual world there is a communication of the affections and consequent thoughts in an endless variety of ways; wherefore a spirit is conveyed to his like, as it were of himself, because he is led to them by his own affection and its delight; indeed, he even turns himself in that direction, for thus he inhales his own life, or draws his breath freely, but not when he turns himself in another direction. It is to be remembered, that communication with others in the spiritual world takes place according to the turning of the face, and that every one has continually before him those who are in similar love with himself; and this, too, whichever way the body is turned; (see above, n. 151). Hence it is that all infernal spirits turn themselves backward from the Lord to the thick darkness, and the darkness, which there occupy the places of the sun and moon of the natural world; but that all the angels of heaven turn themselves to the Lord as the sun and as the moon of heaven; (see above, n. 123, 143, 144, 151). From these considerations it may now be manifest, that all who are in the hells are in evils and in the falses thence derived; and likewise that they are turned to their own loves.

553. All the spirits in the hells, when inspected in any degree of heavenly light, appear in the form of their own evil; for every one there is the effigy of his own evil, because with every one the interiors and exteriors act in unity,—the interiors exhibiting themselves visibly in the exteriors, which are the face, the body, the speech, and the gestures. Thus their quality is known as soon as they are seen. In general, they are forms of contempt of others; of menace against those who do not pay them respect; of hatred of various kinds; also of various kinds of revenge. Ferocity and cruelty from their interiors are transparent through those forms. But when others commend, honor, and worship them, their faces are contracted, and have an appearance of gladness arising from delight. It is impossible to describe in a few words all those forms, as they actually appear, for no one of them is similar to another. Among those, however, who are in similar evil, and thence in a similar infernal society, there is a general likeness, from which, as from a plane of derivation, the faces of all

there appear to bear a certain resemblance to each other.   In general, their faces are hideous, and void of life like corpses ; in some cases they are black ; in others they are fiery like little torches ; in others, disfigured with pimples, warts, and ulcers ; many appear to have no face, but instead thereof something hairy or bony ; and in some instances nothing is seen but teeth. Their bodies also are monstrous ; and their speech is like the speech of anger, hatred, or revenge,—for every one speaks from his own falsity, and in a tone corresponding to his own evil.   In a word, they are all images of their own hell.   I have not been permitted to see what is the form of hell itself in general ; I have only been told that, as the universal heaven in one complex resembles one man, (n. 59–67), so the universal hell in one complex resembles one devil, and may also be presented in the effigy of one devil, (see above, n. 544).   But the specific form of the hells or infernal societies, I have often seen ; for at their openings, which are called the gates of hell, there usually appears a monster, that represents in general the form of those who are within.   The inhumanity of those who dwell there, is then at the same time represented by things shocking and horrible, which I forbear to mention.   It is, however, to be observed, that such is the appearance of infernal spirits when seen in the light of heaven ; but among themselves they appear like men.   This is of the Lord's mercy, that they may not appear as loathsome to each other, as they do to the angels.   But this appearance is a fallacy ; for as soon as a ray of light from heaven is let in, their human forms are turned into monstrous ones, such as they are in reality, as described above ; for in the light of heaven everything appears as it really is.   Hence it is, too, that they shun the light of heaven, and cast themselves down into their own lumen, which is like the light from ignited coals, and in some cases like that from burning sulphur.   But this lumen is also turned into utter darkness, as soon as any light from heaven flows in upon it.   Hence it is that the hells are said to be in thick darkness, and in darkness ; and that thick darkness and darkness signify falses derived from evil, such as are in hell.

554 From an inspection of those monstrous forms of spirits in the hells,—which, as was said, are all forms of contempt of

others, of menace against those who do not pay them honor and respect, and of hatred and revenge against those wno do not favor them,—it was made manifest that, in general, they were all of them forms of self-love and the love of the world; and that the evils whereof they are specific forms, derive their origin from those two loves. I have also been told from heaven, and it has been proved to me by much experience likewise, that those two loves,—namely, self-love and the love of the world,—r:le in the hells, and likewise make the hells; and that love to the Lord and love toward the neighbor rule in the heavens, and likewise make the heavens; also that the two former loves, which are the loves of hell, and the two latter, which are the loves of heaven, are diametrically opposite to each other.

555. At first I wondered why it was, that self-love and the love of the world are so diabolical, and that they who are in those loves are such monsters to look upon; since in the world little thought is given to self-love, but only to that puffed-up state of mind, outwardly manifested, which is called pride, and which, because it appears to the sight, is alone believed to be self-love. Moreover, self-love, which does not so exalt itself, is believed in the world to be the fire of life, whereby man is stimulated to seek employment, and to perform uses; it is contended that, unless he looked to the honor and glory to be thereby acquired, his mind would grow torpid. Who, say they, ever did any worthy, useful, or memorable deed, but for the sake of being celebrated and honored by others, or in the minds of others? And whence, it is asked, does this arise, but from the ardor of love for glory and honor, consequently for self? Hence it is unknown in the world, that self-love, in itself considered, is the love which rules in hell and makes hell with man. This being the case, I will first describe what self-love is, and then show that all evils and the falses thence derived, spring from that love as from their fountain.

556. Self-love consists in a man's wishing well to himself alone, and not to others except for the sake of himself,—not even to the church, to his country, or to any human society; also in doing good to them solely for the sake of his own reputation, honor and glory; for unless he sees these in the uses which he performs for them, he says in his heart, Of what use is it? Why should I

do this? What advantage will it be to me? And so he leaves
the use undone. Whence it is evident that he who is in self-love,
neither loves the church, nor his country, nor society, nor any
use, but himself alone. His delight is only that of self-love; and
because the delight which proceeds from his love makes the life
of man, therefore his life is the life of self; and the life of self is
the life derived from man's proprium; and the proprium of man,
viewed in itself, is nothing but evil. He who loves himself, loves
those who belong to him, who in particular are his children and
grand-children, and in general all who make one with him, whom
he calls his friends. To love these, is also to love himself; for
he regards them as it were in himself, and himself in them.
Among those whom he calls his friends, are also to be reckoned
all who praise, honor, and pay their court to him.

557. From a comparison of self-love with heavenly love, the
nature of the former may be clearly seen. Heavenly love consists
in loving, for their own sake, the uses or good works which a
man performs for the church, for his country, for human society,
and for a fellow-citizen; for this is to love God and the neighbor,
because all uses and all good works are from God, and are likewise the neighbor that is to be loved. But whoever loves them
for the sake of himself, loves them as he does his household
domestics, merely because they render him service. Hence it
follows, that he who is in self-love desires that the church, his
country, human society, and his fellow-citizens, should serve
him, and not that he may serve them; for he places himself
above them, and them below himself. So far, therefore, as any
one is in self-love, he removes himself from heaven, because from
heavenly love.

558. Still further: so far as any one is in heavenly love,—
which consists in loving uses and good works, and in being
affected with delight of heart in the performance of them for the
sake of the church, his country, human society, and a fellow-citizen,
—he is led by the Lord; because that is the love in which He is,
and which is from Himself. But so far as any one is in self-love,
which consists in performing uses and good works for the sake
of himself, he is led by himself; and in proportion as any one is
led by himself, he is not led by the Lord: whence also it follows,

that so far as any one loves himself, he removes himself from the Divine, thus also from heaven. To be led by himself is to be led by his own proprium, and the proprium of man is nothing but evil; for it is his hereditary evil, which consists in loving himself more than God, and the world more than heaven.[1] Man is let into his own proprium, thus into his hereditary evils, as often as he has regard to himself in the good that he does; for he looks away from good works to himself, and not away from himself to good works; wherefore in his good works he presents the image of himself, and not any image of the Divine. That such is the case, has also been proved to me by experience. There are evil spirits, whose habitations are in the middle quarter between the north and the west, beneath the heavens, who are skilled in the art of letting well-disposed spirits into their proprium, and thus into evils of various kinds; this they accomplish by letting them into thoughts concerning themselves, either openly by praises and honors, or secretly by determinations of their affections toward themselves; and so far as they succeed in this, they turn away the faces of the well-disposed spirits from heaven, darken their understandings also, and call forth evils from their proprium.

558. That self-love is the opposite of neighborly love, may be seen from the origin and essence of both. The love of the neighbor with him who is in self-love, commences from self,—for he insists that every one is neighbor to himself,—and from self as its centre, proceeds to all who make one with himself, with dim-

---

[1] That the proprium of man, which he derives hereditarily from his parents, is nothing but dense evil, n. 210, 215, 731, 876, 987, 1047, 2307, 2308, 3518, 3701, 3812, 8480, 8550, 10283, 10284, 10286, 10731. That the proprium of man consists in loving himself more than God, and the world more than heaven, and in making nothing of his neighbor in comparison with himself, except only for the sake of himself, thus that it consists in the love of self and of the world, n. 694, 731, 4317, 5660. That all evils flow from the love of self and the love of the world, when these predominate, n. 1307, 1308, 1321, 1594, 1691, 3413, 7255, 7376, (7480), 7488, 8318, 9335, 9348, 10038, 10742; which are contempt of others, enmity, hatred, revenge, cruelty, deceit, n. 6667, 7372, 7374, 9348, 10038, 10742. And that in these evils every false principle originates, n. 1047, 10283, 10284, 10286.

inution according to the degrees of conjunction with him by love; and they who are out of that consociation, are made no account of; and they who are opposed to him and his friends, and to their evils, are regarded as enemies, whether they be wise or upright, sincere or just, or whatever be their character. But spiritual love toward the neighbor commences from the Lord; and from Him as the centre, it proceeds to all those who are conjoined to Him by love and faith, and is exercised toward all according to the quality of their love and faith.[1] Hence it is evident that the neighborly love which commences from man, is the opposite of that which commences from the Lord; and that the former proceeds from evil, because from the proprium of man, but the latter proceeds from good, because from the Lord, who is Good Itself. It is also evident, that the love of the neighbor which proceeds from man and his proprium is corporeal, but that which proceeds from the Lord is heavenly. In a word, the love of self with the man in whom it rules constitutes the head, and heavenly love with him constitutes the feet

---

[1] They who do not know what it is to love the neighbor, suppose that every man is a neighbor, and that good is to be done to every one who is in need of assistance, n. 6704. And they likewise believe, that every one is neighbor to himself, and thus that neighborly love begins from self, n. 6933. That they who love themselves above all things, thus with whom self-love prevails, reckon also the commencement of neighborly love from themselves, n. 6710. But in what manner every one is neighbor to himself, is explained, n. 6933 to 6938. But they who are Christians, and love God above all things, reckon the commencement of neighborly love from the Lord, because he is to be loved above all things. n. 6706, 6711, 6819. 6824. That the distinctions of neighbor are as many as the distinctions of good from the Lord, and that good ought to be done with discrimination toward every one according to the quality of his state, and that this is of Christian prudence, n. 6707, 6709, 6710, 6818. That those distinctions are innumerable, and that on this account the ancients, who were acquainted with the true meaning of neighbor, reduced the exercises of charity into classes, and marked them with their respective names, and that hence they knew in what respect every one was a neighbor, and in what manner good was to be done to every one prudently, n. 2417, 6628, 6705, 7259 to 7262. That the doctrine in the ancient churches was the doctrine of charity toward the neighbor, and that hence they had wisdom, n. 2417, 2385, 3419, 3420, 4844, 6629.

whereon he stands; and if this does not serve him, he tramples it under foot. Hence the reason why they who are cast down into hell, appear to fall with their heads downward toward hell, and their feet upward toward heaven; (see above, n. 548).

559. Self-love is also of such a quality, that so far as the reins are given it,—that is, so far as external bonds are removed, which consist in fear of the law and its penalties, and of the loss of reputation, honor, gain, employment, and life,—it rushes on in its mad career, until at last it not only desires to rule over the whole terrestrial globe, but also over the whole heaven, and over the Divine Himself. It knows no limit or bounds. This propensity lurks within every one who is in self-love, although it does not appear before the world, where the above mentioned bonds restrain it. That such is the case, is obvious to every one from the conduct of kings and potentates, who are subject to no such restraints and bonds, and who rush on, subjugating provinces and kingdoms, and,—so far as they succeed in their purposes,—aspire after unlimited power and glory. The same truth is still more evident from the Babylon of the present day, which has extended its dominion into heaven, and transferred all the divine power of the Lord to itself, and continually lusts after more. That persons of this character, when after death they enter the other life, are altogether opposed to the Divine and to heaven, and are in favor of hell, may be seen in the little treatise concerning the Last Judgment and the destruction of Babylon.

560. Picture to yourself a society of such persons, all of whom love themselves alone, and love others only so far as they make one with themselves; and you will see that their love for each other is not unlike that of robbers, who, so far as their associates act conjointly with them, embrace and call them friends; but, so far as they do not act conjointly with them, and reject their domination, rush upon and cruelly slay them. If their interiors or minds be examined, it will be found that they are full of bitter enmity toward each other, and that in heart they laugh at all justice and sincerity, and likewise at the Divine, whom they reject as of no account. This may be still further manifest from the societies of such in the hells, treated of below.

561. The interiors belonging to the thoughts and affections of those who love themselves above all things, are turned toward themselves and the world, and thus are turned away from the Lord and heaven. Hence they are filled with evils of every kind, and the Divine cannot flow-in ; for the instant it does, it is immersed in their thoughts about themselves, and is defiled, and is likewise infused into the evils which arise from their proprium. Hence it is that all such, in the other life, look away from the Lord toward the thick darkness which there occupies the place of the sun in the world, and which is diametrically opposite to the sun of heaven, which is the Lord, (see above, n. 123) ; thick darkness also signifies evil, and the sun of the world the love of self.[1]

562. The evils which appertain to those who are in the love of self, are in general, contempt of others, envy, enmity, and thence hostility toward all who do not favor them, hatred of various kinds, revenge, cunning, deceit, unmercifulness and cruelty. And in respect to the things of religion, they not only entertain a contempt for the Divine, and for divine things,—which are the truths and goods of the church,—but even feel anger against them, which is likewise turned into hatred when man becomes a spirit ; and then he not only cannot endure to hear those things mentioned, but also burns with hatred against all who acknowledge and worship the Divine. I once conversed with a certain spirit, who had been in authority when in the world, and had loved himself in an unusual degree. This spirit, at the bare mention of the Divine, and especially at the mention of the Lord's name, was moved by such hatred arising from anger, that he burned with a desire to kill Him. The same spirit also, when his love was left unrestrained, desired to be the devil himself, that from self-love he might continually infest heaven. This, too, is the desire of many who are of the Roman Catholic religion, when they perceive in the other life that the Lord has all power, and themselves none.

---

[1] That the sun of the world signifies the love of self, n. 2441. In which sense by adoring the sun is signified to adore those things which are contrary to heavenly love, and to the Lord, n. 2441, 10584. That the sun growing hot denotes the increasing concupiscence of evil, n. 8487

563. There appeared to me some spirits in the western quarter toward the south, who said that they had been in stations of great dignity in the world, and that they deserved to be preferred above others, and to rule over them. They were examined by the angels in order to ascertain their true quality; and it was discovered that, in the discharge of the duties of their offices in the world, they had not looked to uses but to themselves, and that thus they had preferred themselves to uses. But because they were very earnest and importunate in their desire to be set over others, they were allowed to take their places among those who were consulting about matters of superior importance; but it was perceived that they were unable to attend to the business under consideration, or to see things interiorly in themselves; and that they did not speak upon the subject from a regard to use, but from proprium, and likewise that they wished to act from personal favor according to their arbitrary pleasure. Wherefore they were dismissed from that office, and left to seek employment for themselves elsewhere. They therefore proceeded further into the western quarter, where they were received first in one place and then in another; but they were everywhere told, that they thought only of themselves, and of nothing except on their own account; consequently that they were stupid, and only like sensual corporeal spirits. On this account, wherever they went they were sent away. Some time afterward, I saw them reduced to extreme poverty, and asking alms. Hence also it was made manifest, that however they who are in self-love, may, from the fire of that love, seem to speak in the world like wise men, still it is only from the memory, and not from any rational light. Wherefore in the other life, when it is no longer permitted to reproduce the things of the natural memory, they are more stupid than others; the reason of which is, that they are separated from the Divine.

564. There are two kinds of dominion; one is that of love toward the neighbor, and the other that of self-love. These two kinds of dominion are, in their essence, altogether opposite to each other. He who exercises rule from love toward the neighbor, wishes to do good to all, and loves nothing more than to perform uses, that is, to serve others; (by serving others is meant to seek

their good, and to perform uses, whether it be to the church, to the country, to society, or to a fellow-citizen) ; this is his love, and this the delight of his heart. So far also as he is exalted to dignities above others, he is glad ; yet not on account of the dignities, but on account of the uses which he is then able to perform in greater abundance, and of a higher order. Such is the dominion that is exercised in the heavens. But he who rules from the love of self, wills good to no one but himself alone ; the uses which he performs are for the sake of his own honor and glory, which to him are the only uses. His end in serving others is, that he may himself be served, honored, and exalted to dominion. He courts dignities, not for the sake of the good service which may thereby be rendered to his country and to the church, but in order that he may be in eminence and glory, and thence in the delight of his heart. The love of dominion also remains with every one after his life in the world. Those who have exercised authority from neighborly love, are also entrusted with authority in the heavens ; but then, it is not they who rule, but the uses which they love ; and when uses rule, the Lord rules. But they who in the world have exercised authority from self-love, after their life on earth are in hell, where they are vile slaves. I have seen the mighty ones, who in the world had exercised dominion from the love of self, cast among those of the meanest class, and some of them among those there who inhabit privies.

565. But as to the love of the world, this is not opposed to heavenly love in so great a degree as the love of self, because so great evils do not lie concealed within it. The love of the world consists in desiring to secure for one's self the wealth of others, by every kind of artifice, in setting the heart on riches, and in suffering the world to withdraw him and lead him away from spiritual love,—which is love toward the neighbor,—and thus from heaven and from the Divine. But this love is manifold. There is the love of wealth for the sake of being exalted to honors, which are the only objects loved. There is the love of honors and dignities with a view to the increase of wealth. There is the love of wealth for the sake of the various uses, which afford delight in the world. There is the love of wealth for its own sake, such as

belongs to the avaricious; and so on. The end for which wealth is sought, is called its use; and the end or use is that from which the love derives its quality; for the love is of such a quality as is the end had in view, and all other things are subservient to it.

WHAT IS MEANT BY HELL FIRE, AND WHAT BY GNASHING OF TEETH.

566. WHAT is meant by the everlasting fire, and the gnashing of teeth, which are mentioned in the Word as the portion of those who are in hell, has hitherto been known to scarcely any one. The reason is, because people have thought materially concerning those things which are in the Word, not being acquainted with its spiritual sense. Wherefore by fire, some have understood material fire; some, torment in general; some, remorse of conscience; and some have supposed that the expression is used merely to excite terror, and thus deter men from crimes. And by the gnashing of teeth, some have understood the literal act; some, only a sense of horror, like that experienced when such collision of the teeth is heard. But whoever is acquainted with the spiritual sense of the Word, may know what everlasting fire is, and what the gnashing of teeth; for in every expression and sentence in the Word, is contained a spiritual sense, since the Word in its bosom is spiritual; and what is spiritual cannot be expressed before man otherwise than in a natural manner, because man is in the natural world, and thinks from the things of that world. What, therefore, is meant by the everlasting fire, and the gnashing of teeth, into which the wicked as to their spirits come after death, or which their spirits, which are then in the spiritual world, suffer, shall be told in what now follows.

567. There are two origins of heat; one from the sun of heaven, which is the Lord, and the other from the sun of the world. The heat which is from the sun of heaven, or the Lord,

is spiritual heat, which in its essence is love, (see above, n. 126–140) ; but the heat from the sun of the world is natural heat, which in its essence is not love, but serves spiritual heat or love for a receptacle. That love in its essence is heat, is evident from the fact that the mind, and thence the body, becomes warm from love, and according to its degree and quality ; and this, man experiences alike in winter as in summer. The heating of the blood is a further confirmation of the same truth. That natural heat, which exists from the sun of the world, serves spiritual heat for a receptacle, is manifest from the heat of the body, which is produced by the heat of its spirit, and supplies the place thereof in the body ; but it is more strikingly evident from the effect of the vernal and summer heat upon animals of every kind, which then every year renew their loves. Not that the latter heat produces this effect, but it disposes their bodies to receive the heat which also flows into them from the spiritual world ; for the spiritual world flows into the natural, as cause into effect. Whoever imagines that natural heat produces their loves, is much deceived ; for there is an influx of the spiritual world into the natural, and not of the natural world into the spiritual ; and all love is spiritual, since it belongs to the life itself. He, likewise, who imagines that any thing exists in the natural world without the influx of the spiritual world, is equally deceived ; for what is natural exists and subsists only from what is spiritual. And the subjects of the vegetable kingdom also derive their germinations from influx out of that world ; the natural heat of spring and summer, merely disposes the seeds into their natural forms, by expanding and opening them, so that influx from the spiritual world may act as the cause of their germination. These things are adduced, that it may be known that there are two kinds of heat, namely, spiritual and natural ; and that spiritual heat is from the sun of heaven, and natural heat from the sun of the world ; and that the influx of the former into the latter, and the subsequent co-operation of both, present the effects which appear before the eyes of men in the world.[1]

---

[1] That there is an influx of the spiritual world into the natural world, n. 6053 to 6058, 6189 to 6251, 6307 to 6327, 6466 to 6495, 6598 to 6626. That

568. Spiritual heat with man is the heat of his life, because, as was said above, in its essence it is love. This heat is what is meant by fire in the Word; love to the Lord and neighborly love being meant by heavenly fire, and self-love and the love of the world, by infernal fire.

569. Infernal fire or love exists from the same origin as heavenly fire or love, namely, from the sun of heaven, or the Lord; but it, is made infernal by those who receive it. For all influx from the spiritual world varies according to its reception, or according to the forms into which it flows, just as the heat and light of the sun of the world are modified by their recipient subjects. The heat from this sun, flowing into shrubberies and beds of flowers, produces vegetation, and likewise draws forth pleasant and delicious odors; but the same heat flowing into excrementitious and cadaverous substances, produces putrefaction, and draws forth noisome and disgusting stenches. So the light from the same sun produces, in one object, beautiful and pleasing colors, in another, ugly and disagreeable ones. The case is similar in regard to heat and light from the sun of heaven, which is love. When heat or love from that sun flows, into goods [*i. e.*, into good and orderly human forms], as with good men, spirits, and angels, it renders their goods fruitful; but when it flows into the wicked, it produces the contrary effect, for their evils either suffocate or pervert it. So the light of heaven, when it flows into the truths of good, imparts intelligence and wisdom; but when it flows into the falses of evil, it is there turned into insanities and fantasies of various kinds. Thus in every instance the effect is according to reception.

570. Because infernal fire is the love of self and of the world, it is therefore every lust which springs from those loves; for lust is love in its continuity, since what a man loves, this he continually lusts after; and it is likewise delight, for what a man loves or lusts after, when he obtains it, he perceives to be delightful; nor is heart-felt delight communicated to him from any other source.

---

there is influx also into the lives of animals, n. 5850. And likewise into the subjects of the vegetable kingdom, n. 3648. That this influx is a continual endeavor to act according to divine order, n. 6211 at the end.

51

Infernal fire, therefore, is the lust and delight which spring from the love of self and the world as from their fountain. The evils originating in those two loves, are contempt of others, enmity and hostility against those who do not favor them, envy, hatred, and revenge, and as a consequence of these, savageness and cruelty. And in regard to the Divine, they consist in the denial, and thence in the contempt, mocking, and reviling, of the holy things belonging to the church: and after death, when man becomes a spirit, these evils are turned into anger and hatred against those holy things; (see above, n. 502). And because these evils continually breathe the destruction and murder of those whom they regard as enemies, and against whom they burn with hatred and revenge, therefore it is the delight of their life to wish to destroy and kill; and when they are unable to do this, they still delight in the wish to do them mischief and harm, and vent their rage against them. These are the things which are meant by fire in the Word, where the wicked and the hells are treated of, some passages from which I will here adduce by way of confirmation. *"Every one is a hypocrite and an evil-doer, and every mouth speaketh folly.—For wickedness burn-eth as the fire; it devoureth the briers and thorns, and kindleth the thickets of the forest, and they raise themselves like the lifting up of smoke.—And the people are become the food of fire; no man spareth his brother."* Isaiah ix. 17, 18, 19. *"I will show wonders in heaven and in the earth, blood, and fire, and pillars of smoke; the sun shall be turned into darkness."* Joel ii. 30, 31.' *"The earth shall become burning pitch; night and day it shall not be extinguished; its smoke shall ascend for ever."* Isaiah xxxiv. 9, 10. *"Behold the day cometh that shall burn like a furnace, and all the proud, and every one that doeth wickedness, shall be stubble; and the day that cometh shall burn them up."* Mal. iv. 1. *"Babylon is become the habi-tation of demons.—And they cried when they saw the smoke of her burning.—Her smoke ascendeth for ages of ages."* Apoc. xviii. 2, 18; chap. xix. 2. *He opened the bottomless pit, and there came up smoke from the pit, as the smoke of a great furnace; and the sun and the air were darkened by the smoke of the pit."* Apoc. ix. 2. *"Out of the mouths of the horses went forth fire, smoke, and brimstone; by these the third part of men were killed, by the fire, by the smoke, and by the brimstone."* Apoc. xi. 17, 18. *"Whosoever worshipeth the beast, shall drink of the wine of the wrath of God, mixed with new wine in the cup of His anger, and shall be tormented with fire and brimstone."* Apoc. xiv. 9, 10. *"The fourth angel poured out his vial upon the sun, and it was given him to scorch men with fire; therefore men were scorched with a great heat."* Apoc. xvi. 8, 9. *"They were cast into a lake burning with fire and brimstone."* Apoc. xix. 20; chap. xx. 14, 15; chap. xxi. 8. *"Every tree that bringeth not forth good fruit, shall be cut down and cast into the fire."* Matt. iii. 10; Luke iii. 9. *"The Son of man shall send forth his angels, and they shall gather together out of his kingdom all things that offend, and those that do iniquity, and shall cast them into the furnace of fire."* Matt. xiii. 41, 42, 50. *"The king shall say to those on the left hand, Depart from Me, ye cursed, into everlasting fire, prepared for the devil and his angels."* Matt. xxv. 41. *"They shall be cast into everlasting fire—into the hell of fire—where their worm shall not die, and the fire shall not be quenched."* Matt. xviii. 8, 9; Mark ix. 43–49. *"The rich man in hell said to Abraham, that he was tormented in flame."* Luke xvi. 24. In these, and in many other passages, by fire is meant the lust arising from self-love and the love of the world; and by the smoke thence issuing, is meant the false derived from evil.

571. Since the lust of doing evils which originate in the love of self and of the world, is meant by infernal fire, and since this is the lust of all in the hells, (see the foregoing chapter), therefore also when the hells are opened, there is seen as it were a volume of fire and smoke, like that arising from buildings on fire,—a dense fiery appearance from the hells where self-love prevails, and a flaming appearance from the hells where the love of the world prevails. But when they are closed, this fiery appearance is not seen, but instead thereof, an appearance like a dark mass of condensed smoke. Nevertheless the same fire continues to rage within, which is also perceptible from the heat thence exhaling. That heat is like the heat from burnt ruins after a fire, in some places like that from a heated furnace, and in others like that

from a hot bath. When this heat flows in with man, it excites in him lusts, and in the wicked, hatred and revenge ; and it renders the sick insane. Such is the fire, or such the heat, with those who are in the above-mentioned loves, since, as to their spirits, they are bound to the hells in which those loves prevail, even while they live in the body. But it is to be observed, that they who are in the hells are not in fire, but that the fire is an appearance ; for they are not sensible of any burning there, but only of a heat such as they before experienced in the world. The appearance of fire is from correspondence ; for love corresponds to fire, and all things which appear in the spiritual world, appear according to correspondences.

572. It is to be borne in mind, that this fire or infernal heat is turned into intense cold when heat flows in from heaven ; at such times the infernals shiver like persons seized with a cold fever, and are also inwardly tortured. The reason of this is, because they are utterly opposed to the Divine ; and the heat of heaven, which is divine love, extinguishes the heat of hell, which is the love of self, and with it the fire of their life ; whence come such cold and consequent shivering, and likewise torture. Then, too, thick darkness ensues, and thence infatuation and blindness. This, however, rarely happens ; only when violent outrages increase beyond measure, and require to be quelled.

573. Because infernal fire denotes every lust to do evil which flows from the love of self, therefore it also denotes such torment as exists in the hells. For the lust derived from that love is, with those inflamed by it, the lust of injuring others who do not honor, revere, and worship them ; and in proportion to the anger thence conceived against such individuals, and to the hatred and revenge arising therefrom, is their lust of exercising cruelty toward them. And when such lust rages in every one in a society which is restrained by no external bonds, such as the fear of the law, and of the loss of reputation, honor, gain, and life, then every one, from the impulse of his own evil, attacks his fellows, and as far as he is able, subjugates them, and brings the rest under his control, and takes delight in exercising cruelty toward those who do not submit. This delight is intimately conjoined with the delight of tyrannous rule, insomuch that they exist in a similar degree.

since the delight of doing injury is inherent in enmity, envy, hatred, and revenge, which are the evils of that love, as was said above. All the hells are societies of this description. Wherefore every one there cherishes hatred in his heart toward every other one, and from hatred breaks out into savage cruelties toward him, so far as he obtains the mastery. These cruelties, and the torment which they cause, are also understood by infernal fire; for they are the effects of infernal lusts.

574. It was shown above, (n. 548), that an evil spirit of his own accord casts himself into hell, although such torments exist there; wherefore also it shall be briefly explained how this comes to pass. From every hell there exhales a sphere of the lusts in which its inhabitants are. When this sphere is perceived by one who is in similar lust, he is affected at heart, and is filled with delight; for lust and its delight make one, since whatever any one lusts after, is delightful to him. Hence the spirit turns himself toward the hell whence the sphere proceeds, and from delight of heart longs to go thither; for as yet he is not aware that such torments exist there; and he who knows it, still desires to go there; for no one in the spiritual world can resist his own lust, since the lust belongs to his love, and the love to his will, and the will to his nature; and every one there acts according to his nature. When, therefore, a spirit of his own accord, or from his own freedom, directs his course to his own hell, and enters it, he is at first received in a friendly manner, and is thus led to believe that he has come among friends. This, however, continues only for a few hours. In the mean time he is examined with a view to discover the degree of his cunning, and thence of his power. When this is ascertained, they begin to infest him; and this they do in various ways, and with gradually increasing violence and severity. This is done by introducing him more interiorly and deeply into hell; for the spirits are more malignant, in proportion as the hell they inhabit is more interior and deep. After the first infestations, they begin to torture him with cruel punishments, which they continue until he is reduced to the condition of a slave. But because rebellious commotions continually exist there, since every one in hell desires to be the greatest, and burns with hatred toward others, therefore fresh outrages occur. Thus one scene

is changed into another. Wherefore they who have been made slaves, are taken out of their thraldom, that they may assist some new devil in subjugating others; when they who refuse to submit, and to yield implicit obedience, are again tormented in various ways. And this goes on perpetually. Such are the torments of hell, which are called infernal fire.

575. But the gnashing of teeth is the continual dispute and combat of falses with each other, consequently of those who are in falses, coupled also with contempt of others, with enmity, mockery, ridicule, and reviling; which evils also burst forth into various kinds of butchery; for every one fights for his own falsity, and calls it truth. These disputes and combats are heard out of those hells like the gnashing of teeth, and are likewise turned into gnashing of teeth, when truths from heaven flow-in thither. In those hells, are all they who have acknowledged nature and denied the Divine; in the deeper hells, they who have confirmed themselves in such acknowledgment and denial. These, because they are unable to receive any light from heaven, and thence are unable to see anything inwardly in themselves, are therefore most of them corporeal sensual spirits, or such as believe nothing but what they see with their eyes and touch with the hands. Hence all the fallacies of the senses are truths to them; and it is from these, also, that they dispute. It is for this reason, that their disputes are heard like gnashings of teeth; for all falses in the spiritual world are grating, and the teeth correspond to the ultimate things in nature, and likewise to the ultimate things with man, which are corporeal sensual.[1] That there is gnashing of teeth in the hells, may be seen, Matt. viii. 12; chap. xiii. 42, 50; chap. xxii. 13; chap. xxiv. 51; chap. xxv. 30; Luke xiii. 28.

---

[1] Concerning the correspondence of the teeth, n. 5565 to 5568. That they who are merely sensual, and have scarcely anything of spiritual light, correspond to the teeth, n. 5565. That tooth in the Word, signifies the sensual, which is the ultimate of the life of man, n. 9052, 9062. That gnashing of teeth in the other life arises from those who believe that nature is everything, and the Divine nothing, n. 5568.

THE WICKEDNESS AND DIABOLICAL ARTS OF INFERNAL SPIRITS.

576 THE superior excellence of spirits in comparison with men, may be seen and comprehended by every one who thinks interiorly, and knows anything about the operations of his own mind. For man can in a moment of time consider, think over, and form conclusions upon, more subjects than he can utter or express in writing in half an hour. From this it is evident what superior excellence man has when he is in his spirit, consequently when he becomes a spirit; for it is the spirit that thinks, and the body whereby the spirit expresses its thoughts in speaking or writing. Hence it is that the man who becomes an angel after death, possesses intelligence and wisdom ineffable as compared with that which he possessed when he lived in the world; for when he lived in the world, his spirit was bound to the body, and by the body was in the natural world. Wherefore what he then thought spiritually, flowed into natural ideas, which are respectively general, gross, and obscure, and incapable of receiving the innumerable things which belong to spiritual thought, and which also involve them in the dense shades arising from worldly cares. It is otherwise when the spirit is released from the body, and comes into its spiritual state, as is the case when it passes out of the natural into the spiritual world, which is its peculiar realm. That its state then, as to thoughts and affections, immensely excels its former state, is evident from what has now been said. Hence it is, that the angels think things that are inef fable and inexpressible, consequently such as cannot enter into the natural thoughts of man; although every angel was born a man, and lived as a man, and then seemed to himself to be no wiser than other men.

577. In the same degree in which there is wisdom and intelli gence with angels, there is also wickedness and cunning with infernal spirits. For the cases are similar; because when the spirit of man is released from the body, it is in its own good or in its own evil,—an angelic spirit in his own good, and an infer-

nal spirit in his own evil. For every spirit is his own good or his own evil, because he is his own love, as has been frequently said and shown above. Wherefore, as an angelic spirit thinks, wills, speaks, and acts from his own good, so does an infernal spirit from his own evil; and to think, will, speak, and act, from evil itself, is to do so from all the things which are included in the evil. It was otherwise when he lived in the body. The evil of the man's spirit was then restrained by the bonds, in which every one is held by the law, by his love of gain and honor, and through fear of losing them; on which account the evil of his spirit could not then break out, and manifest itself in its own intrinsic nature. Besides, the evil of the man's spirit then lay wrapped up and veiled in external probity, sincerity, justice, and the affection of truth and good, of which such a man has made an oral profession, and has assumed an appearance for the sake of the world. Under these outward semblances, the evil lay so covered up and concealed, that he was scarcely aware himself that his spirit contained so great wickedness and subtlety, or that in himself he was such a devil as he becomes after death, when his spirit comes into itself, and into its own nature. Such wickedness then manifests itself as exceeds all belief. There are thousands of evils which burst forth from evil itself, among which, also, are such as cannot be expressed in the words of any language. I have been permitted to learn and comprehend their nature by much experience; for it has been granted me by the Lord to be in the spiritual world as to my spirit, and at the same time in the natural world as to my body. This I can testify, that their wickedness is so great, that it is hardly possible to describe a thousandth part of it; and furthermore, that unless the Lord protected man, it would be impossible for him ever to be rescued from hell; for there are with every man both spirits from hell and angels from heaven, (see above, n. 292, 293); and the Lord cannot protect a man, unless he acknowledge the Divine, and live the life of faith and charity; for otherwise, he averts himself from the Lord, and turns toward infernal spirits, and thus becomes imbued as to his spirit with similar wickedness Nevertheless, man is continually withdrawn by the Lord from the evils, which on account of his consociation with those spirits, he attaches, and as it were attracts, to himself; for if he cannot be restrained by internal bonds, which are those of conscience, and which are not accepted if he denies the Divine, still he is withheld by external bonds, which, as was said above, are the fear of the law and its penalties, and of the loss of gain, and the privation of honor and reputation. Such a man may, indeed, be restrained from evil acts by the delights of his love, and by the fear of the loss and privation of them, but he cannot be brought into spiritual goods; for so far as he is led toward these, he meditates cunning and deceit, by simulating and counterfeiting deeds that are good, sincere, and just, with a view to persuade others to think well of him, and thus to deceive them; this cunning adds itself to the evil of his spirit, and gives it a form, and imbues it with a quality like its own.

578. The worst of all, are they who have been in evils originating in self-love, and who at the same time acted from interior deceit,—for deceit enters more deeply than any other evil into the thoughts and intentions, and infects them with its poison, and thus destroys all of man's spiritual life. Most of these are in the hells at the back, and are called genii; and it is their peculiar delight to render themselves invisible, and to flit about others like phantoms, covertly infusing evils which they scatter around as vipers do their poison: these suffer more dreadful torment than the rest. But they who have not been deceitful, and have not been filled with malignant cunning, and yet were in evils derived from the love of self, are also in the hells at the back, but not in so deep ones. But they who have been in evils derived from the love of the world, are in the hells in front, and are called spirits. These are not such evils, that is, they are not such hatreds and revenges, as those who are in evils from the love of self; and consequently they have not such malice and cunning; on which account, also, their hells are more mild.

579. I have been permitted to learn by experience the peculiar quality of the wickedness of those who are called genii. These do not operate upon, and flow into, the thoughts, but into the affections, which they perceive, and smell out, as dogs do wild beasts in a forest. When they perceive good affections in another, they instantly turn them into evil, leading and bending them in a won-

derful manner by his delights; and this so clandestinely, and with such malignant art, that the other knows nothing of it,—for they dextrously guard against any idea of what they are about entering into his thought, since they would thereby be discovered. They are seated, with man, beneath the hinder part of the head. These, when in the world, were men who deceitfully captivated the minds of others, leading and persuading them through the delights of their affections or lusts. But those spirits are prevented by the Lord from approaching any man, of whose reformation there is any hope; for they are of such a nature, that they are able not only to destroy man's conscience, but also to excite his hereditary evils, which otherwise lie concealed. Wherefore, in order that man may not be led into those evils, it is provided by the Lord that these hells should be entirely closed; and when, after death, any man whose character is similar to that of these genii, comes into the other life, he is instantly cast into their hell. Those spirits also, when they are inspected as to their deceit and cunning, appear like vipers.

580. What dreadful wickedness belongs to infernal spirits, is manifest from their nefarious arts, which are so many, that to enumerate them would fill a volume, and to describe them would require many volumes. Nearly all those arts are unknown in the world. ONE kind relates to the abuse of correspondences: a SECOND, to the abuses of the ultimates of divine order: a THIRD, to the communication and influx of thoughts and affections, by conversions [or turning toward the subject of the operation], by inspections [or fixing the sight upon him], and by operating through other spirits distant from themselves, and through emissaries sent forth from themselves: a FOURTH, to operations by means of fantasies: a FIFTH, to ejections out of themselves, and consequent presence in a different place from that in which they are in the body: a SIXTH, to pretences, persuasions, and lies. Into these arts the spirit of a wicked man comes of himself, when he is released from the body; for they are inherent in the nature of the evil in which he then is. By these arts they torment each other in the hells. But as all of them, except those which are effected by pretences, persuasions, and lies, are unknown in the world, I

shall not here describe them specifically, both because they would not be comprehended, and because of their direful nature.

581. The reason that torments in the hells are permitted by the Lord, is because evils cannot otherwise be restrained and subdued. The only means of restraining and subduing them, and of keeping the infernal crew in bonds, is the fear of punishment. There is no other means; for without the fear of punishment and torture, evil would rush headlong into deeds of madness, and all would be chaos, like a kingdom on earth where there is no law and no punishment.

THE APPEARANCE, SITUATION, AND PLURALITY OF THE HELLS.

582. In the spiritual world, or the world inhabited by spirits and angels, there appear objects similar to those in the natural world, or that inhabited by men,—so similar, indeed, that as to outward aspect there is no difference. There appear in that world plains and mountains, rocks and hills, and valleys between them, besides waters, and many other things which are seen on earth. But still they are all from a spiritual origin; on which account they are visible to the eyes of spirits and angels, but not to the eyes of men, because men are in the natural world; and spiritual beings see those objects which are from a spiritual origin, and natural beings, those which are from a natural origin. Wherefore man cannot possibly with his eyes behold the objects which are in the spiritual world, until he becomes a spirit after death, unless it be granted him to be in the spirit. Nor, on the other hand, can an angel or spirit see anything whatever in the natural world, unless he be present with a man to whom it is permitted to speak with angels and spirits; for the eyes of man are adapted to the reception of the light of the natural world, and the eyes of angels and spirits, to the reception of the light of the spiritual world; and yet both have eyes altogether similar

in appearance. That the spiritual world is of such a nature, is something which the natural man cannot comprehend, and least of all the sensual man, who believes nothing but what he sees with his bodily eyes, and touches with his hands, consequently what he becomes acquainted with through the sight and touch; and since he thinks from those things, therefore his thought is material and not spiritual. Such being the similarity between the spiritual and the natural worlds, therefore man, immediately after death, scarcely knows but that he is still in the world where he was born, and from which he has departed; for which reason, also, death is called only a translation from one world to another like it. That there is such a similarity between the two worlds, may be seen above, where representatives and appearances in heaven were treated of, (n. 170–176).

583. In the more elevated places of the spiritual world, are the heavens; in the low ones there, is the world of spirits; beneath both these, are the hells. The heavens do not appear to the spirits who are in the world of spirits, except when their interior sight is opened; yet they occasionally appear as mists or as bright clouds: the reason is, because the angels of heaven are in an interior state as to intelligence and wisdom, and thus above the sight of those who are in the world of spirits. But the spirits who are in the plains and valleys, see each other; yet when they are separated there, as is the case when they are let into their interiors, the evil spirits do not see the good, though these can see the evil; but the good turn themselves away from the evil, and spirits who turn themselves away become invisible. But the hells do not appear, because they are closed; only the entrances, which are called gates, are seen when they are opened to let in other similar spirits. All the gates leading to the hells open from the world of spirits, and none of them from heaven.

584. The hells are everywhere, both under the mountains, hills, and rocks, and under the plains and valleys. The openings or gates to the hells which are under the mountains, hills, and rocks, appear to the sight like holes and clefts of the rocks, some of them widely extended and spacious, others strait and narrow, and most of them rugged. All, when looked into, appear dark and dusky; but the infernal spirits who are within

them, are in such a kind of light resembling that from ignited coals. Their eyes are adapted to the reception of that light, because while they lived in the world they were in thick darkness in respect to divine truths, in consequence of denying them, and in light as it were in respect to falsities, in consequence of affirming them ; in this way the sight of their eyes was formed in accommodation to that light. Hence also it is, that the light of heaven is thick darkness to them ; wherefore, when they come out of their dens, they see nothing. From which facts it was made abundantly evident, that man comes into the light of heaven so far as he acknowledges the Divine, and confirms with himself the things belonging to heaven and the church ; and that he comes into the thick darkness of hell so far as he denies the Divine, and confirms with himself the things which are contrary to those of heaven and the church.

585. The openings or gates leading to the hells which are beneath the plains and valleys, are widely different in their appearance. Some are like those which are beneath the mountains, hills, and rocks ; others are like dens and caverns ; others like great chasms and whirlpools ; others like bogs ; and others like stagnant pools of water. All are covered over, nor are they opened except when evil spirits from the world of spirits are cast in ; and when they are opened, there is an exhalation from them, either like fire accompanied with smoke, similar to what appears in the air from buildings on fire, or like flame without smoke, or like the soot which issues from a chimney on fire, or like a mist and thick cloud. I have heard that the infernal spirits themselves neither see nor feel these things, because when they are in them they are as if in their own atmosphere, and thus in the delight of their life ; and the reason is, because such objects correspond to the evils and falses in which they are immersed ; namely, fire to hatred and revenge ; smoke and soot, to the falses arising therefrom ; flame, to the evils of the love of self ; and a mist and thick cloud, to the falses thence proceeding.

586. I have also been permitted to look into the hells, and to see what sort of places they are within ; for when the Lord pleases, a spirit or angel who is above, can look down into the lowest depths, and observe the character of the objects there,

notwithstanding the coverings. Thus, too, have I been permitted to look into them. Some hells appeared to the sight like caverns and dens in rocks tending inward, and then also obliquely or perpendicularly downward. Some appeared like caves and dens, such as wild beasts inhabit in forests. Some like vaulted caverns and grottoes, such as are seen in mines, with caves tending toward lower regions. Most of the hells are threefold; the superior ones within appear in thick darkness, because inhabited by spirits who are in the falses of evil; but the inferior ones appear fiery, because inhabited by spirits who are in the evils themselves; for thick darkness corresponds to the falses of evil, and fire to the evils themselves; and in the deeper hells reside those who have acted interiorly from evil; but in the less deep, those who have acted exteriorly, that is, from the falses of evil. In some hells there appear as it were the ruins of houses and cities after a conflagration, among which ruins the infernal spirits dwell and conceal themselves. In the milder hells there appear as it were rude huts, in some cases contiguous, resembling a city with lanes and streets. Within their habitations, infernal spirits are engaged in continual quarrels, enmities, blows, and fightings, while in the streets and lanes are robberies and depredations. In some hells there are nothing but brothels, which are disgusting to behold, being full of all sorts of filth and excrement. There are also dark forests, in which infernal spirits roam like wild beasts, and where likewise there are subterranean dens, in which they take refuge when closely pursued by others. There are deserts likewise where all is sterile and sandy; and in some places rugged rocks, with caverns in them; in other places are also huts. Into these desert places are cast out from the hells, such as have suffered the extremity of punishment, especially those who, when in the world, had been more cunning than others in plotting artifices and contriving deceits; their final condition is such a life.

587. As to the situation of the hells specifically, it cannot be known by any one, not even by the angels in heaven, but by the Lord alone. But their situation in general is known from the quarters in which they are. For the hells, like the heavens, are distinguished in respect to the quarters, and the quarters in the

spiritual world are determined according to the loves. All the quarters in heaven begin from the Lord as a sun, who is the East; and because the hells are opposite to the heavens, their quarters begin from the opposite one, that is, from the west; (on which subject see the chapter concerning the four quarters in heaven, n. 141-153.) Hence it is that the hells in the western quarter are the worst of all, and are most horrible, becoming successively worse and more horrible by degrees, the more remote they are from the east. These hells are inhabited by those who, when in the world, were in the love of self, and thence in contempt of others, and in enmity against those who did not favor them, also in hatred and revenge against those who did not pay them respect and homage. In the most remote hells in this quarter, are those who were of the Catholic religion, as it is called, and who desired to be worshiped as gods, and consequently burned with hatred and revenge against all who did not acknowledge their power over the souls of men and over heaven. They still cherish the same disposition which distinguished them in the world, that is, the same hatred and revenge against those who oppose them. Their greatest delight is to exercise cruelty: but this delight is turned against themselves in the other life; for in their hells of which the western quarter is full, one rages like a madman against another who derogates from his divine power. But upon this subject more will be said in the little work on the Last Judgment and the destruction of Babylon. But how the hells in that quarter are arranged cannot be known further than this, that the most direful of that sort are at the sides toward the northern quarter, and the less direful toward the southern quarter. Thus the direfulness of the hells gradually diminishes from the northern quarter to the southern, and also toward the east. To the east dwell those who have been haughty, and have not believed in the Divine, but still have not been in such hatred and revenge, nor in such deceit, as they who are in the deeper regions of the western quarter. In the eastern quarter there are no hells at this day; those which were there, have been transferred to the front of the western quarter. There are many hells in the northern and southern quarters; and those are in them, who, while they lived on earth, were in the love of the world, and thence in various kinds of evils, such as enmity, hostility, theft, robbery, cunning, avarice, unmercifulness. The worst hells of this kind are in the northern quarter, the milder in the southern. Their direfulness increases as they are nearer to the western quarter, and likewise as they are more remote from the southern; and it decreases toward the eastern quarter, and also toward the southern. Behind the hells which are in the western quarter, are dark forests, in which malignant spirits roam like wild beasts; and it is the same behind the hells in the northern quarter. But behind the hells in the southern quarter, there are the deserts which were treated of just above. Thus far respecting the situation of the hells.

588. With respect to the plurality of the hells, they are as many in number as are the angelic societies in the heavens, since every heavenly society has its opposite in some infernal society to which it corresponds. That the heavenly societies are innumerable, and all distinguished according to the goods of love or charity, and of faith, may be seen in the chapter concerning the societies of which the heavens consist, (n. 41–50); and in the chapter concerning the immensity of heaven, (n. 415–420). The case, therefore, is the same with the infernal societies, which are distinguished according to the evils opposite to those goods. Every evil is of infinite variety, like every good. That such is the fact, cannot be conceived by those who have only a simple idea concerning every evil, as concerning contempt, enmity, hatred, revenge, deceit, and other similar evils. But be it known that every one of those evils contains so many specific differences, and every one of these, again, so many other specific or particular differences, that a volume would not suffice to enumerate them. The hells are so distinctly arranged in order according to the differences of every evil, that nothing more orderly and distinct can be conceived. Hence it may be evident that they are innumerable, near to, and remote from, one another, according to the differences of their evils, general, specific, and particular. There are also hells beneath hells. Some communicate with others by passages, and more by exhalations, —the communications being regulated entirely according to the affinities between one genus or species of evil and others. How

great the number of the hells is, I have been permitted to learn from this circumstance, that there are hells under every mountain, hill and rock, and also under every plain and valley [in the spiritual world], and that they extend beneath them, in length, breadth, and depth; in a word, the whole heaven, and the whole world of spirits, are as it were excavated beneath, and beneath them is a continuous hell. Thus far concerning the plurality of the hells.

THE EQUILIBRIUM BETWEEN HEAVEN AND HELL.

589. In order that anything may exist, there must be an equilibrium of all things. Without equilibrium there is neither action nor reaction; for equilibrium is between two forces, one of which acts, and the other reacts; and the state of rest resulting from similar action and reaction is called equilibrium. There is an equilibrium in all things and in every single thing. In general there is an equilibrium in the atmospheres themselves, in which the inferior parts react and resist, in proportion as the superior parts act and press upon them. In the natural world, also, there is an equilibrium between heat and cold, between light and shade, and between dryness and moisture,—the middle temperature being their equilibrium. There is also an equilibrium in all the subjects of the three kingdoms of nature, the mineral, the vegetable, and the animal; for without an equilibrium in those kingdoms nothing exists or subsists,—there being everywhere a kind of effort acting on one part and reacting on the other. All existence, or every effect, is produced in equilibrium; but it is produced in this way, that one force acts, and another suffers itself to be acted upon; or that one force flows in by acting, and another receives the influx and yields in agreement therewith. In the natural world, that which acts and that which reacts is called force, and also effort; but in the spiritual world that which acts and that which reacts is called life and

will.   Life in that world is living force, and will is living effort
and the equilibrium itself is called freedom.   Spiritual equilibrium or freedom, therefore, exists and subsists between good acting on one part, and evil reacting on the other ; or between evil
acting on one part and good reacting on the other.   The equilibrium between good acting and evil reacting, is such as exists
with the good ; but the equilibrium between evil acting and good
reacting, is such as exists with the evil.   That spiritual equilibrium is between good and evil, is because the whole of man's
life has reference to good and evil, and the will is the receptacle
of both.   There is also an equilibrium between the true and the
false ; but this depends upon that between good and evil.   The
equilibrium between the true and the false is like that between
light and shade, which operate upon the subjects of the vegetable
kingdom in proportion to the heat and cold that are in the light
and shade.   That light and shade of themselves produce no effect,
but that heat operates by means of them, is manifest from the
similarity between the light and shade in the seasons of winter
and spring.   The comparison of the true and the false with
light and shade, is on account of their correspondence ; for truth
corresponds to light, the false to shade, and heat to the good
of love.   Spiritual light, indeed, is truth, spiritual shade is
the false, and spiritual heat is the good of love ; on which subject
see the chapter where light and heat in heaven are treated of, (n.
126–140).

590. There is a perpetual equilibrium between heaven and
hell.   From hell there continually exhales and ascends an effort
to do evil, and from heaven there continually exhales and descends an effort to do good.   The world of spirits is in that
equilibrium, for it is intermediate between heaven and hell, as
may be seen above, (n. 421–431).   The world of spirits is in
that equilibrium, because every man after death first enters that
world, and is there kept in a state similar to that in which he
was in the natural world, which would not be possible unless the
most perfect equilibrium existed there ; for by means of this, all
are explored as to their quality, being there left in their freedom,
such as they enjoyed while they lived in the world.   Spiritual
equilibrium with men and spirits, is freedom, as was said just

above, (n. 589). The quality of every one's freedom is there ascertained by the angels in heaven, by the communication of his affections and of the thoughts thence proceeding; and is visibly manifested to angelic spirits by the ways in which he goes. Spirits that are good go in the ways which tend toward heaven; but evil spirits go in the ways which tend toward hell. Ways actually appear in that world; and this is why ways, in the Word, signify truths which lead to good, and in the opposite sense, falses which lead to evil. And it is for this reason also, that going, walking, and journeying, when mentioned in the Word, signify progressions of life.[1] I have often been permitted to see such ways, and likewise the spirits going and walking upon them freely according to their affections and the thoughts thence derived.

591. Evil continually exhales and ascends from hell, and good continually exhales and descends from heaven, because a spiritual sphere encompasses every one, and that sphere issues and overflows from the life of his affections and the thoughts thence derived.[2] And because such a sphere of life flows forth from every one, therefore it also flows forth from every heavenly society, and from every infernal society; consequently from all those societies together, that is, from the whole of heaven and from the whole of hell. Good flows forth from heaven, because all in heaven are in good; and evil flows forth from hell, because all in hell

---

[1] That to journey in the Word, signifies the progression of life, in like manner to go, n. 3335, 4375, 4554, 4585, 4882, 5493, 5605, 5996, (5181), 8345, 8397, 8417, 8420, 8557. That to go and to walk with the Lord is to receive spiritual life, and to live with Him, n. 10567. That to walk denotes to live, n. 519, 1794, 8417, 8420.

[2] That a spiritual sphere, which is a sphere of life, flows forth and issues from every man, spirit, and angel, and encompasses them, n. 4464, 5179, 7454, 8630. That it flows forth from the life of their affections and thoughts, n. 2489, 4464, 6206. That spirits are known as to their quality, at a distance, from their spheres, n. 1048, 1053, 1316, 1504. That spheres from the evil are contrary to spheres from the good, n. 1695, 10187, 10312. That those spheres extend themselves far into angelic societies, according to the quality and quantity of good, n. 6598 to 6613, 8063, 8794, 8797; and into infernal societies according to the quality and quantity of evil, n. 8794, 8797.

are in evil. The good which is from heaven is all from the Lord; for the angels in the heavens are all withheld from their own proprium, and kept in the proprium of the Lord, which is Good Itself; but the spirits who are in the hells are all in their own proprium; and since the proprium of every one is nothing but evil, therefore it is hell.[1] From these considerations it may be evident that the equilibrium, in which the angels in the heavens and the spirits in the hells are kept, is not like the equilibrium in the world of spirits. The equilibrium of the angels in the heavens is the degree in which they desired to be in good, or the degree in which they lived in good, when in the world; and consequently the degree in which they held evil in aversion: but the equilibrium of the spirits in hell is the degree in which they were willing to be in evil, or the degree in which they lived in evil when in the world; and consequently the degree in which they were, in heart and mind, opposed to good.

592. Unless the Lord governed both the heavens and the hells, there would be no equilibrium; and if there were no equilibrium, there would be no heaven and no hell; for all things and every single thing in the universe, that is, in the natural as well as in the spiritual world, subsist by reason of equilibrium. That such is the fact, every rational man may perceive. Suppose there were a preponderance on one side, and no resistance on the other, would not both perish? So would it be in the spiritual world, if good did not react against evil, and continually restrain its insurrections: and unless the Divine alone did this, both heaven and hell would perish, and with them the whole human race. I say, unless the Divine alone did this, because the proprium of every one, whether angel, spirit, or man, is nothing but evil, (see above, n. 591); for which reason, no angels or spirits can possibly resist the evils that continually exhale from the hells, since on account of their proprium they all tend toward hell. From these considerations it is evident, that unless the Lord alone governed both the heavens and the hells, no one

---

[1] That the proprium of man is nothing but evil, n. 210, 215. 731, 874, 875, 876, 987, 1047, 2307, 2308, 3518, 3701, 3812, 8480, 8550, 10283, 10284, 10286, 10732. That the proprium of man is hell with him, n. 694, 8480.

could possibly be saved. Moreover, all the hells act as one, for evils in the hells are connected like goods in the heavens; and the Divine, which proceeds solely from the Lord, can alone resist all the hells, which are innumerable, and which act together against heaven, and against all who are in heaven.

593. The equilibrium between the heavens and the hells is diminished or increased according to the number of those who enter them, which amounts to many thousands every day. But to know and perceive which way the balance inclines, and to regulate and equalize it with precision, is not in the power of any angel, but of the Lord alone; for the Divine proceeding from the Lord is omnipresent, and observes, in every direction, if there be the slightest preponderance; whereas an angel only sees what is near himself, and cannot even perceive within himself what is passing in his own society.

594. How all things are arranged in the heavens and in the hells, so that all their inhabitants, both collectively and individually, may be in their equilibrium, may be manifest in some measure from what has been said and shown above concerning the heavens and the hells; as, that all the societies of heaven are arranged most distinctly according to goods, and their genera and species; and all the societies of hell according to evils, and their genera and species; and that beneath every society of heaven there is a society of hell corresponding to it in the way of opposition, from which opposite correspondence there results an equilibrium. Wherefore it is continually provided of the Lord, that no infernal society beneath a heavenly society shall prevail over it; and as far as it begins to do so, it is restrained by various means, and is reduced to the just measure required for the maintenance of equilibrium. These means are numerous, of which I will mention only a few. Some of them have reference to a stronger presence of the Lord; some, to the closer communication and conjunction of one or more societies with others; some, to the ejection of superfluous infernal spirits into deserts; some, to the translation of certain spirits from one hell to another; some, to the arrangement of those in the hells, which is also effected in various ways; some, to the concealing of certain hells under denser and heavier coverings; also to the

letting of them down to greater depths; not to mention other means, including those employed in the heavens above them. These things are stated, in order that it may in some measure be perceived, that the Lord alone provides that there shall everywhere be an equilibrium between good and evil, thus between heaven and hell; for upon such equilibrium the preservation of all in the heavens and of all on earth, is based.

595. It is to be observed, that the hells are continually assaulting heaven, and endeavoring to destroy it; and that the Lord continually protects the heavens, by withholding the inhabitants from the evils derived from their proprium, and by holding them in the good which is from Himself. It has been frequently granted me to perceive the sphere issuing from the hells, which was nothing but a sphere of efforts to destroy the Divine of the Lord, and consequently heaven. The ebullitions of some hells have also been occasionally perceived, which were efforts to emerge and to destroy. But the heavens, on the other hand, never assault the hells; for the divine sphere proceeding from the Lord is a perpetual effort to save all; and because those who are in the hells cannot be saved, since all who dwell there are in evil and opposed to the Divine of the Lord, therefore their outrages are moderated, and their cruelties restrained as far as possible, in order to prevent their breaking out against each other beyond the limits prescribed. This, too, is accomplished by innumerable mediums of Divine Power.

596. There are two kingdoms into which the heavens are distinguished, namely, the celestial and the spiritual, (concerning which see above, n. 20–28). In like manner the hells are distinguished into two kingdoms, one of which is opposite to the celestial kingdom, and the other opposite to the spiritual kingdom. The former, which is opposite to the celestial kingdom, is in the western quarter, and its inhabitants are called genii; but the latter, which is opposite to the spiritual kingdom, is in the northern and southern quarters, and its inhabitants are called spirits. All who are in the celestial kingdom are in love to the Lord, and all who are in the hells opposite to that kingdom are in the love of self; but all who are in the spiritual kingdom are in love toward the neighbor, and all who are in the hells op-

posite to that kingdom are in the love of the world. From this it was made evident, that love to the Lord and self-love are opposites; in like manner love toward the neighbor and the love of the world. It is continually provided by the Lord, that no efflux from the hells opposite the Lord's celestial kingdom, shall be directed toward those who are in the spiritual kingdom; for if there should be, the spiritual kingdom would perish; the reason of which may be seen above, (n. 578, 579). These are the two general equilibriums, which are constantly maintained by the Lord.

MAN IS IN FREEDOM THROUGH THE EQUILIBRIUM BETWEEN HEAVEN AND HELL.

597. THE equilibrium between heaven and hell has been treated of in the foregoing chapter; and it has been shown that this equilibrium is an equilibrium between the good which is from heaven and the evil which is from hell; thus that it is a spiritual equilibrium, which in its essence is freedom. Spiritual equilibrium in its essence is freedom, because it is an equilibrium between good and evil, and between truth and falsity, and these are spiritual. Wherefore, to be able to will what is good or evil, and to think what is true or false, and to choose one in preference to the other, is the freedom which is here treated of. This freedom is given to every man by the Lord, nor is it ever taken away from him. By reason of its origin, indeed, it is not man's, but the Lord's, because it is from the Lord; nevertheless it is given to man along with life as his own; and the reason why it s given, is, that man may be reformed and saved,—for withou freedom there can be neither reformation nor salvation. Every one from rational intuition may see that man is at liberty to think ill or well, sincerely or insincerely, justly or unjustly; and like-

wise that he can speak and act well, sincerely and justly, but not ill, insincerely and unjustly, by reason of spiritual, moral, and civil laws, whereby his external is kept in bonds. From these considerations it is evident, that the spirit of man, which is that which thinks and wills, is in freedom; not so his external, which speaks and acts, unless it does so in conformity with the above mentioned laws.

598. Man cannot be reformed unless he be in freedom, because he is born into evils of every kind, which yet must be removed in order that he may be saved; nor can they be removed, unless he sees them in himself, acknowledges them, and afterward ceases to will them, and at last holds them in aversion. Then for the first time they are removed. This cannot be effected unless man be in good as well as in evil; for from good he may see evils, but he cannot from evil see goods. The spiritual goods which man is capable of thinking, he learns from infancy by reading the Word, and from preaching; and moral and civil goods he learns by living in the world. This is the primary reason why man ought to be in freedom. Another reason is, because nothing is appropriated to man, except what he does from an affection which is proper to his love. Other things, indeed, may enter, but they penetrate no further than the thought, and do not reach the will; and what does not enter even into man's will, does not become his own; for thought derives all that belongs to it from the memory, but the will derives all that it has from the life itself. Nothing that man ever thinks or does is free, which is not from the will, or what is the same, from an affection which belongs to his love: for whatever a man wills or loves, this he does freely. Hence it is, that the freedom of man, and the affection which is of his love or will, are one. Man, therefore, is endowed with freedom, in order that he may be affected by truth and good, or love them, and that thus they may become as his own. In a word, whatever does not enter into man in freedom, does not remain, because it is not an object of his love or will; and the things which are not objects of a man's love or will, do not belong to his spirit; for the esse of the spirit of man is love or will. It is said, love or will, because what a man loves, this he

wills. This, then, is the reason why man cannot be reformed unless he be in freedom. But more may be seen on the subject of man's freedom in the ARCANA CŒLESTIA, in the passages cited below.

599. In order that man may be in freedom, so that he can be reformed, he is conjoined as to his spirit with both heaven and hell; for there are with every man spirits from hell and angels from heaven. By means of the spirits from hell, he is in his own evil, but by means of the angels from heaven he is in good from the Lord; thus he is in spiritual equilibrium, that is, in freedom. That angels from heaven and spirits from hell are adjoined to every man, may be seen in the chapter concerning the conjunction of heaven with the human race, (n. 291–302).

600. It is to be observed, that the conjunction of man with heaven and with hell, is not immediately with them, but mediately through spirits who are in the world of spirits. These spirits are with man, but none from hell itself and from heaven itself. Through evil spirits in the world of spirits, man is conjoined with hell, and through good spirits there, with heaven. Such being the case, the world of spirits is therefore intermediate between heaven and hell; and in that world is equilibrium itself. That the world of spirits is intermediate between heaven and hell, may be seen in the chapter concerning the world of spirits, (n. 421–431); and that equilibrium itself between heaven and hell is there, may be seen in the chapter immediately preceding, (n. 589–596). From these considerations it is now evident whence man has freedom.

601. Something further shall be added concerning the spirits adjoined to man. An entire society may have communication with another society, and likewise with any individual wherever he may be, by means of a spirit sent forth from that society. This spirit is called the subject of many. It is the same with regard to man's conjunction with societies in heaven, and with societies in hell, by means of spirits adjoined to him from the world of spirits. On this subject see also the ARCANA CŒLES·TIA in the passages cited at the close.

602. Lastly, something shall be said about the innate impres-

54

sion concerning his life after death, which man receives by influx from heaven. There were some of the simple common people, who in the world had lived in the good of faith: they were brought into a state similar to that in which they were in the world,—this may be done with every one when the Lord gives permission,—and it was then shown what idea they had entertained concerning the state of man after death. They said that some intelligent persons had asked them, when in the world, what they thought about their souls after the life on earth; and they replied, that they did not know what the soul was. They were then asked what they believed respecting their state after death; and they replied that they believed they should live as spirits. They were next asked what they believed a spirit to be; to which they answered, that a spirit is a man. Being further inquired of as to how they knew this, they said they knew it because it is so. Those intelligent ones marvelled that the simple had such faith, and they themselves had none. Hence it was made evident, that every man who is in conjunction with heaven, has an inherent conviction that he is to live after death. This inherent conviction comes from no other source than from influx out of heaven, that is, through heaven from the Lord, by means of spirits who are adjoined to man from the world of spirits; and it is possessed by those who have not extinguished their freedom of thinking by notions previously adopted, and confirmed in various ways, about the soul of man, which they say is either pure thought, or some vital principle, whose precise location in the body they try to search out; when yet the soul is nothing but the life of man, but the spirit is the man himself; and the terrestrial body which he carries about in the world, is only an instrument, whereby the spirit, which is the man himself, fitly does its work in the natural world.

603. What has been said in this work concerning heaven, the world of spirits, and hell, will be obscure to those who take no delight in learning spiritual truths, but clear to those who find delight therein; and especially will they be clear to those who are in the affection of truth for its own sake, that is, who love it because it is truth. For whatever is loved enters with light into the

mind's conception; especially truth, when that is the object
loved, because all truth is in light.[1]

---

[1] Extracts from the ARCANA CŒLESTIA concerning the Freedom of Man,
concerning Influx, and concerning the Spirits by whom Communications
are effected.

CONCERNING FREEDOM. That all freedom is of love or affection, because what a man loves he does freely, n. 2870, 3158, 8987, 8990, 9585 to
9591. That since freedom is of love, therefore it is the life of every one,
n. 2873. That nothing appears to be a man's own, but what is from freedom, n. 2880. That there is heavenly freedom and infernal freedom, n.
2870, 2873, 2874, 9589, 9590.

That heavenly freedom is of heavenly love, which is the love of the
good and the true, n. 1947, 2870, 2872; and that since the love of good
and of truth is from the Lord, therefore true freedom consists in being led
of the Lord, n. 892, 905, 2872, 2886, 2890, 2891, 2892, 9096, 9586, 9587,
9589, 9590, 9591. That man is introduced into heavenly freedom by the
Lord through regeneration, n. 2874, 2875, 2882, 2892. That in order to
be capable of being regenerated, man must be in freedom, n. 1937, 1947,
2876, 2882, 3145, 3146, 3158, 4031, 8700. That otherwise the love of good
and of truth cannot be implanted in man, and appropriated by him apparently as his own, n. 2877, 2879, 2880, 2888. That nothing is conjoined
to man in a state of compulsion, n. 8700, 2875. That if man could be reformed by compulsion, all would be saved, n. 2881. That compulsion in
reformation is hurtful, n. 4031. That all worship from freedom is true
worship, but not that from compulsion, n. 1947, 2880, 7349, 10097. That
repentance ought to arise in freedom, and that compulsory repentance is
of no avail, n. 8392. States of compulsion described, n. 8392.

That it is granted to man to act freely from reason, in order that good
may be provided for him, and that on this account man possesses the freedom of thinking and also of willing and doing what is evil, so far as the
laws do not forbid, n. 10777. That man is held by the Lord between
heaven and hell, and thus in equilibrium, in order that he may have freedom as a means of reformation, n. 5982, 6477, 8209, 8907. That what is
inseminated in freedom remains, but what is inseminated by compulsion
does not remain, n. 9588. That therefore freedom is never taken away
from any one, n. 2876, 2881. That no one is compelled by the Lord, n.
1937, 1947.

That man may compel himself from a principle of freedom, but that ne
cannot be freely compelled, n. 1937, 1947. That man ought to compel
himself to resist evil, n. 1937, 1947, 7914; and also to do good as from himself, with the acknowledgment that his power is from the Lord, n. 2883,
2891, 2892, 7914. That man has stronger freedom in temptation-combats

in which he conquers, because then he forces himself to resist more interiorly, although it appears otherwise, n. 1937, 1947, 2881.

That infernal freedom consists in being led by the loves of self and the world, and by their concupiscence, n. 2870, 2873. That the inhabitants of hell know no other freedom, n. 2871. That heavenly freedom is as distant from infernal freedom, as heaven is from hell, n. 2873, 2874. That infernal freedom, which consists in being led by the loves of self and of the world, is not freedom, but slavery, n. 2884, 2890, because slavery consists in being led of hell, n. 9586, 9589, 9590, 9591.

CONCERNING INFLUX. That all things which man thinks and wills, flow into him; from experience, n. 904, 2886, 2887, 2888, 4151, 4319, 4320, 5846, 5848, 6189, 6191, 6194, 6197, 6198, 6199, 6213, 7147, 10219. That man's capacity of viewing things, of thinking, and of forming analytical conclusions, is from influx, n. 1285, 4319, 4320. That man could not live a single moment, if influx from the spiritual world were taken away from him; from experience, n. 2888, 5849, 5854, 6321. That the life which flows-in from the Lord varies according to the state of man, and according to his reception of it, n. 2069, 5986, 6472, 7343. That with the evil, the good which flows-in from the Lord is turned into evil, and truth into the false; from experience, n. 3642, 4632. That the good and truth, which continually flow-in from the Lord, are received in the measure in which they are not opposed by the evil and the false, n. 2411, 3142, 3147, 5828.

That all good flows-in from the Lord, and all evil from hell, n. 904, 4151. That man at this day believes that all things are in himself, and from himself, when yet they flow-in, and that he might know this truth from the doctrinal tenet of the church, which teaches that all good is from God, and all evil from the devil, n. 4249, 6193, 6206; but if man believed according to that doctrinal tenet, he would not appropriate evil to himself, nor would he make good his own, n. 6206, 6324, 6325. How happy the state of man would be, if he believed that all good flows-in from the Lord, and all evil from hell, n. 6325. That they who deny heaven, or know nothing about it, are ignorant that there is any influx thence, n. 4322, 5649, 6193, 6479. The nature of influx, illustrated by comparisons, n. 6467, 6480, 9407.

That the all of life flows-in from the first Fountain of life, because it is from that Source, which is the Lord, and that the influx is perpetual, n. 3001, 3318, 3337, 3338, 3344, 3484, 3619, 3741, 3742, 3743, 4318, 4319, 4320, 4417, 4524, 4882, 5847, 5986, 6325, 6468, 6469, 6470, 6479, 9276, 10196. That influx is spiritual, and not physical, thus that it is from the spiritual world into the natural, and not from the natural into the spiritual, n. 3219, 5119, 5259, 5427, 5428, 5477, 6322, 9110, 9111. That influx proceeds through the internal man into the external, or through the spirit into the body, and not contrariwise, because the spirit of man is in the spiritual world, and the body in the natural world, n. 1702, 1707, 1940, 1954, 5119, 5259, 5779, 6322, 9110. That the internal man is in the spiritual world, and the external in the natural world, n. 978, 1015, 3679, (4459), (4523), (4524), 6057, 6309. 9701. to 9709, 10156. 10472. That it appears as if influx proceeded from the externals of man into the internals, but that this is a fallacy, n. 3721. That with man there is influx into the things of his rational faculty, and through them into scientifics, and not contrariwise, n. 1495, 1707, 1940. The nature of the order of influx described, n. 775, 880, 1096, 1495, 7270. That there is immediate influx from the Lord, and also mediate influx through the spiritual world or heaven, n. 6063, 6307, 6472, 9682, 9683. That the Lord's influx is into the good appertaining to man, and through the good into the truth, but not contrariwise, n. 5482, (5649), 6027, 8685, 8701, 10153. That good gives the faculty of receiving influx from the Lord, but not truth without good, n. 8321. That nothing is injurious which flows only into the thought, but what flows into the will; because what flows into the will is appropriated to man, n. 6308.

That there is a general or common influx, n. 5850; and that it is a continual endeavor to act according to order, n. 6211. That this influx flows into the lives of animals, n. 5850, and also into the subjects of the vegetable kingdom, n. 3648. That thought falls into speech, and will into actions and gestures with man, from this common or general influx, n. 5862, 5990, 6192, 6211.

CONCERNING SUBJECTS. That spirits sent forth from societies of spirits to other societies, and also to other spirits, are called subjects, n. 4403, 5856. That communications in the other life are effected by such emissary spirits, n. 4403, 5856, 5983. That a spirit, who is sent forth as a subject, does not think from himself, but from those by whom he is sent forth, n. 5985, 5986, 5987. Several particulars concerning such spirits, n. 5988, 5989.

INDEX.

just, and right in every work and every employment, 360, 535.

CHILDHOOD.—In childhood spirits are present who are in the affection of knowing, 295.

CHINESE.—The Chinese, 325. See GENTILES.

CHRIST.—From the Spiritual Divine, the Lord in the world was called Christ, 24. See JESUS.

CHURCH.—The Church is the Lord's heaven upon earth, 57. The Church is in man, and not out of him, 57. The Church in general consists of men, in whom is the Church, 57. The Church of the Lord is universal, and with all who acknowledge a Divine, and live in charity, 308. The Church of the Lord is spread over all the globe, 328. The universal Church on earth is before the Lord as one man, 305. The Church specifically is where the Word is, and by it the Lord is known, 308, 318. They who are born where the Word is, and where the Lord is known, are not, on that account, of the Church, but they who live a life of charity and faith, 318. Unless there were a Church where the Word is, and by it the Lord is known in this earth, the human race would here perish, 305. If good were the characteristic and essential of the Church, and not truth without good, the Church would be one, 57. All Churches make one church before the Lord by virtue of good, 57. See ANCIENT CHURCH and MOST ANCIENT CHURCH.

CICERO.—Conversation of Swedenborg with Cicero, 322.

CITIES.—The habitations of angels are contiguous, and disposed in the form of cities, 184.

CLEFT.—For Cleft of a Rock, see ROCK.

CLIMATE.—The differences of the changes of state with the angels, are in general like the variations of the state of days in different climates on the earth, 157.

CLOTHING.—See GARMENTS.

COHABITATION.—In heaven, the conjunction of two in one mind is called cohabitation, 367.

CLOUDS.—Clouds signify the Word in the letter, or the sense of its letter, 1.

COLOR.—That colors in heaven are variegations of the light there, 179. That they signify various things which are of intelligence and wisdom, 179, 356. That colors, so far as they partake of redness, signify good, and so far as they partake of white, signify truth, 179.

COMING OF THE LORD.—That the coming of the Lord is his presence in the Word, and revelation, 1, Arcana Cœlestia, 3900, 4060.

COMMUNICATION.—That in the heavens there is a communication of all good, 49, 199, 200 to 212, 288; and of all thought, 2. In the heavens there is a communication of all with each, and of each with all, 399. Communication with others in the spiritual world is effected according to the turning of the face, 552. The inmost communication of the spirit is with the respiration and with the motion of the heart, 446.

COMMUNION.—Heaven is a communion of all goods, 73, 268.

COMPULSION.—That nothing is conjoined to man which is of compulsion, 293. What is of compulsion in reformation is hurtful, 293.

CONCEPTION.—Conceptions signify the same spiritual things which are of good and truth, or of love and faith, 382.

CONCUPISCENCES.—Concupiscences flow from the love of self, and the love of the world, 396.

CONFIRM.—Whatever is confirmed puts on the appearance of truth, and there is nothing which cannot be confirmed, 352, 353.

CONJOINED.—Whatever can be conjoined to the Divine cannot be dissipated, 435. Good and truth love each other and wish to be conjoined, 319.

CONJUNCTION.—The conjunction of heaven with the human race, 291 to 302. The conjunction of heaven with man by the Word, 205, 208, 254, 303 to 310, 319, 423, 424. That all conjunction in the spiritual world is according to conversion, 255. The conjunction of heaven with the world is effected by correspondences, 112. The conjunction of Angels and Spirits with man, 246, 247, 255. The conjunction of husband and wife in one, 369. The conjunction of truth and good makes an angel, 370. The conjunction of the understanding and the will, 423. The conjunction of good and truth is heaven; that of evil and false is hell, 425.

CONNECTION.—There is a connection of all things by intermediates with the First, and whatever is not in that connection is dissipated, 9, 302, 303, 305.

CONSOCIATION.—Consociations in heaven, 36, 64, 200 to 212, 479. All are consociated in heaven according to spiritual affinities, 205. It is not the angels who consociate themselves, but the Lord, 45. Man has consociation with the angels, and conjunction with the Lord, 304.

CONSONANTS.—The speech of the celestial angels is without hard consonants, 241. In the inferior heavens, the ideas of thought from affection are expressed by consonants, 261. See VOWELS.

CONSUMMATION.—The consummation of the age is the last time of the church, 1.

CONTINUE.—Continuance of the first state of man after death, 498. Term of man's continuance in the world of spirits, 426.

CONTINUOUS.—In what is continuous there does not appear to be anything distant, except from those things which are not continuous, 196.

CONVERSION.—That all conjunction in the spiritual world is according to conversion, 255. Conversion of the interiors and exteriors of man either to the Lord or back from the Lord, 253, 552.

COPPER.—That copper signifies natural good, 115.

CORN.—That standing corn signifies truth in conception, 489.

CORRESPONDENCE.—Correspondence of all things of heaven with all things of man, 87 to 102. Correspondence of heaven with all the things of the earth, 103 to 115. By correspondences the natural world is conjoined to the spiritual world, 106. That all things which correspond signify also the same things in the Word, 111.

CORRESPONDENT.—All that which in nature exists and subsists from divine order, is correspondent, 90, 107.

CUPIDITY.—Cupidity, or lust, is love in its continuity; it is the infernal fire; it springs from the love of self and the love of the world, 570.

Doors.—See Gates.

Doves.—Doves signify intellectual things of the mind, 110.

Drunken.—When angels think of marriage with more than one, they are alienated from internal blessedness and heavenly happiness, and become as drunken persons, because good is disjoined from its truth with them, 379.

Dwellings.—See Habitations.

Ear.—By the ears is signified obedience, 97. In the Greatest Man, those who are in the ears are in hearing, or obedience, 96. The ear corresponds to perception and obedience, and hence signifies them, 271.

Earth.—The earth signifies the Church, 307. The lower earth; its situation, 513, 391. The earths in the universe; that they are innumerable, 417; that their inhabitants adore the Divine under a human form, 321.

East.—In heaven, it is called the east where the Lord appears as a sun, 141. The Lord, in the supreme sense, is the east, 141. The east signifies love and its good in clear perception, 150. Those in heaven who are in clear perception of the good of love dwell in the east, 148, 149. In the hells, those who are in evils from the love of self dwell from their east to their west, 151.

Edifices.—Sacred edifices of the most ancient people, 223. Sacred edifices in the celestial kingdom are not called temples but houses of God, 223. See Temple.

Education.—The education of infants in heaven, 334 to 344. Comparison between infant education in heaven, and on earth, 344.

Effect.—The effect derives all that it has from its efficient cause, 512.

Effigy.—In the other life, every one becomes the effigy of his own love, even in externals, 481.

Egypt.—Egypt and Egyptian in the Word signify the natural, and the scientific thence derived, 307. With the Orientals, and in Egypt, the science of correspondences flourished, 87.

Elect.—That they are the elect who are in the life of good and truth, 420.

Elevation.—Elevation of the understanding into the light of heaven, 130, 131. That there is an actual elevation into the light of heaven when man is elevated into intelligence, 130.

Employment.—Concerning the employment of angels in heaven, 387 to 394.

End.—There is no end to any good thing, because it is from the Infinite, 469. False belief concerning the end of the world, 312.

Ends.—Nothing is regarded by the Lord, and thence by the angels, but the ends, which are uses with man, 112.

Enthusiasts.—Concerning enthusiasts and enthusiastic spirits, 249.

Entrance.—Concerning man's entrance into eternal life, 445 to 452.

Equilibrium.—Concerning the equilibrium between heaven and hell, 589 to 596. Equilibrium is between two forces, one of which acts and the other reacts, 589. On equilibrium is founded the safety of all in the heavens and on the earth, 594. Equilibrium is in the world of spirits, 600. The equilibrium between the heavens and the hells is diminished and increased according to the number of

those who enter heaven, and who enter hell, 593.

Errors.—Those who are in the sense of the letter of the Word, and not enlightened by genuine doctrine come into many errors, 311. Errors of the Learned, see Learned.

Esse.—The Divine Itself was the Esse of the Lord's life, from which the Human afterwards went forth, 44. The will of man is the very esse of his life, and the receptacle of the good of love, 26, 447, 474.

Essential.—The essential of order is Divine Good, 77, 523. The essential of the Church is to acknowledge the Divine of the Lord and his union with the Father—see extract on page 57. The essential of all doctrines is to acknowledge the Divine Human of the Lord, 227. The essential of good and truth is innocence, 281.

Evil.—All that is evil comes from the proprium of man, 484. All evils are from the love of self and of the world; they are contempt of others, enmities, hatred, revenge, cruelty, 359. The hereditary evil of man, in what it consists, 342. Every evil brings along with it punishment, they being conjoined, 509. Man is the cause of his own evil, and not the Lord, 547. Why, in the Word, evil is attributed to the Lord, when yet from the Lord is nothing but good, 545. That every evil has in it what is false, wherefore they who are in evil are also in the false, although some of them do not know it, 551.

Excrement.—Those who have passed their lives in more pleasures, living delicately, indulging appetites, and loving those things as the highest good of life, in the other life love excrementitious things and privies, which to them are objects of delight, 488.

Existere.—The Human was made the existere from that esse of the Lord's life which was the Divine Itself, page 55. That nothing exists from itself, but from what is prior to itself, thus all things from the First, which is the very Esse of the life of all, 9, 37, 304. In man, the understanding is the existere proceeding from the esse, 474.

Extension.—Extension of thoughts and affections, 49, 79, 85, 199, 201, 203, 204, 206, 240, 477.

Extent.—The difference between extense in heaven and extense in the world, 85.

Exteriors.—The exteriors of the spirit are those by which it accommodates the body of man in the world, 492. As compared with interiors, exteriors are more remote from the Divine, obscure and inordinate, 267. See Interiors.

Eye.—By the eyes are signified understanding, because the understanding is internal sight, 97, 145. The eyes correspond to truth from good, 232. That the sight of the eye signifies the intelligence which is of faith, and also faith, 271. In the Greatest Man, those who are in the eyes are in understanding, 96. All the infants in heaven are in the province of the eyes, 333. To lift up the eyes and see, signifies to understand, to perceive, and to observe, 145.

Face.—With the angels the face makes one with the interiors, 143, 457. That the face of man's spirit differs very much from the face of his body, 457. The face of man's body is from the parents, but the face of the spirit is from the affection, of which it is the image, 457.

The face, in the Word, signifies the interiors, which are of the affection and thought, 251, 457. All who form one angelic society are of a like face in general, but not in particular, 47. Angelic faces are the forms of their interiors, 47.

FAITH.—Faith is the light of truth which proceeds from charity, 148. Faith is all that which is of doctrine; it consists in thinking justly and rightly. It becomes charity when what a man thinks justly and rightly he also wills and does, 364. Faith separate from love, is no faith, but only science, which has no spiritual life in it, 474. Faith does not remain with man, if it be not from heavenly love, 482. Merely to believe the Word is not faith, but to love truth from heavenly love, and to will and do it from interior affection, 482. That what is incomprehensible falls into no idea, thus neither into faith—extract on page 59, line 2.

FALSE.—All that is false comes from evils flowing from the love of self and the love of the world, 342, 558.

FEET.—Feet signify the natural, 97. In the Greatest Man those who are in the feet, are in the ultimate good of heaven, which good is called natural-spiritual, 96.

FIBRES.—The nervous fibres in the human body, 212, 413.

FIELDS.—Fields signify those things which appertain to state, 197.

FIRE.—Fire signifies love in each sense; sacred and celestial fire divine love, and infernal fire the love of self and of the world, 13, 118, 134. Concerning infernal fire, 566 to 575.

FIRST.—The First and the Last signifies all and single things, thus the whole, 301. What is not connected by intermediates with the First, does not subsist, but is dissipated and becomes nothing, 37.

FLAME.—Flame signifies spiritual good, 179. In the opposite sense, flames correspond to the evils of the love of self, 585.

FLESH.—The flesh of the Lord signifies his Divine Human, and the divine good of his love, 147.

FLOWERS.—Flowers signify scientific truths and knowledges, 176, 489.

FOOD.—Food corresponds to the affections of good and truth, because these nourish spiritual life as earthly food nourishes natural life, 111, 274. Food, in a spiritual sense, is everything which comes forth from the mouth of the Lord. Spiritual food is science, intelligence, and wisdom, 340.

FOREHEAD.—The forehead corresponds to heavenly love, and by forehead in the Word, that love is signified, 145, 251.

FORM.—Concerning the form of heaven, 200 to 212. The form of everything is from order, and according to it, 201. In the most perfect form, such as the form of heaven is, there is the likeness of the whole in a part, and of a part in the whole, 62, 72, 73. The form of the natural man differs very much from his spiritual form, 99. The human form is the form of the whole heaven, of every society, of each angel, and of everything of thought which is from heavenly love with the angels, 460. In the nature of the world, all things which there exist according to order, are forms of these, 112. See MOULD.

FOUNDATION.—Foundation signifies truth on which heaven, the Church, and doctrine are founded, 187.

FREEDOM.—All freedom is of love and affection, since what a man loves, this he does freely, 45, 293. See concerning Freedom, in the extracts from the *Heavenly Arcana*, on page 427, and in the body of this work, nos. 45, 293, 598.

FRUITS.—Fruits signify the good of love and charity, 176, 185.

GABRIEL.—Gabriel is an angelic society, so named from its function, 52.

GARDEN.—A garden signifies intelligence and wisdom, 111, 176, 489.

GARMENTS.—That garments in the Word signify truths, because these invest good, 129. Garments correspond to intelligence, 179, 365. The garments of the Lord, when he was transfigured, signify divine truth, proceeding from his divine love, 129. Bright garments of fine linen signify truths from the Divine, 179. Concerning the garments with which angels appear clothed, 177 to 182. The garments of the angels do not merely appear so, but are really garments, 181.

GATES.—Gates signify introduction to the doctrine of the Church, and by doctrine into the Church, 187, 307. Gates of heaven and gates of hell, 428 to 430.

GENERALS.—Generals are in an inferior degree as compared with particulars, and are the continents of particulars, 267.

GENERATION.—That generations and nativities signify the same spiritual things which are of good and truth, or of love and faith; and hence they signify regeneration and rebirth by faith and love, 382.

GENII.—Who and of what quality are the infernal spirits called genii, 123, 151, 579.

GENTILES.—Concerning the gentiles, 3. Those who are born out of the Church are called gentiles, 3. The gentiles are saved alike with Christians, 318. The gentiles are afraid of Christians, on account of their lives, 321. The gentiles enter heaven more easily than Christians at this day, 324, 514. How gentiles are instructed in the other life, 321, 512, 513.

GESTURES.—Those things which are of the will set themselves forth in the gestures of the body, 91, 244.

GLORIFICATION OF THE LORD.—See extracts from the HEAVENLY ARCANA on page 56, et infra.

GLORY.—Glory, in the Word, signifies Divine Truth, such as is in heaven, and such as is in the internal sense of the Word, 1.

GNASHING OF TEETH.—Of the gnashing of teeth, 245, 566 to 575.

GO.—To go signifies progression of life, 590. To go with the Lord is to live with him, 192.

GOAT.—Goats, male and female, signify the affections, 110.

GOD.—God is man, 85. That God is man can hardly be comprehended by those who judge all things from the sensual things of the external man, 85. In the universal heaven no other is acknowledged for the God of heaven than the Lord alone, 2. See DIVINE, DIVINE HUMAN, LORD.

GOLD.—Gold from correspondence signifies celestial good, 115, 307.

GOOD.—All good is of love, 23. That is called good which is of the will, and thence of the work, 26. Celestial good is the good of love to the Lord, 23. Celestial good is in the in

angels who are in this good dwell on hills, 188.

HOLE.—A hole in a rock, in the Word, signifies the obscene and the false of faith, 488.

HOLINESS.—Concerning external holiness, 224.

HOLY.— The Holy is divine truth proceeding from the Lord, 140. Of those who have lived a holy life in externals in the world, that they might be honored before others, and accounted saints after death, 535. Every one is holy according to his interiors, 224.

HOUR.—An hour signifies state in particular, 165. Compare *Arcana Cœlestia*, 4334.

HOUSES.—The houses in the heavens, 180, 184. Houses, with the things within them, signify those things with man which are of his mind, thus, his interiors, and consequently which relate to good and truth, 186. A house of wood signifies those things which are of good, and a house of stone those things which are of truth, 186. The house of God signifies, in the supreme sense, the Divine Human of the Lord, as to divine good; and in the respective sense, heaven and the Church, as to good and truth, 187, 223. By the house of the wedding is understood heaven and the Church, from the conjunction of the Lord with them by His divine truth, 180.

HUMAN RACE.—That heaven and hell are from the human race, 311 to 317. The human race is the seminary of heaven, 417.

HUNDRED AND FORTY-FOUR.—A hundred and forty-four, in the spiritual sense, are all truths and goods in the complex, 73, 307.

HUNGER.—They are said to hunger who desire the knowledges of good and truth, 420.

HUNGRY.—In the Word they are called hungry who are not in the knowledges of good and truth, and still desire them, 520.

HUSBAND.—Why the Lord, in the Word, is called the Husband, 180. Husband is predicated of the Lord, and of his conjunction with heaven and the Church, 368. Husband signifies the understanding of truth, 368.

IDEA.—There are innumerable things in one idea of thought, 240. The ideas of thought are various forms into which the common affection is distributed; for no thought and idea at all is given without affection; their soul and life is thence, 236. The natural idea of man is turned into a spiritual idea with the angels, 165. Angelic ideas, when they flow in with men, are turned in a moment, and of themselves, into the natural ideas proper to man, corresponding altogether to spiritual ideas, 168. The ideas of the internal man are spiritual, but man during his life in the world perceives them naturally, because he then thinks in the natural, 243. Man after death comes into his interior ideas, which then form his speech, 243.

IGNORANCE.—Why man cannot but be born into mere ignorance, 108.

ILLUMINATED.—To be illuminated or enlightened, is to be elevated into the light of heaven, 131. The light of heaven illuminates the understanding of man, and hence he is rational, 130. The understanding is enlightened so far as man receives truth in good from the Lord, 130.

IMMENSITY.—Of the immensity of heaven, 415 to 418.

IMPLANTED.— Concerning what is implanted from heaven, 74, 82, 260, 602

INDUSTRY.—All things produced by human industry for use, are correspondences, 104.

INFANCY.—In infancy spirits are present who are in innocence, 295. The good of infancy is not spiritual good, but it becomes so by the implantation of truth, 277. That whatsoever is imbued in infancy appears natural, 277.

INFANTS.—Infants in heaven, 4, 329 to 345. In the Word, infants signify innocence, 278. That infants grow up in the heavens, 4. In the Greatest Man, or heaven, infants of a spiritual disposition are in the province of the left eye, and those of a celestial disposition in the province of the right eye, 333, 339. The ideas of infants when they see objects, the same as in heaven, 338. Temptations of infants, 343. Infants in heaven do not advance in age beyond early manhood, and stop there to eternity, 340. Character of infants on earth, 277. All who die infants are accepted of the Lord, wheresoever they are born, 308.

INFINITE.—No ratio is given between the infinite and the finite, 273.

INFLUX.—See page 425, extracts from the *Heavenly Arcana*, concerning INFLUX: and in the body of this work, Nos. 26, 37, 110, 112, 135, 143, 207, 208, 209, 277, 282, 296, 297, 298, 304, 319, 435, 455, 549, 567.

INMOST.—Man, otherwise than animals, has an inmost, by which he can be elevated by the Lord to Himself; hence also it is that he lives to eternity, 39, 435.

INNOCENCE.—Innocence is the receptacle of the truth of faith, and of the good of love, 330. The state of innocence of the angels in heaven, 276 to 283. Innocence is the very ease of good, 282. Innocence of infants, 277. The innocence of infants is the plane of all the affections of good and truth, 341. The innocence of infants is not true innocence, but true innocence dwells in wisdom, 277. Genuine innocence is wisdom, 341.

INSITUM.—With every man who is in conjunction with heaven, there is an innate [*insitum*] idea concerning his life after death, 602.

INSPIRATION.—In what manner the Lord spoke with the prophets, through whom was the Word, 254.

INSTRUCTION.—Of the state of instruction of those who come into heaven, 512 to 520.

INTELLIGENCE.—Since the light of heaven is divine truth, therefore also that light is divine wisdom and intelligence, 131. Heavenly intelligence is interior intelligence, arising from the love of truth for the sake of truth, 347. Intelligence consists in receiving good and truth from the Lord, 80. What true intelligence is, 351. What spurious intelligence is, 352. What is false intelligence? 353. Intelligence and wisdom make man, 80. See WISDOM.

INTELLIGENT.—Who those are who are meant by the intelligent, 347, 348, 356.

INTENTION.—The intention of man, from which his internal sight or thought is determined, is his will, 532.

INTERIOR.—The interiors of the spirit are those which are of its own proper will, and thence thought, 492. Interior things flow in with successive order into external things, even into the extreme or ultimate, and that there also they exist and subsist, 304, 475. Interior things exist and subsist in what is ultimate

351, 396, 468, 532. Opening of the exteriors, 396. Opening of the degrees of the mind, 468. Opening of the things which are above the rational mind, and of the things which are below it, 430. Opening of the eyes of the spirit, 171. Opening of the gates of hell, 583.

OPINION.—False opinions concerning the angels, the devil, the soul, the resurrection, and the last judgment, 312, 183, 458.

OPPOSITES.—When one opposite acts against another, pain is produced. There is not any thing without relation to its opposites; and from the opposite is known its quality, &c., 541. Between the opposites there is equilibrium, 541.

ORDER, DIVINE.—The Lord is order, inasmuch as the divine good and truth which proceed from the Lord make order, 57. All things which in nature exist and subsist from divine order are correspondent, and have relation to good and truth, 107. Divine order does not rest in the middle, but terminates in an ultimate, and the ultimate is man: thus divine order terminates with man, 304, 315. All things of divine order were collected into man, and man from creation is divine order in form, 30, 202; because he is its recipient, 523. Divine order is heaven with man, 523. So far as man lives according to divine order, so far in the other life he appears as a man, perfect and beautiful, 454.

ORIENTALS.—The science of correspondences flourished with the Orientals, 87.

OXEN.—Cows and oxen correspond to the affections of the natural mind, 110.

PALACES.—Concerning palaces in heaven, 184, 185. The palace of wisdom, 270.

PANCREAS.—The pancreas corresponds to the purification of good and truth, 96, 217.

PARADISE.—Paradise signifies intelligence and wisdom, 111, 176, 489. The magnificence of things paradisiacal in the other life, 176. Why heaven is called paradise, 136.

PARTICULARS.—Those things which are in a superior degree are particulars, and those things which are in an inferior degree are generals; and generals are the continents of particulars, 267.

PATH.—A way, path, road, or street signify truths, which lead to good, and also falses, which lead to evil, 479.

PEACE.—Concerning the state of peace in heaven, 284 to 290. Peace is the inmost of delight from the good of innocence, 285. Peace in the heavens is the Divine inmostly affecting with blessedness every good and truth there, and it is incomprehensible to man, 286, 288. Innocence and peace walk hand in hand, 288. A state of peace in the heavens is as a state of dawn and of spring in the earth, 289. Heavenly peace is given with men who are in wisdom, yet it is stored up in their interiors while they live in the world, 288. Internal peace is not given with those who are in evil, 290. Peace signifies the Lord and heaven, and also heavenly joy and the delight of good, 287. Peace signifies the union of the Divine itself and the Divine Human in the Lord, and the conjunction of the Lord with heaven and with the Church, 287.

PEARLS.—Pearls signify introductory truths, 307.

PERCEPTION.—Perception is internal hearing, 434.

PERFECTION.—Perfection in the heavens increases according to the plurality of the angels, 418, 71. All perfection also increases toward the interiors, and decreases toward the exteriors, 341, 158.

PETER.—The Apostle Peter represented the Lord as to faith, 526.

PIETY.—A life of piety without a life of charity is of no avail, but with the latter is of advantage in every respect, 535.

PLACES.—Places and spaces are presented visible according to the states of the interiors of angels and spirits, 195. Places signify states, 192. Changes of place in the spiritual world, are changes of the state of life, 192.

PLURALITY.—Plurality of earths, 417. Plurality of hells, 588.

POOR.—The poor in heaven, 357 to 365. In the Word, by the poor are understood those who are spiritually poor, that is, who are in ignorance of truth, and still desire to be instructed, 420, 365.

POWER.—The power of the angels in heaven, 228 to 233. The angels are called powers, and are powers, from the reception of divine truth from the Lord, 137, 231. All power is from the Lord, and is of truth from good, thus of faith from love, 232. The false from evil has no power, 233, 539. All the power which man has is from his understanding and will, 228.

PREACHERS.—Of preachers in the heavens, 223 to 226. All the preachers in the heavens are from the Lord's spiritual kingdom, 225.

PREACHING.—Of preaching in the heavens, 221 to 227, 259.

PRESENCE.—The presence of the Lord in the heavens is that He is everywhere, and with every one, in the good and truth which proceed from Him, consequently that He is in his own with the angels, 147, 121. The presence of the angels is not with the Lord, but the Lord's presence with the angels, 142. In the spiritual world, one is exhibited as present with another, if he only intensely desires his presence, 194.

PRIESTHOOD.—Priesthood signifies the good of love to the Lord, 226.

PRIESTS.—Priests represented the Lord as to Divine Good. A priest, in the Word, signifies those who are in the good of love to the Lord, 226. False belief of the priests, 74, 183, 312.

PRIVY.—See EXCREMENT.

PROCEED.—To proceed is to be produced and exhibited in a suitable form, that it may be perceived and appear, 474. The things which proceed are of that from which they proceed, 474. To exist from an esse is what is meant by proceeding, 139.

PROCREATION.—In the heavens there is a procreation of good and truth, 382.

PROFANATION.—Profanation is the commixing of good and evil, also of the true and false, with man, 456.

PROFANE.—To profane is to believe at first, and afterward deny, 456.

PROGRESSION.—All progressions in the spiritual world are made by changes of the state of the interiors, so that progressions are nothing else than changes of state, 192, 195.

PROPHETS.—The prophets had their spiritual sight opened, 76. How the Lord spoke with

See also the collection of extracts from the *Heavenly Arcana*, concerning the sciences, page 233, *et infra*. The science of correspondence, 87 to 102, 114, 114, 487, 488. The science of correspondences excels other sciences; to the ancients it was the chief science, but at this day it is obliterated; it flourished with the Orientals and in Egypt, 87.

Scientifics.—Scientifics are of the natural memory, which man has in the body, 355. To enter into the truths of faith from scientifics is contrary to divine order. From spiritual truth it is allowable to enter into the scientifics which are of the natural man, but not the reverse, because of the manner in which influx is given, 365. See **Science.**

Seers. Why prophets were called seers, 76, 487.

Sense of the Word.—The literal sense of the Word consists of such things as are in the world; but the spiritual sense of such things as are in heaven, and each and all of the things which are there, correspond, 104. In all and each of the things of the Word, there is an internal or spiritual sense, 1. The internal sense of the Word is its soul, and the sense of the letter is its body, 307.

Sensual.—The sensual is the ultimate life of man, adhering to, and inhering in, his corporeal, 267, 353. He is called a sensual man who judges and concludes all things from the senses of the body, and who believes in nothing but what he sees with his eyes and touches with his hands. Sensual men reason acutely and cunningly placing all intelligence in speaking from the natural memory; they are cunning and malicious more than others, 267, 353, 461. See, also, 18, 74.

Separation.—When and how the separation of bad spirits from good spirits is effected, 511.

Separations.—Removals or separations in the spiritual world are according to the differences in the states of the interiors, 193 to 195.

Serpent.—Serpents of the tree of science, is a term applied to sensual men by the ancients, 353. See **Sensual.**

Servants.—See **Master.**

Seventy-two.—The number seventy-two signifies all truths and all goods in the complex, 73.

Sheep.—Correspond to the affections of the spiritual mind, 110.

Shoulder.—By the shoulders is signified power, 231.

Sight.—The sight of the eye signifies the intelligence which is of faith, and also faith, 271. The sight of the left eye corresponds to the truths of faith, and the sight of the right eye to their goods, 118. Internal sight is of the thought, 85, 144; or of the understanding, 208, 462. The things of the spiritual world are seen by man when he is withdrawn from the sight of the body, and the sight of his spirit is opened, 76, 171. The sight of the spirit is interior sight, 171.

Silver.—Silver signifies spiritual good, or truth from a celestial origin, 115.

Similitude.—Similitude conjoins, and dissimilitude disjoins, 427. Similarity causes angelic societies to be together, 42. Concerning likenesses, 16, 47, 72, 582.

Simple.—Concerning the simple in heaven, 346

to 356. Of the simple, see, 74, 83, 86, 183, 268, 312, 313, 322, 464.

Smelling.—See **Senses**, 402, 462.

Smoke.—Smoke corresponds to the falses which proceed from the evils of hatred and revenge, 585.

Society.—The heavens consist of innumerable societies, 41 to 50. Every society is a heaven in a less form, 51 to 58. Every society in the heavens resembles one man, 68 to 72. Every society of heaven has its opposites in a society of hell, 511, 588. Every man as to his spirit, is conjoined to some society, either infernal or heavenly—a wicked man to an infernal society, a good man to a heavenly society, 510. Every one returns to his own society after death, 510.

Socinians.—The Socinians are out of heaven, 3. Their interiors are closed, 83.

Solitary.—Of those who give themselves up to a life almost solitary; how they are in the other life, 360, 535, 249.

Son-in-law.—Son-in-law signifies truth associated to the affection of good, 382.

Sons.—Sons signify the affections of truths, thus truths, 382.

Soot.—Soot corresponds to the falses from hatred and revenge, 585.

Soul.—The soul of man is his spirit, for this is immortal as to all its properties, 432, 602. False opinions concerning the soul, 183, 312, 456. In the Word, the soul signifies understanding, faith, and truth, 446.

Sound.—The sound of speech corresponds to affection; and the articulations of sound, which are words, to the ideas of thought, which are from affection, 236, 241, 260, 296.

South.—The south signifies wisdom and intelligence in clear light, 150. The south signifies a state of light, or wisdom and intelligence, 150. In heaven, those dwell in the south who are in greater light of wisdom, 148, 149. In the hells, those who are in the falses of evil dwell from their south to their north, 151.

Space.—Concerning space in heaven, 191 to 199. To the angels there are neither distances nor spaces, but states and their changes, 192. Spaces in heaven are external states corresponding to internal, 193. Spaces are presented visible according to the states of the interiors of angels, 195. In the Word, space signifies state, 192.

Speech.—Concerning the speech of angels, 234 to 245. The speech of angels with man, 246 to 257. There is spiritual or angelic speech appertaining to man, although he is ignorant of it, 243. After death man comes into his interior ideas, which then form his speech, 243. Man is able to speak with spirits and angels, and the ancients frequently spoke with them; but in this earth at this day it is dangerous to speak with spirits unless man be in a true faith, and be led by the Lord, 249.

Sphere.—A spiritual sphere, which is a sphere of life, flows forth and diffuses itself from every man, spirit, and angel, and encompasses them; it flows forth from the life of their affection, and thence of their thought, 17, 49, 591. Concerning spiritual spheres, see, also, 384, 574, 591.

Spirit.—That every man is a spirit as to his interiors, 432 to 444. That the spirit is the man himself, and that from that the body lives,

that extense which is under the sun, and receives from it heat and light; and of that world are all the things that thence subsist, 89. The natural world exists and subsists from the spiritual world as an effect from a cause, 89, 106; and both from the Divine, 106.

WORLD—SPIRITUAL.—The spiritual world is heaven, and of that world are all things which are in the heavens, 89. In the spiritual world, where spirits and angels are, similar things appear as in the natural world where men are; so similar that as to the external aspect there is no difference, yet all those things are from a spiritual origin, 582.

WORLD OF SPIRITS.—What the world of spirits is, 421 to 431. The world of spirits is not heaven nor hell, but a middle place or state between both, whither man after death first comes, 421. How the world of spirits appears, 429. The world of spirits is in equilibrium between heaven and hell, 590.

WORMS.—Marvellous transformations of worms, 108.

WORSHIP.—Divine worship in heaven, 221 to 227.

57

Varieties of divine worship, 56. Divine worship of the ancients, 111, 188. External acts and the externals of worship do nothing, but the internals from which externals proceed, 495.

WRATH.—Why wrath, in the Word, is attributed to the Lord, 545.

WRITING.—Concerning writings in heaven, 258 to 264. Numerical and literal writing, 263.

WRITING—NUMERICAL.—See NUMBER 263.

YEAR.—Year signifies states of life in general, 155, 165.

YESTERDAY.—Yesterday signifies from eternity, 165. Compare *Arcana Cœlestia*, 3998. See TO-DAY and TO-MORROW.

YOUNG MEN.—Young men signify, in the Word, the understanding of truth, or one that is intelligent, 368.

YOUTH.—In youth, who may be regenerated, are present spirits who are in the affection of truth and good, and thence in intelligence, 295.

ZION.—By Zion, in the Word, is meant the Church, specifically the celestial Church, 216.

INDEX

CPSIA information can be obtained
at www.ICGtesting.com
Printed in the USA
BVHW031431140521
607266BV00001B/116